The Freestate of the Three Leagues in the Grisons, a rural confederation in the Swiss Alps, was one of the most unusual political entities found in early modern Europe.

In the sixteenth century, its inhabitants enjoyed popular sovereignty and remarkable local autonomy, and many of them insisted on political equality among citizens, and on political leaders' responsibilities to their communities. The author uses pamphlets and political documents to trace the Freestate's evolution, focusing on its institutional structure and on the political language used by its inhabitants. This language included radical statements about "democracy" and rule by the "common man." Even so, the Freestate participated in contemporary European political developments; but because it was different, it provides new perspectives on political ideas in sixteenth-century Europe. The Rhaetian Freestate was not typical, but rather represents a political culture distinct from both absolutism and later liberal ideas.

CAMBRIDGE STUDIES IN EARLY MODERN HISTORY

Early Modern Democracy in the Grisons

CAMBRIDGE STUDIES IN EARLY MODERN HISTORY

Edited by Professor Sir John Elliott, University of Oxford, Professor Olwen Hufton, Harvard University, and Professor H. G. Koenigsberger

The idea of an "early modern" period of European history from the fifteenth to the late eighteenth century is now widely accepted among historians. The purpose of Cambridge Studies in Early Modern History is to publish monographs and studies which illuminate the character of the period as a whole, and in particular focus attention on a dominant theme within it, the interplay of continuity and change as they are presented by the continuity of medieval ideas, political and social organization, and by the impact of new ideas, new methods and new demands on the traditional structure.

For a list of titles published in the series, please see end of book

Early Modern Democracy in the Grisons

Social Order and Political Language in a Swiss Mountain Canton, 1470–1620

RANDOLPH C. HEAD

University of California, Riverside

CAMBRIDGE
UNIVERSITY PRESS

Published by the Press Syndicate of the University of Cambridge
The Pitt Building, Trumpington Street, Cambridge CB2 1RP
40 West 20th Street, New York, NY 10011–4211, USA
10 Stamford Road, Oakleigh, Melbourne 3166, Australia

First published 1995

Printed in Great Britain at the University Press, Cambridge

A catalogue record for this book is available from the British Library

Library of Congress cataloguing in publication data applied for

ISBN 0 521 47086 2 hardback

WD

This book is dedicated to the children:
Abigail and Benjamin, Diana and Taia,
Jarrod, Cassandra, and Alexandra

Contents

Illustrations

Tables

Acknowledgments

The fortuitous discovery of certain fascinating political pamphlets set this study in motion; since that time, it has been supported and furthered by many people, some specialists and scholars, but others simply citizens who thought that scholarly historical research was a project worth supporting. Among the former my advisor, H. C. Erik Midelfort, deserves my lasting gratitude for his steadfast support and ready criticism as this project took shape and grew. In Switzerland, Professor Dr. Peter Blickle at the Historical Institute of the University of Bern took me on for a year as a special student, and has contributed significantly to this project. Dr. Georg Jäger in Chur provided both personal and scholarly support, including arranging a colloquium of *Bündner* historians which discussed my project in his home above Chur in the Lürlibad, while Dr. Jon Mathieu listened, argued, and debated with me as my work in Chur progressed. Piotr Gorecki and other colleagues at the University of California at Riverside have commented on drafts of several chapters. I owe thanks to all of the scholars I have worked with.

A historian is also dependent upon the institutions which preserve the sources he relies upon. This project's opening stages took place primarily at the Widener and Houghton libraries of Harvard University. In Charlottesville, various departments at the Alderman library enabled smooth progress over nearly six years. Central to the Swiss part of my study was the Staatsarchiv Graubünden in Chur, whose knowledgeable staff went out of their way to help me despite being confined to a bomb-shelter during remodeling. My thanks also to the Stadtarchiv Chur, the Landesregierungsarchiv in Innsbruck, the Vadianische Sammlung at the Kantons-bibliothek in St. Gallen, the Schweizerische Landesbibliothek in Bern, the Archiv der Evangelisch-Rätischen Synode in Chur, and to many others.

Funds from the Fulbright program and the Eidgenössische Stipendien-kommission für ausländische Studierende made it possible for me to do research in Switzerland, while the University of Virginia provided me with generous support in Charlottesville. The Swiss Benevolent Society of Washington provided financial support for a semester of writing. A field research travel grant from the Academic Senate at the University of California supported my work on revisions during the summer of 1993.

Besides these many intellectual debts, I specially want to thank the non-academics who supported me generously during the execution of this project.

Acknowledgments

Friends and family in Charlottesville, Boston, and Switzerland went out of their way to further an undertaking apparently far from the everyday life of the twentieth century. Ellen, Jon, Abigail, and Benjamin Miller treated me like family as I burrowed in Widener, while Anita and Fritz Kohler lent me a home away from home in Bad Ragaz. Scholarship thrives and is of value when it retains a personal connection with contemporary life – a connection which depends on the interest and support of those outside the scholarly community. To all those who have helped so generously to improve this work, my thanks. Any errors and flaws, of course, remain my own.

Note on languages, orthography, and translations

Although this book bears the title "Grisons" to describe the region it studies – Grisons being the name best known to English-speaking readers – I will generally use "Rhaetian Freestate" or just "Freestate" to refer to the early modern political entity that I discuss here. This is in keeping with the usage of its inhabitants in the early modern period, who named themselves after their political status, rather than according to a foreigners' nickname for them. In the book, I also use "Graubünden," the region's modern name in its majority language, to describe the physical place involved. In an area with three indigenous languages – Romantsch, German, and Italian – it seems preferable to avoid referring to it in yet a fourth, such as French (which is the origin of the English name Grisons). Therefore, despite its appearance in the title, that particular name will not be found in the text. The terms *Bündner* or Rhaetian will generally be used to refer to the inhabitants, especially since Grisons allows only awkward adjectival forms in English.

Any study of a tri-lingual region – especially one written in a fourth language – is bound to run into further difficulties with language and the translation of names. I have tried to follow a few other general rules. Most places are named in the contemporary language of their inhabitants, although the predominance of German in formal documents (including maps) requires some bending of this rule. Thus I speak of Disentis, not Mustér, of Ilanz rather than Glion, of the Engadine rather than of the Agnadina. Similarly, most individuals are named in their native language, with the exception of a few who appear in modern library catalogues under their name in a different language. The most important instance of this is Durich Chiampell, who is known to the scholarly world, and in this book, as Ulrich Campell. For these unavoidable changes, my apologies to the modern speakers of Romantsch, whose language is all too often ignored altogether.

Where I have transcribed manuscripts or sixteenth-century publications, I have tried to cite exactly without any changes. I have not always maintained the distinction between "unnd" and "und" and "vnd" and "vnnd," however. I have consistently rendered the superscript "o" over "u," which is common in German-language sources, as "uo." All of the various forms of the umlaut (from superscript "e" to the modern double dot) have been reduced to the modern German form for the sake of typographical clarity. As few other changes as possible have been made in punctuation, except as noted. Readers who wish to see all translated texts in the original language should consult my dissertation, "Social order, politics, and political language in the Rhaetian Freestate (Graubünden), 1470-1620" (Ann Arbor: University Microfilms, 1992). All translations are mine unless otherwise attributed.

Abbreviations

AHR	*American Historical Review*
ARG	*Archiv für Reformationsgeschichte*
BK	Schiess, Traugott, ed. *Bullingers Korrespondenz mit den Graubündnern.* Vols. XXIII–XXV, *Quellen zur Schweizer Geschichte*, o.s. Basel, 1904–06 (reprinted Nieuwkoop: B. de Graaf, 1968).
BM	*Bündnerisches Monatsblatt*, and its successor journal, *Bündner Monatsblatt.*
EA	*Ämtliche Sammlung der älteren Eidgenössischen Abschiede, 1245–1798.* 8 in 22 vols. Various publishers, 1856–86.
GA	*Gemeindearchiv* (Communal archive).
GG	*Geschichtliche Grundbegriffe. Historisches Lexikon zur politisch-sozialen Sprache in Deutschland.* 7 vols. Ed. Otto Brunner, Werner Conze, and Reinhart Koselleck. Stuttgart: E. Klett, 1972–1992.
HBLS	*Historisch-Biographisches Lexicon der Schweiz.* 7 vols. and supp. Ed. Heinrich Türler, Marcel Godet, Victor Attinger *et al.* Neuenburg: Administration des Historisch-biographischen Lexikons der Schweiz, 1921–34.
HSG	*Handbuch der Schweizergeschichte*, Zürich: Verlag Berichthaus, 1972–77.
HZ	*Historische Zeitschrift.*
JBSG	*Jahrbuch für Schweizergeschichte.*
JHAGG	*Jahresbericht der Historisch-antiquitarischen Gesellschaft von Graubünden.*
JM I, II	Jecklin, Fritz, ed. *Materialien zur Standes- und Landesgeschichte Gem. III Bünde (Graubünden), 1464–1803.* Vol. I: *Regesten.* Vol. II: *Texte.* Basel: Basler Buch- und Antiquariatshandlung, 1907 and 1909.
JSG	Jecklin, Constanz, ed. "Urkunden zur Staatsgeschichte Graubündens." *Jahresbericht der Historisch-antiquitarischen Gesellschaft Graubündens*, 20 (1890): 41–63, and 21 (1891): 21–133 (two parts separately paginated into a single sequence: all citations by this internal pagination).
JVF	Jecklin, Constanz, ed. *Urkunden zur Verfassungsgeschichte Graubündens. (Als Fortsetzung von Mohr's Codex Diplomaticus).* Chur: Sprecher und Plattner, 1883. Also published in JHAGG, 1883, 1885, 1890.
LAI	Landesregierungsarchiv, Innsbruck.
QSG	*Quellen zur Schweizer Geschichte*, old series.

List of abbreviations

RC   Decurtins, Caspar, ed. *Rhätoromanische Chrestomathie*, 13 vols.
Erlangen: A. Diechert and Fr. Junge, 1888–1919. Reprinted Chur:
Octopus, 1982–85.

SI   *Schweizerisches Idiotikon. Wörterbuch der schweizerdeutschen Sprache*. Ed.
Friedrich Staub and Ludwig Tobler. Frauenfeld, J. Huber, 1881–

SSRQ   *Sammlung schweizerischer Rechtsquellen*. Section XV. *Rechtsquellen des
Kantons Graubünden*. Series B, *Die Statuten der Gerichtsgemeinden*.
Part 1: *Der Gotteshausbund*. Ed. Andreas Schorta. Aarau: Verlag
Sauerländer, 1980–. Part 2: *Der Zehngerichtenbund*. Ed. Elisabeth
Meyer-Marthaler. Aarau: Verlag Sauerländer, 1985–.

STAB   Staatsarchiv Bern.

STAC   Stadtarchiv Chur.

STAG   Staatsarchiv Graubünden.

SZG   *Schweizerische Zeitschrift für Geschichte*.

VAD   Kantonsbibliothek St. Gallen (Vadianische Sammlung).

WS   Wagner, R. and L. R. von Salis, eds. *Rechtsquellen des Cantons
Graubünden*. 4 sections in 2 vols. Special imprint from the *Zeitschrift für
Schweizerisches Recht*, vols. 25–28. Basel: C. Detloff's Buchhandlung,
1887.

ZBZ   Zentralbibliotek Zürich.

ZSG   *Zeitschrift für Schweizerische Geschichte*.

ZSKG   *Zeitschrift für Schweizerische Kirchengeschichte*.

Social order, politics and political language in Graubünden, 1470–1620

Among all of the temporal blessings and gifts, which God is accustomed to bestow on the human race, spiritual and worldly liberty of conscience and of self-government is by no means the least, because one can preserve one's soul, honor, body and goods through its legitimate use, and enjoy these things without vexatious compulsion and pressure. Therefore it has always and everywhere been desired and sought after by everyone as a precious valuable treasure.[1]

The form of our government is democratic; and the election and removal of all kinds of magistrates, judges and officers, both here in our free and ruling lands and in those lands subject to us, lies with our common man.[2]

Grawpündtnerische Handlungen deß M.DC.XVIII jahrs (1618)

The statements above, with their unapologetic use of the expressions "democratic" and "common man," appeared in a factional manifesto written in the "Freestate of the Three Leagues in Old Upper Rhaetia" – now the modern Swiss canton known in its three native languages as Graubünden, Grischun, or Grigioni.[3] Effectively separated from the Holy Roman Empire in 1499, the Rhaetian Freestate developed into a polity unique in early modern Europe. Multi-lingual, and after the 1520s multi-religious, the Freestate spent the stormy years of the sixteenth century governed by communal democracy according to majoritarian principles. In an age that celebrated hierarchy and divinely ordained authority, its inhabitants celebrated their "liberty of self-government," maintaining that they had no lord but God himself. Living in a confederation of autonomous political communes, the Freestate's citizens claimed the power, "according to [their] majorities, to create laws and to abrogate them, to form alliances with foreign princes and communities, to regulate peace and war, and to deliberate concerning all other matters pertaining to higher

---

[1] *Grawpündtnerische Handlungen*, A ii[r]. Translated from the 52 page German edition of 1618.
[2] *Ibid.*, A ii[v].
[3] On names for the republic in question, see Oechsli, "Die Entstehung der Namen 'Graubünden' und 'Bündner.'"

and lesser authority."[4] Contemporary observers often described the Freestate in terms of sheer anarchy; yet this polity enjoyed relative autonomy and prosperity, if not always tranquillity, until the rising tides of confessionalism and power politics upset its internal equilibrium and submerged it in the disaster of the Thirty Years' War.

The Freestate's place in European history reflects the ambivalence of its geography, which is both central and isolated. Since the days of the Carolingian empire, the long, high mountain range at the heart of Western Europe has had seemingly contradictory effects on the inhabitants of those mountains. On the one hand, the Alps stood at the geographical center of the medieval German empire, separating two imperial heartlands, southwestern Germany and northern Italy. Almost everyone – French, English, Dutch, Slav – had to cross the Alps to get to the Mediterranean world, while Italians in turn crossed northwards to go to the courts of Germany, the universities of Paris and England, and the merchant centers of the Netherlands and the Hansa. Crowded into a few passes, all of Europe passed before the doorways of the Alpine population. On the other hand, the Alpine regions have always been marginal in a number of ways. The terrain and the climate guaranteed that they would remain economically marginal, thinly populated, and dependent on imported grain. The physical barrier they represented made them a region crisscrossed by boundaries: boundaries between kingdoms and principalities, of course, but also between language groups and cultures. The central Alps, from Sion to Innsbruck, and from Bellinzona to Lucerne, are the source of waters that run to the Mediterranean, to the North Sea, and to the Black Sea. The same watersheds also separated German, French, Italian, and Romantsch speakers, distinct in language and government even as they shared the same high mountain meadows for their cattle and goats.

Under these distinctive circumstances, it is not surprising that the political life of the central Alps was also unusual compared with that of most of Europe. The Rhaetian Freestate violated most of the patterns of early modern state formation. Not only did its inhabitants speak three languages, they were also subjects of at least three different major lords during the late Middle Ages, not to mention half a dozen local dynasties. Some were vassals of the bishops of Chur, others of the abbot of Disentis, still others came under Habsburg dominion by the end of the fifteenth century. With the onset of the Protestant Reformation, grounds for division only increased: some villages became Protestant, while others remained staunchly Catholic. Nor did any dynamic central authority or institutions bind the Freestate into a whole. On the contrary, authority was zealously protected at the local level, allowing a bare minimum of joint action to protect the Freestate's existence. Like

---

[4] *Grawpündtnerische Handlungen*, A ii[v]. This passage continues the second one quoted at the head of this chapter. The word *Demokratie* is very rare in German before the seventeenth century, and in Latin works is generally seen as a negative form of popular government. GG I: 821–900, esp. 844–45.

Switzerland, the Freestate remained a confederation of quasi-sovereign entities; unlike Switzerland, where the entities were mostly large rural communes or good-sized towns, the individual units in the Freestate were mountain valleys, often with no more than a few hundred inhabitants. Yet common political institutions and a common political identity did develop in the Freestate, despite the many divisions among its population. By the late sixteenth century, moreover, this common identity was reflected in common values and shared myths about the region's history.

For all its unique characteristics, Rhaetia underwent economic and social trans-formations similar to those found in the rest of central Europe during this period. Agricultural colonization and political fragmentation in the high Middle Ages, contraction and retrenchment during the plague years, and the emergence of rural and urban communes as a distinctive and decisive form of social organization: all of these phenomena took place in Rhaetia, although they often took on distinctive forms as a result of local conditions. The appearance of a territorial state in Rhaetia paralleled similar developments across southern Germany, while European legal systems penetrated the region. In the southern valleys, notaries drew up Latin contracts that they recorded in their registers, while in the north petty nobles used their seals to guarantee charters written in German. Latin statutes reflecting Italian developments were drawn up in the Engadine even as German-speaking communes codified their common law in the north.

In most of Europe's republics, narrow elites came to monopolize political power during the sixteenth and seventeenth centuries. Many of the Italian city-states became autocratic, or, as in Venice, laid an increasing emphasis on birth over talent as a qualification for office. A similar process was under way in Swiss and German cities, as the ranks of political citizenship were closed to newcomers. Comparable developments began in the Freestate as well, yet in Rhaetia the principle of majority rule actually increased in importance between 1520 and 1620. Such rule was frequently turbulent, however. Modern historiography has generally accepted the judgment of the seventeenth century, that the Rhaetian Freestate was weak and anarchic, and that foreign influence was the primary factor in its eclipse from 1620 to 1639. Even Swiss historians who praise its democratic tendencies conclude that the absence of central authority condemned the Freestate to an impotence remedied only by the more oligarchic regime established after 1639.

Most inhabitants of the Freestate in the late sixteenth century would not have agreed with this assessment. They repeatedly attempted to reform their consti-tution so as to prevent governmental corruption. Moreover, the direction of these reforms was exactly the opposite of what we might expect: in 1603, when the situation seemed graver than ever, the Great Reform devolved *more* authority onto the Freestate's constituent communes, rather than strengthening the central government. Obviously, the reformers' assumptions about what values were para-mount in a political system, and about where the greatest dangers to their freedom lay, were quite different from those held by contemporary theorists of absolutism and centralization. In the early seventeenth century, during a political crisis that nearly destroyed the Freestate, some Rhaetians also claimed that the government they lived under was democratic. This study attempts to trace the political culture and political experience that led up to such statements, looking not only at institutions and at the exercise of power, but also at the social practice of the peasants and village magnates who inhabited the Freestate of the Three Leagues.

An outpouring of political texts after 1607 sought to explain and justify Graubünden's communal government to its participants and to the rest of Europe. Some authors combined feudal and humanist models in defense of Rhaetian liberty, while others drew upon their communal experience to propose a radically populist interpretation of the Rhaetian republic. The latter are particularly interesting because they expressed ideas we otherwise glimpse only in revolutionary manifestos or eccentric utopias – ideas that were usually suppressed or marginalized by a European power structure committed to hierarchy and "natural" authority. But radical political language in Rhaetia was no aberration or individual fantasy: instead, a century's experience of communal politics on a national scale combined with a domestic and international political crisis around 1620 to produce a burst of texts expressing communal ideas about political authority and legitimacy. Despite the sometimes fragmentary and incoherent character of populist texts, they represented a creative attempt to capture their authors' practical experience in a vocabulary drawn largely from quite different political world-views. Radical communal rhetoric from Graubünden provides a window into a conceptual world that extended far beyond Switzerland, moreover, although it was Graubünden's atypical circumstances that made its expression possible.

Aside from their sheer unusualness, political thought and practice in Rhaetia are potentially interesting for two major trends in the study of early modern Europe. First, the Rhaetian situation adds an important viewpoint to current scholarship about European peasants and their relationships to larger political systems. Generations of historians have assumed that most peasants were politically inert, at most rising up unpredictably in the name of "tradition" and their good old customs. Recent work, especially by German and American scholars, has attempted to recreate the peasantry as an actor in the political history of European nations, and to show how peasants' understanding of their own situation and interests influenced the way they interacted with their lords, especially when they chose to rebel. In most of Europe, in fact, rebellion is the only time we see peasants as autonomous political actors, which explains why scholarship has generally focused on events such as the German Peasants' War of 1525.[5] In Rhaetia, in contrast, peasants were actively involved in creating a new and distinctive state. For once, we

---

[5] Most lasting of the wave of scholarship that accompanied the 450th anniversary of the German Peasants' War has been Peter Blickle's *The Revolution of 1525*.

4

can see them acting as the legitimate bearers of political authority, rather than as desperate rebels or sullen subjects. Naturally, the Rhaetian peasants in their communes had to contend with entrenched power structures and ambitious leaders of their own; nevertheless, their position was nearly unique in early modern Europe, and provides a revealing contrast to the much more restricted role they usually played elsewhere.

The history of political culture in Graubünden can also contribute to the study of European political theory in general. Recent work on the history of political ideas has focused on "languages" or "idioms" that European thinkers used to express their understanding of human societies in history. This linguistic metaphor is a powerful way of representing political thought: it can accommodate both dissonance and change without reducing discussion to "unit ideas" or endless strings of "influences." It allows us to outline cohesive political world-views without insisting on perfect systems and total coherence.[6] Anthony Pagden has recently identified the four most important political idioms in early modern Europe as the language of natural law, the language of classical republicanism, the language of political economy, and the modern science of politics.[7] The language of communalism, if we may call it that, that was found in Rhaetia was less clearly articulated and less consistently disseminated than Pagden's major traditions, but for the historian interested in the structure of human action as well as the trans-mission of ideas, it was of comparable importance. Too many historians have demonstrated the tenacious hold that such ideas had for Europe's "common man," both in the towns and in the countryside, for them to be ignored.[8] Communal values displayed the persistent ability to organize and motivate direct action by large numbers of people, and cannot be dismissed in the study of politics and political change during this era. Just as English history and the experiences of common lawyers provide a background for interpreting seventeenth-century rhetoric about the "Ancient Constitution" of Britain, so does the practical organization and the ideology of late medieval village life in Graubünden provide an unusual window on the conceptual world of communal politics across a large part of Central Europe. Much of this study is therefore intended to explain the origins of the "political languages" that appeared in the region's literature, especially around 1620.

Yet a linguistic metaphor for political ideas can be confining if one's object of study is not political texts themselves, but rather the collective experience of a people living in a specific polity. As J. G. A. Pocock and his colleagues freely admit, neither *mentalité* nor human action is central to the kind of research they

---

[6] Pocock, "The concept of a language." See also Melvyn Richter, "Reconstructing the history of political languages: Pocock, Skinner, and the *Geschichtliche Grundbegriffe*," *History and Theory*, 29, 1 (1990): 38–70.

[7] Anthony Pagden's own introduction to Pagden, *The Languages of Political Theory*, 3.

[8] See esp. Blickle, *The Communal Reformation*.

do.[9] Different jobs require different conceptual tools: since this study attempts to trace both language and action from the Rhaetian Freestate's emergence in the mid-fifteenth century until its near destruction in the early seventeenth, it will also draw upon the broader category of "political culture." By "political culture" I understand the whole complex of ideas, assumptions, reflexes, specific language, and expectations that the inhabitants of Graubünden held about the nature and conditions of their collective existence. Such a broad definition ensures that all aspects of political life will be included. It recognizes that political culture organizes action as well as knowledge, providing patterns for response to various situations as well as values useful in interpreting one's predicament.[10]

Political culture can be usefully divided into unselfconscious and self-conscious parts. The former may include unexamined assumptions about how individuals and groups should interact, reflexive reactions to certain problems, and ideas about "human nature" and the nature of the universe – the whole range of phenomena that can also be gathered under the rubric *mentalité*.[11] For the historian, unself-conscious political culture is difficult to investigate; often it must be deduced from the actions of individuals in specific situations. Self-conscious political culture includes openly expressed ideologies, the purposeful self-representation of individuals in their political context, explanations of their situation to outsiders, and all forms of persuasive rhetoric and propaganda directed to political ends. Most of the evidence in textual sources is relevant primarily to self-conscious political culture, although routine documents often contain clues to unselfconscious values as well.

There is no reason to believe that the political culture of the Rhaetian Freestate (or of any polity) formed a single coherent whole. On the contrary, political ideas are almost always controversial, discursive, and entwined with other spheres of interest. Nor should we assume that every *Bündner* had a coherent set of ideas about politics at any given moment: the evidence from Graubünden suggests that people held ideas about politics that seem contradictory if we try to order them into a single system. Indeed, much of our source material is a direct consequence of the controversial nature of political ideas. People argued, disputed, and attempted to convince one another or a more general audience; in doing so, they left evidence about what they thought, or what they wanted others to believe they thought. Their arguments relied on ideas that were emotionally loaded and rhetorically effective, whatever their origins. Even so, there was some consistency to the Rhaetians'

---

[9] Pocock, "The concept of a language," 22, 36–38. More generous about the connections between political ideas and political action is Skinner, *Foundations*, I: xi–xii.
[10] Rohe, "Politische Kultur," 326. Rohe emphasizes that "political culture" is a useful viewpoint because it allows us to analyze the connection between "Einstellungen *und* Verhaltensmuster."
[11] Rohe, "Politische Kultur," 336–37, who agrees that political culture is "mehr oder minder gleichbedeutend mit politischer Mentalitätsforschung," though he emphasizes that it implies an expressive dimension as well as a set of ideas.

political culture. Certain connections among ideas were immediately plausible to audiences within the Freestate, whereas others could be adopted only at the expense of becoming an outsider in the political debates then taking place. People were more willing to act upon some appeals than upon others, and experience and observation about how the Freestate was in fact ruled constrained the ways in which its government could be described.

The study of any real polity therefore requires that one study its institutions as well. To quote John Najemy, "it was in the matrix of institutions that the fundamental assumptions of political life, and ultimately of political thought, gathered concrete significance and precise definition" in the minds of the Rhaetians.[12] By arguing and fighting about which of their institutions were legitimate, and what ought to be changed to increase their legitimacy, Rhaetians often revealed their assumptions about what made a political order legitimate in general. Most of what they said was about the concrete political world they took part in – its specific characteristics, the specific measures needed to improve it, the specific ways in which they could bring their own interests to fruition. To understand the unusual language found in the Freestate around 1620, therefore, we must look both at political values and at institutional practice before that time. The sum of all these considerations should provide an understanding of the Rhaetians' political culture.

Two parallel paths provide the structure for this study. The first is chronological, covering the Freestate's history from about 1450 to 1620. Rather than forming a simple progression, however, the narrative chapters focus on the political predicament faced by the Freestate and its inhabitants during various stages of its history. This predicament changed fundamentally as Rhaetia's internal organization and international environment were transformed. Chapter 2 covers the period before 1520. Why and how communes should join into leagues represented the key issue during the late fifteenth century, as Rhaetians from all estates sought to maintain public peace and establish local autonomy in the face of the collapsing feudal order in the region. Who should inherit what parts of the lords' authority dominated politics during the early sixteenth century, leading up to the promulgation of a group of fundamental constitutional documents between 1524 and 1526. Chapter 4 turns to the consolidation of institutions and power systems that took place after the 1520s, and to the beginnings of a growing rift between the local elite and the remainder of the population. Finally, chapter 6 covers the rise and fall of a reform movement after 1580, and the resultant breakdown of relations among various political forces in the Freestate through the year 1620. After that, foreign manipulation overwhelmed domestic forces in the region, leading to deep-seated changes in the social balance of power between communes and their leaders.

---

[12] John M. Najemy, *Corporatism and Consensus in Florentine Electoral Politics, 1280–1400* (Chapel Hill: University of North Carolina Press, 1982), 15.

Certain themes run throughout this long century of Rhaetian history: the growing power and legitimacy of communal entities, the shifting balance between hierarchical and horizontal models of political authority, and the growing power of a new local elite that was mirrored by the growing frequency of popular tumults. All of these are discussed in detail throughout the book. I have, in contrast, spent little time on economic developments and limited my analysis of religion to its political dimension, not because other approaches would be fruitless, but because attempting a more comprehensive view would make this study conceptually as well as materially unwieldy.

Parallel to the chronological progression described above, the remaining chapters follow a trajectory from social practice to ideological expression, and from the local community to the Freestate as a whole. Chapter 1 investigates the detailed model of rural organization developed by historians of late medieval southern Germany during the last few decades, and illustrates the model's applicability to Graubünden. The resulting paradigm represents a crucial foundation for this study for two reasons: first, because it provides an explanatory framework for the poorly documented early history of communes in Graubünden, and second, because it places Rhaetian history in a larger regional context, thus establishing its relevance to the history of communalism elsewhere. The chapter also considers other models of social order, such as late feudalism and neo-Stoicism, that had some influence in Graubünden. Chapter 3 turns to the specific political practices that evolved in Rhaetian village communes, and shows how these influenced the construction of the entire Rhaetian Freestate. It goes on to describe the institutional structure of the Freestate as it matured during the sixteenth century, and also considers how the Freestate's institutions actually functioned.

Chapter 5 turns from formal organization to the actual exercise of power in Rhaetia. A new social and political elite that appeared after 1500 provides the starting point: wealth, prestige and military leadership all contributed towards defining a new cohort of powerful families who attempted to monopolize offices and decision-making in the late sixteenth century. The reasons they did not entirely succeed form the remainder of the chapter. Even though a relatively small group of men normally kept control over the political process in the Freestate, the universal acceptance of communal values constrained their action in various ways. Towards the end of the sixteenth century, Rhaetian leaders increasingly feared direct political action by the communes. Popular action might find its origin in feuds within the leading group, but it also reflected common men's conviction that final authority in the Freestate belonged to them. Finally, chapter 7 analyzes the propaganda and rhetoric that appeared after 1600, when it became increasingly clear that the Freestate's institutions could no longer bridge the gap between elite self-perception and communal values. Confronted with a crisis of both authority and power, various thinkers tried to justify the Freestate's existence in various ways: both history and abstract liberty were pressed into service as fundamental

8

sources of legitimacy, while a few embittered aristocrats even denied that the Freestate had any right to exist at all.

The following study therefore has both a narrative and an analytic dimension. I hope that the systematic explanation of this particular region's history will expand our understanding about the range of social and cultural orders that were possible in early modern Europe. Sixteenth-century Graubünden was different not only from twentieth-century North America, but also from many European societies of its own era. Its history therefore provides a novel perspective on the process of political and ideological change that was under way around 1600.

Communalism and other political models
in Europe and in Graubünden

Social condition is commonly the result of circumstances, sometimes of laws, oftener still of these two causes united; but when once established, it may justly be considered as itself the source of almost all the laws, the usages, and the ideas which regulate the conduct of nations: whatever it does not produce, it modifies.

Alexis de Toqueville, *Democracy in America*[1]

The source of the Rhine, as custom has it, is a small lake above Disentis known as the Oberalpsee. On reflection, though, this designation may seem arbitrary: why this particular valley and pond among the dozens of valleys and ponds around it? And why down at the lake, rather than high above in some snow-filled col? The historical origins of the Rhaetian Freestate, a polity that took shape amid the Alps near the end of the Middle Ages, and which is the subject of this book, are equally problematical. The traditional beginning, the first identifiable point beyond the scattered and enigmatic finds of archeologists, was identified – or invented – in the sixteenth century by the geographer and historian Aegidius Tschudi. In 588 BC, he wrote, a Tuscan leader called Rhetus fled his Italian homeland to escape the invading Gauls and brought his people into the mountains to live in liberty and peace.[2] This myth explains the Roman name for the region, "Rhaetia," and marks the "beginning" of its history. Tschudi's collection of footnotes from Roman texts thus set the first firm mark in the stream of Rhaetian history. The people who lived there before – probably not very many, since mountains dominate the land, and the scarce flat ground is full of rocks – were dismissed like the rills and trickles above the Oberalpsee.

Today the region draws its name from more recent and better known events, and is known in the three local languages as Graubünden, Grigioni, Grischun – that is, as the land of the Gray Leagues.[3] Rhetus and his followers have been superseded

---

[1] Alexis de Tocqueville, *Democracy in America*, 2 Vols., ed. and tr. Phillips Bradley (New York: Alfred A. Knopf, 1951), I: 46.

[2] Tschudi, *Die uralt warhafftig Alpisch Rhetia*, A iii[v].

[3] The French and English name for the region, the Grisons, naturally shares this etymology. See the note on language.

by the tumultuous fifteenth and sixteenth centuries, when a collection of peasant communes created and defined their nation. This study is about the later period, rather than about the shadowy events of an earlier past. Before setting aside the Rhine and its origins, though, we can draw two other lessons from them. First, the Rhine drains only part of Rhaetia. Just as important are the headwaters of the Inn in the long valley known as the Engadine, and the valleys draining southwards towards the Po. The divergence of waters from the heights of the Rhaetian Alps thus reminds us that we should not expect the history of the region to flow toward a single point. Nor is even a single river always easy to grasp. The modern Rhine leaves Graubünden neatly contained by arrow-straight levees, typical of the tidy borders and administrative order that characterize modern Switzerland. But in the sixteenth century, appropriately enough, the Rhine crossed the border in a swampy tangle of multiple channels, dangerous and uncertain. The Inn, the Ticino, and the Adda, meanwhile, have always taken their own courses, through gorges and swamps inhospitable to human travel. This study follows one historical stream to be found in the region – the social and political history of early modern Rhaetia – but I claim neither that this is the only direction one could go, nor that the well-defined story I am telling represents the natural course of a people's or a region's history.

During the fifteenth and early sixteenth centuries, a distinctive political entity emerged in Rhaetia. It was based on communes – associations of peasants and burghers who regulated their own internal affairs – rather than on existing structures of lordly authority, and it was organized by horizontal alliances rather than according to a vertical hierarchy. Understanding this polity therefore requires understanding the communal entities that created it. Many historians have recognized the commune as a specific social and institutional innovation which appeared during the high Middle Ages in Europe, both in the cities and in the countryside. The overwhelmingly rural character of the Rhaetian Freestate requires us to analyze the rural commune in particular: even the few towns in Rhaetia existed within a political system defined by the needs and interests of rural areas. Yet Rhaetia did not exist in isolation from the rest of Europe, and any consideration of its history must recognize the importance that other models of social and political order played in its development. The end of this chapter, therefore, will briefly turn to two major alternatives during the early modern period: the ideology of local feudalism, and the ideal of administrative order and descending authority that characterized the early modern state.

THE COMMUNALISM MODEL

Although similar movements can be found all over Europe during the same period, communes rarely dismantled lordly authority as completely as they did in the central Alps. Consequently, communal ideas about politics rarely flowered as completely elsewhere, tending instead to remain confined to local disputes.[4] Certainly, republicanism flourished in Italian cities such as Florence and Venice, and Peter Blickle's seminal work has shown that peasants played a larger part in the politics of rural southern Germany than most historians have thought. North of the Alps, though, communalism usually existed only under the watchful eyes of princes and prelates.[5] After the 1520s, princely states and oligarchic city governments predominated in Germany, with communal principles operating only locally. Switzerland and Rhaetia stood at the opposite extreme: lordly authority, where it survived at all, was reduced to a private matter between landholders and tenants, whereas public authority fell to village and regional communes. In many ways Rhaetia represents an extreme case of the communal development that spread across Europe at the end of the Middle Ages, only to fade in the early modern period.

The terms "commune" and "communalism" carry many meanings, but they refer to something quite specific when speaking of late medieval and early modern Europe.[6] Historians have long recognized that horizontally organized associations, including confraternities, guilds, urban communes, and village communities, became ubiquitous in the late Middle Ages. Consisting of men (and occasionally women) who were free enough to swear a common oath, such associations brought about profound social and political changes, especially in Germany and Italy. The term "commune" applies specifically to associations whose ends were primarily political, and whose membership was defined territorially. Best known are the urban communes of Italy and Germany – such as Florence, Venice, Augsburg, and Strasburg – but rural communes endowed with various powers spread widely across the European countryside during the same period.

Most research on rural communes has treated them as a local phenomenon which played a decisive role only in the affairs of face-to-face communities of peasants – something essential for understanding the internal affairs of villages and peasants' relations with their lords, but of lesser importance for the political life of territorial principalities, city-states, and kingdoms. Only recently have historians begun investigating the role peasants played on a larger political scale. In the Rhaetian Freestate, however, a political world-view founded on face-to-face communal organization provided the theory for a sizable territorial state. The principle that linked village and Freestate was the concept of the commune as beneficial

---

[4] On the limits on communal politics in South Germany, see Brady, *Turning Swiss*.

[5] Blickle, *Landschaften*. Recent work by David Sabean and Hermann Rebel emphasizes how effectively princely states intruded into village life during the *ancien régime*. See Sabean, *Power in the Blood;* and Rebel, *Peasant Classes*.

[6] My understanding of both terms is based primarily on the work of Peter Blickle, and thus tends to reflect south German and Swiss circumstances. See esp. his *Deutsche Untertanen*. On the word *Gemeinde*, the entry in Jacob and Wilhelm Grimm, *Deutsches Wörterbuch*, vol. v (Leipzig: S. Hirzel, 1897 (reprinted Munich: Deutscher Taschenbuch Verlag, 1984)), cols. 3219–42, esp. 3233–36, is more instructive than GG ii: 801–62.

corporation (*Nutzungsgenossenschaft*). This idea, which reflected the fundamental practices and political assumptions of local communes, provided the framework as Rhaetians established, ruled, and eventually defended their state from both ideological and political enemies. In a confederation of communes which self-consciously resisted traditional models of feudal authority, communal practice provided the models that guided the Freestate's development throughout the sixteenth century.

Although the social reality of communal life differed from place to place, a consistent conceptual model characterized Europeans' thinking about communes.[7] Most important was the voluntary nature of communal association. Unlike subjection to a lord, membership in a commune was thought to require an act of *will*, usually an oath which was repeated at regular intervals. Even where membership followed from some other criterion, such as living in a certain village or owing service to a certain lord, the idea that participation in communes depended on the voluntary acts of free men decisively influenced the commune's overall development. Since communal oaths could be taken only by someone possessing a certain degree of liberty, slaves could not join communes, although serfs often could. Unlike the oaths which peasants and townspeople swore to their lords, moreover, communal oaths were made not to a person but to the collectivity as a whole. Because all swore the same oath of obedience to the same collectivity, members were in principle equal. Their shared act of will superseded most differences in status or power, although this egalitarianism only extended as far as a commune's membership.

A commune did not necessarily consist of everyone living in a certain place, but rather of recognized members. In rural areas, members might be the tenants of certain farms, the subjects of a certain lord, or even speakers of a certain language.[8] Excluded from membership were women, children, servants, and sometimes poorer or unfree peasants. In regions of older settlement, typically only masters over a landed household enjoyed full membership in the commune, although this applied less to Graubünden, where the primary criterion for membership was bearing arms, and most adult males were included. Even when broadly inclusive in their membership, however, Rhaetian communes carefully restricted immigration, as did communes throughout southwestern Germany.[9]

The voluntarism at the heart of the communal ideal profoundly affected the internal organization of communes. Since communes lacked a charismatically legitimated lord or king, final authority could be exercised only by the membership as a whole: almost all communes had some form of general assembly to choose

---

[7] Otto von Gierke's *Das deutsche Genossenschaftsrecht* is still valuable despite its romantic view. See also Black, *Guilds and Civil Society*, esp. 18–26.

[8] The first two restrictions were common; the last is rare, e.g. WS I: 106–08.

[9] Most of the village statutes printed in WS contain provisions limiting immigration. Cf. Wunder, *Bäuerliche Gemeinde*, 19.

leaders and ratify decisions (even if real power lay elsewhere). From very early on, such assemblies reached decisions by voting, whether by acclamation, by show of hands, or by separation into groups.[10] Meanwhile, every communal association derived some power to command from the fact that its members had sworn obedience to it. The more free its members were, the greater the commune's potential authority. This point is crucial: unlike most lords, whose ability to make law was narrowly constricted by tradition, communes could and did legislate freely within their spheres of competence, establishing new laws and revoking old ones without hesitation.[11]

Even though legitimate authority belonged to the entire membership of a commune, however, individuals actually managed a commune's affairs on a daily basis: guild masters, town mayors, village magistrates, and the like. Under these circumstances, leaders were thought to be mere agents of the whole, operating with delegated authority that the commune could withdraw at any time. Never could they command by virtue of their persons alone. This by itself distinguished the conceptual model of communal organization from the norms of feudal Europe, where a lord's right to command flowed from his person and his house, rather than from those whom he commanded.[12] The principle that the power to command was always delegated from the collectivity, combined with the very real fear that leaders might seize lord-like power, resulted in frequent elections and rapid turnover in many communal offices. Florentine *priori* served for only two months, and most German mayors had to be reelected annually. In Graubünden, too, one- or two-year terms were the rule, and reelection was often prohibited.

Once commoners organized sworn communes, conflict with their lords increased. Late medieval Germany was convulsed by the struggle between princes and urban leagues, while the Italian cities banded together to reject imperial authority and subordinate the rural nobility in their *contado*. Especially in mountain regions such as Switzerland, peasant communes doggedly undermined external control over their daily lives – often at a high cost in money and blood.[13] Nowhere did this process go further than in Graubünden, where lordly dominion had lost its vigor by the late fifteenth century. The rural communes there not only secured extensive internal autonomy, but also became the founders of a federal state able to legislate, to negotiate with kings and princes, and to exercise sovereignty.

An extended struggle for local autonomy dominated Swiss politics from 1350 to 1500, and ended with an unqualified victory for the communes.[14] These communes included towns ruled by various kinds of guild regimes, and rural republics where

---

[10] See Maleczek, "Abstimmungsarten."

[11] Wunder, *Bäuerliche Gemeinde*, 44–45. On communal law, see Ebel, *Die Willkür*.

[12] On the idea of the *Haus*, see Brunner, "Das 'ganze Haus.'"

[13] Blickle, *Deutsche Untertanen*. Blickle's more recent work has stressed the large sacrifices that peasant communes made to increase their autonomy; see e.g. "Rechtsautonomie durch Kirchenkritik."

[14] HSG I: 243–63. See also Meyer, *Bildung der Eidgenossenschaft*, esp. 209–92.

the entire citizenship gathered annually to elect their leaders and to conduct public business. Many historians have demonstrated that neither sort of commune was necessarily very democratic by modern standards: citizenship was limited not only by gender but also by wealth or residence, and office-holding was usually dominated by a few powerful families. In addition, many parts of Switzerland, although communally organized at the local level, were also subject to the sovereign cantons and lacked political rights. Nevertheless, political authority in Switzerland ultimately derived less from lordly concession than from popular will sealed by oath and secured by arms. This characteristic, shared with Italian communal alliances and with the leagues among German Imperial cities, gave the Swiss confederation its contemporary name, the *Eidgenossenschaft*, the "oath-comradeship." The Rhaetian republic, too, was a confederation of communes, and its inhabitants were also given a name reflecting this fact, being known in German as the *Bündner* (Leaguers).

Rural communes

During the last thirty years, historians have analyzed the appearance of both the village (*Dorf*) and the rural political commune as distinct legal and social phenomena in southern Germany and Switzerland during the high Middle Ages. This research, which has included work on settlement patterns, agrarian economies, legal history, and politics, has resulted in a broader understanding of the autonomous communes that played such a large role in the region's history until the end of the *ancien régime*.[15] More recently, Peter Blickle has focused on the political consequences of communal development and on the changes in political culture that followed from it, demonstrating peasants' political participation and authority in late medieval and early modern Germany. In his most ambitious statements, Blickle proposes that an entire era of European history, from the thirteenth to the eighteenth centuries, be characterized as an age of communal organization.[16]

The novelty of the rural commune in the high Middle Ages may come as a surprise to some. Naturally, peasants and their masters lived in groups in earlier periods, but little of the surviving evidence suggests that peasant groups coalesced into self-regulating communes. Under the "older dominion over land" (*ältere Grundherrschaft*), which prevailed in most of Germany before *ca.* 1000, rural labor was closely controlled by landowners and lords, who also retained full control over

---

[15] For the legal history of village communes, Karl S. Bader's work remains fundamental, while the work stimulated by Theodor Mayer and the Konstanzer Arbeitskreis explores local developments in various parts of Germany. Recent surveys by Heide Wunder and Roger Sablonier outline the current state of research on these topics. Wunder, *Bäuerliche Gemeinde*; an English condensation: "Peasant communities"; Sablonier, "Das Dorf im Übergang."

[16] Blickle, *Deutsche Untertanen*, chapter 4, esp. 112–14.

local legislation and justice.[17] Well into the high Middle Ages, many lords managed their own estates, relying on labor from full-time laborers residing on the estate, or from local peasants who owed labor dues. The lords' control over production was paralleled by their judicial authority over the peasants who worked for them. Such conglomerations of land and authority, known as *villae* in Latin or *Höfe* in German, were scattered across a countryside characterized by relatively few nucleated settlements.[18]

The first German reference to a peasant commune appears only in the *Sachsenspiegel*, compiled in the 1220s. By that time, changes that had taken place since 1000 had laid the groundwork for the appearance of rural communes: population growth, internal and external colonization encouraged by lords, and the development of markets for agricultural products. These changes led to the "newer dominion over land" (*neuere Grundherrschaft*), defined not only by changed relations between peasants and their lords, but also by changed relations among peasants themselves. The balance of power between peasant communities and their lords in southern Germany shifted steadily throughout the "newer dominion," resulting in two distinct periods. The heyday of the peasant commune from about 1300–1500 was an age of "dominion shared with peasants" (*Herrschaft mit Bauern*), according to Heide Wunder, in contrast to the later age of "dominion over peasants" (*Herrschaft über Bauern*) that resulted from the rise of the princely state after about 1500.[19]

Changes in the control of agricultural labor were the decisive step towards the *neuere Grundherrschaft*. During the high Middle Ages, lords began to lease their land to autonomously producing peasant households. Instead of managing farming themselves, the lords left control over the details of production in the hands of peasants. The peasants in turn gathered their leased lands into common fields, which enabled the use of more productive systems of crop rotation. The dense population and high grain prices of the high Middle Ages made such an emphasis on grain production profitable to lord and peasant alike. The lord gained secure and steady revenue, often paid in money, while the peasant gained autonomy and the opportunity to expand his holdings by participating successfully in the local market economy. The gathering of scattered parcels into common fields brought about a transformation of settlement patterns and of the peasant family. Nucleated villages replaced the scattered estates of the earlier system, and the individual household became the primary unit of production and consumption.

The new villages, which often contained land belonging to several lords,

---

[17] Wunder, *Bäuerliche Gemeinde*, 26–32; Mayhew, *Rural Settlement*.

[18] The German terminology is confusing, since *Hof* can apply to a single farm operated by a peasant household, as well as to earlier noble demesne operations. Some literature tries to distinguish *Grosshöfe* or *Fronhöfe* from smaller entities; in any case, the context in which the word *Hof* appears is always important.

[19] The periodization and terminology here are Heide Wunder's, from her *Bäuerliche Gemeinde*, 33–79, esp. 61–76.

managed their common fields collectively, even though each separate parcel was leased by a single family from a single lord. Villages also strove to establish clear boundaries against their neighbors, as they took control over the meadows and forests that became more important to their survival as the population grew. Thus, both the demands of internal cooperation and the pressures of competition with other villages acted to increase the importance of village institutions. Peasants responded to this situation with innovative social, economic, and legal changes.[20] The autonomous control over land by separate households required a new social and legal bond, the "union" (*Einung*), which joined households as equals by means of oaths to one another. While each separate household remained subject to a lord, they now possessed a collective framework for cooperation independent from their lords, based on the assumption of equality and mutual responsibility for local affairs. At first these unions controlled only the management of common fields, but they soon extended their reach to other areas of life.

Meanwhile, control of different amounts of land by different families within villages led to the appearance of a village elite that attempted to steer collective decision-making according to its own interests. Both communal authority and internal stratification grew rapidly because of the increasing pressure on resources that resulted from the high population density of central Europe around 1200. As Roger Sablonier points out, the expansion of the social and economic authority of the village:

was far less the result of any vague sense of community than of the imperatives of mutual security, control and differentiation. In village life, the peasant experienced not just solidarity and cooperative action, but also – perhaps even more commonly – hatred, envy, misfortune, daily conflict and competition for land, food, and resources in the broadest sense.[21]

The hard choices of daily life, rather than "Germanic community" or "peasant collectivism" brought forth this new system.[22] In its early phases, this system increased income to the lords as it simultaneously fulfilled the peasant elite's desire for autonomy and familial continuity.

The defining features of the communal paradigm are these: the emergence of the village commune, which functioned as an association of equals, and which comprised a substantial proportion of the households (though often excluding the landless); the consequent growth of horizontal solidarity among the member

---

[20] Wunder, *Bäuerliche Gemeinde*, 65–66.
[21] Sablonier, "Das Dorf im Übergang," 734–35.
[22] Late medieval villages were therefore neither a survival of ancient Germanic tribal gatherings, nor a direct product of rural economic associations (*Markgenossenschaften*). Wunder, *Bäuerliche Gemeinde*, 26, reflects the general opinion among historians today: "Die lange vorherrschende Auffassung, daß für die Siedlungsstruktur und die wirtschaftlich-soziale Verfassung der germanischen Stämme nach Abschluß der Völkerwanderung große Haufendörfer und die Markgenossenschaft der Gemeinfreien bezeichnend gewesen seien, ist wissenschaftlich überholt."

households; the expansion of the commune's control over local jurisdiction, expressed in its power "to command and forbid"; the creation of a local sphere more or less removed from lordly control; and the combination of individual management of labor with the collective management of the means of production, such as fields and forests. These widespread and stable features determined the subsequent expansion of village communes. In a few regions such as Graubünden, where the balance of power between lords and communes favored the latter from an early date, this peasant world was able to expand, and ultimately to determine the organization of an emerging state. This is why understanding the local commune is essential for understanding the Rhaetian Freestate. Communal and federal politics there directly reflected the central and stable elements of the communalism paradigm.

All over Germany, the emergence of village communes during the high Middle Ages displayed a dynamic of its own that soon led to conflict between the newly constituted communes and their lords.[23] By taking over the functions of organizing production and providing social discipline within the village, the new village commune necessarily became a "politically active association."[24] As it did so, its membership became more homogeneous. The members might originally have belonged to different groups – freemen, serfs of one lord or another, and persons in various semi-free conditions – but the village commune tended to dissolve such differences in favor of a generalized peasant estate, which found its first expression in the comprehensive petty jurisdiction of the village court over all subjects living in a village, regardless of who their lord was.[25] The peasant's personal status became less important than the amount of land (whether leased or owned) that he managed. At the same time, the boundary between "free peasant" and "petty noble" became much less permeable. A new social model of orders based on social function replaced the early medieval categories of free and unfree men. Meanwhile, a very specific combination of legal autonomy with collective economic and social decision-making distinguished the late medieval village from the early and high medieval villa. The emerging village commune became both a corporation *and* a community (a *Genossenschaft* and a *Gemeinde*), even though this development had little to do with older Germanic traditions, as historians once claimed.[26]

Not all aspects of this paradigm can be applied directly to Graubünden, where the persistence of scattered settlement patterns and the existence of non-Germanic

---

[23] Blickle, *Deutsche Untertanen*, 55–60; Sablonier, "Das Dorf im Übergang," 739–45.

[24] Sablonier, "Das Dorf im Übergang," 737.

[25] Bader, *Dorfgenossenschaft*, 62–102, *passim*. See Bundi, *Besiedlungs- und Wirtschaftsgeschichte*, 534, 540 for examples of this process in Rhaetia.

[26] Bader, *Dorfgenossenschaft*, 1–29. Wunder, "Peasant communities," 16–17, points out that most German researchers continue to separate the two, defined as "private corporation" and "public corporation." Such legalistic distinctions focusing on the exercise of public power do not do justice to the wide variety of peasant communes found in central Europe.

legal traditions complicated the situation. The ideal type of the compact, hedged in village never predominated among Rhaetian settlements, though a slow tendency in this direction was visible. But Graubünden nevertheless developed legally competent village communes not unlike those in Swabia and other German regions, though often larger and endowed with greater authority.[27]

Peter Blickle takes the theory of communalism much further than agrarian historians do. Like them, he argues that the specific combination of economic and social functions in the emerging village of the high Middle Ages was distinctive. But Blickle is specifically interested in how the emerging commune changed the political order in regions where it was predominant, such as southwestern Germany and Switzerland. He argues unhesitatingly for a progression from communalism to parliaments to republicanism, and studies the political values of the village commune as an influence on the political world of regions and nations.[28] Blickle's definition of communalism emphasizes its political dimension:

Communalism means . . . that the organization of everyday issues (expressed in the power to make statutes, in administration and in the administration of justice) and the maintenance of peace within and outside, together with the legal norms which derived from these two aspects, was exercised in the form of autochthonous rights of a commune by all of its members on the basis of equal entitlement and obligation. Entitlement and obligation developed out of the autonomously exercised labor of peasant and manual laborer within a communal association.[29]

As lords withdrew from the daily management of peasant villages, Blickle argues, the villages had to assume the function of maintaining order.[30] The central organ that emerged to undertake this task was the village assembly. Meeting annually or more often, it managed communal resources, regulated the agricultural cycle on the land gathered into common fields, produced statutes and regulations about village affairs, and elected both a council to oversee village affairs and employees to carry out common tasks.

The corporate character of villages entitled them to have their own courts, which soon competed with the lords' courts as the primary venue for petty affairs.[31] Initially, the lords maintained control over adjudication in the villages by appointing the judge (called *Amman* or *Mistral* in Graubünden) who presided over the communal court. Other members of the court were either appointed by the lord or elected by the village. As the village communes strove for greater autonomy, the right to choose their own *Amman* became a key battlefield against the lords. Various complex compromises resulted across rural Germany: the lord might choose among

---

[27] On Bader's neglect of larger rural communes, Bierbrauer, *Freiheit und Gemeinde*, 72.
[28] Blickle, "Kommunalismus, Parlamentarismus, Republikanismus."
[29] *Ibid.*, 535.
[30] The following analysis is based on Blickle, *Deutsche Untertanen*, 23–60, esp. 30–37.
[31] Blickle, "Kommunalismus, Parlamentarismus, Republikanismus," 534–35.

candidates elected by the village assembly, or the village assembly might elect from candidates chosen by the lord. In most cases, however, the lord retained his right to give the *Amman* the oath of office even after other lordly prerogatives had withered away.[32] Much more rarely, village communes achieved judicial autonomy in capital cases; even in Rhaetia, only the largest political communes bought or usurped this right between the fifteenth and seventeenth centuries.

New forms of local organization manifested themselves in a new model of political life, in Blickle's view. He stresses the importance of assembly and voting in rural communes, which gave peasants practice at governing their own affairs. In addition, he emphasizes that officers and employees were elected out of the village population, which increased the effective autonomy the villagers enjoyed from their lords. The village commune was thus perceived by all of its members as an association that managed collective resources for the general good (*Gemeinnutz*), regardless of how the benefits were distributed.[33] Such a strong view of the commune as beneficial corporation (*Nutzungsgenossenschaft*) is particularly applicable to Graubünden, as we will see.

Blickle's model of communes as voluntary associations, however, does not always take account of the fact that communes also remained *natural* associations, to which members were bound whether they consented or not.[34] They were natural in a geographical and biological sense, in that members were born into them, and that no commoner within the territory of a full-fledged commune could claim exemption from its authority. This aspect of communal organization in Graubünden is illustrated by the fact that the communes there controlled not only the details of agricultural production, but the civil and even criminal behavior of all inhabitants without exception. But late medieval communes were also "natural" in the language of the period because they depended on the authority of their lords.

The dominant social vision during the late Middle Ages portrayed the authority of all lords as natural within the hierarchy of occupational estates. The central medieval social order, based on unfree laborers and free landholders, had divided all men into the free and the unfree. As peasants came to control their own labor

---

[32] This pattern is typical for southwestern Germany, though it varied elsewhere. Wunder, *Bäuerliche Gemeinde*, 35–60.

[33] Wunder, *Bäuerliche Gemeinde*, 66; Blickle, *Deutsche Untertanen*, 56. Both echo Von Gierke, who made equality among members one of the defining characteristics of community. *Community in Historical Perspective*, 18, describes the reemergence of Germanic fellowship in the form of "free union": "That a fellowship did not – or did not solely – owe its existence to natural affinity or to an external unity imposed by a lord, but had the basis of its solidarity in the free will of its members – this was the new idea which built up a branching structure of popular associations from below during the last three centuries of the Middle Ages ... "

[34] My use of the ambiguous term "natural" here is intentional. It contains the idea of a condition connected with one's birth (Latin *natura* from *nasci*, to be born), but also echoes the language of medieval judicial decisions that defended the "natural" rights of lords. GG, "Natur," IV: 215–44, esp. 215, and "Naturrecht," IV: 245–313, esp. 270–78 on the relation of will to late medieval concepts of natural law.

within communes, however, the division between free and unfree men yielded to a new, no less hierarchical model of three occupational estates. High medieval social theorists proposed a tripartite division of society into those who prayed, those who fought, and those who worked, resulting in a divinely sanctioned system ensuring peace and the common weal.[35] Within this system, secular political authority "naturally" belonged to those who fought to protect the other two estates, namely the lords. The lords' authority could be used to authorize the creation of communes and to endow them with certain powers, but this did not (in the lords' view) decrease the natural power of the nobility.

Communalism, with its emphasis on horizontal relations, eventually posed a challenge to this social ideology, to be sure. Village communes persistently sought to increase their autonomy and their own political authority. But communalism developed *within* a society where hierarchy was the predominant world-view, and where power was firmly in the hands of the lords. The result of this situation was a synthesis, in which the emerging communes were given legitimacy by the natural authority of their lords, even as they produced a new sphere of political and social interaction based on the more egalitarian logic of communal values.[36] As long as the communes' sphere of authority was limited to the details of village life, this synthesis served the interests of lords as well as of peasants: the lord's authority was recognized, and his income was maximized by increased agricultural efficiency. Ideally, commune boundaries followed lordship boundaries, communal officers were appointed by or approved by the lords, and each peasant's individual duties to his lord were kept separate from his participation in the commune. Horizontal ties arranged below a vertical hierarchy seemed to be a viable model for social order. Only when communal entities began allying with one another, and began to invade areas formerly reserved to the lords, such as maintaining public peace, did conflict develop.

In fact, the medieval village commune lay at the boundary between "natural" hierarchically constituted communities and purely voluntary associations of free men. Depending on local circumstances, it could share features of both. In some cases, the commune served primarily as a new conduit for lordly authority as agriculture shifted from demesne farming to leasing. Communes firmly under the control of a single powerful lord often degenerated into instruments of his lordship, as he exploited the cooperation of some peasants to control the whole village.[37] A

---

[35] A classic study on this subject is George Duby's *The Three Orders*. For the Germanic world, see Oexle, "Die funktionale Dreiteilung."

[36] Gerhard Oestreich's distinction between "firm relations based on status" (a *Herrschafts-* or *Statusvertrag*), and the "free contractual relationship" (*freies Vertragsverhältnis*) of communal obligation, captures this dual character of communal identity. Oestreich, "The religious covenant and the social contract," in *Neostoicism*, 139–40.

[37] The model of peasants "sharing in their own domination" is developed persuasively in Robisheaux, *Rural Society*.

village commune where dominion was divided among several lords, in contrast, might emphasize membership and oath in order to overcome the legal differences among the peasants. Under these circumstances, the commune might well become a tool for excluding all the lords from the management of village affairs. Most of the rural communes in Graubünden took yet another position on this spectrum of possibilities: they were mostly under the authority of single lords, but those lords were either weak or distant. Consequently, Rhaetian village communes connected their entire population with a single lord, yet they were able to resist and eventually marginalize these lords' prerogatives. In any case, the conceptual difference often blurred between communities defined by their members' subjection within a larger hierarchy, and communities given identity by the (sometimes fictitious) equality among members, especially when the two models overlapped in practice.

The dual nature of the commune was reflected in dual interpretations of the "freedom" of communal entities during the late Middle Ages.[38] One kind of freedom was the guarantee of protection to be given by a lord, the other was an exemption from external authority that was recorded in the concrete form of privileges. Both views of freedom persisted throughout the *ancien régime*, in institutional structures but also in the mentality of the peasants themselves.[39] Each view corresponded to one aspect of the commune at the time: either an association of peasants dependent on a single lord, or else a group of freely deciding peers. By emphasizing the second definition, peasants all over the Germanic world could make local autonomy their legitimate goal; at the same time, the freedom of action implicit in this definition helped create a sphere of peasant politics that could easily be turned against the lords. It is thus not surprising that ideas of peasant "freedom" took on great importance in regions where peasants gained a strong position against their masters, such as southern Germany and Switzerland.

In Germany proper, where lords retained their political authority and social predominance, tension between communal and hierarchical models of order often manifested itself in peasant rebellions and other forms of popular unrest – most dramatically in the German Peasants' War of 1525. When a communally organized confederacy such as the Freestate succeeded in wresting control over maintaining the peace from its lords, in contrast, the tension between these coexisting models of community and freedom shifted in focus. By marginalizing the lords' political authority and privatizing control over land and peasants, the creation of the Freestate allowed communal concepts of community and liberty room to grow. This process can be seen in parts of Switzerland during the fourteenth and fifteenth century, and in the Freestate during the fifteenth and sixteenth. Conflict with lords

---

[38] The idea of "freedom" in medieval and early modern Europe is the subject of a tremendous amount of research. My description here relies on Bierbrauer's review of the literature, *Freiheit und Gemeinde*, 26–43. For a general overview, especially of the German-language literature, see the article in GG IV: 425–542 esp. 446–56, and Jürgen Schlumbohm's *Freiheitsbegriff und Emanzipationsprozeß*.

[39] This point is elaborated in Bierbrauer, *Freiheit und Gemeinde*, 19–81.

in these regions often took the form of outright wars, which the peasant and urban forces often won.[40]

A study of the Rhaetian Freestate, a region containing only one small town, must follow Blickle in laying great emphasis on the way the peasant commune was rooted in agrarian practice and everyday political life. But the village commune's appearance on the historical stage closely parallels that of other sworn associations of equals. High and late medieval towns were also communes, limited in membership and claiming political authority on the basis of their common oath. Similarly, noble estates appeared as a counterpoise to the great princes of realms all over Europe: organized by their common subservience to a single lord, the estates viewed themselves as corporations of equals, who often reached decisions by voting.[41] Both of these elements – common oath or *coniuratio*, and common subjection to a lord whose responsibilities included protection and legal order – played a role in the evolution of the Rhaetian communes. Thus, even though the practical roots of the Rhaetian commune are to be found in local conditions, the forms its development took paralleled other phenomena all over Europe during the same period.

Attributing so much importance to the emerging political functions of the village commune does not require a naive faith that harmony and consensus were the predominant characteristics of village political life. The romanticists of the Germanic commune often fall into this trap, while Blickle's structural approach also puts little stress on village organization's potential to reflect differences as well as cooperation (though he is not blind to the potential for disagreement in village life). Some recent studies, however, have stressed conflict in village life. Local organization in peasant societies might also ensure that a few powerful families could consistently exploit the landless and the marginal, even as it spurred intergenerational and intrafamily hostility.[42] The most convincing work in this vein treats areas such as Württemberg and Upper Austria, where princely rulers built strong administrative states that penetrated into the countryside and soon subverted the communal ideal of cooperation among village citizens. In these regions, peasants often lost control over communal institutions to princely administrators; in other areas, such as Hohenlohe, weaker lords co-opted some peasants into the structure of domination so as to control the rest more effectively.[43] In either case,

---

[40] A string of Swiss victories over invading lordly armies allowed the Confederation to flourish: Morgarten in 1315, Sempach and Näfels in 1386, the Appenzeller Wars in the early fifteenth century, and the Swabian (Swiss) War in 1499.

[41] Näf, "Frühformen des 'modernen Staates' im Spätmittelalter"; Bosl and Möckl, *Der moderne Parlamentarismus*, especially Mitterauer, "Grundlagen politischer Berechtigung im mittelalterlichen Ständewesen," 11–41.

[42] Sabean, *Power in the Blood*; and Rebel, *Peasant Classes*. Critically about earlier examples of this general approach, Bader, *Dorfgenossenschaft*, 270.

[43] Robisheaux, *Rural Society*. Recent Swiss work has also stressed the control exercised by local oligarchies, and the narrow limits within which Swiss "democracy" functioned in this era.

village solidarity often crumpled in the face of internecine hostility, leaving power in the hands of lords and their agents.

The weakness of outside domination in Rhaetia led to a different situation. Conflict, both within communes and between them, remained common, and family feuding and struggles over religion or resources often resulted in bitterly divided communities. Nevertheless, the resolution of conflict also rested firmly in the hands of the communes themselves. Since a modicum of internal harmony was essential if a commune was to maintain its claims against its neighbors, strong incentives were in place to prevent conflict from dominating communal life. In Graubünden, the village commune thus remained a locus of shared action and values, especially against outside forces, even when internal tensions divided it into warring factions. The high value placed on internal harmony is illustrated by the tendency to partition communes in which conflict had become unresolvable. *Bündner* peasants preferred life in a smaller unit which had fewer resources and less political weight, to living in a large commune permanently riven by strife; moreover, the choice to do so was in their hands, not in the hands of outside agents.

To summarize, the following were the essential features of the village commune, particularly in the western and southern parts of the Germanic world:

– It consisted of a finite and concrete membership who collectively benefited from the resources held in common, and who collectively shouldered the burdens of maintaining and defending those resources.
– The most important productive resources, especially cropland, were privately controlled, and individual peasants controlled the disposition of their own labor. But the use of these resources was strictly regulated by collective institutions.
– The commune strove for maximum legal and political autonomy.
– The commune's decisions were ratified at assemblies of the entire membership, where an oath of membership in and obedience to the collective were taken.
– The commune displayed characteristics of both a voluntary association created by an oath among equals, and of a "natural" hierarchically constituted community created by an oath to a lord.

These general principles raise many specific questions about the peasant commune in Graubünden. First of all, what specific forms did the commune take there? What political practices developed within the Rhaetian village commune? In what ways did such political practices influence local alliances and the Freestate as a whole? Because the early evidence from Graubünden is fragmentary, not all of these questions can be answered for periods before the sixteenth century. Still, the surviving evidence suggests that the communal paradigm does apply to Rhaetia, which allows us to fill in some of the historical gaps on the basis of the broader theory.

Communalism and other models

Communalism in Rhaetia

While a first look might suggest that communalism flourished in Graubünden, one could also argue that the underlying structure of settlement and production was quite different from Blickle's Swabian examples. Much of Rhaetia was settled only during the high Middle Ages, and grain production was never the exclusive form of agriculture. Since control over labor and over land play such a central role in this model, such differences cast the theory's usefulness for Graubünden into doubt. Can Blickle's model, based on one specific constellation of circumstances, be extended to the different environment of the Rhaetian Alps without modification? Looking at the scattered evidence about settlement, agriculture, and politics in medieval Rhaetia can help answer this question.

The areas of old settlement in Rhaetia were in fact organized into *villae* or *Höfe* which were managed by lords or their agents: the initial situation was thus comparable to Blickle's model. However, estates managed by lords or their agents were not the only form of agricultural organization, although the *villae* did tend to control the most fertile fields. Instead, "compact closed *villae* [*Hofwirtschaft*] were complemented by a large number of smaller autonomous peasant farms, which led to a greater diversity of economic relationships . . . "[44] As much as half the population farmed land on its own behalf as far back as the evidence reaches.[45] During the high Middle Ages, the two forms of labor management began to melt into one another, leading to the creation of village communes that eventually overcame the distinction between unfree laborers on the *villae* and autonomous peasant farmers. A close study of the village of Zernez in the Lower Engadine revealed that:

Large villae [*Grosshöfe*] consisting of groups of subjects as well as the scattered farms of new colonists were grouped in a more or less scattered fashion around an old village kernel, the *vicus*, which was usually inhabited by an association of free people . . . From the sixteenth century on, a continual process of concentration within the inner zone of the village took place.[46]

Village commune formation in Graubünden took place later than in the long-settled grain-farming regions of the flatlands, but the process itself seems to have been quite similar.

Most of the higher regions in Graubünden were first settled and cleared only

[44] The essential resource on agriculture in Graubünden is M. Bundi, *Besiedlungs- und Wirtschafts- geschichte* (here 190, describing the Upper Engadine).
[45] *Ibid.*, e.g. 540, 511. Note that similar proportions held even where demesne farming was most intensive in the lowland grain country. Wunder, *Bäuerliche Gemeinde*, 28–29.
[46] M. Bundi, *Besiedlungs- und Wirtschaftsgeschichte*, 542. Bundi also notes that "The formation of villages in most Bündner communes appears to have taken a course similar to the case of Zernez described here."

during the boom times of the twelfth and thirteenth centuries, however. In addition, the migration of German-speaking cattle farmers from the upper Rhône valley into the highest valleys in the thirteenth and fourteenth centuries exercised some influence on settlement patterns and political organization during the late Middle Ages. These new migrants, known as Walser, favored scattered settlements, and moved to marginal regions because of the extensive autonomy the local lords offered them.[47] In these regions, a process of village-formation never took place. Nevertheless, local communes similar to those predicted by the communalism theory did appear. The legal status of the Walser, who were at first collectively responsible for dues to their new lords, encouraged the development of strong collective associations, and the pastoralism they practiced was conducive to collective patterns of production.[48] In Graubünden at higher altitudes, then, one might speak of the creation of a commune-based pastoral agricultural system, rather than the transformation of an existing system of noble *villae* into communal villages. In any case, the social and political consequences were similar, though even less advantageous to local lords than in Germany. While the Rhaetian lowlands follow Blickle's model reasonably closely, newly settled regions took a different path to communal organization from the one he describes.

Not only did a process of communalization occur in Rhaetia, then, but the form of agricultural production which came to predominate put an unusually high value on communal control and organization. This was not grain-farming as in Swabia, but rather alpine pastoralism.[49] Indeed, wool, milk products, and cattle may have played the same role in Rhaetia that grain for urban markets did in southern Germany. In the early Middle Ages, pastoralism seems to have been subordinate to grain-raising in the settled part of Rhaetia, which at that time was confined to lower elevations and to the main pass routes. By the high Middle Ages, sheep had become an important product, both for wool and meat. Some *villae* already specialized in animal raising; in most others, every household held a few sheep for its own use. The areas settled by the Walser during the thirteenth century were characterized by a climate too harsh for raising cereal crops, and were therefore entirely dependent on pastoralism; the dues they paid their lords consisted entirely of lambs, wool, and dairy products.[50]

Alpine pastoralism as practiced in Graubünden displayed a combination of individual enterprise and collective management similar to that of communal peasant farming elsewhere, though with an even greater emphasis on the

---

[47] The supposed influence of the Walser and their liberties in Rhaetia has been exaggerated in much of the historiography; as Bundi points out, the original Walser often paid relatively high rents, and were obligated to extensive military support for their lords. M. Bundi, *Besiedlungs- und Wirtschaftsgeschichte*, 142–45. On Walser historiography, see Fontana, "Ländliche Gemeinde."

[48] M. Bundi, *Besiedlungs- und Wirtschaftsgeschichte*, 536.

[49] *Ibid.*, 576ff, *passim*.

[50] *Ibid.*, 595–99.

communal dimension. Many peasant families owned their cattle, and raised hay and perhaps some grain on their own fields. However, the summering of the herd on the high meadows was managed collectively, and the village community restricted the number of animals any individual could own, according to the amount of pasture available.[51] Going beyond the communal supervision of individual labor found in grain-farming regions, the alpine commune not only controlled the summering of the herds, but actually carried it out as well.[52] Cheese production was a collective enterprise carried out by employees of the village commune or alpine corporation – but the resulting product was divided among the individual cattle owners according to complex formulae that considered not only the number of cows a peasant had on a given alp, but also their condition. At the same time, animal husbandry put a premium on the availability of pasture, which in Graubünden had to be either created by communal labor, or leased from neighboring regions. Establishing an alpine meadow required a substantial investment: paths had to be cleared; stalls, cheese-making huts, and dwellings for the cowherds had to be built; and trenches and conduits for irrigating the dryer parts of the slopes were often created.[53] Since grazing took place far from the homes of the peasants, communal organization was essential if large-scale production was to take place. Animal husbandry also implied a greater orientation to markets and monetary exchange than did the limited grain-raising possible in Graubünden; the availability of salable products may have eased the transition from demesne farming to rents in kind or in money. Later, the cash profits from dairy production enabled the communes to purchase political and judicial privileges from their lords.

A shift from sheep to cattle took place in the fourteenth century, just at the time when village communes appeared in many areas. Unlike sheep, many of which could be sold off every winter, raising cattle required year-round collective management to prevent the exhaustion of pastures and winter fodder.[54] Collective control over the cattle-raising cycle – from winter stall to spring pasture to summer meadow and back – fulfilled the same role in the development of Rhaetian village communes that collective control over common fields did in the Swabian grain belt. Thus, Blickle's model of the agrarian foundations of communalism is also applicable to Rhaetia; if anything, the Rhaetian situation was more conducive to communal organization than was the case elsewhere.

Finally, the political and legal organization of Rhaetia presented an environment for the development of communal institutions similar to the areas on which the communalism paradigm is based. Because of its passes, Rhaetia became part of both the Carolingian and the Ottonian imperial systems, so that the struggle for

[51] Some alpine meadows were privately owned, especially in communes where the Walser were strongly represented. For a more detailed analysis, Weiss, *Alpwesen Graubündens*, 170.
[52] *Ibid.*, 202–06; and Mathieu, *Bauern und Bären*, 65–67.
[53] Mathieu, *Bauern und Bären*, 56–60; M. Bundi, *Besiedlungs- und Wirtschaftsgeschichte*, 275–76.
[54] M. Bundi, *Besiedlungs- und Wirtschaftsgeschichte*, 576–607.

authority between imperial agents and local dynasts was not unlike that which took place in Germany and Italy.[55] Of course, Rhaetia's strategic position, perched between Italy and Germany, influenced the specific course of development there, as did its economically marginal position and the long distance from the great centers of imperial authority. Nevertheless, the region was not exceptional within the bewilderingly complex tapestry of legal and political development in the Holy Roman Empire: despite its peculiarities, it was well within the spectrum of possible situations before about 1300. Only in the late Middle Ages did Graubünden, like Switzerland and a few other areas such as Dithmarschen, take a decisive turn away from the most common path of political and social development in Germany. This turn must therefore be seen as a *result* of communal development within the specific Rhaetian situation, rather than as a decisive precondition for it.

In Graubünden, there was an important distinction between village communes and the larger political units shaped by communal organization and values. In some ways, this distinction is artificial: Rhaetians called all sorts of entities communes (*Gemeinden, Comüns*), from parts of a village to entire valleys. *Gemeinden*, whether local or extended, shared similar institutional practices and a similar political logic, and stood in similar relationships to outside lords. Indeed, only the creation of communal entities that extended beyond the immediate village offered the possibility of successfully dissolving lordly authority, as the Swiss experience clearly illustrates. Yet a sociologically convincing analysis of communalism and its importance on the larger scale depends in part on establishing a connection to the structures that regulated the labor and daily life of the population in question. Such a connection must be founded on the face-to-face village community. Any effort to rediscover Rhaetian peasants as autonomous *actors* in their own history must show how their action depended upon their experience, which for most of them revolved around the village commune rather than around the larger communal entities.

Recognizing the importance of social experience, especially the experience of labor and collective organization, does not necessarily imply materialist conclusions. Rather, assuming we accept Blickle's argument that the collective organization of production by peasants who managed their own labor was fundamental to the village commune, we must then ask how the social and political consequences of this form of social order were abstracted and extended to social and political units which were not themselves such groups of producers. The Rhaetian Freestate was organized and held together by a political cosmology that had its roots in village life, but the extension of communal principles to larger units was by no means simple or automatic. Rhaetian peasants and their leaders had to construct a functioning political order, capable of resolving disputes and maintaining itself against outsiders. The creation of the Freestate was not simply a peasant rebellion,

---

[55] Some striking similarities between Swiss and Italian communal development are enumerated in Ruser, "Die Talgemeinden des Valcamonica."

but rather its inhabitants' creative response to the possibilities and to the constraints of their local and ideological environment.

ALTERNATIVE MODELS FOR POLITICAL ORGANIZATION IN THE FREESTATE

Although communal life provided the most important models for organizing the confederation of communes that became the Freestate, it was by no means the only source. The feudal principles that ordered late medieval politics were never formally repudiated in Graubünden, nor was the region's identity as part of the Holy Roman Empire abandoned entirely. Moreover, throughout the sixteenth century many leading Rhaetians encountered firsthand the new bureaucratic and authoritarian forms of government that were developing in France, in the German princely states, and even in the other Swiss cantons. Echoes of all these influences appeared in the Freestate as it consolidated over the course of the sixteenth century.

By the late Middle Ages, a political ideology reflecting the fractured realities of feudalism in the southern regions of Germanic Europe had developed; its most lucid description appears in Otto Brunner's classic study, *Land and Lordship*.[56] Brunner claims to be describing practice as well as theory in late medieval Austria, but his work is most important for illuminating the ideological structure of feudalism in the region. Like many medievalists, Brunner starts his analysis by pointing out the transcendent character of justice in medieval political thought: human justice, embodied in law, reflected divine justice and therefore preceded, rather than derived from, existing political institutions. This assumption allowed every individual enjoying full personhood to resist injustice – not just because injustice represented a violation of human order, but because it represented a direct attack on each individual's connection with the transcendent order ordained by God. Resistance was thus not directed against the state conceived as an impersonal system, but aimed at an unjust ruler who was himself equally subject to the principles of justice and law. This commonplace view lies behind Brunner's outline of the ideology of feudal politics.[57]

As the title of his book suggests, two fundamental concepts for the feudal nobles

---

[56] Translated into English in 1992 (see Bibliography). My research is based on the third German edition, *Land und Herrschaft*. Brunner revised his the book after World War II to excise passages all too friendly to Nazism, but his theoretical standpoint is more clearly visible in the earlier version. On Brunner, see Robert Jütte, "Zwischen Ständestaat und Austrofascismus: Der Beitrag Otto Brunners zur Geschichtsschreibung," *Jahrbuch des Instituts für Deutsche Geschichte (Tel Aviv)*, 13 (1984), 237–62. Brunner's strongly historicist approach permeates *Land und Herrschaft*, e.g., 2; this makes it possible to reject his twentieth-century ideological concerns, while still relying (cautiously) on his analysis of noble ideas in the late Middle Ages.

[57] Brunner, *Land and Lordship*, 114–24. For an analysis of the notion that justice transcended political organization within the communalist context of late medieval Switzerland, see Reibstein, *Respublica Helvetiorum*, chapter 2.

of Austria were "territory" (*Land*), and "lordship" (*Herrschaft*).[58] A *Land* was a territory unified under a single law, whose unity was a historical fact not dependent on dominion by a single lord. Lordship, in contrast, was simply the property (both real and in privileges) of a single lord, even when this property was fragmented among more than one territory. Brunner lays particular stress on the deeply patriarchal character of lordship: a lord is one who controls a *Haus*, a social entity including not only his wife and family, but also his servants and other dependents – including his peasants, who Brunner claims had no political standing or power to initiate actions at law.[59] The *Haus* was a sphere of action dominated by the authority of its father and lord and was sheltered from formal law and actions pertaining to the larger political world. Only the master of a Haus, a *Hausvater*, enjoyed full personhood and freedom: patriarchy and politics coexisted intimately in this scheme of things.

This connection between patriarchal authority and the ability to act in public leads Brunner to a key conclusion: "So the central concepts of 'private-law,' namely guardianship (*Munt*) over persons and dominion (*Gewere*) over things and rights, turn out to be the core of all lordship relations, without which the constitutional structure of the *Land* cannot be understood. What they are is power, legitimate power, '*dominium quoad protectionem*, protection and wardship [*Schutz und Schirm*].'"[60] Political competence as conceived by this model was limited to the minority of fathers who controlled the rest of the population and who possessed all property: they alone were authorized and able to act politically, whether through public legal proceedings or by means of violence. The German phrase *Schutz und Schirm*, "protection and wardship," legitimated the exercise of authority within this system. Since the phrase remained common in Rhaetian documents throughout the sixteenth century, despite the overtly anti-aristocratic views which prevailed there, it deserves our special attention.

According to Brunner, the idea of protection provides the organizing principle for hierarchical relations in the feudal system. Based on the father's protection of his dependents, *Schutz und Schirm* also justified a lord's authority over his vassals, though with one important difference. Whereas dependents within a *Haus* could not act against their "father," either at law or by their actions, a lord's vassals might themselves be fathers with the standing to act both through the law and through feuds. Their relation to their lord was consequently a reciprocal one, in which they provided him "counsel and aid" (*Rat und Hilfe*) in exchange for his

---

[58] Both terms are difficult to translate. On *Land*, Brunner's comment, 151–52, that *Land* and *territorium* cannot be separated inspires my translating it as "territory." On *Herrschaft*, 200–03 conveys the essentially contingent and personal character of *Herrschaft* that Brunner emphasized, leading to a translation as "lordship." In other contexts one might choose "dominion" to stress the broad connotations of the German word in early modern sources.

[59] Brunner, *Land and Lordship*, 211–13, and in more detail, "Das 'ganze Haus.'"

[60] Brunner, *Land and Lordship*, 279.

protection against their enemies. Should he fail to protect them, they could repudiate his authority and conduct a suit or a feud against him on the basis of their own powers as fathers and lords, which empowered them to appeal for transcendent justice. We must note, however, that while *Schutz und Schirm* among lords always implied a reciprocal relationship, it also established a hierarchy: the protector gained the power to command those he protected, at least until his protection failed.

Brunner thus divides late medieval society into two categories: those with the means to conduct a legitimate feud (which represented an appeal to the higher justice above any lord), and those who were dependents of a *Haus*, and thus unconditionally subject to their father's authority. Brunner believes that peasants fell into the latter category: their collectivities were conceptually *within* the *Haus* of their lord, and their assemblies were private events conducted under his authority.[61] Peasants could not fight, according to a social ideology that reserved fighting for a distinct social estate. Brunner even attempts to subsume towns – the quintessential communal entities according to older scholarship – into a similar relationship: "Any understanding of the place of towns in the territorial constitution must recognize that each town possessed a lord, and was included in his *Haus*."[62] Brunner's description of feudal organization thus incorporates, but goes beyond, the medieval idea of a society of three orders – those who fought, those who prayed, and those who labored.

The *Land* consisted of the collectivity of fathers, of all those who controlled a *Haus* and who were entitled to conduct a feud if their privileges were violated. Because the remaining population was both protected and dominated by this group, an assembly of these lords *was* the entire people, and thus the entire territory.[63] Peasants were therefore incapable of legitimate political action, and did not need to be represented (in the modern sense) when the lords in a *Land* gathered to deliberate.[64] The authoritarian bent of Brunner's thinking becomes clear here, along with his interest in subordinating conflict between communes and lords to a framework in which lords alone were entitled to act politically. Whatever Brunner's bias, though, he identified and explained a coherent vision of political life, one that appears in southern German, Austrian, and Swiss sources well into the early modern period. But since he wrote, many studies about conflicts between communes and their lords have shown that his vision outlines the world-view of the

---

[61] *Ibid.*, 285–86.
[62] *Ibid.*, 287. Brunner does admit that *for the individual citizen*, the town took the place of the lord, (and that towns could therefore appear in territorial assemblies), but subsumes this relative lordship under the "real" obedience of the town as a whole to its lord.
[63] Brunner, *Land und Herrschaft*, 471ff, esp. 474. (*Land and Lordship*, 324–33 is somewhat different in thrust.) On 484 (in the English, on 349), Brunner emphasizes that the nobles did *not* represent the *Land*, but rather embodied it.
[64] On the changing meanings of "representation," see Hoffman, *Repräsentation*.

lords, not the "constitution" of the entire society, as he claimed.[65] Nevertheless, this world-view profoundly influenced early modern ideas of authority, serving as one viable model of political organization for Rhaetian thinkers well into the seventeenth century. Even after "lordship" all over Germany had become an alienable, purchasable commodity, feudal theory continued to define public debate about authority and politics. At this level, then, Brunner's characterization of authority and order in feudal terms remains important.

One way to reconcile the social ideology of feudalism with the growing power of communes was to squeeze the latter into the categories established by the former. One might claim that each member of a commune was a lord and father, as feudalism defined them – on a small scale, perhaps, but still entitled to defend his position by law and feud. A non-noble making such a claim would emphasize his right and ability to bear arms, and his freedom from anyone else's protection. Land tenure would also be reconceived, losing its overtones of service and protection and becoming a strictly private and contractual exchange of land for money or products. These are precisely the claims set forth by Rhaetian peasants and communes. They raised and used their own military forces, and made bearing arms the decisive criterion for membership in their communes. They also stressed their "freedom," not merely as a privilege granted by their lords, but as something earned by their military prowess. And finally, in the Second Ilanz Articles of 1526, they reduced land tenure to a private transaction by mandating hereditary alienable tenure. At one level, then, Rhaetian commoners did not challenge the ideology of late medieval feudalism, but simply subverted its principles for their own ends by communalizing it. This partial appropriation of feudal values was only an expedient, though, and as the Freestate continued to evolve, its political theory moved further and further from Brunner's feudal vision.

The *Schutz und Schirm* which a father exercised over his dependents, and a lord over his vassals, could also be made more congenial to communal liberty. Even Brunner recognized that peasants often ignored the authority of lords who failed to protect them, but the Rhaetian communes went much further.[66] By the late sixteenth century, they had turned *Schutz und Schirm* into an obligation that lords owed their subjects, one whose neglect justified throwing off lordly authority altogether. Not just the failure to protect villages from other lords, but any dereliction regarding the "common good" was enough to persuade Rhaetian communes to ignore their nominal masters. Given the fact that most local lords lacked the resources or will to overcome this kind of resistance, effective lordship over the communes in the Freestate became impossible. Neither the local nobility, nor the bishop and the abbot of Disentis, nor even the Habsburg dukes in Tyrol

---

[65] On Brunner's idea of *Verfassung* in German medieval history, see Graus, "Verfassungsgeschichte des Mittelalters," 566–73.
[66] Brunner, *Land and Lordship*, 44–63, 283.

actually controlled the Rhaetian communes after about 1500, even though the formal authority of these lords was rarely questioned.

Another reason that a political model founded on *Schutz und Schirm* persisted in Graubünden long after lordship there had been gutted was that the Rhaetians themselves exercised "lordship" over subjects outside their own communalized territories. The Valtellina, the counties of Bormio and Chiavenna, and the communes of Maienfeld and Malans were subjected to the Freestate on the basis of feudal ties: the Italian valleys had been extorted or conquered from the duchy of Milan, and the two German communes had been bought from their previous lords, all in the early sixteenth century. Since these territories provided the Freestate with much of its income, it remained important to justify the Freestate's dominion there. The idea of *Schutz und Schirm* provided a serviceable legitimation without threatening the autonomy of the communes at home. The Rhaetians thus employed that part of feudalism that justified their collective authority over their subjects, while rejecting the premise that peasants were inherently subjected to lords, which would have threatened their own status.

Later in the sixteenth century, yet another model of political order began to influence the structure of the Freestate. In an era of growing centralization and bureaucratic control in the surrounding regions, some Rhaetian leaders sought to bring about similar changes in the Freestate. Not only the surrounding principalities – Württemberg, Tyrol, Venice and Milan – made increasing use of the administrative methods associated with the absolutist state; Swiss urban cantons such as Zurich and Bern did so as well, limiting political participation to smaller groups, sending officers to rural areas, and claiming divine rather than popular sanction for their authority.[67] The Freestate's character as a confederation made it more difficult to introduce centralized government, however. The kinds of changes that resulted from steady and purposeful pressure on the part of central governments elsewhere in Switzerland – the closing of city councils, the spread of uniform religious and legal codes, the rationalizing of administrative practice – were rare in Graubünden, and when they did occur, they often had a quite different character.

Still, the reorganization of government practice that Rhaetians could observe in the neighboring territories did influence the Freestate's government, as did the rationalization of military administration that Rhaetian mercenary officers experienced during their service abroad. In the early seventeenth century, leading politicians repeatedly tried to create a smaller executive committee – a "Secret Council" (*Geheimrat*) in contemporary vocabulary – that would concentrate power in fewer hands. But communal suspicion of the central government blocked this development, and the Freestate never even established a central treasury.

---

[67] On absolutism in Switzerland, see esp. Peyer, *Verfassungsgeschichte der Alten Schweiz*, 107–42. Comparable material for southern Germany in Vann, *The Making of a State*.

Meanwhile, a reform movement that flourished after 1585 tried to rationalize the administration of the subject territories, and certain improvements were introduced in 1603. On the whole, however, the intense particularism and localism that was built into communal politics combined with popular suspicion of the *Bündner* elite to block the kind of changes that were going on in most European states by the early seventeenth century. Neither foreign pressure nor domestic turmoil could convince the Rhaetian communes to give up their local autonomy to any central bureaucracy.

In addition to administrative centralization, the early modern state is often associated with increasing ideological discipline imposed from above. Following the pioneering work by Gerhard Oestreich, a flood of scholarship has focused on the disciplining effect that new ideas, especially neo-Stoicism, exercised on both elites and on the general population in the later sixteenth century.[68] In much of Europe, the growing authority of princes was accompanied by a new philosophy of internal self-control taught by neo-Stoic thinkers such as Justus Lipsius, who portrayed the ideal government servant as a Christian warrior who overcame the tribulations of political life through his fortitude and self-control. Although this movement found sympathy among the Rhaetian elite, it seems to have had little effect on popular conceptions of politics.[69]

Special caution is necessary when looking for "state discipline" in the Freestate during this period, moreover, because late medieval communalism also assumed certain forms of social and political discipline that superficially resembled the obedience demanded from the subjects of absolutist princes. Sometime before 1600, for example, the city of Chur passed an ordinance requiring all citizens to show obedience to the city fathers:

If any citizen or denizen should be commanded to do something for the city by the lord mayor, the city justice, a judge, guild master, or any other officer of the city, and if he should be disobedient to this command and not carry it out, he or they shall be fined 1£ without any reduction.[70]

While this statute resembles the kind of disciplining measure typical of early absolutism, its meaning in the city of Chur was less clear. Was it a new kind of control imposed on the citizenship, or did it simply reassert the communal principle that all members of a commune were bound to act for the common good and to obey the will of the majority? Statutes like this one validated communal officers over individual citizens, even as they insisted that all important matters be referred to communal assemblies.[71] Insofar as early modern absolutist thought and

---

[68] Oestreich's essays collected in *Neostoicism* and *Strukturprobleme*. A summary of recent research in Hsia, *Social Discipline*.

[69] See, for example, the schoolbook and diary kept by the young Johann von Tscharner of Chur during the late sixteenth century, which contains unmistakable traces of neo-Stoic doctrine. STAG B70.

[70] WS III: 5.

[71] Cf. the statutes of Fürstenau and Ortenstein of 1615, WS III: 109, esp. 116, footnote 1.

political discipline made any appearance in the Freestate, it did so without openly challenging the communal foundations of authority in the communes or in their Leagues.

On the whole, Rhaetian political culture discouraged any effort to adopt the newly organized and energized European states of the sixteenth century as models for the Freestate's own development. Instead, both communal and feudal models – often inextricably intertwined – provided most Rhaetians with the cognitive resources for thinking about political life, at least until after 1620. That the international environment surrounding the Freestate was increasingly dominated by states organized and legitimated by absolutist ideas did not change this fact. Rather, the weakness of statist ideas in Graubünden, in addition to the decay of traditional lords' power, left room for the unusual flowering of communal principles.

2

Graubünden to 1520: geography, society, history

God himself wrought the ringwalls so well,
the high mountains that enclose the land,
and we withdrew there to enjoy our free estate.

Fortunat Sprecher von Bernegg, 1615.[1]

Geography has imposed significant constraints upon human activity in Graubünden throughout its history. The Rhaetian Freestate's sovereign heartland consisted of two major river valleys flowing out of the jumbled center of Europe. To the north is the Rhine: from its source at the Oberalpsee, it flows east along a nearly impassable line of mountains that separate Graubünden from the rest of Switzerland. All of the Rhine's major tributaries during its eastward course flow out of a series of deep-cut valleys from the south; the larger ones, especially the Domleschg, provide access to the passes that connect Rhaetia to northern Italy, most notably the Splügen (2117 meters) and the Septimer (2311 meters). The Rhine itself, having lost nearly 1500 meters of altitude, reaches the end of the confining northern range at Chur (585 meters), and turns north to flow towards the Lake of Constance. The lower reaches of the Rhine in Graubünden are one of the few relatively flat and fertile parts of the region: from Ems above Chur down to Fläsch, the valley broadens out into a "U" shape with gently rising fields on the eastern side of the river. Not only grain and pasture but also vineyards are found here.

Fifty kilometers to the southeast, parallel to the Rhine, the Inn begins its course down to the Danube. Unlike the Rhine, which starts high among the peaks, the Inn begins in a group of lakes that lie in a glacier-cut trough known as the Upper Engadine. The flat valley floor of the Engadine extends nearly thirty kilometers northeast down to Zuoz (1692 meters), its chief village in the sixteenth century. Unlike the flatlands below Chur, the Upper Engadine was too high for efficient grain-farming; instead, the broad meadows under the shadow of the Piz Bernina provided the base for intensive cattle raising. Below Zuoz the valley narrows, as the

---

[1] "Ein schön neu Lied zu Ehren der drei Bünde," in Zinsli, "Politische Gedichte," 6.

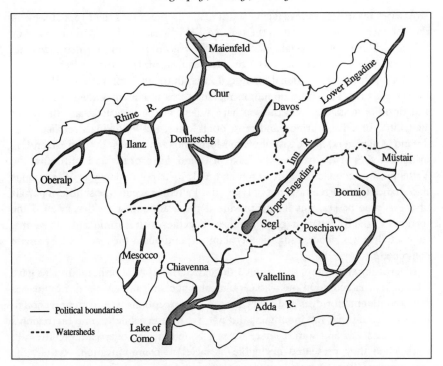

Illustration 1   Graubünden's rivers and watersheds.

Inn drops rapidly through the Lower Engadine to depart the Freestate's territory below Ramosch (1236 meters).

The mountainous territory between the Rhine and the Inn – the "land of 150 valleys" – was more thinly populated and linguistically and culturally more fragmented than the two major river valleys. The routes leading up to the major passes depended on international trade and politics, whereas the smaller valleys formed cul-de-sacs despite the lesser passes that connected them with one another. Nonetheless, the location of the valuable mountain meadows, high on the slopes rather than down on the valley floor, ensured that even dead-end valleys would stay connected with their neighbors. Villagers met in the pastures during summer, negotiating over boundaries and raiding one another's cattle.[2] Mountain ridges established connections as well as barriers; indeed, in some Rhaetian valleys, the gorges deeply cut into their centers were a more formidable obstacle to communication than the mountains around them.

---

[2] For an example of the intensity of such contacts far back into the medieval period, see Deplazes, *Alpen, Grenzen, Pässe.*

A series of smaller valleys facing south made up the rest of the Freestate. From the Val Mesocco in the west to the isolated Val Müstair in the far southeast, they helped establish the Freestate's control of the pass routes, and formed a channel connecting the Romance south with the Germanic north of Europe. After 1512, the Freestate ruled over additional territory to the south, an "empirette" as Benjamin Barber calls it.[3] This little dominion included two mountain valleys, Chiavenna and Bormio, nestled among the southern valleys of the Freestate, and the larger Valtellina. Broader, warmer, and most of all lower, the Valtellina stretched from Tirano (429 meters) in the east down to Morbegno (255 meters) in the west, ending in the marshes at the head of the Lake of Como. Historically and culturally, the Valtellina was connected with Como and Milan. Its possession was of enormous importance to the Freestate: not only did the Valtellina secure the southern portals of the Alpine passes, but it also produced the grain and wine that swelled the fortunes of the Rhaetian magnate families. Together with Bormio and Chiavenna, the Valtellina was richer, and probably about as populous as the rest of the Freestate combined.[4]

By creating the valleys that formed the basic geographical unit, mountains gave Rhaetia its character. On the whole, political, linguistic, and economic boundaries followed mountain ridges and valley gorges. Yet exceptions were common enough to demonstrate that the mountains did not by themselves determine the region's fate. Watersheds and watercourses formed boundaries all over Europe, after all, even when they presented negligible obstacles to communication. Rather, the geography of Rhaetia represented a constraining grid, favoring certain kinds of development, hindering others. Understanding what the inhabitants made of the terrain they inhabited requires looking more carefully at the lives they led.

ECONOMY

Graubünden's high altitude and harsh climate severely constrained its rural economy. Only in the lower valleys could enough grain be grown to cover local consumption; settlement in the rest of the region demanded other forms of agriculture, primarily animal husbandry. The mountains of the region are characterized by an abundance of high meadows that provide rich pasture during the summer, although long, wet winters require careful planning if the herds are to survive. Unlike some mountainous regions, though, Graubünden was poor in mineral resources. A few mines operated before the modern era, but they were rarely profitable and never developed into large-scale operations like those found in late medieval Tyrol. A third dimension of ongoing importance was the concentration of

---

[3] Barber, *Death of Communal Liberty*, 148–56.
[4] Horatio Brown's discussion of the Valtellina and its diplomatic situation, based on Venetian reports, is still useful. On population, Brown, "The Valtelline," 35.

38

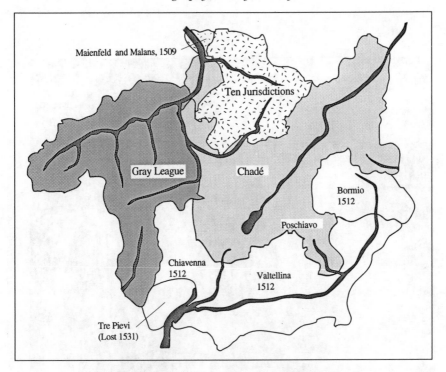

Illustration 2 The Three Leagues and their subject territories.

trade through mountain passes. The Rhaetian routes through the Alps remained attractive to overland merchants throughout the premodern period, though always in competition with the Brenner to the east and the Gotthard to the west.[5] The passes represented both an economic and a cultural resource: travelers paid well to have themselves and their goods transported across the Alps, and in the process, the local population was exposed to European affairs – exposed in more than one sense, as the events of the early seventeenth century were to show. Armies as well as merchants needed to pass the Alps, not always to the benefit of the Rhaetians.[6]

Even though the mountains constituted an overwhelming feature in Graubünden's geography, geographical elements constrained and shaped economic, social, and political developments in complex ways. Neither agricultural products nor the mode of production remained the same from the early Middle Ages until the end of the *ancien régime*. The earliest records portray an economy limited primarily to the lower altitudes, in which the farming of grain including

[5] The standard study is Schnyder, *Handel und Verkehr*.
[6] A strategic overview in Parker, *Army of Flanders*, 70–79.

Chur

Illustration 3   Chur, *ca.* 1640. Engraving by Matthäus Merian, in *Topographia Heluetiæ, Rhætiæ, et Valesiæ*, 2nd edition (Frankfurt am Main: Merianische Erben, 1656).

wheat, rye, and barley, predominated.[7] In addition, the major pass routes were settled very early, since a trickle of trade persisted throughout the Middle Ages, providing a livelihood for a limited population. After the sixth or seventh century, steady progress took place in clearing the forests in the more important valleys, still at lower altitudes.[8] The *Tello-Testament* of 765 describes a flourishing villa in Sagogn (779 meters), consisting of twenty-three buildings and about twenty hectares of grain fields; it was worked by eight families tied to the central villa, together with twelve outlying families.[9] The villa already used some of the higher areas around Sagogn as well, to judge from their inclusion in the *Testament*.[10] Nevertheless, the economy seems to have revolved primarily around food crops in the limited areas where this was possible.

In the high Middle Ages, a qualitative change developed out of earlier conditions. An improving climate and increasing population pressure spurred the first colonization of the high valleys. Often organized by cloisters or priories, a net of cultivation and more importantly of animal husbandry spread across the mountains. In the high Middle Ages, sheep were the most important product, but the monks in particular also encouraged cattle-raising. The major wave of colonization undertaken around 1300 by the German-speaking Walser increased the emphasis on cattle, with important consequences for local organization and political change.[11] Less hardy but more productive, cattle required increased communal cooperation both in the development of fodder supplies, and in the marketing of cheese, butter, and meat. Related to these changes in agrarian products were changes in rural organization: from lordly villa to scattered commune to compact village, the settlement patterns and local institutions found in Graubünden changed fundamentally between the eleventh and the seventeenth centuries.

Even where geographic conditions were similar, however, social organization could vary widely. Mathieu's detailed study of the Lower Engadine shows that the agrarian system was not predetermined by the mountainous conditions and the climate, but rather responded flexibly and creatively to the challenges posed by the natural environment.[12] Still, pastoralism was the only form of intensive exploitation possible in much of Graubünden. The most favored communes, such as the Lower Engadine, could practice balanced agriculture that produced nearly enough grain for local needs, allowing the export of dairy products for profit. But for most Rhaetians before 1800, cattle and dairy products had to be traded for grain.

---

[7] The following survey follows M. Bundi, *Besiedlungs- und Wirtschaftsgeschichte*. On grain varieties, see 564–66. On the predominance of grain raising over animal husbandry in the early period, 576f.

[8] *Ibid.*, 25.

[9] *Ibid.*, 27.

[10] *Ibid.*, 38–39.

[11] *Ibid.*, 584.

[12] Mathieu, *Bauern und Bären*, 296. Mathieu's work, by far the best detailed study of local society in early modern Graubünden, concentrates on the seventeenth and eighteenth centuries.

A distinctive characteristic of the region was its lack of self-sufficiency, making it dependent not only on the economics, but also on the politics of grain and cattle markets outside Graubünden.

LANGUAGE AND CULTURE

Not least among the boundaries that divided Graubünden in the Middle Ages were linguistic ones. The original tide of Alemannic colonization in Switzerland barely reached the region. Thirty-five kilometers to the northwest lay the Walensee, whose name, meaning "lake of the strangers," indicates an early boundary between Germans and Romance-speaking Rhaetians.[13] As German crept towards the headwaters of the Rhine, the Vulgar Latin of the region was itself becoming a distinct Romance language, now known as Rhaeto-Romance or Romantsch.[14] Not until the fifteenth century was the city of Chur germanized, and the language boundary remained there for several centuries. Higher in the mountains, German-speaking settlers formed islands among their Romantsch neighbors, as at Obersaxen and Rheinwald. Meanwhile, the Engadine remained firmly attached to Rhaeto-Romance, even influencing the Italian of the valleys to the south. Italian speakers formed the third language group; while they were least numerous, possession of the Valtellina gave Italian a disproportionate role in the Freestate's affairs, as did the widespread use of Italian in diplomacy during the fifteenth and sixteenth centuries.

Not only did speakers of three distinct languages inhabit the Freestate, but sharp dialect differences further separated the population. This was noticeable even for German, since the old German settlements around Maienfeld spoke a quite different dialect than the late-arriving Walser colonists. In Romantsch, the difference was even greater. Developing in separated valleys for nearly a thousand years, the Surselvan dialects of the Upper Rhine became nearly incomprehensible to the Ladin-speakers of the Engadine. When religious fervor after the Reformation stimulated the publication of vernacular texts, the different dialects were frozen in print, and have survived to the present. Still, the differences can be overstressed: the first great composer of Surselvan texts was himself an Engadiner by birth, who only took up work in the Surselva as an adult.[15]

Despite such a confusion of tongues and dialects, language does not seem to have been a profoundly divisive issue until the nineteenth century, and linguistic boundaries seemed to have had little impact on other affairs.[16] Even though the early Reformation in the region was profoundly divisive, for example, major

---

[13] The name Walensee derives from the Germanic root for "stranger." Jacob and Wilhelm Grimm, *Deutsches Wörterbuch*, vol. XIII (Leipzig, S. Hirzel, 1922), cols. 544, 1327–53.

[14] The spelling of the latter name varies: Romontsch and Romansh are also current, as is Rhaeto-Romanic. A careful study of the history of the language is Billigmeier, *Crisis*, 49–82.

[15] Stephan Gabriel, who published his Surselvan *Il vêr sulaz dal pievel giuvan* in 1611.

[16] Billigmeier, *Crisis*, considers language differences to have been of greater importance, e.g. 49–51.

divisions did not follow linguistic lines. In the Surselva, Romantsch Disentis and the German enclave of Obersaxen stayed Catholic, while Romantsch Ilanz and German Tamins adopted the Reformed faith. Further south, both Romantsch Schams and the neighboring German Rheinwald reformed, while the adjacent Romantsch communes of Obervaz and Oberhalbstein split between the two faiths. The Italian Mesocco became a bastion of Catholicism, whereas Bregaglia and Poschiavo reformed.

Two reasons may explain the relative insignificance of language boundaries in Graubünden. The first was that only two languages, Latin and German, were used in legal documents before the seventeenth century. Both were in some respects foreign languages for the local population: for a Romantsch villager or an Alemannic husbandman, Chancery German and medieval Latin were equally alien tongues, thus muting potential resentment about local language differences. More-over, the line separating the notarial and Latin legal sphere to the south from the charter-based and German legal sphere in the north cut right across the Romantsch regions: Engadiners conducted their serious business in Latin, Surselvans often in German. The second reason is the high degree of local autonomy in Graubünden, which ensured that village life could proceed quite well in a local dialect. No distant lord or central administration needed to approve the decisions of each Rhaetian commune, freeing the communes to use whatever language suited them.[17] Only individuals who wanted to be active beyond the borders of the village needed to learn another language: traders and politicians learned whatever idioms they needed because they had good reason to do so. Different languages often functioned in different spheres, as illustrated by the case of a young patrician from the Engadine. Sent off to Basel to the university, he corresponded with his father in Latin (improving as his studies progressed), with his brothers in Italian, and with his mother and sisters in Ladin Romantsch.[18]

Yet the lack of overt conflict is not evidence that people were unaware of lan-guage differences. The sixteenth-century historian and minister Ulrich Campell, for example, proudly inserted Romantsch passages into his Latin works.[19] More practically, the Rhaetian parliament, the *Bundestag*, sometimes postponed awkward petitioners by begging extra time to translate documents into Romantsch and Italian. Language differences could also become an obstacle. When Johannes Guler toured the Freestate in 1605 to renew the oath of confederation, for example, his eloquence may have been muffled by the fact that in many villages his oration had to be translated.[20] The statutes of the Val Lumnezia issued in 1457 went so far as to

---

[17] *Ibid.*, 22.
[18] Letters by Rudolf von Salis-Samedan, son of Johann von Salis-Samedan. Letters to his father in STAG D II a3a and D II a28, to others in Italian in D II a28, ca. 1585; to his sister Eva in D II a25 and D II a28.
[19] E.g. in his *Historia Raetica*, I: 92–93.
[20] Guler, "Die Erneuerung des Bundesschwures," 180.

require immigrants to be "of Romantsch descent from this side of the mountains, in paternal line, or subjects of the Bishop . . . "[21] On the whole however, language itself rarely provided the criterion for important divisions within the Freestate.

SOCIAL AND POLITICAL ORDER

Since the forms of social organization found in Rhaetia and their political consequences lie at the heart of this book, the following passage will give only an overview of the situation before about 1500. Two paradigms of human relations permeated late medieval Rhaetian society: one, eventually becoming dominant, centered on the community and may be called communal; the other, which remained influential even as practice diverged from it, revolved around dominion and lordship, and is usually called feudal. Neither, of course, was unique to this region: rather, the coexistence and eventual competition between these two social cosmologies characterized much of Europe during this period.

Lordship in the region showed few systematic differences from anywhere else in Europe. Local lords pursued family aggrandizement, while more powerful dynasts sought to draw the whole region into their holdings.[22] Nor was communal organization in the region especially precocious. While early evidence for communes abounds from the twelfth century onwards, especially in Rhaetia's southern valleys, they did not at first carry any political weight. Instead, they mostly regulated relationships among peasants, taking over the supervision of local agriculture from lords' agents in a slow but steady process.[23] Corresponding to this process was the slow spread of relatively free land tenures, especially *Freie Erbleihe*, which gave peasants *de facto* property rights while maintaining the fiction of lordly ownership. Personal freedom was on the increase, too, although by no means all Rhaetian peasants were free in the thirteenth, or even in the sixteenth century.[24] None of these characteristics set Graubünden apart from neighboring regions.

In the fourteenth century, however, communes not only dominated the local affairs of peasants, but started to become political players on a larger scale. In the constantly shifting alliances among the region's greater and the lesser lords, support from the communes became an increasingly important resource, especially since the Rhaetian peasants were armed. Most of the local nobles were too poor to draw on mercenary or vassal troops, so that the local peasants formed the only military forces available. Moreover, as the Habsburg experience in Switzerland was showing at the time, properly motivated peasant militias could be devastatingly effective against mounted knights, especially in mountainous terrain.

---

[21] WS I: 106.
[22] Sablonier, *Adel im Wandel*; more accessible, although dated, is Isler, *Verfall des Feudalismus*.
[23] The southern communes seem to have been the earliest. Keller, "Mehrheitsentscheidung und Majorisierungsproblem."
[24] Castelmur, "Die Leibeigenen der III Bünden in der Herrschaft Maienfeld," 377–80.

Geography, society, history

The age of the commune in Rhaetian history began when the communes started forming leagues with one another and with the local noble families. Such leagues demonstrated that the communes had achieved enough internal cohesion to affect the outcome of political struggles. The boundaries of league formation at first matched the borders of the highest feudal authority in the region, the see of Chur. Even though the bishops' real authority was fractured by innumerable allods, immunities, and usurpations, the see continued to define the extent of alliances among rural communes: only the town of Chur sought broader horizons in the late fifteenth century by reaching for connections with more distant towns, including Zurich.

During the century after 1350, a complex tapestry of alliances developed in Graubünden. By the mid-fifteenth century, three associations of communes had emerged that between them contained nearly the entire territory of the subsequent Rhaetian Freestate. These leagues expanded within the see until checked by several more powerful territorial states that were also expanding into the region. The Rhine valley between Sargans and the Lake of Constance, for example, never joined the Freestate, even though it originally belonged to the see of Chur. Instead, a contest took place during the early fifteenth century between the Swiss, the villagers of Appenzell, and the local nobility; the end result was Habsburg control or patronage over part of the valley, and Swiss domination of the rest.[25] Similarly, the dominion of Tyrol's consolidation from its centers in Innsbruck and Trent cut off some Tyrolean parts of the see of Chur from participation in the Freestate – a process that ended only when the lower part of the Val Müstair, Untercalven, was lost to the Freestate around 1600. Consequently, the boundaries of the Freestate itself, particularly to the east and northwest, reflected the territorialization of dominion in the larger region: the competing efforts of Habsburg and Swiss to round out their territories set the limits to the Freestate's growth. Although the see of Chur provided outer limits, the realities of communal and lordly power determined which areas belonged to the Freestate, and which ended as parts of Tyrol or subject to the Swiss cantons.

The emergence of alliances as a politically creative force was not unique to Graubünden. One need only look to the neighboring Swiss Confederation, or before that to the Lombard League, to find earlier examples of similar phenomena. What distinguished Graubünden, though, was the relative importance of alliances in the formation of a territorial state there. Federal consolidation on the basis of communal entities went further than anywhere else in Europe, as will be shown below. The particular circumstances of late medieval Graubünden – weak episcopal authority beset by local allodial magnates and ambitious territorial dynasts such as the Habsburgs, combined with unusually strong communal development founded on local social and agrarian conditions – produced a political

---

[25] Bilgeri, *Der Bund ob dem See.*

45

Illustration 4 The Rhine valley above Chur, *ca.* 1640. Engraving by Matthäus Merian, in *Topographia Heluetiae, Rhetiae, et Valesiae*, 2nd edition (Frankfurt am Main: Merianische Erben, 1656).

entity and political culture that represented the most extreme example of communal and federal state-building to be found in Europe at the time.

THE ORIGINS OF THE THREE LEAGUES

On September 23, 1524, delegates from the Rhaetian communes sealed a document now known as the *Bundesbrief*, the Letter of Alliance, which consolidated and superseded a variety of older alliances in the region. By 1524, three particular leagues had become the primary actors: the Gray League to the northwest, the Chadè in the center and south, and the Ten Jurisdictions to the northeast. The *Bundesbrief* merely affirmed the close cooperation that these three had established during the previous half-century – cooperation that included joint military campaigns, a common foreign policy, and even common legislation. Before the period of consolidation between 1471 and 1524, however, each of the three Leagues had a history of its own. The differences between their histories illustrate the various routes that communes could take toward forming a federal polity.

Like most political developments in southern Germany during this era, the emergence of the three Leagues and their consolidation was a complex process. The object of the following pages is to penetrate through the myriad details to illuminate the key points in the development of each League, and show how they coalesced after 1450 into a single entity capable of concerted action in the diplomatic and military environment of the late fifteenth century. Such an approach must ignore the fine web of detail that has been painstakingly cataloged by earlier historians of the Freestate: each commune, each village had its own history of lordship and political development that helped explain both its internal organization and its position in its League. Instead, I will focus on one key dimension of each separate League, in hopes of illustrating the three primary processes that furthered communal alliances in general. The reader should remember that all three processes took place in each of the Leagues.[26]

First of all, however, we must define these three Leagues. While patriots have always argued about their relative priority, I will describe them in the order ordained by an arbitrational court in 1551, which decreed that the Gray or Upper League (*Grauer Bund, Oberer Bund, Ligia Grischa*) came first, followed by the League of the House of God (*Gotteshausbund, Chadè*), and finally the League of the Ten Jurisdictions (*Zehngerichtenbund*). For the sake of brevity, the following short forms will be used: "Gray League," the Romantsch "Chadè,"[27] and "Ten

---

[26] In this I follow the methodology (though not always the conclusions) of Peter Liver's seminal "Die staatliche Entwicklung," esp. 220–22.

[27] *Chadè*, a term current in the sixteenth and seventeenth centuries, should not be confused with the term *Cadi*, used more recently to refer to the Catholic portion of the Romantsch Surselva, especially the commune of Disentis. The two are identical in their etymology, both meaning "house of God," but the first refers to the see of Chur, the second to the abbey of Disentis.

Jurisdictions." The Gray League also gave its name to the entire Rhaetian confederation. Inhabitants of the region were known all over Europe as the Gray Leaguers, as in the French Grisons and the Italian Grigioni.

From its earliest beginnings, the Gray League's history reflected the mutual desire of quite different partners to restore the peace in their region and to undertake campaigns against their neighbors. Included in the League were most of the valleys of the upper Rhine above Chur.[28] Late in the fifteenth century, the southern valley of Mesocco also joined the League. The Gray League's first forerunner appeared in a treaty among the most important lords of the area in 1395 that temporarily ended a period of unusually vicious feuds among them. Abbot Johann of Disentis, Lord Ulrich Brun of Rhäzüns, and Lord Albrecht of Sax-Misox agreed to submit their disputes to an arbitrational panel rather than continuing their battles. Significantly, several communes also took part in the treaty, though in a subordinate role. Along with Johann, the commune of Disentis was a party, just as the Val Lumnezia participated along with the lord of Sax-Misox. The document included not only provisions for solving conflicts between the lords, but also guaranteed that "every lord and every man should be treated according to his law."[29] Already visible in this document was the central purpose of the Gray League: establishing peace and order in a region divided among a number of lords and dynasties and subject to devastating feuds.[30]

The importance of maintaining the peace motivated subsequent alliances in this part of Rhaetia, based on the hope that voluntary agreements among more or less equal partners could restore order. Various combinations of lords and communes formed alliances during the decades after 1395, including both members of the later Gray League and regions that subsequently belonged to the Chadè. Increasingly, communes also formed leagues of their own without their lords' participation. In 1396, for example, the bishop of Chur's subjects in the area allied with subjects of the counts of Werdenberg, although the letter of alliance acknowledged that it was written "with the benevolent scrutiny, with the grace, will and knowledge of our noble gracious lords . . . "[31] The entire Domleschg valley formed a league in 1423, whose peace-keeping purpose appeared unmistakably in article 4:

All those among us who belong to this alliance or who shall join it in the future, whether they be noble [*Edel*] or not noble, who at any time had to speak or negotiate with one another, or who came into conflict about any matter whatsoever within the boundaries of the league, shall seek their satisfaction at law from one another at those places where each one should do so according to law . . . [32]

---

[28] For a general overview of constitutional history in this period, see Planta, *Geschichte von Graubünden*; Moor, *Geschichte von Currätien*; and Pieth, *Bündnergeschichte*. On legal history, Meyer-Marthaler, *Studien*, is the best study.

[29] Planta, *Geschichte von Graubünden*, 115.

[30] See esp. Meyer-Marthaler, *Studien*, 68–110.

[31] JVF, 7.   [32] JVF, 17.

The provisions of this treaty applied to all inhabitants in the region regardless of their feudal status. Article 2 provided for military action against any peace-breakers, especially the bishops of Chur or the lords of neighboring Rhäzüns.

The actual Gray League was founded in 1424 when three major lords joined with some fourteen communes in forming a common league to protect one another, to keep the roads safe, to allow free trade and movement within the league, and to establish a common law.[33] The league was intended to be eternal, and the founding charter included provisions about accepting further members and about resolving conflicts between members. The latter were particularly important: article 12 not only established that the League could not be dissolved because of any dispute among its members, "whether because of manslaughter, stabbing or beating, or because of other disputes or statements of great import,"[34] but also established a fixed arbitrational panel to judge all matters by majority vote. The panel was to have twelve members. The abbot and commune of Disentis appointed three, the lords of Rhäzüns and Sax each appointed three, and the free communes of Rheinwald and Schams appointed two and one respectively.[35] Linking the local nobility and increasingly autonomous communal entities in a common league, the Gray League resembled other late medieval peace alliances (*Landfriedensbünde*) in the Holy Roman Empire during the fifteenth century. Not revolutionary in its goals or in its form, "the League's sole purpose was to ward off violence and the denial of justice."[36]

That such peace-keeping leagues could also be turned against the local nobility and against the bishop became strikingly evident in 1450, however. That year, the episcopal vice-regent joined the count of Werdenberg-Sargans and the lord of Rhäzüns in an effort to suppress the commune of Schams, which was resisting a new bailiff's efforts to reestablish control. The Schamser called upon their allies in the Gray League, and the communal militias decisively defeated the combined forces of the three lords at the Bärenberg. The lord of Rhäzüns was captured and sentenced to death by an impromptu military court at Valendas, since he had violated his oath to the League by supporting the bishop and the count.[37] By mid-century, then, the Gray League had become an effective bulwark against noble efforts to control the peasant communes of the region, even though its founding documents never explicitly challenged the principle of lordly dominion. What made this shift possible was the fundamentally egalitarian principle embodied in the

---

[33] Planta, *Geschichte von Graubünden*, 117. JVF, 19–25.
[34] JVF, 23.
[35] *Ibid*. The panel eventually became a standing appeals court for the Gray League, known as the Court of XV.
[36] Moor, *Geschichte von Currätien*, I: 350. Like many Swiss historians, Moor overlooks the League's aggressive potential.
[37] A highly romanticized narrative about this *Schamser-Fehde* in Moor, *Geschichte von Currätien*, I: 370–75.

Bund, the league, in which all partners were equal because they all swore the same oath to observe the same articles. Even though lords continued to enjoy some priority in actual documents – not only were they listed first, but they also appointed more members to arbitrational panels – all League members were bound by the League and were subject to prosecution should they violate its provisions. In the absence of any single agent who could maintain the peace, such a freely willed alliance provided the only hope of restraining violence. The consequence of such a league, however, was to make the communes partners with their lords, rather than subjects.

The Chadè arose from a different constellation of circumstances, as its name "League of the House of God" implies. The geographical and social situation was similar to that of the Gray League – a mountainous region organized into communal entities – but the political context was distinguished by common rule over the area by a single lord, the bishop of Chur, and by the weakness of independent dynasts. The Chadè was geographically more fragmented than the other two leagues: in the watershed of the Rhine, it included Chur and its surrounding villages, along with the eastern side of the Domleschg and a few other valleys. South across the mountains, all of the Engadine and the southern valleys of Bregaglia, Poschiavo, and Val Müstair belonged to the Chadè. The separation between the League's political center at Chur and the communes south of the Alps gave the southern communes, and the magnate families that dominated them, unusual independence from the bishop.

Although the exact form of subjection to the bishop varied from commune to commune, the League's central problem was defining and constraining the bishop's authority.[38] In contrast to the Gray League, where independent lords organized the League and set its tone, the most important political group in the Chadè consisted of the bishop's ministerial servants within the communes, who were aided by the cathedral chapter in Chur.[39] Consequently, the early organizational principle of the Chadè was entirely different from the Gray League: rather than being a cooperative effort in which the contracting parties enjoyed equal status, the Chadè consisted of parties of differing legal and social position, who were bound primarily by their shared interest in limiting the bishop's power. Only over the course of nearly two centuries of development did the Chadè become a League similar to the other two – a development made possible only by the extraordinary status rural communes gained in the region.

When the bishop's ministerials, the cathedral chapter, and the citizens of Chur met in 1367 to prevent Bishop Peter of Bohemia from handing the region's

---

[38] The following survey based primarily on Liver, "Die Stellung des Gotteshausbundes," here 134; and Clavuot, "Kurze Geschichte des Gotteshausbundes."

[39] Ministerials or *Dienstadel* were those who gained semi-noble status because of their personal service to a feudal lord. Looked down on by the high nobility because of their allegedly servile origins, the ministerials nevertheless enjoyed many of the privileges of noble status by the late Middle Ages.

immunities over to the Habsburg rulers of Austria, their action followed a pattern common to regional estates all over the Germanic world. At the same time, the participation of several mountain communes mirrored events in neighboring Switzerland, where rural communes joined towns in resisting territorial consolidation by the Habsburgs. Even though the events of 1367 did not lead to any permanent institutions, they highlighted one issue that would catalyze political development in the Chadè well into the sixteenth century: a single lord's relations with his subjects, who included not only nobles but also clerics and peasant communes.

During the decades after 1367, maintaining regional peace became a second unavoidable problem in the Chadè. Although the presence of a single lord gave the alliances that resulted a rather different flavor from the Gray League, the concern for regional peace and the practice of settling disputes through voluntary alliances moved the Chadè in the same direction as its future allies. Still, the distinctive character of the Chadè was accentuated during the reign of Bishop Hartmann von Werdenberg-Sargans (1388–1416); the latter was intent on expanding his (and his dynasty's) influence by military means, but he was remarkably unsuccessful in doing so and suffered numerous defeats.[40] The resulting weakness of the see encouraged both dimensions of the Chadè's identity: the conflict between estates and their nominal lord, and the formation of peace-keeping alliances based on free will. On the one hand, the bishop's repeated military failures (he was twice captured by his Austrian enemies and ransomed by the Chadè) enabled communes and petty lords alike to extort privileges from the impoverished see. Each estate benefited from the estates' common relationship with a powerless lord, whose nominal overlordship shielded them from outside meddling even as they dismantled his real power. On the other hand, political weakness made the see unable to preserve peace in the region. The resulting disorder encouraged further alliances, as communes tried to protect their citizens from noble warfare and from banditry. Communal alliances intended to preserve the peace in the Chadè sometimes rejected the bishop's authority explicitly. When Oberhalbstein and Avers allied with Rheinwald in 1407, they stated:

We have also agreed that if our lords demand our [military] service outside these boundaries, every man should be willing and obedient to his lord, with this limit, that none of us shall act against his allies [*aignossen*], or assist in action against them, in good faith without any deceit.[41]

The bishop's subjects thus denied his authority to order them against their allies: their alliance outweighed their feudal duties to their lord. Similarly, the

---

40 Liver, "Die Stellung des Gotteshausbundes," 136–37; Clavuot, "Kurze Geschichte des Gotteshausbundes," 537–38.
41 JVF, 13–14.

peace-keeping league in the Domleschg, mentioned above, explicitly identified the bishop as a potential aggressor who could be resisted by force.[42] The 1407 alliance also illustrated the bishop's dependence on military support from the communes. After his defeat by the Austrians in 1409, the bishop even handed over the administration of his seat in Chur to a bailiff and two counselors appointed by the Chadè.

Over the course of the fifteenth century, therefore, the communes – led by the ministerial nobility who lived in them – took more and more control over the machinery of episcopal administration. Not only petty and capital jurisdiction, but sources of income, castles, and policy towards the see's neighbors came under League supervision. The bishop remained nominal head, but actual control slipped to two parties: the ministerial families, and the city government of Chur. As the Habsburgs gained increasing control of the cathedral chapter, in contrast, the chapter lost influence in league decision-making. In 1468, a meeting of the Chadè demanded that the bishop accept a permanent council of twenty-four members with authority to approve all important matters, but the bishop refused.[43] In 1480, Chur purchased control over imperial jurisdiction there, effectively ending the bishop's sovereignty over the city. Finally, after the bishop took the Austrian side in the Swabian War of 1499, the Chadè took more or less permanent control over the see's political authority, although the bishops continued to enjoy some privileges throughout the sixteenth century.[44]

Seen in one light, the history of the Chadè involved the process of regional estates eroding their lord's authority to the point that they, not he, became the most important political force in the region. From another perspective, the emancipation of the Chadè resembled the emancipation of German episcopal cities, except that the beneficiaries were not urban burghers, but a collection of rural communes headed by local families. In any case, the process of communal takeover went further than anywhere else except the Republic of the Valais, where rural communes stood in a similar relationship to the bishop of Sion. The relative weakness of the bishops of Chur, especially after Bishop Hartmann's disastrous military undertakings, accelerated the shift to collective authority. The Chadè differed from the Gray League and the Ten Jurisdictions, however, in that it never had a formal letter of alliance. Its cohesion derived from subjection to a single lord, and opposition to him grew out of older power

---

[42] JVF, 17.
[43] See Castelmur, "Ein Versuch zur Einführung," 96–108; Liver, "Die Stellung des Gotteshaus-bundes," 138–39. The distribution of the twenty-four illustrates the location of power in the Chadè. The cathedral chapter and the city of Chur were each to appoint four, and the rest were to be appointed "by the valleys," that is, by the magnates in the rural communes. The demands of 1468 are published in JM II: 21–24 (no. 10).
[44] Liver, "Die Stellung des Gotteshausbundes," 140–46. See also Vasella, "Die bischöfliche Herrschaft."

centers rather than deriving from a common oath between equal members of an alliance. Communes of peasants became the decisive element in the Chadè only towards the end of the fifteenth century. Matured by the demands of peace-keeping, the communes succeeded in taking over their League, especially when the bishop's ministerials decided to participate through their communes rather than to form a separate estate of their own.[45] By the time the Three Leagues consolidated their permanent alliance in 1524, the communes of the Chadè took their place alongside those of the Gray League and the Ten Jurisdictions as full partners. Unlike the situation in princely territories elsewhere in southern Germany, the peasants became the dominant estate.[46]

Smallest and latest of the three Rhaetian Leagues was the Ten Jurisdictions, which did not emerge until the mid-fifteenth century.[47] Its history shares features from both of its more powerful partners. Squeezed between the other two Leagues and the Austrian Vorarlberg, the League included two valleys flowing into the Rhine, the Schanfigg and the Prättigau, together with two communes in the Rhine valley proper below Chur. Like the Gray League, the Ten Jurisdictions resulted from a freely willed association, but like the Chadè, all of the communes were originally subject to a single lord, the house of Toggenburg. Most decisive was the relationship between the communes and their lord: unlike the Chadè, where subjects from different estates cooperated to negotiate with and thus influence their lord, the communes that made up the Ten Jurisdictions joined initially to stay together under a single lord who could guarantee their privileges. Later, after lordship over most of the Ten Jurisdictions fell to powerful outsiders, the League opposed any efforts to assert feudal rulership over the communes.

The region had come into the hands of the powerful Toggenburg dynasty, which had holdings all over eastern and central Switzerland, in the fourteenth century. In contrast to the autonomy common in the Chadè and the Gray League, the Ten Jurisdictions appear to have experienced effective, though not burdensome, dominion under the Toggenburgers. When the last count of Toggenburg died in 1436, a series of wars broke out over his lands, as the Habsburgs, the city of Zurich, and the rural Swiss all hastened to seize a share. The ten communes in Rhaetia allied in 1436 to protect their unity and the privileges that they had gained up to that point.[48] Unlike the Gray League or the Chadè, the League of the Ten Jurisdictions included only communes: no lords appeared as parties, and no exceptions for lords

---

[45] On the role of ministerials and magnates in the communes, especially in military affairs, see Padrutt, *Staat und Krieg*. Blickle discusses the Chadè in "Kommunalismus, Parlamentarismus, Republikanismus," 546–47.

[46] Bundi *et al.*, *Geschichte der Stadt Chur*, II: 160–67.

[47] In early documents, it is often referred to as the *eleven* jurisdictions rather than the ten, counting separately the priory of Schiers (the *Chorherrengericht*). Cf. the original alliance of 1436, JVF, 29.

[48] Moor, *Geschichte von Currätien*: I: 353–57.

were made within the document. Instead, the communes clearly stated their intentions with regard to any future lord:

2. Item, the aforementioned lands and jurisdictions desire to render to a hereditary lord [*Erbherren*] whatever is owed to him, provided it is established that he is their hereditary lord.

3. Item, we have also discussed and decided that if these lands and jurisdictions should gain a hereditary lord, we will stay united by the oaths described above, and we will help anyone to that which is his by right, in good faith without deceit, now and later, and we will not let ourselves be forced from this point.[49]

In short, the subjects proposed to determine the conditions of their own future subjection by acting decisively at the moment when their rulers were weakest, during a succession dispute.

The communes were divided in 1438 between the families of Montfort, Sax-Monsax, Brandis, Mätsch, and Aarberg – all relatively impoverished houses who proceeded, one by one, to sell their rights to the steadily expanding Austrian house of Habsburg. By 1500, lordship in eight of the Ten Jurisdictions belonged to the Habsburgs; the other two, Maienfeld and Malans, escaped this fate when they were purchased by the Three Leagues themselves in 1509. All of the communes used the disorderly years after 1438 to expand their privileges and exemptions from lordly control. In 1450, without permission from their various lords, the Ten Jurisdictions expanded an old anti-Austrian alliance with the communes of the Chadè into a peace-keeping league. When the Habsburgs purchased eight of the communes in 1470, the Ten Jurisdictions sought further protection by allying with the Gray League as well. By creating a new link between the Chadè and the Gray League, the Ten Jurisdictions' efforts to maintain their own autonomy thus helped lay the foundations for the Freestate of the Three Leagues. The loose set of alliances made in 1471 marked the beginning of the Freestate's concerted action in both domestic and foreign affairs.[50]

As the most overtly anti-aristocratic of the three Rhaetian Leagues, the Ten Jurisdictions continued to catalyze consolidation among the other two Leagues after 1471. Because their sovereign lords represented a real threat to their newly gained autonomy (unlike the impoverished bishop in the Chadè or the fractious petty dynasts in the Gray League), the Ten Jurisdictions had every reason to emphasize communal authority. Centralization of lordship in the hands of the Habsburgs also eliminated lesser nobles as a force in the Ten Jurisdictions, leaving the field free for wealthy peasant families to consolidate their power in the communes. Meanwhile, both strategic considerations and the military superiority that the Three Leagues

---

[49] JVF, 29–30.
[50] On the alliances of 1471 (and the non-existence of a supposed *Vazeroler Bund* linking all three Leagues), Jenny, *Traditioneller Vazeroler Bund*.

demonstrated during the Swabian War of 1499 hindered the Habsburgs from defending their rights as lords. Throughout the sixteenth century, therefore, the Ten Jurisdictions functioned as an alliance of equals without any reference to their lords, embodying the most extreme form of communal autonomy. Only a century later did Austria attempt to resume its authority by invading the communes in 1621. The status of the Ten Jurisdictions was finally resolved by the sale of all Austrian rights to the inhabitants in 1647.[51]

The emergence of the three separate Leagues in Rhaetia illustrates the processes that favored communal autonomy and federal organization. The fractured political situation in the high and late Middle Ages made peace-keeping one central problem, as seen particularly in the Gray League. Where several weak lords squabbled, communes could take a share in maintaining public order on a larger scale, and their success at this task nurtured their political self-consciousness and ambition. Where communes could raise effective military forces by working together, their collaboration could lead to both peasant autonomy and a high degree of cooperation between them. In many respects, the history of the Gray League replays events that took place in central Switzerland a century earlier during the foundation of the Swiss Confederation. Weak lordship could also spur communal efforts to gain autonomy in the context of regional estates. In the Chadè, the bishop provided a focus for political organization not only among communes, but also among his cathedral chapter and the local petty nobility. The early history of the Chadè resembled that in Tyrol, the Valais, or in parts of southern Germany, where representative institutions often included peasants. The Chadè diverged from these situations, however, because it took over responsibility for peace-keeping, and because the petty nobility decided to lead the communes rather than to fight them. Finally, communal efforts to control the conditions of their dominion could also result in freely willed alliances, but ones that excluded rather than included the regional nobility. Although they never explicitly challenged the principle of lordship itself, the Ten Jurisdictions were more anti-aristocratic than the other two Leagues. Lords were founding members of the Gray League, and the Chadè manipulated a weak lord's prerogatives to its own benefit. The Ten Jurisdictions, in contrast, thrived by limiting lordly authority to a bare minimum. Not only was their League contracted without the permission or consent of their lords, but its primary goal was to prevent new lords from separating or effectively controlling the individual communes. From its beginnings, therefore, the League of the Ten Jurisdictions attested to its inhabitants' political consciousness, which developed in an increasingly populist direction throughout the sixteenth century.

---

[51] The sale is analyzed in detail (but from a confessional standpoint) in Maissen, *Drei Bünde*.

THE THREE LEAGUES

The early history of the three Leagues is thus a history of differences. But as they developed individually, they also began to cooperate. Both geographical proximity and political necessity furthered this trend, visible from the mid-fifteenth century on. By 1471, all three Leagues were indirectly allied, and they campaigned together during the Italian wars. In 1509, all three purchased the lordship over Maienfeld and Malans, and in 1512 they conquered the Valtellina together. Rulership over the common subject territories added impetus to the consolidation of the Freestate, which finally took place in 1524, when a single alliance joined all three Leagues within a common framework. The decisive institutional trend between 1470 and 1520 was homogenization, as communes from all three Leagues took on increasingly similar roles within the Freestate (whatever the remaining differences in their internal affairs or in their relationships to their lords).[52] After 1450, relations among entire Leagues were the focus of future changes.

Alliances between Leagues rather than between individual communes became the most important form of political consolidation in the second half of the fifteenth century. Two sets of circumstances external to Graubünden accelerated this process by encouraging both tighter organization within the Leagues and increased cooperation between them. The first was the sustained tension between the Swiss Confederacy and the Habsburg dynasty from the late fourteenth century until 1499, especially after the Habsburgs became undisputed rulers of the Tyrol. As major territorial blocks within the Holy Roman Empire consolidated, the borderlands between them – including Graubünden – came under greater pressure to align with one of the greater powers. In 1499, the Swabian (or Swiss) War broke out between Swiss and Habsburgs; the defeat of the Habsburg forces ensured that Graubünden would remain in the Swiss sphere of influence, rather than coming under renewed princely rule. The second impetus for Rhaetian unity came from the south, when disruption and warfare in northern Italy opened opportunities for southward expansion, provided that the Three Leagues could work in concert. At the peak of the Italian crisis, the Rhaetians took advantage of Milan's weakness to seize the Valtellina in 1512, and thus gained new subjects and new administrative responsibilities. As a result of the pressures for common action, the Rhaetian Leagues had grown close enough by the 1520s that they were able to contain the Protestant Reformation's divisive potential. In 1524 they broadened their shared alliances into a single, comprehensive confederation including all three Leagues. This new polity – the Republic of the Three Leagues, as it came to be known – proved just strong enough to survive the religious, social, and political challenges it faced between 1525 and 1540, thanks largely to the foundations that had been laid after 1471.

Close relations among the Leagues started well before the 1470s, of course. An

---

[52] Meyer-Marthaler, *Studien*, 9.

early step was the alliance established between the Gray League and the town of Chur in 1440.[53] In 1450, the Chadè and the Ten Jurisdictions sealed an eternal league to ensure the preservation of legal order between their members, and to provide for common defense against attacks from outside. Only communes joined this alliance: the bishop and the cathedral chapter were not included.[54] Increasing cooperation among the Leagues tended to reinforce their communal and federal character, effectively squeezing out non-communal members or partners such as the lords in Gray League and the cathedral chapter in the Chadè.

Although communes played an increasingly independent role after 1450, they nevertheless continued to respect the nominal authority of their lords. As was customary, each treaty listed the specific exceptions each party needed to make because of previous obligations. The evolution of these exception clauses from treaty to treaty provides an important clue to the Freestate's consolidation during this period.[55] In 1450, the Ten Jurisdictions and the Chadè excepted not only the pope and emperor, but also their own immediate lords. The Chadè also guarded its alliances with Zurich and with the Gray League; the Ten Jurisdictions, still in an earlier stage of consolidation, even made an exception for their own league among themselves, suggesting that they saw their alliance with the Chadè as a matter pertaining to individual communes rather than to their collectivity.[56] By 1471, in contrast, the exceptions in the league between the Gray League and the Ten Jurisdictions were much vaguer: "Item, we have also reserved in general such promises and oaths we may have made before this league, and everything to which we are bound by honor and oath should be excepted"; the rights, customs and privileges of "every lord, land, jurisdiction, towns, villages, noblemen and commoners without any exceptions" were also protected.[57] Although these provisions formally protected the rights of various lords in the regions, the absence of specific mention of Emperor or Pope is striking. Subsequent leagues, including the *Bundesbrief* of 1524 remained equally vague.[58] The Leagues' growing power allowed them to give less and less consideration to their lords' claims over them.

Each of the Leagues, even the Ten Jurisdictions, was well on its way to a common identity by 1450. When the communes of Maienfeld and Davos resisted joining an alliance with the Chadè, the other eight communes in the Ten Jurisdictions charged them with violating the League charter of 1436. The dispute was arbitrated by the mayor and council of Zurich, who forced the two recalcitrant communes to join the new alliance and swear an oath of loyalty to it. The Gray League had a standing civil appeals court by this time, too, while the Chadè was

[53] Moor, *Geschichte von Currätien*, I: 365–66; and Bundi *et al.*, *Geschichte der Stadt Chur*, II: 113–33.
[54] JVF, 41–42.
[55] Meyer-Marthaler, *Studien*, 52ff.
[56] JVF, 42–43.
[57] JVF, 61, articles 13 and 14.
[58] For a slightly differing interpretation of these specific articles, Meyer-Marthaler, *Studien*, 30.

already proposing a collective council to control the Bishop and manage the see's affairs. By the mid-fifteenth century, then, each of the three Leagues had become strong enough to enforce certain obligations over its individual members.

A Habsburg effort to establish a bridgehead in both the Chadè and in the Ten Jurisdictions during the 1460s motivated the final phase in the consolidation of the Three Leagues.[59] After purchasing the small lordship of Tarasp in the Lower Engadine, Duke Sigmund of Tyrol was able to buy eight of the Ten Jurisdictions in 1470 from the last of the lords of Mätsch.[60] The *Bündner* responded with a flurry of new alliances among themselves, the most important of which linked the Ten Jurisdictions directly to the Gray League. Moved as they said,

for loyalty, for affection and the good, for greater security, for the protection and for the preservation of the honor and goods of our lands and our people, we have faithfully and affectionately agreed on a good, faithful, firm, eternal and permanently effective League, and together we have assured, promised and sworn in person to God and the saints, and all taken a learned oath with raised hands all together and each one separately, that we and all our heirs and descendants, whom we also firmly bind to this agreement, shall always firmly hold and fulfill in good faith without reservation all the items, points, and articles found in this letter as follows . . . [61]

Of the noble members of the Gray League, only the abbot of Disentis joined, while the Ten Jurisdictions had no such members in the first place: this was unmistakably a communal and anti-feudal treaty.

The actual contents of the alliance were not at all innovative, however. The document repeated large parts of the Gray League's founding treaty of 1424, often copying its language directly.[62] The 1470 treaty stressed legal security and mutual protection on demand and provided conflict-resolving procedures in case of disputes. This document's importance lay not in its novelty – the inhabitants of the Three Leagues clearly knew how to write an alliance by this point – but in its closure of the connections among the Three Leagues. For the next forty years, the Three Leagues acted as one unit on the international stage without feeling any need for a formal treaty to link them.[63] Not until domestic tensions were exacerbated by the early Reformation was such a document drafted and adopted – the *Bundesbrief* of 1524.

Even before 1470, all three Leagues had been meeting to establish common policies, especially in their foreign relations. Early deliberative assemblies drew

---

[59] Baum, *Sigmund der Münzreiche*, 264–72. Moor, *Geschichte von Currätien*, I: 382–87.
[60] Although Tyrol itself was technically only a county, its Habsburg rulers were called *Herzöge* (a term traditionally translated as "dukes") because they ruled a complex of territories considerably larger than the original county of Tyrol.
[61] JVF, 59.
[62] Meyer-Marthaler, *Studien*, 22–23.
[63] In this respect the Three Leagues in Rhaetia from 1471 to 1524 resembled the Swiss Confederation. Peyer, *Verfassungsgeschichte*, 21–43.

upon the provisions found in the separate alliance documents that regulated disagreements among members. The 1450 treaty between the Chadè and the Ten Jurisdictions, for example, provided that "if it should happen that all of us who are part of this alliance should come into conflict, (may God prevent it!), or if it seemed to either part that we needed each other's help or counsel, or if we needed to come together because of perils to or opportunities for our league and our lands," then delegates from both Leagues should assemble, meeting alternately in Chur and Davos.[64] Such provisions were easily extended to all three Leagues. Regular rotation among locations probably began before 1471 as well.[65] An assembly of the Three Leagues represented the nascent Freestate to Milan in a dispute about tolls in 1464 and 1465, and another met to negotiate with the duke of Tyrol's representatives in 1467.[66] In the following years, common assemblies of the Leagues became more frequent, as increasing tension in Italy and growing French interest in Swiss and Rhaetian mercenaries drew the Swiss Confederation and its allies into international affairs. Given the bishop's political weakness and the impoverishment of the local dynasts, the Leagues that had grown during the previous half-century represented the best way to respond to new challenges – a way, moreover, that came naturally to the commoners and local ministerials who controlled the communes' military and political resources.

The alliances of 1471 also highlight the anti-aristocratic dimension of the Rhaetian Leagues, a characteristic that linked them closely to the contemporary Swiss Confederation. Graubünden lay not only between territorial power centers, but also between conflicting political world-views. To the west lay the federal model of the Swiss, based on horizontal bonds among commoners, which began taking on an ideological as well as a practical dimension late in the century.[67] To the east lay the dominion of Tyrol, where a territorial prince was busy consolidating his authority over the local nobility and peasants. Despite the advantages Tyrolean commoners enjoyed compared to others in Europe, both the rhetoric and reality of princely authority were growing there in the late fifteenth century. The Rhaetian alliances after 1471, which included neither the bishop of Chur nor any of the local dynasts, represented a clear choice for communal over lordly power, and was seen as such by contemporaries.[68] It was thus entirely consistent that the Rhaetian Leagues began to strengthen their ties to the Swiss during the same years.

Neighborly relations between the upper Rhine valley and some of the Swiss cantons dated far back. The abbey of Disentis had long struggled against Uri for

---

[64] Cited from Meyer-Marthaler, *Studien*, 119. The passage is slightly revised from the version in JVF, 46.

[65] Meyer-Marthaler, *Studien*, 119. The earliest reference to rotation dates to 1469.

[66] *Ibid.*, 21, 39, footnote 76.

[67] On contemporary Swiss ideology, see Marchal, "Nouvelles approches des mythes fondateurs."

[68] On the difficulties the Habsburgs had in obtaining obedience from the inhabitants of the six (later eight) communes they owned in the Ten Jurisdictions, see Baum, *Sigmund*, 268–70.

control over the Urseren valley, where disputes continued until 1407.[69] Disentis also entered into relations with neighboring Glarus during the fourteenth century, evidently to prevent mutual raiding across the mountain meadows lying between the two.[70] An agreement to this effect from 1343 was expanded into a full-fledged alliance in 1400. Both parties promised military support and mutual access to legal proceedings. Signatories were the *Amman* and commune of Glarus on the one hand, and the abbot, the Gray League's dynasts, and "the League in general," on the other.[71] Bordering on the heartland of the Swiss Confederacy, the Gray League naturally maintained close, though not always friendly, contact with its Swiss neighbors.

The Chadè's connections with the Swiss rested on a quite different basis. The principal approach to Graubünden's passes ran from Zurich along the Lake of Zurich and the Walensee to Chur, where the road branched to either the Septimer or the Splügen passes. The city-state of Zurich sought to control as much of this route as possible, directly or indirectly. One motive behind the Swiss civil war of the 1440s was Zurich's efforts to seize the Toggenburg inheritance, which would have given the city control over key points on the road to the passes. Farther afield, Zurich made alliances in Rhaetia to help secure its routes and to gain advantages for city merchants. In 1419, the bishop, chapter, and subjects of the see in Chur became "external citizens" of Zurich, on which occasion the penniless bishop also sold Zurich the strategic castle of Flums.[72] When the agreement expired in 1470, it was duly renewed for another twenty-six years. While Zurich and the Chadè were formally equal in the treaty of 1470, the provisions reflected the actual balance of power between the two. Zurich was then at the peak of its influence, whereas the Chadè, as we have seen, was still in the process of consolidating its connections with the other two Rhaetian Leagues. The Chadè therefore had to pay Zurich a yearly fee of twenty-six Rhenisch guilders, and Zurich was not obliged to assist the Chadè if the League entered disputes without the city's knowledge and permission.[73]

After 1471, a new phase of Swiss–Rhaetian relations began. For the next half century, Swiss mercenaries took a prominent place in European affairs, a place shared by their Rhaetian fellows.[74] At the same time, the constitutional order of the Swiss Confederacy was reaching maturity, and the Swiss Diet (the *Tagsatzung*) looked as if it might develop into an effective central legislature.[75] For a time, it

---

[69] JSG, 5–8, 14–17. See esp. the explanatory note on p. 8.

[70] JSG, 9.

[71] JSG, 10: the document lists the abbot, the lords of Rhäzüns and Sax, the commune of Rheinwald ("denen vom Rine"), and then concludes the contracting parties with a reference to "und mit dem teil gemeinlich." The editor suggests that *Teil* is a translation of the Romantsch *la part*, an early term for the Gray League.

[72] JSG, 17–20; the practice of making alliances by taking on outsiders as "external citizens," (*Ausbürger*) was frequently used by Swiss and south German cities to extend their spheres of influence.

[73] JSG, 23–24, esp. articles 3–7.

[74] An overview in HSG I: 336–67. [75] HSG I: 415–16.

appeared that the Three Leagues might formally join the Confederacy, too. In mercenary agreements reached during this period, for example, the Rhaetians sought to be treated like the Swiss, at first insisting that the Three Leagues receive the same pensions and contingents as one full member of the Confederacy, but later demanding that each League be accorded the same treatment as a single canton.[76] Faced with increasing Habsburg and imperial pressure, the Swiss Confederacy and the Rhaetian Leagues came even closer to full partnership in the late 1490s. When the death of Duke Sigmund of Tyrol in 1496 united Tyrol with the other Habsburg lands controlled by Emperor Maximilian, the Gray League approached the Swiss Diet with a proposal for an alliance. The legates claimed that both France and the anti-French alliance headed by the pope were seeking an alliance with the League; a public assembly in Disentis, however, had decided to ally with no one but the Swiss.[77] Negotiations went swiftly, soon drawing in the Chadè as well. In June, 1497, the Gray League and seven of the eight Swiss cantons signed and sealed a treaty of friendship and alliance. A nearly identical alliance was established between the Chadè and the seven cantons in December, 1498, just before the outbreak of the Swabian War in 1499.[78]

Even at this moment of closest Swiss–Rhaetian cooperation, however, their formal alliances remained relatively loose. The treaties of 1497 and 1498 differed noticeably from the stricter ones that united the Swiss cantons to one another.[79] Both parties, for example, preserved the right to make subsequent alliances at will, although not to the detriment of the present agreement.[80] More importantly, neither treaty made any mention of military obligations between the parties. Article 9 of each alliance established only that "If both parties were to become involved in a war or feud against someone, then neither party should negotiate or accept any truce or peace unless the other party is also included in its provisions";[81] the leagues among the Swiss and among the Rhaetians, in contrast, carefully detailed each party's right to call upon the others for military aid, including details about the geographical extent of such support, the distribution of costs, and the partition of any booty. Even the previous alliance between Zurich and the Chadè had contained such provisions. The alliances of 1497 and 1498, in contrast, were little more than expressions of friendship and mutual support between equal partners. Graubünden and Switzerland shared enemies, and they shared consti-tutional and ideological principles, since both were federal and anti-feudal. The latter point was particularly visible in the documents of 1497 and 1498: none of the aristocratic members of the Rhaetian Leagues were among the contracting parties, neither the abbot of Disentis, nor the lords of Rhäzüns and Sax, nor the Bishops of

[76] Plattner, *Entstehung*, 225–26.
[77] *Ibid.*, 226. Plattner anachronistically calls the assembly a *Landsgemeinde*.
[78] JSG, 30–39.
[79] Plattner, *Entstehung*, 231.
[80] JSG, 32–33, Article 8. Identical language in JSG, 37.   [81] JSG, 33.

Chur. Still, the friendship between Switzerland and Graubünden did not lead to formal union.[82]

The events of 1499 put their friendship to the test. Habsburg hostility toward the Swiss and Swiss resistance to the imperial reforms of 1495 combined to bring about a full-scale war fought on fronts from Basel to the South Tyrol. The emperor, the Swabian League, and the south German nobility sought to dam the growing influence of the Swiss, whereas the Swiss fought, in effect if not according to their stated intentions, to expand their patchwork of privileges and liberties into full exemption from both princely and imperial control. The outcome was determined by a dramatic string of Swiss and Rhaetian military successes. While the Ten Jurisdictions cautiously took a neutral stance, the other two Leagues defeated the Austrians not only in pitched battle, but in a series of skirmishes all around the Freestate's borders. Much of the war consisted of raids, as both parties used the occasion to steal livestock and goods from their neighbors: the Lower Engadine was particularly hard-hit when troops from Tyrol burned several villages and seized most of the local cattle.[83] In Graubünden, the most important battle took place at Calven in the Val Müstair, where a Rhaetian force managed to encircle and destroy an entrenched Tyrolean army. In the Treaty of Basel that ended the war, the Swiss and Rhaetians (except the Ten Jurisdictions) were acknowledged to be Imperial subjects who owed obedience to no other lord, and who were not subject to new imperial legislation or taxation. In effect, Switzerland and Rhaetia no longer belonged to the Holy Roman Empire, although this was not formally acknowledged until 1648.[84]

The situation in Italy provided a second stimulus to closer cooperation among the Rhaetian Leagues. The Italian valleys at the southern feet of the Alpine passes became attractive targets for expansion when the Lombard states that had previously controlled them dissolved. Not only were these areas relatively prosperous, but control over them also offered opportunities to exploit the pass trade more effectively. The communes to the north seized the opportunity to storm down from the summits: the Valais over the Simplon into the Val d'Ossola, Uri and Schwyz over the Gotthard into the Val Leventina, while Rhaetian military adventurism was directed at Chiavenna, Bormio, and the Valtellina. In 1486, the bishop of Chur and the Chadè sent troops into Bormio and Chiavenna, allegedly to reassert the bishop's claims to lordship over these valleys.[85] The attack was preceded by deliberations

---

[82] Graubünden only became part of Switzerland in the Napoleonic period. Before that it was considered *Zugewandt*, meaning it was allied without being either part or subject to the Swiss Confederation.

[83] Described in nationalistic terms by Planta, *Geschichte von Graubünden*, 137–38.

[84] Peyer, *Verfassungsgeschichte*, 75–77.

[85] The see's claim derived from a deed of gift signed by Mastino Visconti in 1404 – hardly a compelling legal document in view of the fact that Mastino was in exile at the time of its signing. It was never confirmed by anyone who actually ruled Milan. Moor, *Geschichte von Currätien*, II: 41–48.

among all Three Leagues, however, and the Gray League rushed to support the Chadè's "with our banner and all our forces," although no territory was gained.[86]

Only after the Italian wars had shattered Milan were the Swiss and the Rhaetians able to seize the valleys south of the Alpine summits. In 1512, the *Bündner* contingent of a French army swept into the Valtellina and the counties of Bormio and Chiavenna. The local population swore fealty to their new lords, who in turn guaranteed all privileges and customs in the three territories they had conquered. Thus the nascent Freestate gained its subject territories.[87] For the next three centuries, administering, exploiting, and defending these territories became a central task for the Republic of the Three Leagues. Their possession promoted the development of the Republic's central institutions even while provoking strife among the leading families, and between the leading families and the common citizens.

Technically speaking, the subject territories also included the communes of Maienfeld and Malans, where the Three Leagues purchased all feudal rights and privileges in 1509. But these two communes were also members of the Ten Jurisdictions, putting them in an unusual position. They were feudal subjects, but they also owned a share of their own lordship. Since the right to appoint the highest magistrate in Maienfeld and Malans rotated among the communes of the Three Leagues, they themselves exercised this right from time to time. In fact, however, feudal rights in the two communes were limited to a few dues and the modest income from the courts; politically, the communes were more members than subjects of the Three Leagues. These communes' unusual status does illustrate how feudal authority could be marginalized in Rhaetia without ever being rejected outright. The essential feudal nexus among ownership of property, jurisdiction, and political authority was fractured: the peasants owned the land, officers appointed by the Three Leagues exercised jurisdiction, and political authority fell into the hands of the communes themselves.[88]

The Three Leagues exercised considerably tighter control over the Italian subject territories. Unlike the citizens of Maienfeld and Malans, who remained "fellow confederates," the inhabitants of the Valtellina were always called "subjects" (*Untertanen*). Meanwhile, the need to provide for the administration of the Valtellina required sustained cooperation among the Rhaetian Leagues. Judges and magistrates had to be appointed, taxes collected, and borders defended. The practice of appointing magistrates for short terms meant that communal delegates had to meet regularly to make such appointments. Moreover, the Valtellina's strategic location between the Freestate, Tyrol, Venice, and Milan created endless

---

86 Cited in Meyer-Marthaler, *Studien*, 56.
87 Barber, *Death of Communal Liberty*, 148.
88 Gillardon, "Erwerbung der Herrschaft Maienfeld," 161–82.

diplomatic complications that required frequent deliberation as well as the creation of governmental organs capable of reacting quickly to changing circumstances.[89] The government in Milan always sought to regain control of the territory for economic and political reasons. Once Spain established itself in Milan, moreover, the Valtellina gained importance as the best route between Milan and Habsburg Austria (via the Umbrail and Stelvio passes). Meanwhile Venice maintained a growing interest in good relations with the Freestate, since the Valtellina provided the only land route over which the Venetian Republic could obtain German mercenary troops.

Particularly in the early sixteenth century, pressure from outside remained high. Possession of the Valtellina increased the Freestate's involvement in the tangled diplomatic situation in Italy. Important now not only as providers of mercenaries, but also as masters over strategic roads and passes, Rhaetian leaders had to find a way through complex negotiations with the Italians, the Swiss, the Austrians, and the French. These pressures led to institutional innovations. For example, the first evidence of the Freestate's interim council, the *Beitag*, comes from the 1520s: this council, usually consisting of a few delegates meeting in Chur, received correspondence and could react to fast-breaking situations, but called upon the communes for advice when more weighty matters arose. Its earliest recorded meetings involved negotiations with the French in 1522, and with Gian Giacomo de Medici in 1528.[90]

In addition, the Freestate's territory had to be defended militarily. Milan twice sought to regain control of its lost mountain territories by encouraging a noble adventurer, Gian Giacomo de Medici, who sought to seize the Valtellina with Milanese complicity in 1525–26, and again in 1531–32. The Rhaetians succeeded in warding off the attack in 1525, after which the Swiss helped mediate a truce. When the war broke out again in 1531, the Rhaetians failed to drive out the invaders, who had captured the town Morbegno in the lower Valtellina. Only a substantial army from the Protestant Swiss cantons enabled the Freestate to regain control, although three villages on the Lake of Como were ceded to Milan in the process. The need to face military threats pulled the communes closer together, even though they never had a well-organized army. Instead, the communes each sent a company when the need was pressing. The assembled troops elected their own generals, and the feelings of the common soldiers often influenced tactics in the field. While the organs of the emerging state made the key political decisions, non-state institutions and customs guided the army's behavior once assembled.[91] Nevertheless, the need for military action on a scale beyond the resources of any single commune hastened the process of consolidation. As early as 1486, delegates from all three Leagues

---

[89] Peyer, *Verfassungsgeschichte*, 68–74.
[90] JM I: 82 (no. 398), and JM I: 95 (no. 457) respectively.
[91] Padrutt, *Staat und Krieg*, esp. 226ff.

signed a common document providing for military discipline. In an attempt to control the warriors sent from the communes, the Three Leagues asserted "that everything which is commanded or forbidden for the honor and good of our lands and communes by those who are given authority by our lords and the communes, whether they be captains, officers, or councilors," should be obeyed on pain of punishment and general outlawry.[92] In addition, military leadership by the local magnates who headed these communal armies helped strengthen social consensus and collective identification within the Three Leagues. The experience of fighting side by side, whether in defense of their Leagues as in 1499, 1525, and 1531, or in pursuit of new territories as in 1486 and 1512, contributed to the stability of the polity that was emerging during this period.[93]

THE REFORMATION AND THE CONSTITUTIONAL FOUNDATION OF THE FREESTATE

External pressures on the Rhaetian Freestate from the 1470s to the 1530s encouraged increased cooperation and institutional maturation, but internal divisions in the 1520s threatened to block this process, or even destroy the Freestate. As in all of Switzerland, the early Reformation was extraordinarily divisive in Graubünden: the autonomy enjoyed by members of both federations allowed differing responses to the Protestant challenge, thus leaving neighboring communes divided about religious affairs. In addition, the Reformation heightened social divisions, as peasants demanded the abolition of tithes and the elimination of clerical jurisdiction in what was nominally an episcopal principality. Along with its neighboring regions, the entire see of Chur, including parts outside the Three Leagues, experienced a storm of popular unrest from 1522 to 1526.[94]

Diplomatic, religious, and social tension combined during the 1520s to transform the Freestate in other ways. Until this point, the long process of commune formation and communal alliance had not challenged the essentially feudal framework of property and productive resources. As lords and bishops lost most of their political prerogatives during the fifteenth century, many of their economic powers also slipped into the hands of communal elites, but without changing the forms of possession. The peasant continued to pay traditional tithes and dues even as he became a political and military actor endowed with considerable power and

---

[92] JVF, 73. I disagree with the editor's identification (footnote 4) of the *houpt lüt* with the later *Häupter* of the Three Leagues; the passage clearly refers to military captains appointed by the Three Leagues.

[93] Padrutt, *Staat und Krieg*, 197–225.

[94] The scanty documents from Graubünden in the 1520s have been exhaustively examined by Oskar Vasella. Vasella writes from a conservative and Catholic, but rarely polemical viewpoint, and his research may be regarded as definitive on the *Bündner* Reformation. The other standard work on the Reformation in Graubünden, Emil Camenisch's *Bündnerische Reformationsgeschichte*, is much less useful.

autonomy. That the collector of traditional payments was increasingly likely to be someone himself not far removed from peasant roots further undermined the logic of the old system.[95] After 1520, however, impelled largely by movements originating outside the Freestate, the social as well as the political landscape burst into movement. The results were enshrined in the Rhaetian Freestate's three most fundamental constitutional documents: the First Ilanz Articles of 1524, the *Bundesbrief* of the same year, and the Second Ilanz Articles of 1526. These documents regulated the place of the churches in the Freestate, established the authority and powers of the central government, and responded to popular pressure for changes in the organization of agriculture and property. Together with the final collapse of lordship in the region, these documents signaled the maturation of a new political sphere in Graubünden.

A specific combination of social organization and political circumstances shaped the outcome of the early Reformation in Graubünden. In its earliest phases, the demand for doctrinal reform was closely connected with demands for changes in the church's role in society, especially in the rural communes. Peasant unrest over tithes, clerical jurisdiction, and the inadequate provision of spiritual services broke out all over the northwestern part of the see of Chur in 1523. Swiss subjects around Sargans, Austrian peasants in the Vorarlberg, and Rhaetian commoners in the flatlands around Chur made similar demands.[96] Meanwhile, the city of Chur itself was engaged in a quite different struggle with the bishop: lordship and jurisdiction, rather than economic complaints, lay at the core of the conflict, which was exacerbated by political tension caused by the incumbent bishop's close connections with Habsburg Austria. Chur and the transalpine communes in the Chadè were primarily interested in limiting the bishop's political and religious prerogatives, since they had already gained control over many of the see's economic resources.[97] Indeed, leading magnates in and outside the city at first resisted peasant demands to abolish the tithe, since they were major beneficiaries of tithe payments by this time. The conflicting goals of rural commoners and city magnates shaped the events from 1523 to 1526.

In 1523, the Swiss peasants in Sargans drafted a set of articles laying out their program with regard to the church: debts were no longer to be collected under threat of excommunication, priests should be able to absolve their parishioners for all sins, trials between clerics and laymen should be held in a local court, and appeals to the bishop's court should be prohibited except for matrimonial cases.[98] These articles inspired similar manifestos in the Vorarlberg and Graubünden; but whereas the Sarganser and Vorarlberg articles remained without lasting effect, the *Bündner*

---

[95] Grimm, *Anfänge*, 22–29, gives a detailed description of one family's rise out of the peasantry.
[96] Vasella, "Bauernkrieg und Reformation," 1–18; "Zur Entstehungsgeschichte," 185–88.
[97] Bundi *et al., Geschichte der Stadt Chur*, 2: 113–69.
[98] Vasella, "Zur Entstehungsgeschichte," 185–86.

version, the First Ilanz Articles, became a key document in the Freestate's constitutional history. The strength of the communes, united by long-established and well-practiced alliances, together with the resulting weakness of the bishop, provide the best explanation for this difference.[99] Whereas peasants in Sargans and the Vorarlberg were politically divided and unable to form a common front in the face of well-organized and determined rulers, Rhaetian peasants already possessed a political tradition that enabled them to act in a concerted fashion.[100] By the time the *Bundesbrief* of 1524 was drafted, Bishop Paul Ziegler had fled the Freestate to his Tyrolean castle in Fürstenburg, never to return to Chur during the remaining sixteen years of his reign.

The First Ilanz Articles were thus not only evidence of a strong, rurally based Reformation, but also represented a decisive step in the political maturation of the Three Leagues. These eighteen articles, drafted and promulgated without the least reference to traditional channels of authority, confidently regulated the place the church should take in Rhaetian society.[101] Many of the articles, such as those regulating the competence of clerical courts, priests' obligations to their parishioners, and the role of priests as citizens, established practices similar to those already well-established in the Swiss Confederation.[102] The First Ilanz Articles went further, though, also foreshadowing some of the claims that later appeared in the German Peasants' War of 1525. Article 2, for example, established the general right of parishioners to participate in the election of parish priests; the Twelve Articles of the Swabian peasants made a similar demand in 1525.[103] Other articles cut even more deeply into the church's economic and legal foundations. Article 9 provided that perpetual masses and similar endowments (known as *Jahreszeiten* in local parlance) could be collected only if verified by a sealed document, thus putting the burden of proof on the endowment's possessor and effectively canceling many of them.[104] Article 17 denied the church the right to collect fees from chaplains and local priests for special dispensations. The articles as a whole reveal a striking confidence in the Leagues' authority and ability to regulate social and religious affairs. The political organization of the Three Leagues provided both the ideological framework and the social consensus necessary for this kind of action because political power had already fallen to the communes, which were led in turn by a newly emerging social elite.

---

[99] Vasella, "Bauernkrieg und Reformation," 4.
[100] The term "political tradition" here is Vasella's, "Bauernkrieg und Reformation," 18. On Bishop Paul Ziegler's problems, 19–25. See also Vasella's "Der Bruch Bischof Paul Zieglers," 271–78.
[101] The articles made no exceptions for emperor, pope, bishop, or lords. Only the recently reached *Erbeinung* treaty with the Habsburgs was mentioned as excepted from the articles. JVF, 79, 82.
[102] Both rural and urban Swiss communes had wrested control over many aspects of clerical life from other authorities during the fourteenth and especially fifteenth centuries. Blickle, "Rechtsautonomie durch Kirchenkritik."
[103] Blickle, *Revolution of 1525*, 195–201.
[104] Vasella, "Der bäuerliche Wirtschaftskampf," 71–80, discusses the effect of this provision.

Immediately on the heels of the First Ilanz Articles came the *Bundesbrief* of 1524. Unlike the Articles, the *Bundesbrief* was neither legally nor socially innovative: it contained few new provisions, and those that were new did not directly challenge the political principles of the surrounding world. The lordly members of the Gray League appeared at the head of the *Bundesbrief* as contracting parties, along with "the communes in common of the Three Leagues,"[105] thus emphasizing the document's continuity with the earlier alliances within and between the Three Leagues. Almost nothing is known about the exact circumstances that led up to the *Bundesbrief*. Among its causes were probably social unrest, diplomatic and military challenges, and growing administrative duties that made it timely to reorganize the relationship among the Leagues by means of a single comprehensive document.[106] Only the desire to consolidate what was already generally accepted can explain the essentially conservative character of the *Bundesbrief* amid such turmoil: aware of the difficulties surrounding them, the Rhaetians needed to affirm what they agreed on. The establishment of the *Bundesbrief* at exactly this moment further attests that the communes *did* in fact agree on a good deal, starting with the principle that the proper way to constitute political relationships was by means of a common act of will. If the First Ilanz Articles vividly illustrate the extent to which communal representatives felt empowered to intervene in church affairs, then the *Bundesbrief* documents the body of shared assumptions and practices – already existent in 1524 – that justified the communes' feeling of empowerment.

Particularly important is the dual role of the *Bundesbrief* in the Freestate's future and its past. On the one hand, it was a conservative document that drew its language from a well-developed legal tradition of communal Leagues. Drawing upon a conceptual universe familiar to its drafters and readers, it embodied five decades of shared practice since the 1470s – practice that included both common action and lengthy internal disputes. This dimension of the *Bundesbrief* is best captured by noting that ten of its thirty-one substantive articles were devoted to a meticulous catalog of how disputes among the partners ought to be resolved.[107] On the other hand, the *Bundesbrief* by its very existence redefined the dimensions of political struggle in the Freestate after 1524. Even though it produced no immediate changes in the course of regional politics, the *Bundesbrief* became the fixed point in *Bündner* politics thereafter. Its authors must have known what they were doing: in article 31, they explicitly canceled all previous alliances among themselves, clearing the slate for a coherent political future. The only exception they made was for the First Ilanz Articles, themselves the expression of the Three Leagues' confidence and authority by this time. The genuinely constitutional character of the

---

105 JVF, 83. Early drafts of the *Bundesbrief* included the Bishop as a party, but his name disappeared when it became clear that he would not seal the document.
106 The causes here based on Meyer-Marthaler, *Studien*, 24. Other historians have almost nothing to say.
107 Articles 8 through 17, JVF, 84–86.

Bundesbrief was reinforced by its close association with both sets of Ilanz Articles, which further specified the Freestate's character, not only politically, but also socially and economically. The true measure of these documents' effectiveness in defining the Freestate is illustrated by the course of political struggle for the rest of the century. Bills of articles remained a common way to resolve all sorts of conflicts as the century went on, yet later articles never returned to the issues discussed between 1524 and 1526. These had been solved definitively, and later generations moved on to deal with the consequences, rather than the preconditions, of living in a federal and communal state.

Whereas the *Bundesbrief* synthesized half a century of political practice and presented it as the foundation for future action, and the First Ilanz Articles demonstrated the communal leadership's willingness to regulate social and religious life on the basis of common will, the Second Ilanz Articles were forced upon the Rhaetian polity by direct pressure from below. Many commentators have observed their striking resemblance to Michael Gaismair's project for a peasant republic in the Tyrol, as well as to the Twelve Articles of the Swabian peasants of 1525.[108] A key difference, however, was that the Second Ilanz Articles represented legislation by a sovereign polity, whereas both the Twelve Articles and Gaismair's plans were rejected and suppressed after noble victory in the Peasants' War.[109]

Even though the broad peasant revolt in Germany and Austria had been suppressed before 1526, the leadership in Rhaetia had little cause to relax. Peasants around Chur, in the Vier Dörfer, and in the Domleschg had been withholding tithes and dues for at least two years, while the Prättigau remained in a ferment – partly due to the personal presence of Michael Gaismair, who had fled there after the defeat of the peasants in the Tyrol.[110] In 1525, local peasants in cooperation with some urban citizens even tried to assault the episcopal quarter of Chur.[111] Meanwhile, the political situation outside Graubünden was threatening. An unstable peace had just been concluded with Gian Giacomo de Medici and with Milan, but both the pope and the French were seeking Rhaetian mercenaries for the Italian wars.[112] Outside help in suppressing the peasants was unavailable: calling foreign nobles into the land would be disastrous for all parties in the Freestate, while the Swiss were themselves divided to the point of immobility by religious conflict between Zwingli's 'Zurich and the Catholic cantons. Under these

---

[108] Bücking, *Michael Gaismair*. On Gaismair in Graubünden see Vasella (disapprovingly) in "Bauernkrieg und Reformation," 53–65.
[109] Liver, "Die staatliche Entwicklung," 227. Note however Vasella's reservations in "Die Entstehung der bündnerischen Bauernartikel," 71–73, esp. footnote 33, and his direct criticism of Liver, 77–78.
[110] Vasella, "Die Entstehung der bündnerischen Bauernartikel," and "Bauernkrieg und Reformation," 25–32.
[111] Vasella, "Bauernkrieg und Reformation," 32–33. See also Bundi *et al.*, *Geschichte der Stadt Chur*, II: 299–301. On cooperation between urban commoners and peasants during the Peasants' War, see Blickle, *The Revolution of 1525*, 105–24.
[112] See e.g, JM I: 89–90, (nos. 429, 432, 433, and 435).

circumstances, social peace in the Freestate could be reestablished only by a conciliatory document.

The situation was all the more complex because leadership and rebels were often hard to tell apart. The men who led the communes against episcopal lordship opposed the peasants on the question of economic burdens. We know almost nothing about the actual individuals involved, but the struggle was three sided by the very structure of the situation. On one side were the bishop and his supporters, weakened but by no means eliminated.[113] At the opposite pole were the common peasants who sought to escape the feudal dues, tithes, and alienated religious endowments that burdened them economically. Caught in between was the third party, the various magnate and elite families who had controlled the nascent Freestate since the 1470s. Comprising episcopal ministerials, ambitious peasant families, and successful Chur merchants, this heterogeneous group had thrown its lot in with the communes late in the fifteenth century.[114] Now, however, popular hostility towards the bishop and all lords threatened the economic foundations of their power, even as peasant hatred of any elite undermined their political authority. A century of successful communalism had taught every farmer that he, too, was a free confederate as good as any other. The leading figures in the Three Leagues had to find their way through this minefield without bringing about an open rebellion against their own authority.[115]

The Second Ilanz Articles not only succeeded at this task, but also fulfilled several of the Freestate's political goals, especially against the bishop.[116] Focusing peasant hostility against the bishop, article 1 asserted the Freestate's complete autonomy by excluding him from all deliberations, and by prohibiting the election of his agents as delegates to common assemblies. In addition, the bishop and all clerics were denied the right to appoint any magistrate or officer in the communes; instead, every commune was to elect its own officers freely.[117] While this article reflected early Protestant ideas about the need to separate clerical from lay authority, its effect was to establish nearly unlimited communal sovereignty. The Articles also laid down Graubünden's solution to the problem of religious division by ordaining that each commune could elect and depose its own clerics at will. This provision made religious confession, too, a communal decision. After 1526, the Freestate was characterized by the legally sanctioned coexistence of Catholic and Protestant worship, side by side.[118] Finally, the Articles addressed peasant

---

[113] Vasella, "Die Entstehung der bündnerischen Bauernartikel," 70–71.
[114] Grimm, *Anfänge*, 180–81.
[115] E.g. Padrutt, *Staat und Krieg*, 221, as early as 1499.
[116] The text of the articles is the only record of the assembly where they were composed. We know neither the authors nor the path to ratification.
[117] JVF, 89–90.
[118] JVF, 92–93. It has been claimed that the Second Ilanz Articles established religious freedom and toleration in Graubünden; see Steiner, *Die religiöse Freiheit*, 33–34. In fact, they did not, at least not for individuals: Vasella, "Bauernkrieg und Reformation," 50–51.

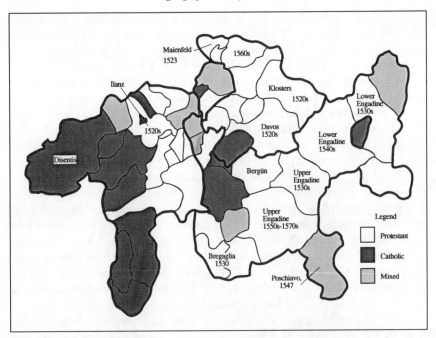

Illustration 5   Religious confession in Graubünden, *ca.* 1600.

grievances, both religious and economic. Articles 6 through 10 regulated the tithe, limiting it to cereal crops and dairy products, specifying how it was to be collected, and establishing every commune's right to redeem tithes that had been converted to secular purposes. Article 11 stated that the only acceptable form of land tenure was free and hereditary (*Freie Erbleihe*), and gave local courts the authority to adjudicate all changes in tenurial burdens.[119] Even though these provisions were not universally implemented, their result was to leave the Freestate as a land of peasant freeholders with limited burdens on their land.

Although the text of the Second Ilanz Articles reflected more than one political agenda, the entire document presupposed a communal view of social and political order. Protestants, rising families in the communes, and the citizens of Chur all increased their independence from the remnants of noble power in the region, whether clerical or secular. Beyond their immediate purpose – to quell broad-based unrest in the communes by means of concessions to the peasantry – the Articles therefore instituted far-reaching changes in the structures of political and religious

---

[119] JVF, 91–92. As both Vasella and Liver have shown, the provision throwing adjudication to local courts was used to reaffirm the general duty of peasants to pay dues to landholders. Vasella, "Der bäuerliche Wirtschaftskampf," and Liver, *Vom Feudalismus zur Demokratie*, 107–36, esp. 118ff.

authority in the Freestate. [120] They captured a revolution in mental frameworks about what sort of a state the Freestate was to become, as much as one in agrarian organization and feudal dues. In both Ilanz Articles and in the *Bundesbrief*, the pressure and turmoil of the 1520s brought about a surprisingly clear formulation of the Freestate's political, social, and religious foundations. These documents were in one sense conservative, in that they gathered and gave expression to the experience of two generations of federal politics. At the same time, the most radical of the Freestate's three constitutional documents of the 1520s, the Second Ilanz Articles, illustrated the future locus of political conflicts in the Freestate, namely the problem of economic and political power in a collective state.

After 1526, communal principles provided the fundamental legitimating principles for political life in the Freestate, even though the forms and rhetoric of feudal law lingered on in countless individual situations. Just to absorb the immediate implications of this change took another generation, while its larger consequences took the rest of the sixteenth century to appear in full force. But the direction of internal development was never seriously in question after the mid-1520s (barring outside intervention). Any serious observer could see that the people in the communes ruled the Freestate, not the bishop or any lords. [121] Communal rule was founded on the principle that authority derived from mutual obligation between freely choosing partners. More than even the Swiss Confederation or the Republic of the Valais, the Rhaetian Freestate seemed to embody democratic principles. In fact, however, the political practice immanent in the documents drafted between 1524 and 1526 developed only slowly during the sixteenth century, while the rhetoric of populism in the Freestate reached its peak only around 1620.

---

[120] Oskar Vasella was quite right to describe the Second Ilanz Articles as revolutionary. His purpose in doing so was to discredit them, and he constructed a powerful argument showing that their revolutionary intent had not in fact been carried out in the following years. Vasella, "Der bäuerliche Wirtschaftskampf," esp. 167ff.

[121] For example Jean Bodin in his *Six Books of a Commonweale* (original 1606, facsimile Cambridge: Harvard University Press, 1962), 247: "In the like matter the tribes of the Grisons, which are of others most popular, and most popularly gouerned of any Commonweale that is, make their common assemblies for the choice of their Aman."

3

Local practice and federal government in the Freestate

Just as the Rhaetians, joined by their Leagues
Divide all offices among them, to noblemen
But also to men from the people,
So they are accustomed to gather as a common resource
All the taxes that are paid to them each year;
Then they divide it, partly by heads,
Dividing it man by man,
And partly according to wealth,
In the opinion that they can better protect their freedom
And control the powerful in this fashion,
By keeping absolutely nothing in a public treasury.

Franciscus Niger, 1543[1]

Throughout the fifteenth and into the sixteenth centuries, Rhaetians drew upon their experience of communal life to construct the system of alliances that culminated in the *Bundesbrief* of 1524. After 1524, communal values and practices continued to provide organizational models for the institutions and political culture of the Freestate. Public assembly, majority decision, and publicly controlled division of benefits and resources were characteristic practices that deeply influenced both the form of the Freestate and the political ideas of its inhabitants. Yet the application of local practices to larger problems was not automatic and reflexive; instead, federal institutions derived from a range of possibilities among which local practice was only one. The extension of communal values to the Freestate did not, therefore, result in *structures* identical to those found in the communes. Rhaetians also drew on other models of political order to arrive at results consistent with, but not directly based on, communal principles. Some institutions reflected earlier feudal structures, while others were based on the vestiges of imperial authority. The result was a complex institutional structure that coexisted with myriad informal or local customs and practices.

---

[1] Niger, *Rhetia*, 56. The text above follows Schiess's translation from the Latin.

THE PRACTICE OF COMMUNAL POLITICS

Every viable political entity must reach legitimate decisions – ones accepted by a preponderance of its members – and must distribute benefits and burdens in a predictable way. The village and political communes of the Rhaetian Freestate developed distinctive (though by no means unique) solutions for these tasks: legitimate decisions were those reached by a majority of the assembled male members, and political goods were distributed proportionally among the membership, either by dividing them when possible, or else by rotating access to them among eligible members. These two principles reflected both the social practice and the conceptual principles of late medieval village communes. In practice, the village was a group of cultivators, each of whom worked his own land under collective management. The fact that most material benefits from the commune were divided among the members rather than being held in common reflected this. Conceptually, though, the village commune was an association of equal members. This equality was expressed in the duty of all members to participate in village assemblies and to share in public burdens. The humanist poet Franciscus Niger captured this system in his poem "Rhetia," cited above. Along with the conviction that public resources should be distributed among an association's members, Niger also vividly conveyed the distrust of established authorities that characterized communal politics.

Equality in political affairs was unqualified in this model, in that every member of the commune had an equal vote in formal assemblies (although, as was typical for late medieval communes, not all inhabitants were necessarily members, and equality within the commune did not follow from any supposition that all humans were equal). Equality in economic matters, in contrast, was proportional, since an equal part in ownership was expected to provide an equal share of benefits. Each of these two principles could be extended to the political life of the Freestate, and both in fact appeared in the institutions and customs that developed. Majoritarian principles were most often applied to problems of decision-making, while proportionality more often became the solution to problems of distribution, although the reverse occurred as well. Rhaetians were flexible in their application of familiar principles to new problems.

Communalism also shaped the Freestate in another, more subtle way. We have seen that communes could be perceived as the result of two separate principles: the will of their members, or the natural subjection of the members to their lord. Of the two conceptual models, Rhaetians drew primarily on the first – the ability of free men to form voluntary associations – to construct the Freestate. Like their neighbors in the Swiss Confederacy and among the Swabian cities, the *Bündner* applied communal principles to the confederations they created. In effect, though, the extension of communal decision-making practices to the confederation implied that the latter was also a kind of commune.[2] The blurred distinction between commune and confederation that resulted from this uncertainty became important during the ideological struggles of the late sixteenth and early seventeenth centuries.

Majoritarian practices

Common assembly and majority voting were decision-making practices well suited to communes that conceived of themselves as collections of equal peers. The first step to understanding the role such practices played in the Rhaetian communes is to establish who was entitled to participate. Certain categories of person were excluded from membership altogether. As was usual elsewhere in early modern Europe, women, children, and foreigners were excluded from active citizenship, although some of them enjoyed the considerable benefits of passive citizenship: Graubünden was and remained a male-dominated society in this respect.

Many scholars argue that early modern Europe was also patriarchal in the sense that public roles were reserved for fathers – or *Hausväter*, as they were called in contemporary German. The strongest ideological expression of such a view could be found among the nobility, as Otto Brunner showed in his work. A similar model often applied to peasant households. Peter Blickle, for example, defines the village commune as a "corporate-communal association of household heads [*Hausväter*], who exercise state-like functions within a relatively closed settlement."[3] The political life of peasants in much of Europe was consistent with this view: the master of each household was enfranchised, whereas his children and servants had only limited rights to participate. A somewhat different model of public enfranchisement seems to have applied to Graubünden, however. Although the available evidence is extremely fragmentary, the essential criterion for having a voice there seems to have been the ability to bear arms. The village commune as a political assembly consisted of a group of potential arms-bearers, rather than of a group of privileged tenants or landowners.[4]

Several kinds of evidence support this view. First, village and communal statutes in Graubünden that specified who ought to attend the annual assembly gave only gender and age as criteria for attendance. The statutes of Safien, for example, state: "Further it is the law, that when attendance at an assembly [*Gmeind*] is commanded according to the statute, the commune's men who are fourteen or

---

[2] GG, "Bund", I: 599.
[3] Blickle, *Deutsche Untertanen*, 57. See also Sablonier, "Das Dorf im Übergang," 734.
[4] Padrutt, *Staat und Krieg* emphasizes the close connection between military service and political entitlement at all levels of sixteenth-century Rhaetian society. Some evidence for the importance of *Hausväter* does survive, as well. In Davos in 1603, for example, the village council made them responsible for seeing that everyone under their authority participated in a day of public fasting and prayer. GA Davos, B 50, entry for December 11, 1603.

older should attend the assembly and appear . . . "[5] While such statutes do not exclude the possibility that some men might not be members of the commune, they do indicate that more than one man per household could be politically enfranchised. Second, the better-documented political assemblies in the neighboring Swiss rural areas included all adult, honorable, arms-bearing men – and occasionally even women.[6] Those attending assemblies as members were often required to carry a sword or knife to prove their good honor and military standing. Thus, a broad militarily based conception of membership in the communes was the norm in the region with which Rhaetia had the closest connections.

Finally, the typical form of political unrest in the Freestate is revealing on this question. When the Rhaetian communes were dissatisfied with the state of affairs in the Leagues, one common recourse was to raise their military standards at a protest assembly (called a *Fähnlilupf* in Graubünden). Such events, documented from 1450 on, included all of a commune's fighters and claimed extensive authority to make political decisions: the commune as a *political* entity was embodied in its arms-bearing members. These quasi-military assemblies demonstrate the close connection between military participation and political empowerment in Graubünden.[7] The large numbers of men reported at such gatherings, moreover, make it impossible that they were just assemblies of *Hausväter*, since far more men attended than there were households in the communes. Consequently, we cannot argue that only the heads of households were politically active in the Rhaetian communes.[8]

Regardless of the exact composition of assemblies within individual Rhaetian communes, the principle that a majority of those attending should decide any and all issues was deeply embedded in political practice. The very terminology used gives a clue here. When the individual communes of the Freestate sent their opinions to central assemblies, these opinions were called "majorities" (*Mehren*), even from those communes where they were reached by methods other than a majority vote. More concrete evidence abounds in communal statutes, which often describe how decisions were to be reached. One of the most detailed statutes dates from 1657, when the commune of Langwies finally achieved full freedom from Austria; the procedures it describes were probably not new at that time, but

---

[5] WS I: 128, undated but from the seventeenth century. WS II: 124ff has a similar statute from Churwalden, dating from 1650 but based on the statute of 1569. None of the statutes collected in WS make wealth a criterion for maintaining citizenship, although to become a citizen one normally had to pay a substantial fee.

[6] See Carlen, *Landsgemeinde*, 12–13. Only the semi-urban canton of Zug specifically excluded those accepting public alms.

[7] Valèr, *Bestrafung*, 48–59, gives a detailed discussion of the legal connections between military service and Rhaetian justice.

[8] Some evidence suggests that the active troops were organized by the young men's associations in most villages. Caduff, *Knabenschaften*, 3, 21–22.

customary. The provisions regarding the election of the highest magistrate, the *Landamman*, were as follows:

Article 18: And if there should be more than one candidate, each one who has been proposed shall choose two honorable non-partisan counters from the district of the commune, who will count the clump [*hauffen*]of those who vote for one or the other candidate, and the one who has more shall be Landamman for that year.
Article 19: No one shall push, pull, or force another to go with him when one is voting.
Article 20: Rather everyone shall be free to go where he wants, and anyone who violates this shall pay a fine of 1£ to the commune.[9]

These articles not only followed the principle of majority decision, but described the means by which this principle found practical application. Moreover, the Langwiesner were clearly aware of the possibilities for abuse in their system of public voting, and established safeguards and penalties to ensure that the process produced a valid result.

That statutes like the one from Langwies described actual practice in some communes, rather than merely expressing pious hopes, is shown by the reports and letters by various observers of political life in the Freestate. Reports written by foreign diplomats are extremely revealing here. Faced with the responsibility of gaining a majority of communes for their proposals, ambassadors paid close attention to how political decisions were actually reached. The despatches of Giovanni Battista Padavino, Venetian ambassador in the early seventeenth century, echo the statutes of Langwies both with regard to the importance of majoritarian practices and their potential for abuse:

In taking the vote of the people, everyone who is fit to carry a sword being entitled to have his say, they use various methods that it would be very tedious to describe in all their diversity. In some places the decisions are made by the largest number of heads, in others by estates, or by parishes, or by clans [guilds?] as in Chur. But the general custom is to call the people on Sunday with a bell, and the magistrates, who are similar to *degani*, publicly read the content of the letters written by the presidents [of the Leagues], after which everyone then has to give his opinion; [the magistrate] then announces that those who desire to accept the matters that have been proposed should raise their hands, and then they count how many are raised, and which ones remain down to indicate the contrary opinion, just as in the ancient elections by show of hands in the Republics.[10]

Padavino was not a theoretician, but a practical politician with a mission to accomplish; therefore his description of decision-making by public majorities ought to be reasonably accurate. But Padavino went on to confirm what the Langwies statute above suggested, namely that Rhaetian voting was not immune to manipulation:

---

[9] WS II: 143. [10] Padavino, *Relatione del Segretario*, 22.

A large part [of the communes] usually have some chiefs in such deliberations, who are able through their authority or through other means to persuade the common people, ignorant and entirely deprived of other information except about tending their flocks, to whatever end [the chiefs] desire; and quite often they beguile them with false reports, with sinister allegations, by paying for drinks, and sometimes they use blows of their fists to force those who are near them to raise their hands.[11]

As Padavino's account illustrates, the fact that majorities were necessary to reach most decisions does not limit the means that could be employed to create a majority. The public decision-making process was not identical with the exercise of power.

The extremely visible and public forms of voting chosen for village assemblies helps reveal Rhaetian ideas about the sources of public authority. Inhabitants of the Lower Engadine during the seventeenth and eighteenth century made use of many different methods of election in their communes, for example, but never employed the secret ballot. "The old methods [before the introduction of secret ballot in 1843] were based on a popular desire for balance and participation . . . the modern democrats, in contrast, emphasized the capabilities and the decision of every individual."[12] The secret ballot protects each individual's freedom to vote as he or she will without fear of retribution, guarding individual choice even within the "social contract" of the community. The common Rhaetian method of separating into groups, a process in which the anonymity of the voter was *minimized*, shows that individual choice was not a key value in this system. Rather, the members of the commune were expected to stand by their choices publicly, thus creating a strong incentive for communal solidarity and even unanimity. At the same time, public voting reflected the principle that political rights proceeded from membership of the commune, rather than from any inalienable natural rights of its members.[13] Just as communal agriculture balanced individual labor and profit against the collective management of resources, Rhaetian communal voting balanced individual choice against the individual's subservience to collective authority.

An incident that took place during the tumults of 1607 illustrates the strength of the Rhaetian tendency to turn to majority rule when decisions had to be made. The court established by the military companies of the communes that spring seized one of the leading figures in the Freestate, Georg von Beeli, and sentenced him to be executed for corruption (see further pp. 180–83). The chronicler Bartholomäus Anhorn describes how Beeli was taken to the place of execution, where he spoke

---

11 *Ibid.*, 22.
12 Mathieu, *Bauern und Bären*, 198. The quote refers to the village commune of Guarda in the Lower Engadine.
13 Barber, *Death of Communal Liberty*, gives this distinction a central role in his argument, e.g. 133–39, 171–80.

before a crowd of several thousand onlookers. After a stirring speech, Beeli made one last request of the crowd:

I also ask you in God's name that you will not hold my death against my honorable relatives, but receive them loyally; beyond that I also ask you to respect my last wish, and allow my relatives to bury my body where they will . . . Thereupon a vote [*Mehr*] was taken with raised hands, that one ought to give his body to his relatives for burial.[14]

The assembled crowd felt that it was entitled to make such a decision on the spot, rather than referring it to the judges or to any political authorities. The people were accustomed to decide, and turned immediately to a show of hands as the appropriate method. This incident reveals the practical, unreflective character of majoritarianism in the Freestate.

The authority of the majority was also recognized in religious affairs after the Second Ilanz Articles of 1526 gave each commune the power to choose its own priest or minister. This decision defused the divisive potential of the early Reformation on the Freestate, and became a broadly accepted principle by mid-century. For example, when a group of Protestants in the commune of Bergün asked in 1573 that the commune support a Reformed minister as well as a Catholic priest, the bishop formulated the situation in these words:

You should consider carefully in this, dear loyal people of the Chadè [*gotzhusleütt*], since you well know what the practice in Graubünden has been until now – that in all cases the minority has to follow the majority . . . But if the opinion [that the Protestant minority was entitled to a minister at public expense] spread among the confederates, then it would be correspondingly legal and just that a Protestant commune be required to maintain a priest, if three or four Catholics were found there . . . [15]

The Freestate's central government generally applied majoritarian principles to the religious disputes that periodically flared within the communes. They ordained that majority opinion on confessional questions be ascertained and followed in Mesocco in 1560, in the Valtellina in 1577, and in the entire Gray League in the secessionist articles approved there in 1620.[16]

Despite the abundant evidence for the principle that the minority ought to follow the majority, however, the high value that Rhaetians put on unity and concord ensured that majority decision-making was only one side of the picture. For most *Bündner*, the best majority was one which included everyone. Moreover, once a decision was made, members of a commune were not free to disagree with it.

---

[14] Anhorn, *Püntner Aufruhr*, 131. A description in the Austrian archives differs slightly in that the question was put to the assembly by the judges: "darauf der Richter dem Volkh zuegesprochen wellich in diß sein herren Belis begern khain bedenckhen, der solle die handt aufheben, welliches von ieder menigelich geschechen." LAI Hofregistratur, Akten, Reihe C, Fasz. 168.

[15] JM II: 438 (no. 426).

[16] JM II: 299, STAG AB IV 1/4, p. 85, and STAC CB III Z45.2, pp. 71–72, esp. the second and third articles.

It took only a majority to elect a *Landamman*, but then all members of the commune had to swear obedience to him. The city statutes of Chur were even more explicit: once a majority on both councils had reached a decision, no one was to appeal the matter to the councils again, or to the commune. Violations could be punished with death.[17]

Occasional evidence also suggests that *Bündner* sometimes thought about the weaknesses of majoritarianism. As one might expect, there were always voices that questioned the "common man's" ability to participate in government, but these were not unique to Rhaetia, and have little bearing on the evolution of communal politics there. More interesting are complaints from those communes that had been outvoted. Majority rule among the communes always coexisted with the conviction that each commune's privileges and traditions were sacrosanct. Each League charter and treaty contained a clause specifically protecting the contracting parties' customary privileges. When communes found themselves in the minority on some issue, therefore, they often claimed that the Freestate was infringing on matters beyond its competence. The endless dispute about how to divide the Upper Engadine into two communes dragged on partly because each party claimed that custom supported its view, and therefore refused to yield to majority decisions made by the Freestate.[18] Even within communes, custom and majority could be competing principles; once communes attained internal autonomy, however, the communal assembly became the final arbiter of what custom might be, limiting the effectiveness of appeals against the majority's will. In the Freestate as a whole – where the federal principle outweighed the idea of any broad national authority – the central government never gained the power to judge local custom, with the result that the majority's power was sometimes curtailed.

Having established that majority decision-making became an ingrained habit within the Freestate's individual communes by the end of the Middle Ages, let us now examine its formal role in the Freestate's legal and institutional arrangements. In this respect, the Rhaetian leagues took a distinctive turn in the early fifteenth century, and subsequently developed in a direction different from the Swiss Confederacy's path. Unlike Switzerland, where the development of majority rule was so slow that it was ultimately blocked by the divisions of the Reformation, majoritarianism grew steadily more influential in Rhaetia until it became insti-tutionalized in the *Bundesbrief* of 1524.[19] Even after 1524, majoritarian procedures continued to gain importance and were extended to further spheres of politics.

In examining the role of majority decisions in various Rhaetian alliances, the same criteria that we applied to the villages are relevant: what sorts of things could

17 JM II: 4.
18 Documents in STAG Asp. III 6b, esp. the one dated August 13, 1576.
19 On majority rule in Switzerland, Elsener, "Zur Geschichte des Majoritätsprinzips"; and "Das Majoritätsprinzip." See also Kopp, *Geltung des Mehrheitsprinzips*.

be decided by a majority, and who could take part in the decision? The earliest surviving alliances between communes did not mention decision-making methods at all, since they were primarily treaties of mutual support. The only mention of a majority in the 1396 alliance between subjects of the bishop of Chur and those of the counts of Werdenberg-Sargans proclaimed that the bishop's subjects would follow the majority of the cathedral chapter in the absence of a unanimously elected bishop.[20] The document that created the Gray League in 1424 went a decisive step further. Should any confederates come into a conflict that could not be resolved satisfactorily by a communal court, a panel of judges was to be appointed by the three lords who led the Gray League. Once this court had heard the case, "what the majority decides, the minority must follow"; moreover, all the confederates were bound to enforce the verdict with their goods and with their lives.[21] This provision went considerably beyond the contemporary practice of allowing a deadlocked arbitration panel to appoint an extra member to decide the case.[22] The appeals court that developed from this provision, the Court of XV, gave the Upper League the most consistent judicial practice to be found in the later Freestate.

Article 11 of the original League of the Ten Jurisdictions in 1436 was the first to extend majority decision-making to the political affairs of the alliance. Concerning the possibility of future treaties, it stated that:

Item if it should occur that we the aforementioned communes [*Gericht*] wanted to form Leagues or make alliances in the future if they were necessary, what the majority of the aforementioned communes and lands decides should also be followed by the minority.[23]

This article went much further than anything earlier. It signaled the shift to a more thoroughgoing application of majority rule to the Leagues, a process that culminated in the majority provisions of the *Bundesbrief* of 1524. There, article 18 established the broad authority of a majority of the Leagues over all common affairs:

It is further agreed that whatever we the aforementioned confederates have to negotiate or to distribute, or gain in common, our assemblies should consequently be held . . . ; and after written announcement we should seek obedience [i.e. attendance], and sit in common all together; and everything that two of the Leagues agree upon, should be followed and observed by the third League and its delegates on their oaths.[24]

The majority specified here consists of two Leagues against the third. Only decades later did the majority of communes, regardless of their distribution among the Leagues, become accepted as the final authority in the affairs of the Freestate. This development was evidence of the increasing consolidation of the Freestate as a locus

---

[20] JVF, 9.
[21] JVF, 23.
[22] On additional arbitrators, Lutz, *Wer war der Gemeine Mann?*, 19–20.
[23] JVF, 31. The article was actually enforced in 1450, see JVF, 52–53.
[24] JVF, 86.

of political decision-making, as well as of the spread of majoritarian principles beyond the specific terms of the *Bundesbrief*. By the late sixteenth century, a majority of communes could decide any kind of political, legal, or constitutional question that came before the Three Leagues.

Proportional division of political goods and burdens

Along with establishing a general principle for reaching legitimate decisions, a second crucial task facing any political entity is finding a method for distributing goods and burdens among its members. Medieval hierarchs argued that distributive justice should be controlled by the emperor, pope, or king, acting as God's viceregent on earth; locally, feudal contractualism was based on the principle that lords were entitled to control the distribution of goods such as land because they protected and defended local society. Meanwhile, the appearance of a communal order in Graubünden, in which individuals owned many resources and deployed their own labor within collective constraints, produced its own principle of distributive justice, based on the partition and rotation of common goods.

The problem of distributing goods (and burdens) was different from decision making *per se*, and had a logic of its own. Whereas politics in the village commune rested on the nominal equality among its members – equally subject to the lord, or equally free in their ability to associate – distributive justice in Rhaetia usually rested on proportionality of resources. In the daily practice of the late medieval Rhaetian commune, the ideal was to distribute benefits in proportion to each member's share of ownership in them. Moreover, whereas political equality could be practiced by giving all members at an assembly an equal vote, not all resources could be divided, equally or otherwise. Instead, villagers had to develop more complex systems that took into account both the kind of resource involved and each communal member's just share in it. As they consolidated, the Rhaetian communes and Leagues were soon characterized by remarkably complex systems to divide or rotate collective resources and burdens.

The analytical distinction between political equality and economic proportionality often blurred in practice. Should the benefits of political lordship over subjects be divided equally among the communes, or in proportion to their population, or in proportion to their part in conquering the subjects? By what principle ought military booty be split among captains, soldiers, and their communes? During the formative period in the Freestate, these questions were addressed and answered, testimony to the practical foresight of those who drafted the leagues and alliances. Sometimes their solution emphasized the equality of all members, and sometimes they chose solutions that reflected the population or influence of the communes involved. But in every case, solving such problems remained a central issue in the political life of the Freestate.

As with majoritarianism, everyday life in the village communes provided both accepted principles and practical methods for managing the problems of distributive justice. This can be seen both in the organization of agriculture, and in the distribution of common labor, known in Graubünden as *Gemeinarbeit*. As the Rhaetian communes expanded their political autonomy, they moved towards distributive systems, both within the commune and in relations with allies, that were consistent with communal values and concepts. These systems were characterized by careful attention to each individual member's share, on the one hand, and by public control of the mechanisms of distribution, on the other.

One of the clearest examples of communal distribution in agricultural organization was the practice, known as *Wechselalpen*, of rotating access to alpine meadows among the members of a village commune, or between neighborhoods and communes.[25] The practice evolved to resolve the difficult problem of maintaining fairness in the distribution of valuable access rights to mountain pastures. A neighborhood or commune normally controlled several such pastures, each capable of supporting a fixed number of cows each summer. The problem arose because not all pastures were equal: cows grazing on some produced more milk and cheese than on others. Since cows were owned by individuals, and because each owner's share of cheese production was based exactly on the productivity of his individual cows, access to richer pastures directly affected each peasant's income. Yet spreading each owner's cows among many meadows would have hindered the individual care and local cooperation that helped maximize production. To prevent systematic unfairness in the distribution of a communal resource from creeping in, some communes responded by periodically redistributing grazing rights among members or fractions of a village, often by lot. Particularly in the south, this practice increased during the sixteenth century: in the Val Bregaglia, for example, the seven alps belonging to the fraction Ob Porta were redivided every five years.[26] In Ardez, the village was divided according to house numbers, so that clusters of neighboring houses shared a pasture. Every seven years, the exact number of grazing slots belonging to each quarter was readjusted to prevent overgrazing; every twenty-eight years, the alps themselves were redivided among the quarters. In Silvaplana, the periods were five years and fifteen years, respectively; in Sils, such a system was already in operation in 1545.[27] By the mid-sixteenth century, then, during the period when the Freestate was consolidating its structure, individual communes were organizing complex systems for dividing communal resources without detracting from the principle that individuals owned the actual productive resources, the cows.

An example of the communal distribution of burdens at the local level was the

---

25 Not all communes used this method to distribute alp-rights. See in general Weiss, *Alpwesen*, 202–06. Weiss's evidence is primarily from the nineteenth and early twentieth centuries. For earlier evidence, see Mathieu, *Bauern und Bären*, 64f.
26 Weiss, *Alpwesen*, 204; on the Bregaglia, 202 (documented in 1812).
27 *Ibid.*, 203–04.

practice of opening almost all village land to grazing at certain times of the year. This practice, known as *Gemeinatzung*, ensured that the commune's cattle would have sufficient fodder in the spring and fall, when the higher meadows were not available. Minutely regulated by village custom and statute, almost all fields were opened to the village herd, regardless of the wishes of each parcel's owner or lessor. In this case, the entire village corporation was the unit of use and distribution: all of the commune's land was used for all of its cows.[28] However, since landholding closely correlated with the number of cattle each individual household owned, this system did represent a proportional distribution of a collective burden. The rich owners of many cows gained the greatest benefit, but they also had to endure the greatest restraint over the use of their fields. In fact, villages carefully regulated how many cows each member could own.[29] In this way, the commune effectively partitioned grazing access to the fields around the village in proportion to each member's wealth. On the whole, though, the practice of *Gemeinatzung* was atypical in that it paid less regard to the exact distribution of burdens among individuals than did most agricultural practices in the communes. In this case, the demands of alpine pastoralism led to a solution that might best be called collectivist, although constrained by certain communalist elements.

In Rhaetia, shared labor for the benefit of the commune was another widespread and important distributive institution organized along communal lines. Roads and paths had to be maintained, meadows had to be cleared and irrigated. By investing their labor together, Rhaetian communes were able to overcome the handicaps of their harsh physical environment, and could markedly increase the productivity of their communal resources. The alpine meadows belonging to the commune of Mesocco, for example, were most productive during the period when they were communally managed and maintained. The commune built access paths through gorges and over mountains, erected substantial structures high up on the mountains, and fenced off parts of the meadow to provide for emergency fodder. When the Mesoccans chose to divide their alps in the mid-fourteenth century, the new owners often lacked the resources to continue such investments, with a resulting decline in production.[30]

Under these circumstances, common labor that was levied from all members equally became an important force for village discipline and integration.[31] Individuals from all parts of a commune worked side by side for the common good. A detailed description of communal road repair survives from the eighteenth century:

---

[28] Barber, *Death of Communal Liberty*, 113–14.
[29] On ownership restrictions and the detailed regulation of *Gemeinatzung* in the Lower Engadine, see Mathieu, *Bauern und Bären*, 62–64.
[30] M. Bundi, *Besiedlungs- und Wirtschaftsgeschichte*, 275–76.
[31] Barber, *Death of Communal Liberty*, 176–78, lays great stress on the integrating effect of common labor in the communes.

The evening before, the village head posts notices on the corners of the houses about what needs to be done the next day, and naming who will be called up. Normally this involved one person from each house . . . On the morning of the common labor, the call was made with three different signals with the village bells. By the third signal, everyone had to assemble in the village square, equipped with shovels, picks, and hatchets. The four village heads counted those present – absences were punished with a fine – and led them to the area where the roads needed to be repaired.[32]

Common labor could also involve work on the alpine meadows. Here the most frequent practice was to demand an equal share of work from every member who summered cows on the alp in question. The equality of membership outweighed the fact that members derived unequal benefits from common work, in proportion to the number of cows they owned.[33]

Thus, partition of common resources, whether equally or in proportion to each individual's ownership, and rotation of access to indivisible resources became characteristic forms of agricultural practice in Graubünden. The same principles applied to the problem of distributing political goods, both within communes and among the Leagues and the Freestate. As the Leagues and the Freestate coalesced, new burdens and new sources of income were distributed among their members almost entirely according to the principles described above, rather than being left for any officials or assemblies to distribute at will. Moreover, the tendency in this direction continued throughout the sixteenth century. More and more distributive authority was taken from the central institutions, and codified instead in complex systems of rotation not subject to anyone's discretion. Division or rotation replaced the idea of collective control: each member took his share or managed a resource in turn.

The division of larger valley communes into villages or neighborhoods provides the most visible evidence of the distribution of political goods by means of partition. Certain large communes had the right to send a delegate or two to central assemblies of the Freestate. In most cases, this right was distributed by rotating it among individual villages or neighborhoods within the larger, political commune. Such partition could be very complex: the commune of Vier Dörfer, for example, was divided into seven fractions by the end of the *ancien régime*: Trimmis and Zizers were each two-sevenths, while Haldenstein, Untervaz, and Igis each were one-seventh. Ramosch was also divided into seven parts, in which Ramosch controlled four, Stalla two, and Avers one share.[34] The process of dividing communes and precisely specifying each fraction's rights to common goods continued throughout the entire history of the Freestate, reflecting common political assumptions held by all *Bündner*. As the Three Leagues' government

---

32 Translated from STAG A 722, *ca.* 1770, and cited by Mathieu, *Bauern und Bären*, 30–31.
33 This gave the wealthy a relative advantage. Mathieu, *Bauern und Bären*, 70.
34 F. Jecklin, "Einteilung der Hochgerichte," 35–42.

consolidated, it often became the arbitrator between neighborhoods competing for their turns to name delegates or to appoint federal officers.[35]

When the communes began to form alliances and leagues, another distributive problem that faced them was military: how were the cost of military action and the spoils of military victory to be shared? Following Swiss practice, the costs of military help were usually paid by the party who appealed for support; only in particularly close alliances did each party have to support its allies at its own expense. But as the Leagues grew, and as they became aware of their military prowess, the problem of spoils took on greater importance. This progression can be illustrated by comparing the alliance between the communes of Oberhalbstein and Rheinwald in 1407 with the foundation of the Gray League in 1424. Article 5 of the former merely stated that the costs of any military support should be distributed by a commission consisting of two members from each commune.[36] The much broader alliance of 1424, including both lords and communes, established a general obligation of every party to support all the rest within their borders. "And whenever we the aforementioned confederates campaign together against an enemy, the things of all kinds that are won or taken should be distributed equally and in common."[37] Equal division remained the method for dividing spoils in all of the subsequent alliances before the *Bundesbrief* of 1524.[38] The experience of winning entire territories such as the Valtellina in addition to transportable booty led the framers of the *Bundesbrief* to create a more complex system of distribution. The *Bundesbrief* distinguished between spoils and territory: the men who had actually fought divided the former, whereas territory was split evenly among the Three Leagues.[39] Moveable goods thus went only to those who had participated in gaining them – a form of proportionality – whereas lordship was divided on the principle that the Three Leagues were all equal to one another. As it turned out, the Freestate undertook no further conquests, and these provisions never had to be exercised again.

Rather, the newly acquired lordships generated a new debate about distributing control over them among the Leagues and communes. Conquered or purchased by the Three Leagues in common, the subject territories were universally viewed as the common property of the whole Freestate. How, then, were the offices and income from this source to be managed? Many Rhaetians competed eagerly for the offices, which brought both income and prestige to their holders. Little evidence

---

[35] An early example of such action in STAG AB IV 1/2, p.1 (from 1570).

[36] JVF, 13.

[37] JVF, 21–22. Cf. Meyer-Marthaler, *Studien*, 48–51.

[38] An alliance proposed in 1451 between the Engadine and the Gray League, but never ratified, suggested that any spoils be given to the alliance in common, and distributed by majority decision. Here, majority decision was given priority before equal partition, showing how the two principles could contradict one another. JVF, 49.

[39] JVF, 84 (article 6).

survives from the early years of Rhaetian dominion, but by mid-century, the principle was well established that each commune in turn should choose the incumbents for the lucrative offices. During the reform effort and political trials of 1542, for example, the Three Leagues ordained:

Second, concerning the offices in the Valtellina, it is established that they should henceforth be distributed equally to each commune according to number [of population?], and that each commune should then be able to select someone as the officer, when and how it suits the commune.[40]

The exact mechanism by which the offices should rotate among the communes remained controversial throughout the sixteenth century, becoming the source of many conflicts. For example, the office of *vicari* in Teglio was specifically exempted from rotation in 1541 and again in 1573, but in each case the language of the exemption suggests that the office had in fact been rotating among the communes. A complex compromise was suggested in 1574, but in 1603 the office was once again included in a reformed system of rotation.[41] The 1603 rules, which remained in effect for the rest of the Freestate's history, blended equal partition, proportional division, and rotation of the right to fill federal offices.[42] These shifts were part of an important power struggle in the Freestate. The more powerful families preferred that officers be chosen during the central assemblies of the Freestate, where they were better able to influence the outcome. Lesser families and small communes attempted to move the entire selection process to the communes themselves, so that they too had a chance to gain a share of the spoils. The conceptual framework for this struggle, however, came out of the communal tradition of rotation and partition.

In fact, the institutions of the Freestate were never strong enough to enforce such complex schemes, so that the offices remained a battlefield on which the great families used bribery and intimidation to install their members. Nevertheless, the surviving evidence suggests that the rules forcing offices to be distributed widely had some effect in the sixteenth and seventeenth centuries. Almost all officers in the early years of the Freestate's reign in the Valtellina came from magnate families. By 1580 in contrast, a year for which a complete list of public offices survives, elite families controlled only six of the ten offices in the Valtellina.[43] The distribution of offices by family over the seventeenth century was relatively broad: the 358 office holders in the Valtellina who can be identified came from no fewer than 134

---

[40] JM ii: 208. The text decrees distribution "nach Antzal," ("according to number"), without further detail.
[41] In 1541, JM ii: 203. In 1573, STAG AB IV 1/3, p. 120. The 1574 compromise at STAG AB IV 1/2, p. 48. In 1603, the Vicari's office was firmly incorporated into the rotation system confirmed that year. JVF, 120, 126.
[42] See JVF, 119–29.
[43] Grimm, *Anfänge*, 170–71.

families. Even if we consider only the highest office, the forty-three known captains of the Valtellina came from twenty-six families.[44] Not everyone had a chance to fill a lucrative public office, to be sure, but the situation in Graubünden never resembled the narrow oligarchies in cities such as Zurich and Bern, and in rural Swiss cantons such as Glarus.[45]

Not only offices and income, but also burdens needed to be distributed in the Freestate. Naturally, everyone was much less eager to undertake their share of these, so that many burdens were simply left to the Freestate as a whole. Still, when matters were pressing, burdens were in fact divided more or less equally. This appears most clearly in military affairs: each commune or League had to provide troops when the Freestate needed to be defended.[46] Normally, each commune or district provided a single company, whose standard size was about 300 men.[47] Since the individual Leagues contained different numbers of districts, the resulting forces were unevenly divided among the Three Leagues: according to a Venetian observer, the Gray League and the Chadè each could provide about 10,000 men, the Ten Jurisdictions about 5,000.[48] In addition, since the communes' populations varied widely, military burdens were never distributed equally by population. Nevertheless, in the case of military service, the principle of equality between the communes – the contracting parties of the confederation – outweighed any resulting inequalities.

When it came to financial burdens, the communes and the Freestate strove to prevent having to distribute them at all. The easiest way to do this was to deduct common expenses from the Freestate's income before it was distributed to the communes. The city of Chur paid for the Freestate's executioner and for various messengers and correspondence, and was recompensed out of income from tolls and from the Valtellina.[49] Delegates at common assemblies received their pay out of common funds as well, although some communes objected to this.[50] The costs of the war preparations in the Valtellina in 1585 were charged mostly to the subjects there, so that the communes did not have to contribute beyond paying their own contingents.[51] Paying common costs out of common income did conform to the principle of equal distribution, even if it reduced the communes' control over the affairs of the Freestate. The *Bundesbrief* of 1524 provided little guidance here, since it merely stated that everyone should render taxes according to the custom of his

---

[44] Data from Färber, *Bündnerische Herrenstand*, 135–36.

[45] For the Swiss urban oligarchies, see Peyer, *Verfassungsgeschichte*, 110ff. For Glarus, see Mathieu and Stauffacher, "Alpine Gemeindedemokratie."

[46] E.g. JM II: 464, to raise 800 troops per League; JM II: 508, to raise 3000 troops per League and 3000 from the Valtellina; STAC CB III Z 45.2, p. 82, to raise 3000 troops per League.

[47] Valèr, *Bestrafung*, 7, with extensive evidence.

[48] Figures from Brown, "The Valtelline," 35, based on reports by Padavino.

[49] Account books in STAG A II/4.

[50] Vasella, "Bischöfliche Herrschaft," 66–67.

[51] JM II: 528, article 6; 529, article 9.

League, and that in case of war, clerical goods should also be taxed.[52] Since the Freestate did not undertake any large capital expenditures during our period, however, these clauses hardly ever had to be invoked.

As in any well-ordered polity, then, the problem of how to distribute benefits and burdens remained central to the Freestate's political life. The distinctive solutions that evolved directly reflected two facts: the Freestate remained a confederation, and this confederation was perceived as a kind of beneficial corporation, according to the model provided by the individual communes. The interplay between these facts helps explain the institutional evolution of the Freestate as a whole: while the formal structures that developed reflected its federal foundations, the generally accepted principles that guided the operation of those structures derived from the practical experience of political life in the communes. Majority decision-making and sophisticated division of common resources represented the communalist core of the Freestate's political culture. While similar ideas can be seen at work elsewhere in contemporary Europe – not only in other Swiss cantons, but also in many parts of Germany and the Netherlands, and in northern Italy – rarely did they appear so clearly in the construction of an institutional state.

THE FREESTATE'S INSTITUTIONS

After 1524 at the latest, the emancipation of the Freestate had gone far enough to justify referring to Graubünden as a functioning state. Once the *Bundesbrief* bound the Three Leagues to common policies, once the Freestate ruled over a relatively large number of subjects in the Valtellina, and once treaties established firm relations with Austria and France, the reality of political power created great incentives to regularize the Freestate's internal structure as well. Communal leaders had been meeting on an *ad hoc* basis since the 1470s to reach decisions on issues of common concern, a pattern that matured into a recognizable, if weak, central government by the mid-sixteenth century.

The Freestate's fundamental identity as a confederation of communes also provided the guiding principle for its formal institutions. Being incorporated into a larger political entity, in turn, reshaped the political communes that constituted the Freestate, and gave their institutions greater importance compared to the village and neighborhood communes within them. Conceiving a larger state required that the political communes, too, be more clearly defined, and that their authority and boundaries be established. The following analysis will therefore proceed from the communes – viewed as part of the entire Freestate rather than as autonomous political spheres – through the assemblies where the communes contributed to national decision-making, to conclude with a description of the limited central administration and its operation. Some discussion of both formal organization as

---

[52] JVF, 86–87, articles 21–22.

well as of the actual course of making and executing decisions is needed to illustrate how politics in the Freestate worked.

Formal political institutions: the communes

Even though individual communes still lived under feudal ties, the Freestate as a whole existed entirely outside the feudal–hierarchical structure of authority that dominated the late medieval Holy Roman Empire. The *Bundesbrief* of 1524 rested on no lord's authority, but was rather a common act of the communes (and of two lords who stood on an equal footing with the communes). The preamble stated that the document represented an agreement between the abbot of Disentis, the lord of Rhäzüns, "and we, all the communes of the common three leagues, on this side and the other side of the mountains, wherever we lie in our regions [*kraysenn*]."[53] After the Second Ilanz Articles in 1526, the importance of Rhaetian lords declined even further, leaving the will of the communes as the only source of formal political authority in the Freestate. The Freestate's consolidation thus created a new political sphere of action – comparable to the Swiss Confederation or the Dutch Republic – whose structure was shaped by the events and struggles that took place in the following century. The absence of a single source of authority within the Freestate, meanwhile, required the creation of novel, federal methods for reaching decisions. As the contracting parties who created the Freestate, the communes took the most important role in the resulting institutional structure.

Surprisingly enough, unlike earlier Rhaetian alliances, the *Bundesbrief* of 1524 did not name the contracting communes individually, so that their exact number remains rather hard to determine. If every community entitled to send a delegate to the common assembly, the *Bundestag*, was counted, one might come to a number in the high fifties, but with increasing institutional consolidation, the official count settled around fifty-two.[54] Contemporaries and historians have used different criteria to define the communes, which only increases the confusion. Jurists and legal historians often base their definition on the boundaries of criminal or civil jurisdiction (which is mostly correct), even though this definition disregards the essentially political function of the communes in the Freestate. Sociologically inclined authors, in contrast, focus on face-to-face communities and shared labor and decision-making in defining the communes.[55] Although such a view captures an important dimension of communal life, it applies to all communal spheres in

---

[53] JVF, 83.

[54] After the commune Unter Calven was lost to Austria during the Thirty Years' War, the number became fifty-one. Liver, "Die staatliche Entwicklung," 211, footnote 2, counts forty-nine. Pieth, *Bündnergeschichte*, 114–16, comes to either forty-eight or fifty-two communes, depending on the period and exact criteria used.

[55] The most important analysis of Graubünden from this angle is Benjamin Barber's in *The Death of Communal Liberty*.

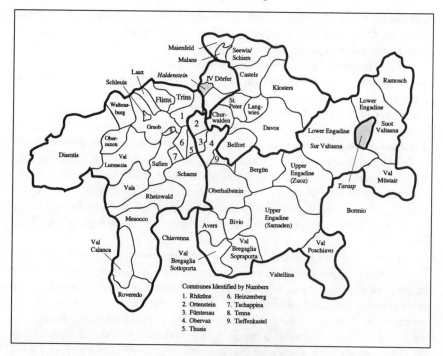

Illustration 6 Communes in the Rhaetian Freestate, 1450–1620.

Graubünden, not just to the specific communes that created the Freestate and remained the highest authority within it. For the purposes of this section, the *political communes* in Graubünden will be defined as units that autonomously managed their internal affairs and courts, and that constituted the Freestate and sent delegates to the *Bundestag*. This definition, like any other, leaves a few communes in anomalous positions, but it reflects the political communes' role in the Freestate as a whole.

Political communes were only one of several levels of organization, although they were the most decisive in shaping the Freestate's institutions. The communes themselves were almost all divided into "fractions" or "neighborhoods" (*Fraktionen, Nachbarschaften*), and were also joined into "districts" (*Hochgerichte*) and into Leagues (*Bünde*). The result was a complex tapestry of overlapping and competing jurisdictions and interests, which led to incessant quarreling within and between the communes about where courts were to be held, about who could elect which officers, and about who had the authority to appoint delegates to the *Bundestag*. Once the Freestate's common institutions stabilized in the mid-sixteenth century, however, each commune enjoyed essentially identical rights and duties with respect to the Freestate. The differences in their formal positions were trivial compared to the situation in neighboring southern Germany, where certain towns or districts maintained highly privileged positions and the rest of the countryside was completely disenfranchised.[56]

Judicial functions were central to contemporary definitions of the political commune, and older historiography is therefore correct in inquiring whether a commune exercised capital justice.[57] Since lordship during the late Middle Ages was often equated with the right to impose and carry out capital punishment, high justice was more than a legal technicality, and its exercise was *prima facie* evidence that a political entity was an autonomous "prince over itself."[58] As the inhabitants of the commune of Avers put it while revising their statute book in 1622, "we have our own [judicial] staff and seal, stocks and gallows, and thanks to God we do not owe any foreign prince or lord anything, but are subject only to Almighty God . . . "[59] The exercise of judicial authority over capital cases, symbolized by the stocks and gallows, represented tangible evidence of a commune's political independence.

Yet not all of the Rhaetian political communes could claim such authority. Among those not possessing the right to exercise high jurisdiction in the sixteenth century, most were subject in some way to the Habsburg family. These included two communes in the Lower Engadine, eight of the Ten Jurisdictions, and the commune of Rhäzüns in the Gray League. In the Lower Engadine, capital cases were heard before a Tyrolean administrator in Nauders, outside the Freestate; in the Ten Jurisdictions, the Habsburgs appointed a bailiff (*Landvogt*) who lived in Castels, and who presided over capital cases, confirmed the local officers responsible for petty justice, and accepted the local population's oaths to their lords. Finally, the lords of Rhäzüns were non-hereditary Habsburg feudatories who exercised high jurisdiction on the basis of the rights of the lordship of Rhäzüns itself.[60] Despite Austrian control over capital jurisdiction, all of these communes were full members of the Freestate.

Aside from the Habsburgs, the most important lord exercising high jurisdiction was the bishop of Chur – in fact, jurisdiction was exercised in his name in the entire Chadè. But the Second Ilanz Articles severely limited the bishop's rights, and the balance of power between the bishop and the communes was such that he could

---

[56] Some large communes in the Freestate had more than one vote in federal affairs, and a few communes did enjoy privileged positions in their separate Leagues. In Württemberg, by contrast, representation in the duchy's estates was monopolized by a few towns who claimed to speak for the rural regions as well. Vann, *Making of a State*, 41–48.

[57] Liver, "Die staatliche Entwicklung," 209; Planta, *Geschichte von Graubünden*, 188–89.

[58] The term *civitas sibi princeps* was of great importance in Italian republican thought. On capital jurisdiction and Switzerland's sovereignty, Reibstein, *Respublica Helvetiorum*, 61–65.

[59] Reprinted in Weber, *Avers*, 129. A similar statement from Langwies, in 1652, WS, II: 140–42.

[60] A compromise reached in Rhäzüns in 1615 acknowledged the nominal authority of the Austrian appointee as lord, while leaving most authority in the hands of the village: LAI Ferdinandea, Fasz. 206, Rubrik 193, undated document (*ca.* 1615) accompanying a letter dated September 22, 1622.

exercise little influence even where his privileges were legally intact.[61] Certain other lords had residual rights in various communes, which provided the stuff for many legal wrangles without playing an important role in the political evolution of the Freestate. Most unusual were the communes of Maienfeld and Malans in the Ten Jurisdictions: after the Three Leagues purchased the two communes in 1509, capital justice there was exercised by the Freestate as a whole.[62] All of these cases illustrate that control over capital jurisdiction was not the defining characteristic of the Freestate's communes, even though jurisdictional boundaries often coincided with communal boundaries.

Despite the symbolic prestige of criminal jurisdiction, control over civil law was equally important in practical terms. The Lower Engadine, where three civil districts formed the basis of the three political communes found there, represents a good example of this fact, since criminal jurisdiction there did not follow communal boundaries.[63] By the sixteenth century, all of the Freestate's communes had almost complete autonomy over their internal affairs, whatever their feudal status, and a majority held an annual public assembly to pass new civil laws, to elect the judge and jurors of the local court, and to debate the major policy decisions for the coming year.[64] The unchallenged authority of these annual assemblies over civil jurisdiction confirmed a sense of communal identity that was reinforced by the fact that individual members swore an oath of obedience and loyalty to the commune at such meetings. Evidence for the internal autonomy of the communes can also be found in the communal record books, the *Landbücher*, that preserved statutes and decisions made over the years. Describing the rights and obligations of the commune's members, the rules of agriculture and trade, and the resolution of civil disputes within the commune, these record books have been described as "little masterpieces of rural legislation."[65] Significantly, many of them were either compiled for the first time or reedited during the sixteenth and early seventeenth centuries, as the political structure of the Freestate as a whole was consolidating.[66]

---

61 Article 8 of the First Articles of Ilanz prohibited appeals to clerical courts; article 1 of the Second Ilanz Articles said that neither the bishop nor any cleric could appoint a bailiff, *Amman*, or council in any commune of the Three leagues. JVF, 80, 89–90. A survey of the bishop's rights in Vasella, "Die bischöfliche Herrschaft," 50–54. The communes still under the bishop's lordship – Poschiavo, Greifenstein (Oberhalbstein/Bergün), and several communes in the Gray League (Ilanz, Gruob, Lumnezia, Flims) – bought out the bishop's rights between 1526 and 1537. Moor, *Geschichte von Currätien*, II: 160.

62 Pieth, *Bündnergeschichte*, 103–04; JM I: 71–72.

63 Liver, "Geschichtliche Einleitung," for detailed description.

64 Cf. Liver, "Die staatliche Entwicklung," 217.

65 A selection is published in WS and in SSRQ, Serie Dorfordnungen/Tschantamaints. Characterized by Wagner, editor of WS II: 215.

66 According to my survey of surviving *Landbücher* and similar legislative collections in WS, the distribution is as follows: before 1500, seven; 1500–10, one; 1510s, one; 1520s, none; 1530s, one; 1540s, five; 1550s, seven; 1560s, none; 1570s, three; 1580s, one; 1590s, five; 1600–10, five; 1610s, three; 1620s, two. Total counted: forty-one.

The emergent political order stimulated a clearer definition of the communes as well as the creation of central institutions.

As a result of their very different feudal and judicial histories, Rhaetian communes had quite different internal organizations, ranging from mini-oligarchies to relatively open democracies. A few examples can illustrate the range of possibilities.[67] In the Upper Engadine, where there was no popular assembly, only members of a few aristocratic families from the village of Zuoz could be elected to the highest offices. In Davos, a small council representing the fractions of the commune wielded final authority, so that popular assemblies took place only occasionally. In the Val Bregaglia Sotto Porta, there were fewer formal restrictions on political participation, but the commune was thoroughly dominated by one family, the Salis. Popular assemblies there served primarily to ratify the decisions reached by a few powerful Salis leaders. In Poschiavo, seven or eight powerful families struggled to dominate the commune, but were not always able to exclude other families from the most powerful and lucrative public offices. Finally, in Schams there was little evidence of a stable elite: the commune had a relatively open system in which public assemblies retained significant control over public affairs. Clearly, the fact that all of the communes were self-governing did not by itself determine the way individual communal governments functioned.

Given such a wide spectrum of local conditions, it is significant that each commune exercised essentially identical powers and responsibilities within the Leagues and in the Freestate; large differences in internal organization resulted in little distinction as far as the Freestate was concerned. Each commune had its vote, could send representatives to common assemblies, and was entitled to a share of the Freestate's resources. The differences among the communes might influence the policies they favored and the threats they most feared, but did not affect each commune's status with regard to the Freestate's central government. Instead, federal policies were in theory established independently from the communal affairs of the internally sovereign communes.

The political life of the individual political communes was already removed from the face-to-face village communalism found in smaller units such as neighborhoods. Nevertheless, the connection between village life and the affairs of the political commune remained relatively close: the political commune might form a large sphere in the mind of a small peasant or the landless worker, to be sure, but he could still see the connection between its affairs and his fate. Even though his economic and social life took place primarily in his village or neighborhood, he marched to war with his commune, witnessed capital punishment ordained by the commune, and swore an oath to his commune and its

---

[67] Based on Färber, *Der bündnerische Herrenstand*, 43–85.

banner.[68] Contemporary terminology reflected the connection between political communes and face-to-face neighborhood communities by calling them both *Gemeinden* or *comüns* – a term that was not applied to the Leagues (*Bünde*, *Lias*) or to the Freestate as a whole. The step from commune to confederation was a major one, both in the daily experience of a commune's members and in the different conceptual categories employed. League business took place sporadically, far away from most of the communes, and was usually in the hands of a few leading families. Confederates from other communes might speak a different language, sell at different markets, and worship according to different principles. Only the free will of the parties involved, sealed through their oaths, bound men together across communal boundaries. This was a very powerful bond, one which echoed the way Rhaetians thought about their communes, but it lacked the additional reinforcement provided by the natural sense of community that held together villages and communes.

The Institutions of the Three Leagues: Formal assemblies

The formal government of the Freestate took place at regular assemblies. The *Bundesbrief* of 1524 established the official framework for all future assemblies in article 18:

whatever we the aforementioned confederates have to negotiate or to organize or to distribute in common, our meeting days should consequently be held first at Ilanz, second at Chur, third again at Ilanz, fourth again at Chur, and the fifth at Davos . . . [69]

Article 19 provided that each League should keep a written record of the deliberations, so that the decisions of the Three Leagues might not be forgotten. The *Bundesbrief* thus specified how and where assemblies were to be held; other developments of the early sixteenth century, meanwhile, especially the conquest of the Valtellina and the purchase of Maienfeld, made such assemblies necessary on a frequent basis. Officers needed to be appointed, income had to be accounted for and distributed to the communes, and appeals from the new subjects had to be heard. The few surviving protocols of such assemblies from before the 1560s suggest that the organizational pattern of these meetings was already well-established at an earlier date.[70]

Assemblies were of two types: ones where all communes were represented, called *Bundestage*; and smaller ones, known as *Beitage*, led by the presiding officers of the

---

[68] I say "he" because the Rhaetian political system left women outside the political sphere, which was defined by fighting, voting, and sharing in communal resources. Only in the third of these could women take part.

[69] JVF, 86.

[70] STAG A II Landesakten 1/615 and 1/755 for early examples.

Three Leagues.[71] Either kind of assembly could take place at any time during the year, but three regular *Beitage* soon emerged, one during the St. Martin's market in Chur in November, another around the feast of St. Paul in February, and the last at the Chur market in early June, the so-called Churerkilbi. *Bundestage*, which were never as regular, had to be announced well in advance, especially if held during winter months when delegates from south of the mountains would have to cross the high snowed in passes.

The larger *Bundestag* was the more important assembly. It consisted of sixty-six delegates from the communes, presided over by the presidents (*Häupter*) of the Three Leagues, namely the *Landrichter* for the Gray League, the mayor of Chur for the Chadè, and the *Landamman* of Davos for the Ten Jurisdictions.[72] The location of the *Bundestag* rotated among the Three Leagues' chief towns – Chur, Ilanz, and Davos – as stipulated in the *Bundesbrief*. Important decisions had to be sealed by all Three Leagues to be valid. The presiding officer at each meeting had no special personal authority, but merely represented his League. The presidents naturally gained considerable practical influence, though, because of their control over the agenda and because they always came from influential communes. The presidents could call a *Bundestag* by writing the communes when important matters arose, such as foreign alliances, although no formal procedure specified how they should do so: the broad principle found in the *Bundesbrief* that common business required a meeting was sufficient justification for their authority. Nor were the presidents the only ones authorized to write the communes. Communal councils could also write their peers to suggest a meeting, while after the 1550s, the episcopal chamberlain in Chur regained the right to announce business to the communes of the Chadè.[73] In addition to *Bundestage* called for special occasions, others met biennially to appoint officers over the Valtellina, and to review the accounts of the officers whose terms had ended.

The meticulous concern the *Bundestag* showed for rotating the leadership of the Freestate among the Leagues and communes illustrates how far from traditional lordship the Rhaetians had come. Meetings, like the existence of the Freestate itself, depended on the will of the confederates, rather than proceeding from any person's authority. Any commune could call for a *Bundestag*, and every commune could attend. In contrast to most of the parliaments and estates in Europe, the Rhaetian *Bundestag* did not claim to "counsel" a prince, but rather established and executed public policy in the name of the communes, who were always referred to as "our lords." Its procedures did not revolve around a prince's desire for money and his subjects' desire for the redress of grievances, but rather on the desire to maintain

---

[71] Some Romantsch and Italian texts transliterate the German names. Others texts call a *Bundestag* a *Comöna* (e.g. RC v: 310), or a *Dieta* (e.g. RC xi: 3–4).

[72] JVF, 37–8.

[73] Vasella, "Bischöfliche Herrschaft," 84–86.

domestic peace and international standing. Everything we know about its organization illustrates its character as an assembly of equals not subject to any higher authority except their own shared oaths.

Because it was the most comprehensive deliberative body in the Freestate, the *Bundestag*'s decisions commanded considerable authority, but they were by no means final. Delegates to the *Bundestag* were described as "messengers" (*Boten*), not as representatives, and the communes retained final authority to accept or reject the decisions that any of the Rhaetian assemblies might reach. In any case, the *Bundestag* was never a flexible and responsive organ for managing the Freestate's affairs. Gathering delegates from over fifty communes scattered across three major watersheds separated by high mountains was never easy, as frequent injunctions against absenteeism indicated.[74] In addition, the provision that business needed to be announced in advance limited the *Bundestag*'s competence, especially when complex negotiations or rapidly changing situations were involved. The Freestate, if it was to function at all, needed another organ that could respond to emergencies, and that could also oversee routine business. This need was fulfilled by the smaller *Beitag*, which met frequently but irregularly in addition to its three regular annual meetings.

A *Beitag* always included the presidents of the Three Leagues, who might also consult with as many additional delegates as they saw fit – usually six or twelve, but occasionally with a full complement as at a *Bundestag*.[75] Quite often, a *Beitag* consisted of only the three presidents, who almost always met in Chur. Each of these dignitaries held his position because of his office within his own League, although each was chosen by his League in a different way. The *Landrichter* of the Gray League was nominated in rotation by the three noble members of the Gray League, namely the abbot of Disentis, the lord of Sax, and the lord of Rhäzüns (the *Hauptherren*). In the century after the founding of the Gray League in 1424, these rights had devolved upon specific communes: Disentis exercised the abbot's choice, Ilanz/Gruob had acquired the rights of the lords of Sax after their extinction, while the lord of Rhäzüns eventually had to share his right of nomination with the commune of Rhäzüns.[76] In the other two leagues the situation was simpler. The mayor of Chur, elected by the guilds, sat for the Chadè, and the *Landamman* of Davos, elected by his commune, sat for the Ten Jurisdictions. Two of the three presidents therefore held their offices because of their positions in their communes, while the third was appointed on the basis of the rights of certain lords and their legal heirs.

The *Beitag* was useful not just for reacting to changing events, but also for

---

[74] E.g. STAG AB IV 1/3, p. 86; AB IV 1/4, pp. 14, 18; AB IV 1/6, p. 386.

[75] The latter, known as a "Beitag volkhomenlich wie in einem Pundtstag," or a "Bytag von all gmeynden gemeiner dreier Bünden," was rare; examples in STAG AB IV 1/3, pp. 183, 215.

[76] After 1486, the *Landrichter* was formally elected by all communes of the Gray League, so that the special rights of the three lords and communes were limited to nomination. Grimm, *Anfänge*, 114.

Table 1. *Assemblies of the Three Leagues by type, 1500–1620*

Bundestag	116	24%
Beitag	264	55%
Unspecified membership	(171)	(36%)
Larger than three presidents	(93)	(19%)
Unclear	100	21%
Total meetings	480	100%

Figures are based primarily on JM I and II and on STAG AB IV 1 / 1–8. They assume that protocol entries within five days refer to a single *Beitag*, and that entries within fourteen days refer to one *Bundestag* (unless there is clear evidence to the contrary).

collecting the opinions of the most powerful communes and families, who were likely to have influential members present in Chur at any given time. The *Bundestag*, in contrast, was unwieldy but derived its greater power from its inclusiveness. The different roles of the two assemblies influenced their relative frequency: of the 480 identifiable meetings between 1500 and 1620, about one-fourth were *Bundestage*, while over half were specifically labeled as Beitage (see Table 1). Most of the remaining ones were probably *Beitage* too, although no positive identification is possible.

When did all these assemblies meet? *Bundestage* were distributed much more evenly than other meetings, normally averaging one to two per year. The most *Bundestage* in one year, four, occurred in 1530 and again in 1603, in each case because of increased diplomatic activity as well as domestic problems.[77] The longitudinal distribution of documentable *Beitage* is quite different from that of *Bundestage*. After relatively scarce meetings (or records) during the early part of the century, with the exception of the years around the Rhaetian Reformation, *Beitage* became far more common in the late 1560s and 1570s. A slight lull in the 1590s was followed by another burst of meetings early in the seventeenth century. Meetings became rarer again (or more records were lost) until well into the *Bündner Wirren*, when the new military and diplomatic situation led to a rapid increase in the number of assemblies after 1616.

Two general conclusions follow from this evidence. One, based on the growing frequency of assemblies during the sixteenth century, is that they represented a genuine forum for the Freestate's political life. Foreign observers and contemporary chronicles both attributed great importance to assemblies and to the decisions they reached. This is not to say that all politics in the Freestate took place

---

[77] In 1530, due to negotiations about helping Zurich and Bern in their struggle with the Inner Swiss cantons, in 1603 due to both the constitutional questions about the Great Reform and to negotiations with Venice about an alliance.

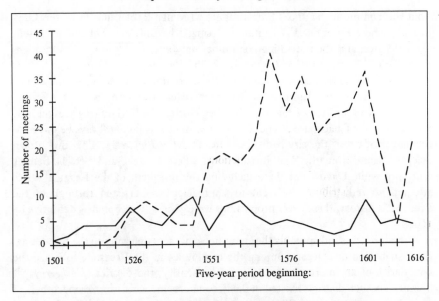

Illustration 7   Chart of the *Bundestage* (solid line) and other assemblies
(dotted line), per five-year period, 1500–1620. Figures based primarily on
JM I and II and on STAG AB IV I/1–8.

at *Bundestage* and *Beitage*, but it does mean that they had become institutionally
indispensable for the decision-making process by the late sixteenth century.
Logically enough for a polity that lacked any alternate focus for power such as a
princely court, assemblies dominated the political process in Rhaetia. The second
conclusion is that a substantial routinization of the Freestate's institutions took
place during the same period. The competence and practices appropriate to each
assembly were refined and made predictable. The number and identity of delegates
were known, and the meeting places of *Bundestage* and *Beitage* became predetermined. Everyone knew that the *Beitag* would meet at least three times a year
during the Chur markets, that a regular *Bundestag* would take place every few years
in January, and that a special *Bundestag* would be convened if foreign ambassadors
proposed an alliance. This predictability, in turn, helped reinforce the assemblies'
importance for political life.

Make-up of the Rhaetian assemblies

The powers and function of any representative assembly depend on what entities
can send delegates, and who becomes a delegate. By the mid-sixteenth century,
established practice in the Freestate required the attendance of sixty-six delegates

99

from the communes of the Three Leagues. Twenty-eight came from the Gray League, where Disentis, Val Lumnezia, Ilanz, Rhäzüns, and Schams each sent two delegates, and the remaining communes only one. In addition, the president of the Gray League, the *Landrichter*, sat in the *Bundestag ex officio*; since he was always from Disentis, Ilanz, or Rhäzüns, these communes effectively sent a third delegate in rotation. Another twenty-three delegates came from the Chadè, including two each from Chur and the Vier Dörfer. As in the Gray League, the president of the Chadè also attended *ex officio*; since this honor always belonged to the mayor of Chur, the city had three votes at every *Bundestag*. The final fifteen delegates came from the Ten Jurisdictions, where Castels, and Seewis/Schiers sent two, while Davos sent three including the president of the League. While attempts to redistribute the right to send delegates persisted throughout the Freestate's history, these exact proportions were generally accepted as definitive by 1600.

Although it was indisputably the communes that sent delegates to the Bundestag, the distribution of delegates among the communes in the Freestate followed the boundaries of an intermediate organizational entity, the district (*Hochgericht*).[78] Twenty-six such districts existed in the Freestate, some consisting of one, others of two or three communes. Their origins may have been early medieval judicial districts, or the immunities of local dynasts.[79] In the sixteenth century, they no longer had any independent institutional existence: no officials held their offices from a district, and the districts exercised no authority either judicial or political. Most historians have consequently treated the districts as "purely administrative" divisions of no great importance. Yet a crucial aspect of the districts lay in the fact that each district – rather than each commune – provided a company of troops when the Freestate gathered its forces. Legal and constitutional historians tend to overlook the military origins of the Freestate, and the continuing power of the idea – characteristic of Swiss rural regions – that a commune's gathered fighters were competent in all other spheres as well.[80] Seen from the common soldier's viewpoint, the regular communal delegates were only messengers for the arms-bearing citizens as a whole. When those citizens gathered in arms, however, they did so by district, not by commune.[81]

---

[78] Although the term *Hochgericht* suggests a judicial function, the districts actually had none; I have therefore chosen the neutral 'district' as the English translation.

[79] Valer, *Bestrafung*, 5–26, suggests the former. Plattner, *Die Entstehung*, part II, attempts to trace the role of immunities in creating the districts. See also Clavadetscher, "Herrschaftsbildung," 150.

[80] The assembled military companies "were" the Freestate in exactly the same sense that the assembled nobility elsewhere "were" the *Land* according to the perception of late medieval feudal ideology as described by Otto Brunner.

[81] On *Hochgerichte*: Liver, "Die staatliche Entwicklung," 212, footnote 3; Valèr, *Bestrafung*, 1–22. See also Albert and Berty Bruckner, *Schweizer Fahnenbuch* (St. Gallen: Zollikofer, 1942), 238f. Padrutt, *Staat und Krieg*, 25–34. For Swiss comparisons, see Möckli, *Schweizerischen Landsgemeinde-Demokratien*, esp. 31–32.

Local practice and federal government

Thus it is not surprising that many *Bündner* thought that each *district* ought to be represented at the *Bundestag* with two delegates – even though the *Bundesbrief* had been authored by the *communes*. For example, a *Bundestag* protocol of 1557 reports:

complaint had been made against the lords and confederates from the Gray League, and it had been requested of them that only two delegates and not more should sit from each large district [*grossen gericht*], according to repeated decisions; but the men from the Gray League did not want to do this without the knowledge and approval of their lords the councils and communes . . . [82]

The dispute arose because the Gray League's twenty-eight seats in the Bundestag came from only eight districts; the Chadè, in contrast, had twenty-three seats for its eleven districts, the Ten Jurisdictions fifteen seats for seven districts.[83] Nevertheless, even though the districts provided organizational boundaries for various purposes, the communes possessed the resources and continuity to actually manage the Freestate: when delegates appealed back home, it was always to the "honorable councilors and commune" – a standard formulation – never to the district.

In addition to the districts, the individual Leagues remained an important part of political life in the Freestate until it was reorganized during the Napoleonic period. The Leagues continued to meet, to legislate, and to act as separate units long after they had joined into an eternal confederation in 1524. A certain legal and institutional ambiguity remained between Leagues and Freestate, therefore. Because the communes, not the Leagues, were the contracting parties in the *Bundesbrief* of 1524, some scholars argue that the Leagues were superseded after that point.[84] But the *Bundesbrief* itself contained frequent references to the Leagues as organizational entities, particularly in the sections on resolving conflicts among the confederates. It was also a majority of Leagues, not of communes, that determined Freestate policy, at least according to the letter of the *Bundesbrief*.[85] By the early seventeenth century, a vote by communes rather than by Leagues became the norm, but during the troubles after 1607, the individual Leagues reemerged as important loci for decision and action. In 1620, the Catholic majority in the Gray

---

[82] JM II: 269. The objections of the other two Leagues make sense only if they are speaking of districts with the term *grossen gericht*, since no commune in the Grey League sent more than two delegates to the Bundestag, but many districts did. Meyer-Marthaler reads the term *grossen Gericht* as a simple reference to the size of the commune involved, (*Studien*, 122).

[83] Each league had one additional seat for its president. Thus the Chadè and the Ten Jurisdictions sent exactly two delegates per district.

[84] Peter Liver makes the strongest claims for this point. He argues that the Freestate as a whole, constituted by the communes directly, was the only subject of the law of nations in Rhaetia, even though its sovereignty in other areas was questionable. "Die staatliche Entwicklung," 206. His view is moderated by Meyer-Marthaler, *Studien*, 111, 116f.

[85] See JVF, 86, article 18, cited above.

League even passed a set of articles that amounted to secession from the Freestate, although these were never implemented.[86]

The individual Leagues possessed a continued sense of separate identity. A particularly clear statement of this sentiment can be seen in 1574, during a dispute among the communes of the Chadè about precedence at their meetings. A settlement proposed by the League was rejected by the communes Lower Engadine and Vier Dörfer, raising the threat that the other two Leagues might be called in to mediate, as the *Bundesbrief* provided. At an assembly of the Chadè in Chur on February 1, 1574, the protocol records:

> Thereupon it was resolved to speak to [the two obstinate communes] earnestly . . . and to request an answer from them once again, in which they reveal whom they consider partisan, and whether they think that the entire Chadè [*gemeiner Gotshuß*] should hand its privileges over to the other two leagues . . . [87]

Each League remained very sensitive about its own internal autonomy and prerogatives, even though the Three Leagues' common organs increased in importance after 1524.

The characteristic quality of federal organization, that authority flowed upwards from the constituent elements as well as downwards from the common magistrates, was omnipresent in the Freestate. It would therefore be mistaken to view the Freestate as a simple hierarchical structure with village communities and communes on the bottom, districts in the middle, and the Leagues and the Freestate at the top, just as it would be incorrect to view only the communes and the *Bundestag* as the institutional core of the Freestate.[88] Rather, various judicial and political divisions, mostly based on the tangled feudal history of the region, cooperated (or often competed) in the fulfillment of various public functions. Despite this complexity, however, by the mid-sixteenth century the formal structure of assemblies was well established: the number of delegates each commune should send to assemblies, the approximate schedule of meetings, and the places where they ought to take place were all well known. A communally organized sphere of political action was appearing.

Actual participation at the Bundestag *and* Beitag

We must also ask whether actual participation in these assemblies conformed to the formal arrangements made at the time. In fact, both *Beitage* and *Bundestage* varied in their actual membership from period to period. Often enough, it is impossible to

---

[86] STAC CB III Z 45.2, pp. 70–79.
[87] STAG AB IV 1/2, p. 52.
[88] Giatgen Fontana points out that such descriptions represent the projection of nineteenth-century liberal ideas about the state onto the phenomena of the sixteenth century. "Ländliche Gemeinde," 57.

determine which communes attended a given assembly, since the recess or protocol merely stated that the assembly was a *Bundestag*, or that the "presidents and delegates" or "all Three Leagues in common" met at a *Beitag*, without specifying the exact size or composition of the assembly. The regular *Beitage* (Martini in November, Pauli in February, Churerkilbi in June) probably always included delegates from many of the communes, but the absence of lists prevents any systematic analysis of attendance.

The personal identity of delegates to *Bundestage* and *Beitage* is also difficult to determine. Considerable evidence suggests that, at least in normal times, communes almost always sent their chief magistrate (*Amman, Vogt, Mistral, podestà*) to the assemblies, especially to *Bundestage*: the highest officer of a commune served as a messenger to the Leagues and to the Freestate.[89] The *Landbuch* of St. Peter in the Ten Jurisdictions, for example, states that the *Landamman* shall have the right to attend two *Bundestage* along with other assemblies during his two years of office.[90] Other evidence suggests that delegates might be specially elected by assemblies in their communes. In disputes over who was the legitimate delegate, a claimant often pointed to his election by the commune to bolster his position. Three neighborhoods of the commune Oberhalbstein complained about the delegate sent to a *Bundestag* in Davos in 1570; however, since the protesters had helped elect (*erwöllen*) the sitting delegate, their protest was denied.[91] In 1588, two competing delegates from Schleuwis each claimed authority from their commune. One said that he, as *Amman*, had called an assembly to deliberate on the issues for the upcoming *Bundestag* as was customary, but that "certain specific individuals" had hindered this assembly, only to hold an unauthorized meeting of their own soon after. His opponent also appeared, saying simply that "he had been elected delegate by his commune which had the authority to do so, and ought to be protected in his claim."[92] The first rather than the second claimant was seated in the assembly, illustrating the presumptive claim that an *Amman* had to the office of delegate.

Most likely, the method by which a delegate to the *Bundestag* was chosen varied from commune to commune. In the larger or more oligarchic communes, popular assemblies, if they existed at all, played a smaller role. Only if several factions among the magnates had to compete for popular approval did the common man have any influence in such a commune. In smaller communes where an assembly was easier to call, direct election of delegates may have been the rule. The surviving evidence is simply too sparse to establish any clear pattern beyond the fact that chief magistrates were the favored candidate, whatever the form of selection.

---

[89] Meyer-Marthaler, *Studien*, 118, for before 1524. Färber, *Herrenstand*, 28.
[90] The surviving text of the *Landbuch* is from the 1650s, but the article in question states that these rights of the *Landamman* to act as delegate are "alle[s] wie vor altem." WS II: 174.
[91] STAG AB IV 1/2, p. 1.
[92] STAG B 1538/6, pp. 58–59.

Because no well-accepted rules determined membership at *Beitage*, they tended to become the preserve of a small, self-perpetuating group of oligarchs. Especially from the 1590s to early in the seventeenth century, a few names appear over and over again in the *Beitag* protocols: Johann Bavier, repeatedly mayor of Chur; Johann Guler, *Landamman* of Davos from 1592–1603; Johann Baptista Tscharner, the standard-bearer of Chur; Johann Baptista von Salis, from one of the two most powerful Rhaetian clans; former *Landrichter* Gallus Demont from the Gray League, and several others. These dozen or so men, all either current or former occupants of important communal and league offices, consulted together, appointed one another to arbitrational panels and embassies, and seem generally to have controlled the daily political process of the Freestate.[93] They took part in deliberations primarily because of their power and influence, and were able to manage the Freestate's business without being elected by the communes.

Such practices caused considerable resentment: it was one thing for communes to elect their leading men to represent them, quite a different thing for a few leaders to coopt one another into *Beitag* after *Beitag*. The *Bundestag* and some communes demanded repeatedly that the excessive number of *Beitage* be curbed, and that a larger number of *Bundestage* – where every commune was entitled to participate equally – should be held.[94] The *Beitag* was too useful to disappear, however: it could be called quickly and could add members as needed in response to rapid changes. Such an organ functioned better, moreover, when its members were men of significant personal influence. Indeed, influential leaders tended to dominate all assemblies, as can be seen in the surviving protocols and recesses. Attendance at central assemblies thus displayed a pattern typical for the Freestate's entire political life: a limited circle of leaders dominated affairs in most cases, yet the persistent principle that the communes ought to appoint and control all of the delegates acted to constrain the elite, either by restricting their legal authority, or if that failed, by open resistance.

The assemblies' business

How did these assemblies proceed, and what functions did they carry out? Unlike other federal assemblies in sixteenth-century Europe, such as the Swiss *Tagsatzung* and the Dutch Estates-General, the *Bündner* assembly reached its decisions by simple majority vote. The *Bundestag* also adopted a distinctive procedure, known as the *Bündner Referendum*, which referred the most important issues to the communes for final ratification. The second question, the actual business of

---

[93] A typical list appears in STAG AB IV 1/8, p. 37. For exhaustive biographical information and the partisan attachments of these and other leading men, see Färber, *Herrenstand*, 204–325.
[94] The Gray League requested that the *Beitag* be limited as early as 1550. STAG A II Landesakten 1/637. Later examples: STAG AB IV 1/1, p. 74; AB IV 1/3, p. 62; AB IV 1/4, p. 21, AB IV 1/6, p. 41; AB IV 1/7, p. 71.

Rhaetian assemblies, has never before been analyzed systematically. From the Freestate's beginnings, certain functions, such as foreign policy, were reserved for central assemblies. Over the course of the sixteenth century, however, both the *Bundestag* and *Beitag* began making decisions covering a much broader range of topics, reflecting the Freestate's growing political integration. Older historiography, concentrating on the importance of the referendum system for reaching the most important decisions, tended to neglect the wide variety of routine matters which Rhaetian assemblies handled by the late sixteenth century.

In principle, neither the *Bundestag* nor the *Beitag* had the power to reach binding decisions without consulting the communes. The common interpretation claims that since the Freestate was constituted by the communes, only the communes could commit themselves to any course of action.[95] The only independent authority held by the *Bundestag*, according to this view, was to gather the opinions of the communes, and to announce the final result. This interpretation also implies that the communes reached their own decisions on matters referred to them by means of a local assembly, or at least that they ought to have done so. The whole system has come to be known by the name *Bündner Referendum*, and has been hailed as an important contribution to democratic practice and theory.[96] A close analysis, however, suggests that the actual procedure was more complex.

The official procedure at Rhaetian assemblies was sketched with exemplary clarity by a Spanish ambassador who negotiated with the Freestate in 1565:

> When any ambassador from a prince or republic comes to negotiate with the Rhaetians, he calls the three Presidents [*Cabeças*] together . . . before whom he proposes his request. The three convoke a Beitag, which is an assembly of some officials from nearby valleys and communes, and if the matter is very important, they appoint a place and a day where all the valleys and communes of the three Leagues can send their delegates . . . When the delegates are assembled, the Mayor [of Chur] asks what instructions they carry from their communes. They answer in order, and if the majority (which they call the "more") is of one mind, the minority concedes without any dispute.[97]

When some business became pressing, the three presidents assembled in a *Beitag* and wrote to all the communes, setting a date for a *Bundestag* and describing the issues to be resolved. The process of informing the communes was called *Ausschreiben*, "writing out." On the appointed date, the delegates arrived at the *Bundestag*, deliberated, and reached a conclusion, which was recorded as an *Abschied*, a recess. The recess would be copied by the delegates and taken home to their communes. If the matter was important – a treaty with a foreign power, an

---

[95] Liver, "Die staatliche Entwicklung," 208, neglecting the strong language in article 18 of the *Bundesbrief*. The seminal description of the *Bündner Referendum* is in Ganzoni, *Beiträge*; a summary is in Pieth, "Das altbündnerische Referendum."
[96] E.g. Barber, *The Death of Communal Liberty*, 180–94.
[97] Cited in Haas, "Sancho de Londoño," 261.

important constitutional change, a major policy decision about the subject territories – the *Bundestag* would request written answers reflecting each commune's
opinion, and set a date for collecting these opinions and announcing the result. The
presidents would meet as arranged, collate the answers (which did not have to be
simply acceptance or rejection of the *Abschied*, but could also contain suggestions,
modifications, or reservations), and issue a sealed document containing the
majority's decision. If no majority was found, the whole process could be repeated,
or the issue could be dropped.

Interpreting *Bündner* politics through the referendum model is attractive, but
this model is flawed by its juristic outlook and excessive idealization. In some
respects, those who adopt it project a system developed in the late seventeenth and
eighteenth centuries onto the much less clear-cut circumstances of the sixteenth
century.[98] The emergence of the referendum around 1570 was important, because
it demonstrated the continuing legitimacy of communal authority, and it is true that
foreign alliances and major constitutional changes usually took place according to
the method described above. But it was scarcely the case that *everything* in the
Freestate had to be decided by referendum. Before 1600, only very few decisions
went through the entire referendum process. A systematic analysis of the
deliberations of *Bundestag* and *Beitag* from 1570 to 1580 reveals only seventy-seven
cases of referring an issue back to the communes through *Ausschreiben* (out of over
1500 entries in the protocols), and only forty examples of collecting a formal
majority in the form of a referendum.[99]

Instead, an extended struggle took place throughout the late sixteenth century
about how decisions should be made. No one disputed the final authority of the
communes, at least in theory, but in fact, the *Bundestag* and *Beitag* often acted
without – or even against – the communes' instructions. Instituting the formal
referendum represented an effort to curb this practice, at least for important
decisions; similarly, reformers throughout the period insisted that delegates carry
written instructions from the communes, and return with written recesses so that
the communal councils could be sure that their delegates had not exceeded their
authority. For matters of great importance, referring an issue to the communes for
a final vote helped build consensus and increased the legitimacy of the final
outcome. But over the course of the sixteenth century, Rhaetian assemblies began
deciding far more issues than the referendum system could possibly accommodate.
A wide variety of business shows up in the surviving protocols of the *Bundestag* and
Beitag, as Table 2 indicates.

The *Bundestag* and *Beitag* heard many appeals of judicial decisions in civil affairs,

---

[98] Barber, *The Death of Communal Liberty*, 182–203. The earliest evidence for the referendum system
appeared during the 1560s, as the *Bundestag* began to specify which issues should be brought before
the communes for approval: cf. JM II, nos. 280 and 281 (1557), 358 (1565), 394 (*ca.* 1568), 410 (1572),
411, 412.
[99] Based on STAG AB IV/1, vols. 3, 4, and 5, to the end of 1580.

Local practice and federal government

Table 2. *Issues decided by the Freestate's assemblies, 1570–1580*

Issue	Bundestag	Beitag	Other	Percentage of total
Diplomatic affairs	32	106	6	9
Public affairs appeal	67	225	7	19
Private appeal	103	372	5	31
Constitutional affairs	19	64	4	6
Administration	86	206	13	20
Social affairs	11	30	0	3
Religious affairs	27	43	2	5
Military affairs	5	23	0	2
Internal affairs of assembly	2	23	0	2
Other/uncertain	6	44	2	3
Total	358 (23.4%)	1136 (74.1%)	39 (2.5%)	100

Counted in the table are all protocol entries for the Three Leagues found in STAG AB IV 1/3, 1/4, and 1/5 between 1570 and 1580 inclusive. Entries pertaining only to the Chadè are not included. The categories reflect the kinds of material recorded in the (mostly very short) protocol entries.

both from the subject territories and from the communes. Appeals of judgments in cases involving private parties made up over 30 percent of all transactions before the Three Leagues recorded in the protocols, while appeals involving public issues, or in which some public entity was a party, constituted another 19 percent. About half of the judicial appeals that appeared in the protocols of the Three Leagues originated in the Italian subject territories, where the Freestate as a whole was the lord and could therefore hear appeals from its subjects. The remainder came from within the Freestate, mostly from the Chadè, despite the communes' tenacious resistance to the *Bundestag*'s arrogation of authority to hear appeals. In the Gray League, the existence of an established civil appeals court in Trun hindered many appeals in that League from reaching the Freestate's institutions, while in the Ten Jurisdictions, the nominal judicial sovereignty of the Austrian bailiff also blocked some. The communes' resistance to appeals of criminal cases was more successful, and the *Bundestag* heard hardly any criminal appeals.

The *Bundestag* not only made policy and heard appeals, it also oversaw administration of the Freestate's collective resources. Most important were the subject territories in the Valtellina and Maienfeld. One of the original and most important of the *Bundestag*'s functions was to appoint the officers, sent for two-year terms, who administered the subjects. In the early sixteenth century, the *Bundestag* apparently chose candidates freely, but the authority to designate candidates soon devolved upon the Leagues, and then upon the individual communes. By the early seventeenth century, a complex system for dividing the various offices among the communes was in operation.[100] However, even after implementing the principle that the communes should choose the officers, the actual appointments took place at the *Bundestag*, where appointees took their oath of service to the entire Freestate. Since such positions were extremely profitable to their holders, intense competition and considerable corruption developed around the selection procedure. Jan Aliesch's verse chronicles his dismay at a 1579 *Bundestag* in Chur:

> In Chur all three leagues elected
> Officials for the Valtellina, (which complains to God),
> Since so many [corrupt] practices were carried on there,
> That every good man ought to have been ashamed.[101]

Evidently the *Bundestag* retained enough control over the selection process for bribery to be worthwhile.

Besides choosing administrative and judicial personnel, the *Bundestag* legislated for the subjects of the Three Leagues, and taxed them in the event of unusual expenses.[102] The *Bundestag* also regulated religious life in the Valtellina, often protecting the local Protestant minority, and maintained military forces there. Few of these activities were subject to the referendum process or to close communal scrutiny, the only exception being religious policy. There, the central authorities usually used the *Bundestag*'s procedures to ensure communal support for difficult policy choices. The Protestants in the Freestate were thus able to use their greater numbers to legitimate the *Bundestag*'s decisions about religion, which were unpopular among the Catholic subject population of the Valtellina.

The *Bundestag* and *Beitag* made decisions about a wide range of public affairs in the Freestate. The vague language in article 18 of the *Bundesbrief* established the assemblies' authority over matters of "common concern" without setting specific limits on the Bundestag. As in many federal systems, therefore, the real problem lay in deciding which matters were in fact "common." A spectrum of possibilities existed. Everyone agreed that matters such as foreign alliances could only be decided by all the communes collectively, whereas others such as criminal jurisdiction should be the business of individual communes. But most affairs fell between these clear poles: both the communes and the central assemblies dealt with them at times, each claiming that tradition and custom were on their side. The surviving documents show the *Bundestag* and *Beitag* making hundreds of decisions that technically required communal approval. The practical authority of the central assemblies thus went far beyond the limited consultative role envisioned by the

---

[100] The system is laid out in a chart, STAG B1538/7, pp. 239–40 (eighteenth-century copy of an undated document, probably 1603.) Early evidence for rotation in office in JM II: 208, (1542) and STAG A II 1/1509 (1566).

[101] RC V: 299–30, lines 131–34. Repeated complaints about corruption, e.g. JM II: 318 (1561); STAG AB IV 1/2, p. 2 (1570); or JM II: 504 (1581).

[102] E.g. JM I: 240–41 (nos. 1041–43).

model of "referendum democracy." While far more decentralized than other early modern European polities, the Freestate still exercised many of the functions of an emerging state.

The assemblies in action: procedures, information flow, and enforcement

Evidence about the procedures at Rhaetian assemblies is even scarcer than information about the delegates. One kind of evidence comes from foreign delegations reporting back to their homelands. Unfortunately, the most detailed of these were written in disturbed times, so that they represent an unreliable indicator of everyday procedure.[103] The records in the assemblies' protocols also give a few hints. Proceedings were probably not open to the public, since non-members usually had a specific invitation to attend and speak. Most of the business was brought by petitioners of one kind or another, but the *Bundestag* rarely reached a decision without attempting to hear the other side of the story. Matters were often postponed for this purpose, or to solicit communal opinions before reaching an important decision. The only certain thing is that formal meetings of the *Bundestag* and *Beitag* always went together with energetic politicking among the assembled leaders, and sometimes among the common citizens as well.

According to the *Bundesbrief*, decisions reached by two Leagues at a *Bundestag* also bound the third League, and this seems to have been the general practice at least until the 1550s. The first record of voting by communes rather than by Leagues comes from 1565, during the renewal of the French alliance that year. Although a majority of the communes supported renewal, most of the Gray League was opposed. The French ambassador rightly feared that forcing the Gray League to accede to the majority of the other two Leagues would cause resentment, and suggested a vote by communes to prevent such an embarrassment. In the end, a majority of communal votes (forty-six out of sixty-six) was recorded for the alliance.[104] Despite such an inauspicious beginning, the practice of voting by communes rather than by Leagues soon took over. By the 1570s, a typical protocol entry for an important decision ran: "We then gathered the decisions [*Mehren*] of the communes, and it was decided with far more than a majority, with forty-five votes . . . "[105]

A system in which authority was so broadly distributed among the scattered communes required a considerable flow of information back and forth between the center and the periphery. The most important official forms of communications

103 Reports from 1607 are found in Innsbruck (LAI Hofregistratur, Akten, Reihe C, Fasz. 168, "Prothocoll vom 14. Mai Anno 1607 . . . ") and in Switzerland (EA v.1.1: 820–23.)
104 The result triggered widespread unrest despite the French ambassador's precautions. Schiess, "Einleitung" to BK II: lv; and F. Jecklin, "Engadiner Aufruhr," 19.
105 STAG AB IV 1/3, p. 130. The introduction of the practice of voting by communes can be traced through the protocols, although no formal discussion of the change seems to have ever taken place.

from the Rhaetian assemblies to the communes were the invitations and recesses (*Ausschreiben* and *Abschiede*). These specified the issues which needed to be decided, and laid out the solutions that the assembled delegates found best. Preparing these documents was inconvenient, however, since the Freestate lacked a standing chancery of its own. Instead, most documents were drafted in the episcopal and city chanceries of Chur, where the assemblies usually took place. The work required was considerable: a list prepared by the episcopal chancery in 1635 called for forty-nine copies to be prepared "when something is sent to the honorable communes."[106] The relative scarcity of these documents in communal archives suggests that, at least in the sixteenth century, such matters were more often handled verbally.[107]

The decentralized structure of decision-making in the Freestate made control over the flow of information an important political resource. Official correspondence such as that described above was important, but many other parties wrote to the communes as well. Private individuals, the subject communities in the Valtellina, and foreign representatives all tried to promote their interests by informing or lobbying the communes. Such lobbying rarely ceased after the *Bundestag* had come to a final majority decision, moreover, but rather increased when a result unfavorable for one party occurred. The *Bundestag* therefore viewed the uncontrolled flow of information to the communes as dangerous – both to the orderly process of reaching decisions, and to the power of a few magnates to influence the outcome – and tried to monopolize the right to communicate with the communes. The resulting tension between a central monopoly on strategic information and the periphery's desire to know made room for propaganda about the politicians in Chur who were "selling out the Fatherland." A particularly egregious example occurred in 1564, after the *Bundestag* had rejected Spanish–Milanese overtures for a military alliance in favor of a French connection. The Spanish ambassador took his case to the communes in the following words:

It did not seem equitable to me that all should suffer because of those who put their own benefit before the honor, benefit and freedom of all of you and of your fatherland . . . Moreover I will not be satisfied with an answer from those who denied me a Beitag or the right to appeal to you, and who wanted to ally you with another power without your knowledge, but I rather [want an answer] from you, all the communes, not from private persons. For I consider you – and not them – the lords here.[108]

The inflammatory content of this letter contributed significantly to popular unrest during the winter of 1564–65.[109]

The authorities in the Freestate responded to efforts to bypass their decisions by

---

[106] JVF, 137–38.
[107] This supposition is also supported by the recurring demands from the communes that written instructions and *Abschiede* be used. See below for a more detailed discussion.
[108] JM II: 349–50.
[109] Jecklin, *Engadiner Aufruhr*, 35.

prohibiting most direct appeals to the communes. A 1551 statute entitled "Prohibition, that no one should go before the communes" claimed that it was intended to prevent "separation, bribery, rebellion or unrest."[110] In 1574, after several years of tumultuous disorder, the Three Leagues passed a new constitutional document, the *Drei-Sigler-Brief* (the Three-Seal Letter), that again attempted to limit access to the communes. Nevertheless, various parties continued to appeal directly to the communes, and the communes continued to hear them. In the end, a mass assembly not only revoked the *Drei-Sigler-Brief* in 1607, but "cut it into pieces and trampled it with their feet."[111] In the rigorously federal atmosphere of the Freestate, attempts to monopolize power by controlling the flow of information to the communes soon generated powerful opposition.

The communes also tried to control the flow of information, though with a somewhat different emphasis. For them, the crucial problem was ensuring that delegates actually carried out instructions, rather than acting on their own. The *Bundestag* was often considered a nest of corruption, bribery, and political pressure. The leading men who usually acted as delegates were often related to one another and from the same stratum of society, and it was feared that they might represent the interests of their class rather than of their communes.[112] Reformers and populists were convinced that delegates who ignored the will of their communes were a profound source of corruption weakening the Freestate. Larger popular assemblies, in which non-elite voices played a greater role, usually demanded that delegates follow written instructions bearing a seal from their communes. In 1564, some rebellious communes in the Engadine went even further:

> It was also established that every village or commune should send a man to the upcoming Bundestag, who should oversee . . . what matters are handled and how. And they should reveal it if there were a delegate who acted against these articles we have established. And if one of them [the overseers] were found, who did not reveal and accuse, then he should be punished with the same penalties.[113]

So little did the communes trust their delegates that they appointed observers to control their behavior. Restless communes also demanded that the recesses and decisions of the *Bundestag* be written down and sealed, so that the communes would have an accurate report of what had been decided.

Access to political information also suffered from the geographic and linguistic barriers to communication within the Freestate. Outlying communes speaking

---

[110] JVF, 109–12.
[111] Ardüser, *Rätische Kronik*, 226–27.
[112] In the restless year 1565, for example, Johan Corn von Castelmur, a leading figure in Bregaglia, revealed such a tension in a letter to Chur: "die furnimst opporta [the upper part of the Bregaglia] sind merer theil mit uns, als die Eid und Treuw trachtig sind. Aber der gemein Pöfel vermeint es sey alles mit gelt verrathen und verkhoufft, und man mueß ietz ir furnemmen folenden lassen . . . " STAC Ratsakten, 1566/1, February 11, 1565.
[113] JM II: 344.

Romantsch or Italian felt very far indeed from the center of decision-making. An unusual letter in the city archive of Chur illustrates this point. The head of one of the fractions of the Val Müstair, the most isolated commune in the Freestate, wrote desperately to the city in 1561. A letter had arrived in the commune, he wrote, but the *Amman* and a few associates had seized it, after which no one from the writer's part of the commune had been able to find out what it said. He asked the city to write him "this very hour," and promised "And if you write about the matter to the village heads, it will be heard publicly before the common man, and you may be confident that we will be good members of the Chadè until the day we die."[114] Far from Chur, separated by two high passes and by the local language, information about the proceedings in the political center could become a precious commodity.

The dissemination and enforcement of decisions made by the Freestate presented another set of thorny questions. This problem was by no means unique to federations, since all sorts of European states grappled with the problem of enforcing uniform laws during the sixteenth century, but federations found it particularly difficult. Many of the leagues erected during the late Middle Ages in southern Germany and Italy were merely defensive alliances that foresaw few binding policies; others, such as the Swiss Confederacy, produced a very limited federal jurisdiction with all enforcement in the hands of the confederated units. The treaties creating the Three Leagues in Rhaetia, especially the *Bundesbrief* of 1524, went further than this: they made majority decisions binding upon all confederates. Moreover, the *Bundesbrief* gave the Three Leagues the power to enforce obedience:

And if anyone among us should not be satisfied with and obedient to such a judgment, then we the aforementioned confederates shall, by our sworn oaths, with our lives and goods, make the disobedient obedient, as soon as we are called upon to do so.[115]

The Freestate had some power over its constituent communes, therefore – power that derived not from any dominion over the communes, but from the oaths that everyone swore to uphold the Bundesbrief.

It would be naive, however, to assume that the *Bundesbrief* by its words established working central control over the scattered communes of Graubünden. Instead, the *Bundesbrief* only created a framework that could organize action and policy that all the parties were willing to accept. The communes zealously protected their autonomy in every possible area of public life, however, and frequently ignored or violated the *Bundestag*'s pronouncements on law, politics, and religion. Since the Freestate lacked its own administrative or military institutions, moreover, only the communes could actually enforce a policy. The typical response to difficult problems therefore consisted of endless negotiations and appeals. Losers appealed against their losses to yet another assembly, while the winners appealed

---

[114] STAC Ratsakten 1561/4, May 21, 1561.   [115] JVF, 86.

for the enforcement of their victories. Various jurisdictions often gave conflicting opinions, so that substantive questions were always tangled in complex jurisdictional debates. Under the circumstances, many disputes proved unresolvable.

Still, the Freestate did on occasion try to enforce its mandates against recalcitrant communes, as provided for in the *Bundesbrief* – or at least it threatened to use its authority. During the troubles of 1564 and 1565, for example, the Bundestag proposed establishing a force consisting of 100 men from each commune to suppress an assembly of malcontents gathered in the Engadine.[116] In 1575 and 1576, events in the Engadine provoked an even stronger reaction from the *Bundestag*. After several judgments by the Three Leagues failed to settle a drawn-out dispute about the partition of the Upper Engadine, the Bundestag in January of 1575 raised the question "of how and whether, with force or in some other way, one ought to make them obedient."[117] In August of 1576, the exasperated *Bundestag* set forth its official decision:

we decided by unanimous consent, to apply all humanly possible ways, means and methods once again to bring the parties to agreement and to avoid the use of weapons. But should our good offices again lead to no results, we have decided according to our majorities that we shall mobilize our banners, arms and weapons to invade those from Ob Fontana Merla, and bring them to obedience by force . . . [118]

In fact, no force was ever sent, so we cannot know how the communes would have responded to such an appeal for troops. Nevertheless, this incident illustrates the Freestate's willingness to employ coercive methods if worse came to worst.

A method more commonly applied to persuade recalcitrant communes was financial pressure. The *Bundestag* distributed the cash pensions paid by foreign powers, especially France, together with the direct and indirect income from the subject territories. In addition, the *Bundestag* also kept control over the lucrative offices in these territories. Refusing a commune its turn in the rotation of offices was an effective way to apply pressure both on leaders and the common people there, since both stood to gain by filling an office. In 1582, for example, the commune of Mesocco was embroiled in a dispute with the Gray League and the Three Leagues about the toleration of Protestants. The Gray League asked the *Bundestag* to exclude the commune "from councils and actions of the common Three Leagues, and also from the benefits of the same"; after hearing the representatives of the commune promise to be obedient, the other two Leagues told the Gray League that "their annual subsidy and pensions, because they are sequestered, one ought to leave sequestered until they have demonstrated their obedience."[119] Here financial pressure seems to have been effective in getting the delegates from Mesocco to comply with the judgments of the Leagues.

---

[116] JM II: 360.   [117] STAG AB IV 1/4, p. 16.
[118] JM II: 464.   [119] STAG AB IV 1/6, p. 69.

The finances of the Three Leagues

Despite occasional uses of financial pressure, however, the Freestate carried out only very limited fiscal functions, and did not even have a central treasury. Its most important fiscal duty involved the simple distribution of income, including the profits from the administration of the Valtellina and Maienfeld, certain tolls, and pensions from foreign powers. Of these, only the foreign pensions produced substantial amounts of cash that the *Bundestag* actually controlled. The income from the Valtellina, in contrast, was spent mostly on salaries and administration in the subject territories, and much of the remainder was collected directly by the officers and their communes.[120] The *Bundestag* also ordered its officers to use other Valtellina income directly to pay specific debts, rather than collecting and disbursing the money centrally.[121] Another important source of cash, the Freestate's share of the toll in Chiavenna, was used mostly to cover running expenses such as military purchases and a pension to the bishop of Chur, so that little profit remained to be distributed.[122]

Despite these fiscal expedients, the wealth of the Valtellina remained crucial to the fiscal health of the Freestate. Substantial amounts of money flowed not through the *Bundestag*, but through the offices there, which were filled by the communes. The communes considered these offices public property, and sold them to candidates who paid the commune for the privilege of filling them. In 1602, Davos carefully listed the offices available to its citizens, and the fees they would owe the commune should they gain a position. A captain paid 500 gulden, the *podestà* of Morbegno 300, the *podestà* in Piuro only fifty gulden.[123] The contemporary author Fortunat von Juvalta bemoaned the corruption that resulted:

not only private individuals haggled over these wares; whole districts negotiated about them, and did not blush to sell the highest offices in a commune, together with the office of delegate to the Bundestag...and the offices in the Valtellina at publicly announced fixed prices for periods of many years. That there might be no doubt, they confirmed these sales with public charters. This was unworthy of their precious freedom, which they profaned and abandoned in this fashion.[124]

---

[120] Surprisingly, the oldest surviving account book from the Valtellina dates only to 1659 (STAG B 781); it suggests an annual income of about 8,000 gulden (p. 7), and a total for two years of 16,848 gulden.

[121] The officers (not including Bormio and Maienfeld) were entitled to salaries totalling 3,900 gulden before 1603, and 9,500 gulden after the Great Reform of that year. The salaries were to be paid half by the subjects directly, and half out of the League's income from dominion over the subjects. JVF, 125–26. In 1583, the Three Leagues ordered that the Leagues' debt to Chur be paid out of the Valtellina income. JM II: 516.

[122] Cf. STAG AB IV 1/6, p. 34f. An agreement between the Three Leagues and the bishop in 1530 had ended the latter's rights over the Valtellina in exchange for a biennial payment of 573 florins from the toll at Chiavenna. The agreement was renewed in 1574. Sprecher, *Geschichte*, I: 28.

[123] GA Davos, B 50, entry for April 25, 1602.

[124] Juvalta, *Denkwürdigkeiten*, 7.

Local practice and federal government

Those who bought offices from their communes naturally expected to make a profit, as did purchasers of offices all over Europe during this period. But whereas venality of office in most states benefited the king or central government, office-holders in Graubünden returned a significant part of their gains to the communes, either through the direct purchase cost, through widely distributed bribes to the voters, or through meals, drinks, and gifts during annual assemblies.[125]

Because the *Bundestag* retained the final right to appoint officers, candidates for office had to distribute money not only in their own commune, but also around the entire Freestate. Several lists of such payments have survived. In 1582, for example, Johann von Salis-Samedan paid out some 500 gulden for the office of *vicari* in the Valtellina. Three hundred and ten were paid to a single member of the Planta family in the Chadè, but the rest was handed out in amounts of less than twelve gulden. One of his largest payments was to Johann Guler in the Ten Jurisdictions, "to spread around."[126] Equally interesting is the list of payments made by Guler to parties in the Gray League when he sought the *vicari*'s office himself: aside from a payment of eighty gulden to the *Amman* of the Val Lumnezia, small payments of five to twenty gulden were distributed to the *Amman* of each commune, presumably as gratuities for their votes.[127] By spreading small amounts among many recipients, such bribes for office effectively distributed the income from the Valtellina around the Freestate. Of course, the recipients did not always pass the bribes on to their communes; but if they themselves had bribed or entertained poorer citizens in order to be elected *Amman* or delegate to the *Bundestag*, the money might trickle down quite widely. In this indirect fashion, then, the income from the Valtellina could benefit the communes, even though much of it followed the lines of political patronage rather than any bureaucratic procedure.

In the Valtellina, where an office-holder had only a single two-year term to recover his investment, this system had pernicious effects, since it encouraged unfettered exploitation of the subjects. To limit the corruption of justice and administration, therefore, the *Bundestag* began appointing two commissioners (*commissari*), who audited the accounts of all the important offices in the Valtellina at the end of each incumbent's tenure. But the office of commissioner soon rotated as did other offices, and so became part of the same system of exploiting the subject population. The powerful families in the Freestate drew a lion's share of the benefits, especially after 1639, yet the common perception of these offices as communal property limited the scope of reform efforts. The communes wanted to

---

125 Mathieu and Stauffacher, "Alpine Gemeindedemokratie," 320–60; and Heidi Lüdi, "Praktizieren und Trölen: Wahlkorruption und Ämterkauf in den Landsgemeinde-Orten der alten Schweiz" (unpublished ms., University of Bern, 1990).
126 STAG A II 1/2221 (1582); VAD 219, loose leaf.
127 VAD 219, loose leaf.

115

shift the flow of benefits from a few families to the communes as a whole, but had little interest in allowing the *Bundestag* (seen as a nest of elite corruption) to take control of the entire system.[128]

Foreign pensions directly to the Freestate were the most important form of financial transaction that remained entirely in the hands of the central institutions. Both France and Austria had treaties with the Freestate that included substantial annual payments in return for access to Graubünden's passes and military manpower. The *Bundestag*'s role consisted simply in distributing the sums received to the communes. The Austrian alliance of 1518 provided that each League would receive 200 Rhenish gulden a year. The French outbid this contribution in the treaties of 1521 and 1523, agreeing to pay the three Leagues an annual pension of 3000 French *livres*. When Venice established an alliance in 1603, it agreed to pay 3600 *ducati* a year.[129] Of the surrounding powers, only Spanish Milan never paid a public pension to the Freestate, although delegations to Milan often received private gifts and bribes.[130] Because the sums involved were widely known, the *Bundestag* had little choice but to divide such income among the communes immediately upon receipt.

The Freestate had few other financial functions. Delegates to the Freestate's assemblies collected a salary, which evidently took up most of the income from the Valtellina that actually reached the *Bundestag*.[131] Other costs were managed by the city treasurer in Chur, including gifts and entertainment for foreign dignitaries, sending messengers within the Freestate and abroad, and paying for an executioner who lived in Chur. In a sample of the accounts from the second half of the sixteenth century, the city never spent more than £200 annually on behalf of the Three Leagues.[132] In addition, the three presidents had considerable out-of-pocket expenses for correspondence and travel. Given the strong pressure to distribute income to the communes as soon as it was collected, both the city and individuals who spent money on behalf of the Freestate had great difficulty in recovering their expenses. The protocols record several cases of former officers

---

[128] The popular view that the elite tended to monopolize the benefits of ruling the Valtellina is described in a letter from Johannes Fabricius to Bullinger in 1561: "So man es unter den gemeinen mann last kommen, das Phillipus [II of Spain] ein groß, unsäglich gelt uffs Veltlyn byete mit erbietung nachpurlich fruntlich ze halten, so wirt mengglich sprächen: by dem Veltlyn habe man gelernet die empter verkouffen; nütze die land nit um ein haller es genüssind sy allein die großen hansen etc." BK II: 338 (no. 384).

[129] Sums from Moor, *Geschichte von Currätien*, II: 154–55, 272, and Sprecher, *Geschichte*, I: 34.

[130] Rudolf Bolzern's meticulous analysis of the career of the Milanese delegate in Switzerland, Alfonso Casati, does not find any outright payments to the Three Leagues. Bolzern, *Spanien*.

[131] See Färber, *Herrenstand*, 35–36. Meyer-Marthaler asserts that delegates were paid by their own communes. While this may be technically correct, in that the cost of delegates was deducted from the sums otherwise distributed to the communes, the income used was that of the Three Leagues, rather than coming from local sources. Meyer-Marthaler, *Studien*, 121.

[132] STAG A II 4, A II 1/1765, and A II 1/1827.

or their heirs tenaciously trying to regain their money, though without much success.[133]

Other kinds of expenses characteristic of the early modern state, such as domestic administration and military preparation, fell directly to the communes. The *Bundestag* repeatedly ordered the communes to ensure that everyone was provided with weapons and armor, without ever proposing to pay for these items. The central government occasionally purchased powder and shot to stock the arsenal at Chur, and arranged for the maintenance of the artillery it had obtained from the counts of Mesocco early in the sixteenth century. Such efforts were sporadic, however, and the Freestate never established any permanent military organization.[134] When large numbers of troops were sent to defend the Valtellina, the costs were borne either by the communes, or by the subjects themselves.[135]

Close examination of the Freestate's administrative functions thus reveals a mixed picture. On the one hand, the *Bundestag* and *Beitag* tried to control many different matters, often without consulting the communes explicitly. Moreover, the idea that the Freestate as a whole could impose its decisions on recalcitrant communes was accepted in theory, even if it was rarely put into effect. On the other hand, the Freestate lacked the strong centralizing tendencies found in many contemporary principalities. Neither military organization nor public administration of unified law – typical means in contemporary European states – provided the Freestate the opportunity to erect a strong central government. Fiscal centralization, the third pillar of the typical early modern state, was completely absent. Communal autonomy and the perception of the Freestate as a free alliance among equals conserved the federalism that had characterized the Freestate's institutions since their earliest beginnings.

---

[133] E.g. the debt the Leagues owed Mayor Ambrosi of Chur and his heirs in the 1570s. STAG AB IV 1/4, pp. 167, 193.
[134] Padrutt, *Staat und Krieg*, 47–61.
[135] After the Chiavenna campaign of 1585, the Three Leagues taxed the subjects to pay for it. JM I: 240–41 (nos. 1041–43)

4

From consolidation to communal politics: the Freestate. *ca.* 1530–1580

No republic under heaven today has such a form as among us in Rhaetia.

Johannes Fabricius, 1560[1]

Throughout the mid-sixteenth century, the Rhaetian Freestate enjoyed effective autonomy and constitutional stability. During this period, moreover, the exercise of power changed steadily to accommodate both institutional maturation and slower developments in popular concepts of authority and legitimacy. The changes of 1524 to 1526 had brought about new preconditions for political life, but practice took some time to catch up. Despite the incomplete triumph of communal politics, however, Rhaetia was unique in that communal principles continued to evolve there in the context of a functioning state. Although political and ideological change in the Freestate continued to reflect multiple, sometimes conflicting tendencies, we can for the sake of clarity identify three phases of development after the 1520s, each characterized by its own dominant trends. First came a period of political consolidation from the mid-1520s to the mid-1540s; second was a period of conflict among elite factions from the 1540s on; the third phase, from the 1560s to the end of the century, saw increasing political activity by the communes in opposition to the new elite.

During the first phase, retrenchment after the internal and external storms of the 1520s dominated the course of politics. Domestically, the Ilanz Articles and the *Bundesbrief* required adjustments from the episcopal castle to the humblest hamlet. The bishop's position in the Freestate was not clarified until 1541, when the death of the exiled Paul Ziegler and the election of a local candidate to the see allowed a reconciliation between the bishop and the Chadè. Ziegler had remained in exile in the Austrian section of the see until his death. When he died, the cathedral chapter in Chur elected a *Bündner* candidate, Lucius Iter, on the condition that he subscribe to a set of articles regulating his authority over the Chadè. The final document, the Six Articles of 1541, reflected the Chadè's *de facto* control over the see throughout:

---

[1] BK II: 223 (no. 281): "Reipublicae forma non est sub coelo hodie talis, qualis apud nos in Rhetia."

after the death of the late honorable prince and lord, lord Paul, former bishop of Chur, the honorable cathedral chapter at Chur assembled and deliberated according to the ancient and praiseworthy custom of the chapter to elect another Bishop and ruling lord, but did not wish to undertake this without the particular favor, knowledge, and permission of the pious, noble, upright, distinguished, honorable and wise, our dear and faithful communes of the entire Chadè.[2]

After this introduction, the Six Articles established the conditions under which the new bishop might assume his seat. In effect, he accepted oversight from both chapter and Chadè.[3]

During the 1530s, meanwhile, the Reformation spread to more and more communes, eventually leading to a Protestant majority at the *Bundestag*. A Reformed synod for all of the Freestate began meeting in 1537, headed by the two ministers in Chur. Despite support from Zurich, however, the Synod never established disciplinary authority over the communes. It had the power only to dismiss ministers for heresy, and communes often ignored its judgments.[4] Tension between Catholics and Protestants grew steadily, but the local character of Rhaetian Protestantism dampened the potential for broad conflict. Protestant leaders were absorbed with organizing their own church and combating doctrinal threats from Anabaptist and Italian religious radicals, while the communes seemed more interested in economizing on pastors' salaries than they were in proselytizing their neighbors. When the Synod urged that the Catholic see be abolished in the 1550s, leading Protestants blocked the plan.[5]

Despite the See's weak position in 1541, the bishops managed to recover some lost ground during the following years. In 1544, Bishop Iter participated in reswearing the *Bundesbrief*, thus affirming his better relations with the Three Leagues. Later, the See regained the privilege of sending episcopal officers to attend the *Bundestag*, despite the prohibitions contained in the Second Ilanz Articles. Eventually, the episcopal chancery even reasserted its right to send the agenda of the Chadè's assemblies to the communes.[6] Nevertheless, the See remained politically weak. When Bishop Iter was called to the Council of Trent in 1545, for example, the Chadè denied him permission to go. Iter's successor, Thomas Planta, was also called to Trent, and stopped there on his way home from Rome. The Chadè immediately sent a messenger to warn him against any concessions: "The Bishop was warned that he should not make any promises, but should remember that he had no power at all, for he would bring great trouble on himself if he did any such thing."[7] The long and the short of it, according to

---

[2] JVF, 99–100.
[3] In 1549, the Chadè even formally ratified the election of the next bishop, Thomas Planta. JVF, 102.
[4] The synod's struggles to discipline its members are best documented in BK, esp. vols. II and III.
[5] On the history of the Synod, see Truog, *Aus der Geschichte*.
[6] Liver, "Die Stellung des Gotteshausbundes," esp. 170–73.
[7] BK I: 229 (no. 170).

Chur's Protestant minister, was that "The bishop is the lord, but the peasants are master."[8]

Meanwhile, social conflict between peasants and landlords reached an equilibrium in the early 1540s. In many cases, peasants or communes purchased their masters' economic and political privileges; elsewhere, political authority was more clearly separated from the property rights of noble and non-noble landowners. The legal enshrinement of free tenures (*Freie Erbleihe*) gave peasants more effective control over the land they worked, and the abolition of serfs' dues and labor services guaranteed their control over their own labor as well. Nevertheless, the more radical parts of the Second Ilanz Articles, such as releasing religious endowments to the communes, were not implemented. Powerful local families had a vested interest in tithes and church funds, and used their control of communal courts to slow peasant emancipation from such burdens. The new situation gave the small peasant more leverage than before, though. The annual communal elections put some limits on abuses by the powerful, since they could not afford to make too many enemies; at the same time, peasants saw communal action, rather than rebellion or flight as the most promising avenue to improve their situation. Agrarian conflict did not vanish from the Freestate in 1526, but it took second place to political issues during the next half-century.[9]

Foreign affairs during the 1530s and 1540s were tumultuous, since the Italian wars and conflict in the Holy Roman Empire drew the Freestate into the affairs of greater powers. The failure to defeat Gian Giacomo de Medici without Swiss assistance in 1525 clearly illustrated the limits on its autonomy in international affairs. Consequently, the Freestate strengthened its ties to the Swiss Confederacy during the following years.[10] The apparent equilibrium reached in 1532 was short lived, moreover. The death of the last Sforza in Milan brought about a fundamental shift in the Freestate's diplomatic environment. Milan moved from French protection to Habsburg control, with the result that the Freestate's passes became a key communications route among the Habsburg domains. After 1535, the Habsburg governors of Milan pursued two goals with regard to Rhaetia: first, to build up a faction of their own among the Rhaetian magnates, who might end the Freestate's French tilt and thus ease access to the crucial mountain passes and to mercenary troops; and second, if the first goal failed, to destabilize the Freestate so that economic and military pressure from Milan could more effectively hinder French policies.[11]

Only direct support from the Swiss allowed the Freestate to maintain control

---

[8] *Ibid.* Plànta stayed in Trent only briefly. Moor, *Geschichte von Currätien*, II: 167–70.

[9] Vasella, "Bäuerliche Wirtschaftskampf," 42, notes that local courts unanimously upheld tithes and dues. The rest of the article discusses the economic dimension of the Ilanz Articles.

[10] E.g. EA IV.1.d: 377, cited in Blumenthal, *Die Drei Bünde*, 137, footnote 1.

[11] On Habsburg strategies, Bolzern, *Spanien*, provides the most detailed analysis. For Rhaetia, see Blumenthal, *Die Drei Bünde*, 171–76.

From consolidation to communal politics

over the Valtellina in 1532, and close cooperation with Switzerland characterized Rhaetian foreign policy for the rest of the century. Alliance with the Swiss also drew the Freestate into the French diplomatic network: after regularizing relations with Austria with the *Erbeinung* treaty of 1518, the Freestate allied with France in 1521 and 1523 and remained a French client throughout the sixteenth century. At the same time, the *Bündner* attempted to preserve friendly relations with Austria. In the long run this was an unstable policy, since Austrian lordship in parts of the Freestate, along with Habsburg control of the markets in Milan and Constance, gave the Austrian government too many ways to apply pressure on the Freestate. But during the mid-sixteenth century, the Habsburgs preferred negotiation and compromise over direct intervention. Meanwhile, both Habsburgs and the French sought to promote local leaders in Graubünden sympathetic to their cause. Milanese diplomats used the same tactics as French agents, distributing bribes and pensions to leading men in the Freestate. There is little evidence that foreign agents made efforts in these years to influence the communes directly.[12] It was primarily the Rhaetian elite who eagerly sought connections with the great powers, which brought both income and prestige. Factions among the leading families soon aligned into French and Spanish (i.e. Habsburg) parties, and eventually a Venetian party emerged as well. Many Rhaetians recognized the corrupting effect such attachments could have on the Freestate, but little could be done to prevent them.

The second phase in sixteenth-century Rhaetian politics extended roughly from 1545 to 1585. During these years, families that had risen to prominence early in the century struggled to gain control over the Freestate's resources and policy. The resulting conflicts were quite different from the feuding that had divided the petty nobility during the fifteenth century, because, rather than seeing themselves as above communal politics, the new magnates fought for local control by means of patronage networks and clientage among the peasantry.[13] Nor were the new magnates a well-defined legal or social class: old ministerial families and merchants from Chur competed with successful peasant landowners and *coqs du village*.[14] Much of the infighting among the elite involved multiple parties who had divergent motives and goals. By mid-century, however, two families had risen to positions of singular influence: the Planta of the Upper Engadine and the Salis of the Val Bregaglia.

The first open outbreak of conflict among the factions took place in 1542, when repeated Habsburg efforts to disrupt the Freestate's military agreements with France bore their first fruit. Foreign pensions to private individuals were forbidden in a statute dating back to 1500, although the law had never been enforced. In the early 1540s, Bartolome von Stampa, an important Austrian partisan, traveled

---

[12] Blumenthal, *Die Drei Bünde*, 131–38.
[13] A recent overview of clientage in early modern Switzerland: U. Pfister, "Politischer Klientelismus."
[14] Grimm, *Anfänge*, 17–21, 183–87.

around the Freestate, entertaining restless men and encouraging them to take action against those who received French pensions.[15] Popular resentment against the pensioners was already high, reinforced by the Protestant ministers' preaching against foreign military entanglements. When Johannes Comander, the minister in Chur, described the uproar to Heinrich Bullinger in Zurich, he claimed that "the common people have begun to correct the pensioners."[16] Perhaps to forestall a violent outbreak, the *Bundestag* appointed a court in February 1542 to punish anyone who had accepted foreign money. The authorities' fear of greater disorder can be seen in their decree forbidding anyone summoned to the court from appearing with more than five companions.[17] Popular anger against the French pensioners faded quickly, however, when it became obvious that Stampa's accusations resulted largely from his own attachment to Austria. Once it was known that the whole affair was mostly a struggle between French and Habsburg partisans, the court handed out only mild sentences.[18] The French party's control over the Freestate's foreign policy remained unbroken, moreover, as shown by the brusque rejection of Milanese diplomatic approaches in 1543 and 1544.[19]

In 1550, French and Habsburg competition in the Freestate once again broke out into the open. The French capitulation that had been in effect since 1523 was due to expire that year; consequently, each side sought to gain influence over the Freestate by attracting the most influential men to its cause. A Milanese document entitled "How to set up a *Bundestag*" argued that France's success rested exclusively on its influence with the three presidents of the Leagues, "despite the rest of the people, who are Imperial in sentiment . . . "[20] According to the anonymous author, only three key figures needed to be brought around; spending money on people in the communes, in contrast, would be fruitless.[21] Both France and Milan sent special legates to promote their causes, but it was the French who succeeded in 1549 in renewing their alliance at the *Bundestag* and in gaining formal ratification from the communes. The French legate's methods included not only generous bribes and the payment of all expenses at the Bundestag of July 1549, but also an appearance there by nearly 2000 troops from communes that supported the French.[22]

Such blatant tactics aroused widespread discontent.[23] In the Ten Jurisdictions, 300 men from Klosters and Castels assembled and seized the leaders who had

---

[15] JM I: 124 (no. 580). Blumenthal, *Die Drei Bünde*, 139–42.
[16] BK I: 40 (no. 31).
[17] JM I: 124 (no. 581).
[18] JM II: 208 (no. 220).
[19] Blumenthal, *Die Drei Bünde*, 135.
[20] Cited in Blumenthal, *Die Drei Bünde*, 172, footnote 4. Similar advice in LAI, Ferdinandea, Fasz. 206, "Anthony von Salis Bericht."
[21] Cited in Blumenthal, *Die Drei Bünde*, 174, footnote 3.
[22] *Ibid.*, 181.
[23] Blumenthal, *Die Drei Bünde*, 182–87; Valèr, *Bestrafung*, 155–59.

negotiated the French alliance at the *Bundestag*. The president of the Ten Jurisdictions was fined heavily and excluded from public office for seven years, as was a captain suspected of taking French bribes; some sixteen others, mostly the *Ammänner* of communes, received milder sentences. Too little is known of the details of this outbreak to determine whether it was instigated by the pro-Habsburg faction among the magnates, or whether popular discontent was the key element. Most likely, both played a part. Even though this tumult and subsequent penal court were limited to a single League, the events of 1550 were important because they demonstrated the increasing importance of communal opinion. Disputes between factions supported by foreign powers provided the trigger for unrest, but communal action often influenced the subsequent course of events.

One rivalry stood out above all others in the competition among the factions in the Rhaetian Freestate: the Planta clan, whose original base was the Upper Engadine, faced the Salis with foundations in the Val Bregaglia. Both clans had expanded far beyond their home communes by the mid-sixteenth century. The Planta dominated the Lower Engadine, as well, and Johann von Planta became lord of Rhäzüns in 1558 and lord of Hohentrins in 1568.[24] Other branches of the family were settled in Bergün, the Val Müstair, Castels, and Chur. The Salis spread in a similar fashion into the Engadine, Schiers, Stalla, Castels, Malans, and Chur. In addition, the Salis were well established in the Valtellina and Chiavenna, where estates and control over trade provided much of the clan's income.

The most visible clash between the clans was their fight to control the see of Chur. Bartholomäus von Salis, archpriest of Sondrio in the Valtellina, was the Salis candidate for bishop in 1541, but Lucius Iter from Chur was elected. Although some Salis-dominated communes refused to swear the new bishop fealty for several years, Iter made his peace with them and with the Salis when his sister married into the family. Upon Iter's death in 1549, Bartholomäus von Salis proposed himself again, only to be defeated by Thomas Planta.[25] Efforts to block Planta's appointment, including the accusation that Planta leaned toward Protestantism, failed, and Planta held office as Bishop from 1549 until his unexpected death in 1565.[26] During the same years, the Planta network gained increasing political weight in the entire Freestate by shifting to a pro-Habsburg position, and through Johann von Planta's rapidly growing influence in the Gray League.

The aged Bartholomäus von Salis and his cousin Dietegen, Austrian bailiff in the Ten Jurisdictions, saw their opportunity in 1565 and again proposed Bartholomäus for the episcopal seat. Hostility between the Salis and the Planta was already at a peak because the Salis had suffered disproportionately in the tumults earlier that

---

[24] Valèr, *Johann von Planta*, 14–16.
[25] Salis, *Die Familie von Salis*, 66–68.
[26] Planta was briefly imprisoned in Rome, but eventually cleared of accusations against him. Planta, *Chronik der Familie Planta*, 114–17. Salis, *Die Familie von Salis*, 69–80.

year, which the Salis saw as a Planta-instigated plot.[27] When the cathedral chapter unanimously elected Beat à Porta, a Planta client, Dietegen von Salis responded with an armed coup in which the communes of the Chadè forcibly installed Bartholomäus as bishop in Chur. According to Chur's Reformed minister, Dietegen set his hesitant cousin upon the cathedral's altar with the words, "Up with you even in the Devil's name!"[28] Bartholomäus's hopes for papal confirmation of his usurpation were quickly dashed, and the two other Leagues, the Emperor and the Swiss applied every possible pressure on the Chadè to depose him. Not until December 1566 did the Salis faction and the Chadè acknowledge defeat, though, by which time the episcopal castle had burned, the see was deeply in debt, and bitterness between the Salis and Planta had reached new heights.[29] Tension between these two clans thus represented an additional dimension of conflict in the tumults that divided the Freestate in the late sixteenth century. Yet even during this period, the two families did not dominate Rhaetian politics completely. Too many other families, and too many other interests, persisted for the Freestate to fall into two clear camps.[30] Moreover, the rising intensity of elite factional conflict stirred up a new development: the increasing opposition of the communes to the magnates.

Rhaetia's liberation from noble rulership benefited from the internal coherence of the communes as they struggled against their lords. Especially during the late fifteenth century, local leaders were tightly integrated into communal life. They commanded respect through their wealth and family connections, and also by personal leadership in military expeditions and by force of personality at communal assemblies.[31] While exercising such leadership was not necessarily safe or easy, it did ensure the political effectiveness of the communes' campaign to dilute, and eventually eliminate, noble power. When a new cluster of leading families rose to power in the early sixteenth century, however, signs of strain began to appear. Peasant unrest in 1525 and 1526 was directed primarily against feudal and church burdens – especially at the tithe and at dues symbolizing serfdom – yet the collection of such exactions had already fallen into the hands of the new magnates. As a result, hostility that had been anti-feudal could easily become anti-oligarchic. The Second Ilanz Articles, which limited such dues, thus represented a partial magnate capitulation to peasant demands, even though they also reinforced the magnates' position against the bishop and lords.

In the long years of peace after 1532, anti-oligarchic feeling increased. The

---

[27] Salis, *Die Familie von Salis*, 85–87. The events of 1565 are discussed below and in Ch. 5.
[28] BK II: 613 (no. 702).
[29] Salis, *Die Familie von Salis*, 100–12.
[30] Färber refutes the idea that politics in Graubünden was simply polarized along the Salis–Planta division in *Bündnerische Herrenstand*, 168–76.
[31] Padrutt, *Staat und Krieg*, esp. 36–39.

From consolidation to communal politics

Freestate's effective sovereignty created a new political sphere for magnate action, and provided the consolidating elite with new sources of income and authority. Federal offices, particularly over the Valtellina, were lucrative and honorable, and did not depend on direct contact with the common people of the communes. Foreign blandishments, too, became increasingly tempting to the most powerful families: service to a foreign monarch offered chances for advancement and wealth far beyond what the Freestate could bid. As the most powerful families turned their attention to politics above the communal level, however, local resistance to their authority increased. Whereas the communes played a relatively reactive role in the struggles about foreign alliances which took place in 1542 and 1551, by the 1560s the population of the communes became much more active in limiting the magnates' freedom of decision. As the division between elite and commoners grew, the coherence that had characterized the era of communal emancipation soon dissolved.

This is not to say that Rhaetian political leaders lost all control over the communes after 1540: quite the contrary was true. During the course of routine political decision making – following the institutional framework described above – the average peasant in his commune had little influence on federal decisions compared to the wealthy patrician with his connections across the Freestate. But a weak federal structure, along with the divisive presence of competing foreign interests, made it certain that conflicts within the elite regularly spread beyond the framework provided by the Freestate's central institutions. Again and again, one party or another appealed to "the common man" to defeat its opponents, thus drawing the communes into the fight. In 1542 and 1551, the instigators of such outbreaks were able to enlist communal support without losing control over it. During conflicts in 1565 and 1572, in contrast, factional struggles allowed the communes to slip out of the magnates' grasp and to become independent actors – actors, moreover, who were generally hostile to the leading families. The dangers inherent in popular action had been evident to Rhaetian leaders much earlier, but the reality of a communal threat to the elite only materialized later in the century. After 1585, the communes' increased freedom of political action spurred a comprehensive reform movement. The period from 1550 to 1585 or so, however, was characterized by a dualism between intra-elite conflict, on the one hand, and latent hostility between the communes and an elite that was increasingly distanced from them, on the other.

The actual course of events was complex: shifts in the international situation, the fitful expansion of Protestantism among the communes, and the consequences of the economic changes that followed from the Ilanz Articles meant that the domestic situation was in constant flux. The administrative machinery of the Freestate, meanwhile, was still in its infancy, whereas the chanceries of the bishop and other lords were moribund or had been abolished. Documentation from this period is accordingly scarce, making it even harder to follow the labyrinthine twists in factional politics. A few critical moments stand out, however, where the normal

125

course of politics was interrupted by extraordinary events that left a documentary record. For the rest of this chapter, I will focus mostly on the tumults of 1565 and 1572–73, when domestic political struggle in the Freestate displayed its full range of complexity.

The renewal of the Freestate's alliance with France was again the proximate cause of the popular uprising that took place in 1565.[32] People unhappy with the French connection had been at work for some time before the communes in the southern valleys raised a revolt in February, 1565. One of the agents fanning popular discontent was the Spanish ambassador, who passed through on his way back to Milan spreading money and anti-patrician rumors; he also publicized the names of the French pensioners in the Engadine and the Val Bregaglia.[33] During the protracted negotiations over a new alliance in 1564, the southern communes had consistently voted against the French, and non-magnate delegates had gathered in the Engadine at the end of 1564 to block the alliance and to reform the organization of the Chadè. Elite factions were involved as well: the most influential members of the Planta had taken a pro-Austrian line since 1558, whereas the majority of the Salis, led by Friedrich von Salis-Samedan in the Upper Engadine, had actively promoted an alliance with France. Finally, social tension played a role, since the first violence took place when the village of Ramosch burned its castle. Ramosch was the last commune in the Lower Engadine to owe the bishop tithes, and the bishop's steward was roundly hated in the village.[34]

The *Bundestag* ratified a new French alliance early in 1565. Late in the negotiations, the Spanish representatives had tried at least to block the French, seeing that they had no chance of obtaining an alliance between the Freestate and Spain. They wrote the communes to point out that trade with Milan would be embargoed if the French alliance was ratified, and accused a small group of politicians in Chur of selling out the Freestate against the wishes of the communes, "as I consider you [the communes] – not them – the lords."[35] Since the Engadine imported most of its grain from and exported its dairy products to Milan, such a threat was effective in mobilizing popular opinion. The Val Bregaglia and the Upper Engadine sent two messengers from village to village in the Lower Engadine, who carried letters that accused the *Bundestag* of ratifying the treaty only because of massive bribery by the French ambassador:

Because of this, our communes have reached the decision to topple this alliance again, with your help . . . Our intention is to do this in a legal way, if it is possible, otherwise we will use open violence. Everything is prepared for the latter. The troops are raised, and all the things needed for war are ready.[36]

---

[32] F. Jecklin, *Der Engadiner Aufruhr*, 7.
[33] *Ibid.*, 33.   [34] *Ibid.*, 24–27.
[35] JM II: 350.
[36] Based on Ulrich Campell's chronicle, cited in F. Jecklin, *Der Engadiner Aufruhr*, 34–35.

Late in February, the village of Ardez responded by raising the banner of the Lower Engadine (which was kept there) and began marching up the valley to meet the Upper Engadiners. By mid-February, some 2000 armed men had gathered in Zuoz to oppose the French alliance. One of their first acts there was to swear a common oath to their banners. Many other communes also voiced their support, though without sending troops. In the end, though, events in 1565 ended without any general assembly of the communes outside the Engadine.[37]

Foiled in their attempt to spur a broader uprising, the forces gathered in Zuoz instead established a court to try the magnates who had allegedly taken foreign pensions. An armed band seized Rudolf von Salis, while Friedrich and Johannes von Salis had to flee to save their lives. Fifty armed men remained in Zuoz to guard the court and the prisoners awaiting trial. It soon became clear, however, that the court was proceeding only against the French party; not only did Spanish partisans go unprosecuted, but the Spanish ambassador was closely involved in the court's affairs.[38] When the court attempted to dissolve after fining several defendants, the Lower Engadine and other communes sent new judges with instructions to prosecute the pro-Spanish magnates as well.[39] The new court's hostility towards all foreign pensioners became evident when the imprisoned Rudolf von Salis was tried and tortured, not for supporting the French alliance, but rather for his connections with Venice and Spain.[40]

By 1565, it seems, two different processes that could stimulate public unrest had become so closely intertwined as to be indistinguishable. On the one hand, the tumult reflected a political struggle at the level of the Freestate, in which magnate clients of different foreign powers stirred up the communes in order to stymie their opponents and increase their own local power. On the other hand, popular concern about the effects of the Freestate's policy on the local economy and growing peasant resentment against the magnates combined to make the communes tinderboxes of hostility against the elite. The formal organization of the communes, especially the annual election of magistrates by the entire citizenry, convinced the peasants that they were collectively the masters, just as the institutional practice of the Freestate made it clear that the communes were the rulers of the entire state. Under these circumstances, the peasants were ready to respond to calls for action against powerful "miscreants," even if the calls originated during struggles among the dominant families.

When feuding magnates appealed to the communes after other weapons had

---

[37] Cf. F. Jecklin, *Der Engadiner Aufruhr*, 47, 82–83. The uprising in the Engadine came to be known as the *Speckkrieg*, the "bacon-war," because the region's store of bacon was the only enemy the companies ever defeated.

[38] F. Jecklin, *Der Engadiner Aufruhr*, 41, 46–51.

[39] BK II: 610 (no. 698).

[40] In his analysis, F. Jecklin ignores the factional dimension of the proceedings in Zuoz almost entirely. See BK II: 597–98 (no. 689).

failed them, the response often escaped elite control. As accusations of corruption flew back and forth, the peasant-dominated penal courts set out to punish everyone who had "failed the fatherland," regardless of factional affiliation. Even though direct action by the communes was not formally part of the political process, the reality of communal power meant that it was always possible. But as leaders from all factions often discovered, popular anger made such appeals to the communes hazardous: the peasants were too erratically informed, and too easily influenced by bribery and economic threats, to be safe partners in any political project.

By 1570, the Freestate's leadership saw that other developments in the communes also threatened political order. More and more men were influencing political decisions by bribing the communes directly: lucrative federal offices distributed by the communes, local positions of authority, even judicial decisions made by communal assemblies could be bought. Candidates for office often provided free food and drink to participants at assemblies, a practice called *Kesseln* after the cauldrons of food set up for the peasants. Bribing commoners was in fact an increasingly common practice wherever rural communes exercised power, especially in Switzerland. Normally, such bribery served as a kind of tax on the local leadership's control over lucrative common resources, but it could become a source of conflict when several contenders sought to influence the peasant voters.[41]

A new Rhaetian statute, the *Kesselbrief* of 1570, addressed the problem directly. The first article stated that every delegate to a *Beitag* or *Bundestag* had to swear a formal oath that he had not gained his office by bribery, and the second established that if it was discovered that any communal, League, or federal officer had done so, he should lose the office and be excluded from all future offices. The seriousness of the statute's intentions appeared in the third and fourth articles. A commune that did not punish its malefactors could be charged before its League, and if the League refused to prosecute, then the other two Leagues were to establish a special court "so that the aforesaid commands shall be followed by the councils and communes, and so that we may follow in the footsteps of our pious ancestors, for the promotion of God's honor so that our land and people may be governed fittingly in fear of God."[42] The *Kesselbrief* thus overrode the judicial sovereignty of the communes in favor of collective jurisdiction exercised by the Leagues and the Freestate. Even so, like earlier anti-corruption measures, the *Kesselbrief* had little effect.

The course of politics in the late-sixteenth-century Freestate was turbulent at best, but the crisis that broke out suddenly late in 1571 went far beyond earlier struggles. During the previous two decades, Johann von Planta had established himself as the richest and most influential man in the Freestate. Doctor of canon and civil law from Bologna, he had settled in the Gray League where he leased the

---

[41] SI III: cols. 520–21; similar practices became institutionalized all over Switzerland under the name *trölen*.
[42] JVF, 115.

lordship of the Austrian territory of Rhäzüns in 1558, and bought the privileges belonging to the domain of Hohentrins in 1568. An active participant in the Freestate's affairs, he had been an ambassador to foreign powers, had served in the Valtellina, and had arbitrated disputes in Rhaetia and in the neighboring Swiss cantons.[43] Unlike many in his immediate family, including two of his brothers, Johann had remained a Catholic when his native village of Zernez accepted the Reformation. His son Conradin became dean of the cathedral chapter in Chur, and after the episcopal election in 1549, Planta had accompanied his cousin, Bishop Thomas, to Rome. Such a powerful man naturally had many enemies: a faction of the Salis family led by Dietegen hated him as leader of those who had blocked Bartholomäus von Salis's election to the see, the Reformed ministers saw him as an obstacle to the further spread of the Reformation, and the common people of Rhäzüns resented his successful efforts to restore lordly privileges there.

The storm broke in 1571 over a priory in Teglio in the Valtellina. The order of monks there had been dissolved by the pope, but the priory's property had been seized by the Three Leagues. The endowment was administered by a wealthy local family, the Guiccardi, who used some of the proceeds to support Reformed ministers in the Valtellina. In 1570, the papacy sought to remedy this situation by giving Planta the authority to appoint his son Conradin administrator of the endowment. Two papal briefs to this effect were supplemented with a bull in February 1571, which gave Planta general authority to reclaim church property that had fallen into heretic hands anywhere in the Three Leagues. While it seems probable that Planta did not actually request such a bull, his reliance on outside authority to seize the priory in 1571 made him terribly vulnerable to his enemies.[44] The Reformed ministers in the Valtellina obtained copies of the incriminating documents and immediately sent them to their brethren in Chur, Tobias Egli and Ulrich Campell.

The subsequent course of events illustrates the multipolar political situation in the Freestate by this time. The struggle proceeded on three quite distinct levels. First, Dietegen von Salis undertook every possible action to bring down his foe, including marching on Chur with troops from his home commune of Castels. The Reformed pastors Egli and Campell, meanwhile, felt that they had to speak out in defense of their church, even though they hoped to avoid a public tumult. Finally, the commoners in the communes, not only in Rhäzüns but throughout the Freestate, were suspicious of the leading families. Not only common peasants, but locally prominent families felt squeezed out by the increasing power and arrogance of a few dominant clans, and were willing to take up arms against the overmighty magnates.

When local leaders supported the exhortations coming from the Reformed

---

[43] Planta, *Chronik der Familie von Planta*, 124–26; Valèr, *Planta*, 14–16.
[44] Valèr, *Planta*, 31–54. Planta steadfastly denied having requested the bull.

pulpits, the ingredients for an explosive outbreak of communal power were present. The charge that Planta wanted to "make himself lord over *Bünden*" may not have been literally true, but his preeminence certainly represented a threat to communes and lesser magnates alike.[45] A first turning point came during secret negotiations between the ministers and Planta in December 1571, in which the ministers demanded he give up not only his claims on clerical property in the Three Leagues, but also the priory in Teglio. Only when these talks failed did the ministers publicize the bull, a move they knew would arouse public anger.[46] By this time, Planta was willing to surrender the papal bull by tearing it to pieces before the ministers' eyes, but he demanded in exchange that his son retain possession of the priory in the Valtellina. Planta's concession was too little and too late: Egli began preaching against the bull and against Planta in Chur, while translations of the bull circulated throughout the Freestate.[47] The rapidly rising storm of outrage put Planta on the defensive, and the *Bundestag*, too, found itself forced to act more and more strongly against him. On January 2, Planta gave the bull to the *Beitag* and promised to yield the priory; on February 2, the *Beitag* decided to destroy the bull without sending copies to the communes, while Planta agreed to pay the costs of the *Beitag* and of restoring the priory, and to pay a fine of two hundred gold crowns. By March 11, the threat of military action from the communes forced the *Beitag* to establish a special penal court to try Planta and several others, including Dietegen and Baptista von Salis.[48] Planta fled from the Engadine to the Gray League, where he thought himself safe, but was seized by the (Catholic) commune of Laax and returned in dishonor to Chur.[49]

Events now slipped entirely out of the *Bundestag*'s and the ministers' hands: commune after commune sent contingents of troops to Chur to observe the court trying Planta. Whereas the *Beitag* had provided for a court with one member from each district and eleven from each league, the military companies added some six hundred "overseers" (*Gäumer*) to ensure that "justice" was done.[50] Planta was tortured, tried, and publicly executed. The main charges were that he had used a papal bull to exercise authority "without the knowledge or permission of his sovereign lords the Three Leagues";[51] that he had sought foreign help to increase his power; that he had tried to establish "absolute dominion" (*einer absolut herrschafft*)[52] over the lordship of Rhäzüns; and in sum, "that he had sought to make

---

45 STAG B 707/3, item no. 7, contains a list of charges against Planta, including that he sought to make himself lord. There is no evidence that Planta had in fact conspired with Austria to do so. See G. Bundi, "Dr. Johann v. Planta-Räzüns," 33–48
46 BK III: 276 (no. 268). Valèr, *Planta*, 55–59. Valèr's conspiratorial theory is implausible.
47 Egli's actions described in his secret letter to the Reformed clergy. BK III: 528–40 (*Beilage*).
48 STAG AB IV 1/3, pp. 50–51, 52–53, 65–66.
49 Valèr, *Planta*, 73–74.
50 STAG AB IV 1/3, 65.
51 F. Jecklin, "Eine neue Quelle," 73.   52 STAG B 707/3, item no. 7, fol. 3.

himself lord over Graubünden."[53] Having disposed of the main foe, the court turned to his family and to other "enemies of the fatherland" who had aroused popular ire. Thirty-seven men were tried, some in absentia, resulting in six death sentences, along with fines totaling over ten thousand crowns; nine defendants were acquitted, although some of these were required to pay court costs. The most powerful clans in the Freestate appeared among those convicted, including Planta, Salis, Raschèr, Beeli, Capaul, Marti, von Castelberg, and Demont.[54]

Most contemporary commentators deplored the populist dimension that dominated the events of 1572. The *Beitag* itself repeatedly begged everyone to remain quiet, since it hoped to forestall direct action by the communes.[55] The magnates, naturally enough, were hostile to direct action too: in 1573, Johann von Planta's brother Balthasar was prosecuted for allegedly "letting it be known, and saying these words, that it would be better and more beneficial if the Three Leagues had a lord, than that they should be governed by common men themselves."[56] Even the ministers who had contributed so decisively to popular unrest were deeply disquieted by it. Campell condemned the court in his chronicle, and Egli worried about the "peasants who now prevail."[57] On March 23, Egli wrote to Bullinger that "the [other communes] are all here in full strength, and yesterday evening the common man was still so embittered, that their leaders simply couldn't open their mouths, and anyone who urges them to do good is viewed with suspicion." In short, "the very least now wants to be lord and master."[58] Indeed, the ministers' main concern during and after the tumult was to dissociate themselves from it and to deny that they had incited it. Even though Egli had encouraged the ministers to preach against Planta and the bull, he insisted that he and his colleagues were only doing their duty. Torn between fear of popular unrest and the imminent threat they perceived from the "papal Antichrist," Egli could only respond: "This labor is imposed on us ministers, that we teach the common people. Unless we do it, they will be seduced; if we do it, we will be suspected of corruption."[59]

Unrest in the Freestate did not end when the tribunal in Chur disbanded in the summer of 1572. The court decreed the confiscation of Johann von Planta's goods, but implementing this sentence proved to be extremely difficult. Not only was Planta wealthy in his own right, but he also controlled the lordship of Rhäzüns, having mortgaged it from its Habsburg overlords. The communes, led by the inhabitants of Rhäzüns eager to be free from lordly control, demanded that the Freestate seize the lordship, whereas Austria protested that its servant had been

---

53 Mayer, "Hinrichtung," 198.
54 F. Jecklin, "Eine neue Quelle," 72–84.
55 E.g. STAG AB IV 1/3, pp. 51, 52, 66.
56 STAG ASP. III, 6b, 2 (May 18, 1573).
57 Campell cited in Valèr, *Planta*, 114. Egli in BK III: 321–22 (no. 289).
58 BK III: 319 (no. 287); the second quote reports the words of Hans Ardüser, *Landamman* of Davos.
59 BK III: 326 (no. 294).

illegally prosecuted, and that the lordship was Habsburg property. Meanwhile, Planta's heirs demanded that their rights to his estate be protected. The complicated legal situation was made more difficult by the fact that the communes monitored every step of the negotiations, eager to maximize the payments they might receive. Caught between Austria, the Planta, the other clans, and the communes, the *Bundestag* managed to forge several compromises, none of which satisfied anyone. For example, its acceptance of only 7,000 crowns to fulfill all claims on the Planta estate enraged the communes. Meanwhile, other magnates demanded that the *Bundestag* remit their penalties as well. Early in 1574, the exasperated scribe of the Chadè added his own thoughts to the official minutes of a League assembly: "Oh, it's pointless to deal with our big shots, and it won't get better unless we start another tumult and lop off all of the big shots' heads."[60]

Discontent with the magnates and their endless infighting was widespread among the communes as well, and exploded into a second tumult in 1573. Not only had the French ambassador caused unrest through his efforts to renew the alliance – particularly distressing to Rhaetian Protestants after the St. Bartholomew's Day massacre the previous summer – but the magnates were all too visibly up to their usual tactics. By late February, the rumor was widespread that the communes would raise their banners again, and in early March, the expected uprising of the peasants took place.[61] At least ten districts sent troops to Thusis, where another court began to proceed against the guilty, once again with six hundred overseers. Unlike the previous year, however, the assembled troops also proposed institutional changes to correct persistent abuses. Bypassing the regular *Bundestag*, still convened at Chur, the troops passed a set of reform articles that were the first evidence of a tenacious reform movement that continued well into the seventeenth century.

The articles established in Thusis took clear aim at the magnates. Article 1 stated that all pensions from France should be divided among the communes, article 2 forbade anyone from leaving the Freestate to serve a foreign prince or from receiving money or gifts from one, and article 3 excluded all pensioners from public offices in the Freestate. Articles 4 through 8 addressed the corruption surrounding the Valtellina offices. They limited everyone to a single turn in office and insisted that the communes, not the *Bundestag*, should fill all offices in rotation. Articles 9 and 10 turned to the Freestate's own assemblies: the *Beitag* was abolished except for emergencies, in which case every commune should be represented, and delegates to the *Bundestag* were instructed to arrive with written instructions

---

[60] STAG AB IV 1/3, p. 212: "Ey es ist mit unseren grosen hansen vergebens, und würdt nit besser werden, wir fachen dan ein nüwe ufrhuor widerumb, und howent dann solchen grosen hansen die köpf allen ab." This extraordinary remark comes at the bottom of a page describing the negotiations, without any other explanation.
[61] Egli specifically describes the opposing parties at the time as pensioners and peasants (*Puren*). BK III: 410–11 (no. 355/2).

and return to their communes with a written report, so that the communes might approve what had been decided. The final article, interestingly, provided that no commune should raise its banner for political reasons in the future, thus excluding the possibility of future assemblies such as the one drafting the articles.[62] The participants in the Thusis assembly did not see their purpose as revolutionary, but sought rather to ensure that "we may follow in the footsteps of our pious ancestors, so that God's honor may be promoted and the land may be ruled fittingly in the fear of God."[63] The fact that the articles were sealed by all three presidents of the Leagues suggests that opposition to magnate corruption included many influential men, who were able to channel popular discontent into reform measures of this kind. The events of 1573 also show, however, that popular unrest was a real political force in the Freestate by this time, something to be feared as well as reckoned with. During the weeks before the actual outbreak, Egli's letters to Bullinger from Chur took on apocalyptic tones.[64]

Reform efforts continued after 1573. A statute of 1574 repeated the prohibition against raising communal banners for political purposes, and added restrictions intended to make it more difficult for both foreign legates and domestic demagogues to manipulate communal opinion.[65] At the same time, however, the power of the magnates rebounded quickly from the setbacks of 1572 and 1573, which limited the effectiveness of the nascent reform movement. Bribery, corruption, and the misuse of office continued during the 1580s and 1590s, and foreign powers continued to buy magnates and even whole assemblies. Nevertheless, the situation after 1572–73 was different than before: the real power of communal resistance had been brought home to the leading families by the torture and execution of Johann von Planta. Even though formal statutes against corruption were rarely obeyed, leading men in the Freestate now knew that certain actions could endanger not only their careers, but also their lives.

What offended the communes most, it seemed, was the perception that their ultimate authority was being ignored, or that the communes were not getting their share of common resources. Bypassing the communes had brought about the death of Planta, who appealed to a power outside the Freestate in order to seize an asset that the communes felt was their own. Fear that public resources had been sold for private gain also motivated the prosecution of foreign pensioners. In 1565 and 1572, commoners rose against their own leaders and attempted to discipline them, reflecting their growing conviction that the Freestate should be governed according to the political values that organized life in the individual communes. The basis for this conviction lay in the fifteenth century, when the communes had fought under local leaders for autonomy from the regional nobility. In the sixteenth century,

---

[62] Articles in JM II: 430–32 (no. 422).
[63] JM II: 432.
[64] See esp. BK III: 408–09 (no. 354).   [65] JVF, 107–12, col. 2.

however, communal values constrained non-noble leaders as well – first in the reform movement which peaked in 1603, and then in the violent outbreaks of 1607 and later.

Magnates continued to accumulate wealth and influence during the period as well, and the great families began adopting aristocratic habits and values.[66] The institutional maturation of the Freestate's central organs, removed from the immediate scrutiny of the common people, actually gave the powerful more room to expand their influence over everyday affairs. Yet at the same time, Rhaetian leaders no longer enjoyed as much freedom from popular discipline as during the early sixteenth century. The risings in 1572 and 1573 became models for direct action by the communes against the established elite. From the 1570s until the Thirty Years' War, the great question in Rhaetian politics was whether an oligarchic elite would accumulate enough power to dominate affairs, or whether the communes and the lesser families would succeed in setting limits on the magnates' power.

---

[66] This process is described in the following chapter, and in greater detail in Head, *Social Order*, chapter 7.

5

Elite power and popular constraint in sixteenth-century Rhaetia

Oh, it's pointless to deal with our big shots, and it won't get better unless we start another tumult and lop off all of the big shots' heads.

Protocol of the Chadè, 1576[1]

Wealthy and powerful families came to dominate the political life of the Rhaetian Freestate during the sixteenth century, filling the void left by the extinction or marginalization of the feudal dynasts. These families increased their influence by means of tactics common to patricians all over early modern Europe, such as patronage networks, control of public offices, and education in the law, although they adapted their methods to the decentralized structure of the Freestate. In many respects, they represent no more than a local variation on phenomena that could be found in other regions at the time. Unusual, however, were the nature and extent of the constraints on the Rhaetian elite. Whereas non-feudal patricians in Europe's monarchies and principalities faced competition from the hereditary nobility and distrust from their princes, and even the Swiss patriciates were limited primarily by factional divisions among themselves, the Rhaetian *grosse Hansen* repeatedly saw their power swept away by populist unrest. Both the political culture of the Freestate, with its emphasis on communal rule, and the demonstrated willingness of common Rhaetians to seize control of the Freestate's institutions set limits on the dominant group.

Like all power struggles, this one took place on several levels simultaneously. Individuals and families competed for the resources essential for power, such as land, money, education, and prestige. Since wealth was a decisive tool for influencing the decision-making process, families bought land, traded, occupied lucrative offices, and sold their military service to foreign princes in order to build their fortunes. But prestige gained through birth, education, ennoblement, or courage also opened the doors to political influence. As the Rhaetian ruling families became more conscious of their power towards the end of the sixteenth century, they began to exclude outsiders and newcomers from their ranks, although this

---

[1] STAG AB IV/1/3, p. 212.

process did not really become effective until after the tumultuous unrest, known as the *Bündner Wirren*, that took place between 1607 and 1639.

During the same period, the Freestate produced unusual opponents to the new ruling class. After 1550, Rhaetians from different social groups increasingly disagreed about the origins and exercise of political authority, in ways quite different from contemporary French or Germans. The communal solidarity that had seemed unbreakable when communes struggled with their lords fragmented with the onset of a long struggle not simply for power, but also for legitimate authority. Influential leaders who gathered at the *Bundestag* or *Beitag* complained increasingly that the common man should not meddle in politics, yet the importance of decisions reached by assemblies and majorities steadily increased. Political customs that vested control in a few families were challenged by egalitarian outbreaks that asserted the unlimited authority of the common man. The key struggles in Rhaetia after 1550 took place not between reactionary nobles, ambitious commoners, and a centralizing state, but rather between the communes and the new oligarchs.

By the end of the century, a clear dichotomy had been established: the effective power of some powerful families within the Freestate stood in contrast to the widely accepted legitimacy of principles and practices derived from communalism, such as majority rule by public assembly, and publicly controlled distribution of common resources. This dichotomy also brought forth recurring political crises in the Freestate. Both conflicts among elite factions and growing hostility between commoners and patricians played a role in triggering large and often violent public assemblies that disrupted the normal course of political action. The net effect of such crises, as well as of the persistent political reform movement that accompanied them, was to constrain the new elite even as its power seemed to be growing most rapidly. This chapter will sketch first the origins of the new ruling group, and then the limits it confronted by the early seventeenth century.

THE NEW RHAETIAN ELITE

Recent research has revealed a profound change among Graubünden's dominant families between the fifteenth and the seventeenth century. The feudal dynasts – the counts of Toggenburg and Werdenberg-Sargans, the counts of Sax-Misox, the lords of Brandis and Mätsch – faded from the scene between 1450 and 1500, bankrupt and powerless. When Jürg von Werdenberg and Gaudenz von Mätsch died in 1504, the regional nobility disappeared completely and permanently from Rhaetian history.[2] Two very different parties stepped into their shoes. On the one hand, the great princes of the region, especially the Habsburg dukes of Tyrol, bought or inherited many of the rights belonging to the local nobility. In fact, Austria's efforts

---

[2] Grimm, *Anfänge*, 11–12.

to bring the Rhaetian passes into its sphere of influence was one of the causes of the Swabian War of 1499. On the other hand, a group of families based in the Freestate's communes took over most practical authority in the region. These families soon coalesced into a new elite that dominated the Rhaetian Freestate until the end of the *ancien régime*, and in some ways up to the present.[3] Some forty-eight families were particularly prominent during the sixteenth century, and some forty dominated affairs during the seventeenth. Twenty-six families took leading roles for both centuries: theirs are the names most commonly found in leadership positions everywhere in the Freestate, and they formed the true heart of the Rhaetian social and political elite.[4] The foundations of their influence were wealth, political office (in the communes and in the Freestate), education, and military leadership. Their dominance perpetuated itself, bringing them more wealth, a near-monopoly on federal offices, and deference except in times of social turmoil.

All the available evidence suggests that wealth rather than noble background was the most important qualification for membership in this new cohort. Not one of the elite families in sixteenth-century Graubünden descended from the feudal nobility, and only about a third of them started as agents of the regional dynasts. Moreover, the leading families never became a legally separate estate from the general population, even after their members began intermarrying and closing themselves off biologically and socially.[5] Well into the eighteenth century, the most distinguished Rhaetian aristocrats from the Planta or the Salis clans could advance politically only if they were willing to sit down as equals with the common peasants of their communes. A liberally inclined Austrian observer in 1774 noted:

It is harmonious to see how the natural equality between the nobleman and the peasant is maintained all around here – except that the latter gives the former a leading position in farming, and usually also in carrying out, foreign affairs. But the nobleman must be a good tobacco and drinking companion to the peasant.[6]

The prestige of the wealthy patricians always existed in tension with the sense of equality inherent in a communally based society.

Their wealth did set the Rhaetian leadership apart from the rest of the population, however. Land ownership provided the foundation of most families' wealth, although trade, credit operations, and foreign pensions usually supplemented direct income from agriculture. The best-documented commune is the Upper Engadine (Sut Fontauna Merla). In a study of its central village, Zuoz

---

[3] *Ibid.*, 13.
[4] The twenty-six are: Bavier, Beeli, Brügger, Buol, Capaul, Castelberg, Enderlin, Florin, Gugelberg, Guler, Jecklin, Jenatsch, Juvalta, à Marca, deMont, Planta, Raschèr, Ruinelli, Salis, Scarpatetti, Schauenstein, Schmid, Schorsch, Sprecher, Travers, and Tscharner. Both Grimm and Färber also identify an inner core of families, all of whom are among the overlapping group. Färber, *Herrenstand*, 10; Grimm, *Anfänge*, endleaf.
[5] Färber, *Herrenstand*, 5; Grimm, *Anfänge*, 17–21.
[6] Cited in Mathieu, *Bauern und Bären*, 273.

(known for its concentration of powerful families), Paolo Boringhieri categorized 26 out of a total of 255 households as magnates.[7] These households, whose estates were reckoned over 9000 florins, controlled 50 percent of the total wealth, whereas the 25 households in the next category, with estates valued between 4000 and 7000 florins, controlled only 17 percent.[8] Magnate wealth within the village of Zuoz included land and rights to summer pasture for their cows. The wealthiest households had over 30 alp-rights each; if we gather related households belonging to a single clan, the Planta in Zuoz alone controlled 117 alp-rights, the Raschèr nearly 70.[9] Still, even the wealthiest *Bündner* in the sixteenth century bore no comparison with the great nobility of the European monarchies: the Rhaetian elite were wealthier than their fellow citizens, to be sure, but the difference was one of degree rather than of kind.

Direct income from agriculture formed only part of the income of the leading Rhaetian families. Profits also came from investments in land, or from entirely different sources such as foreign pensions and political office. The rise of the family of Capaul in the Gray League shows how these kinds of income could mix.[10] Starting in the mid-fifteenth century, the previously unknown Capauls began buying land and rents in the region around Flims. This property was then leased, or sold advantageously to others. Starting in 1488, Härtli I von Capaul also began collecting an annual pension from Austria of 30 florins; to this was added a Milanese pension of 50 florins in 1498. His son Wolf collected pensions from Austria and France totalling 113 florins in 1517, for which he was censured by the Gray League. In 1483, Hans von Capaul bought the toll in Ilanz from the counts of Sax for 200 florins, suggesting an annual income of about 10 florins. Although the Capaul acted as episcopal bailiffs in the late fifteenth century, they shifted their focus to the public offices of the Three Leagues after 1500, serving in the Valtellina and in Maienfeld. By the mid-sixteenth century, they were deriving income from "rents, tithes, tolls, from mercenary fees, pensions and gifts, also from their share of fines as communal officers, from being bailiffs, and from offices in the Valtellina."[11] The period from 1450 to 1520 brought fertile opportunities for enterprising commoners

---

[7] Ten percent of the village's households belonged to the economic group of magnates, probably an unusually high proportion. The individual magnate households were not exceptionally wealthy, however. Boringhieri, "Geschlechter," 187.

[8] This information is for 1591. Boringhieri, "Geschlechter," 186–87. Surprisingly, the single wealthiest individual in 1591, the widow of Noli Dusch, was not from one of the families generally included in the Rhaetian elite, though she herself was a Jecklin, and her husband had been elected *mastrel* of the Upper Engadine in 1565, 1575, and 1583. Boringhieri, "Pussaunza," 104.

[9] *Ibid.*, 96–97 (for the year 1586). The magnate families of Zuoz owned 515 of the 1106 alp-rights controlled by the village in 1591. Boringhieri, "Geschlechter," 174–75. These figures document the Planta family's wealth in only one section of one commune: it needs to be multiplied many times to account for their holdings in other neighborhoods of the Engadine, and elsewhere in the Freestate.

[10] The following description based on Grimm, *Anfänge*, 22–30.

[11] *Ibid.*, 29.

to get rich: the feudal nobles sold more and more of their land and rights, and the conquest of the Valtellina in 1512 offered new opportunities for gain. Wealthy peasant families such as the Capaul, urban merchants, and the families that had previously served the dynasts all hastened to improve their positions however they could.

The Rhaetian elite's political influence remained rooted in the communes, as one would expect for a decentralized federation like the Freestate. At the lowest level in the villages, members of the leading families appeared regularly as *cuvihs* or village heads. In Samaden in the Upper Engadine, Joachim Bifrun, Friederich von Salis, and Georg Travers were all *cuvihs* of their neighborhoods before becoming chief magistrate of their entire political commune.[12] In the Lower Engadine,

[the lists of village officeholders] contain nearly the entire aristocracy . . . , as well as many names from the village elites...The powerful families had other goals, and were in any case ubiquitous in village politics. When an office was given to them, however, they could not scorn it.[13]

Even men who later appeared in much more important offices participated in local politics in the Freestate.[14] The fact that offices changed hands every year or two, meanwhile, ensured that almost every family would eventually serve.[15]

Access to offices in the larger political communes and to federal offices was much more limited. As the highest magistrate over a population that might number several thousand, the *Landamman, Mistral,* or *podestà* was a figure of considerable respect and influence. Competition for the position was usually fierce, and in many communes a few families dominated. During the sixteenth century, members of the elite families constituted 90 percent of the communal chief magistrates still approved by lords, and 75 percent of those where the commune could choose autonomously.[16] Research on the better-documented seventeenth century shows similar overall results, although a few communes chose officers from a larger circle of families.[17] Offices in the Valtellina were similarly distributed. The right to appoint to offices theoretically rotated among the communes, but this did not prevent a small number of families from filling most of them as well. The forty-five captains of the Valtellina during the sixteenth century came from only sixteen communes, all of them seats of influential families. The Salis, the Planta, and the

---

[12] From the period 1532–54, for which records survive. *Ibid.*, 103.
[13] Mathieu, *Bauern und Bären*, 196–200, cite from 200. Färber, *Herrenstand*, 26, reaches a similar conclusion.
[14] Grimm, *Anfänge*, 102–04.
[15] This in contrast to regions where higher offices were filled by territorial princes, and there was little overlap between higher and lower magistrates. E.g. Vann, *The Making of a State*, 40–41; Blickle, *Landschaften*, 449–61.
[16] Lords retained nominal powers of appointments in a number of communes. Grimm, *Anfänge*, 112.
[17] Färber, *Herrenstand*, 49, 57, 68, 69, 75, 89–90, 97, 110–11. For the Upper Engadine, see also Boringhieri, "Pussaunza," 88–90.

Travers clans alone provided eighteen of the incumbents.[18] Communes were thus willing (or could be coerced) to nominate members of magnate families to the highest political offices.

Another important way that certain families gained respect and wealth was through military leadership of two kinds: leading communal forces in defense of the Freestate, and leading mercenary troops in service to foreign princes. Because bearing arms was such an important part of communal identity, political leadership was closely connected to military leadership: successfully leading communal troops brought a man enormous prestige and was a sure foundation for political influence.[19] Foreign military service, meanwhile, brought captains and families both fortune and prestige. The conflicts in Rhaetia and in Italy from the 1470s to the 1530s allowed new families to rise into the leading class through military leadership at home.[20] During the long domestic peace from 1532 to 1620, other families rose to prominence in the service of foreign princes, notably the Hartmannis of Churwalden and the Schmid of Ilanz.[21] Members of the Salis and Planta families, meanwhile, led a steady stream of regiments into foreign service, bringing their families large profits and occasional knighthoods and titles of nobility.

As the elite families increased their wealth, power, and prestige during the sixteenth century, they also began closing themselves off from the rest of the Rhaetian population. The disappearance of the dynastic nobles around 1500 had loosened older patterns, so that rising families could marry into older ministerial clans, but the social sphere within which the elite chose spouses narrowed again after 1550.[22] Some turned to local marriage compacts, in which a few families in a region customarily married one another, but the greater families created a new elite marriage circle across the entire Freestate, which narrowed after mid-century to include only about a dozen of the most powerful clans.[23] The process of narrowing was paralleled by an increasing use of marriage contracts specifying the financial and political dimensions of an elite marriage. Not only dowries and property arrangements, but also support in gaining political offices might be included in such contracts.[24]

An unusual feature of Rhaetian elite families was their tendency to seek a foothold in as many separate communes as possible. A direct consequence of the Freestate's federal structure, this pattern resulted in networks of kin spread across

---

[18] Grimm, *Anfänge*, 119.
[19] Padrutt, *Staat und Krieg*, 36–46.
[20] *Ibid.*, 39.
[21] Grimm, *Anfänge*, 225–26, 202.
[22] *Ibid.*, 78.
[23] Grimm, *Anfänge*, 83. This dozen is substantially the same as Färber's inner elite of fifteen families; Färber, *Herrenstand*, 10.
[24] Grimm, *Anfänge*, 84–86.

the Freestate. The Planta spread from their original seat in the Upper Engadine into nine other communes, from Chur to the Val Müstair. The Salis also spread widely, but favored the Ten Jurisdictions: influential branches of the family were to be found in Malans, Grüsch, and Schiers.[25] Chur, the only city and *de facto* capital, was the most important commune for an ambitious family. Twelve of the most influential families from throughout the Freestate had powerful branches in Chur, while other elite families became citizens without being active in the city's political life.[26] Outside Chur, the rich landscapes of the Domleschg and Maienfeld attracted wealthy families.[27] Finally, several families expanded into the subject territories in the Valtellina. Particularly in the seventeenth and eighteenth centuries, much of the Salis family's substantial wealth derived from their control over the wine and grain trades there.

Spreading into more than one commune magnified the influence of a family, even though such a move could have complex causes. The Schiers branch of the Salis, for example, was created when young Hercules von Salis found it impossible to gain office in his native Bregaglia. Not that his family had no influence there – the Salis controlled the Val Bregaglia – but certain of his relatives "had fixed themselves so firmly in the favor of the people, by whom the magistrates and officers were elected" that he had little chance of advancement.[28] Instead, he married an influential heiress in the Ten Jurisdictions, and soon took a leading role in his adopted commune. Individuals might move to other communes to escape the influence of their clan, not just to further it. Still, the effect of Hercules' move was to broaden the Salis presence in the Freestate as a whole.

Being distributed among several communes could also result in disagreement or even enmity between branches of a family. Elite factions in the Freestate did not always divide along clan lines. While certain elective affinities did appear – the Salis were more often associated with the French party, the Planta with the Austrian and Spanish parties – members from all the important clans appeared in every faction.[29] Even members of the same nuclear family could be found as members of opposed factions. To cite just one example from the early seventeenth century, Luci von Mont was the leader of the pro-Spanish faction in the Gray League in the late 1610s, where he was supported by one brother, whereas another brother, Albert, supported the pro-Venetian party.[30] Despite the great importance of kinship in Rhaetia, political interests often cut across family ties.

---

[25] *Ibid.*, endleaf.
[26] Grimm, *Anfänge*, 177, noting that well over half of his forty-eight elite families could be found in Chur. See also Färber, *Herrenstand*, 108–09.
[27] Grimm, *Anfänge*, 177–78, who also mentions Zuoz and Disentis as attractive communes for expansion.
[28] Salis-Marschlins, *Denkwürdigkeiten*, 3.
[29] See Färber, *Herrenstand*, 168–83.
[30] *Ibid.*, 178–79.

Even so, a family's presence in several communes buttressed both the individual family and the collective influence of the elite. Control over several communes multiplied a family's influence in the central institutions, and also ensured that catastrophes affecting one branch would not eliminate a family from national influence. Similarly, a clan with branches on both sides of important disputes could be sure that one branch would be on the winning side, thus providing a kind of insurance in troubled times. Meanwhile, the collective influence of the elite was enhanced because a Planta or a Salis who moved into another commune had the resources to squeeze out locally prominent families. The Hercules von Salis who moved to Schiers immediately began filling high offices for his adopted commune:

[He] . . . settled in Grüsch, where he was able to win the favor of the population so quickly, through his friendly and upright demeanor, that he was not only accepted as a citizen, but thereupon elected to the office of Podestà of Tirano in 1590, with the support of his relatives. This occurred with great applause from the people, but at the expense of irrevocable animosity from some otherwise influential men in the commune, who saw themselves thrust aside in this way by a newcomer.[31]

Strengthened by their growing tendency towards endogamous marriages, the Rhaetian elite sought to infiltrate as many communes as possible, guaranteeing their collective social and political control.

By the end of the sixteenth century, then, the Rhaetian Freestate was spanned by a social elite that had dissociated itself from the communes even though it depended on them for offices and authority. Consisting of branches spreading from home communes to richer waters elsewhere; sustained by commercial farming, the pass trade, foreign pensions, and mercenary service; and exercising power in communal and federal offices, the new elite transcended the Freestate's communal foundations. Conscious of their wealth and prestige, members of the elite were inevitably tempted by social ideologies that recognized their special status more explicitly than communalism ever could. This temptation was multiplied because the European world outside of Rhaetia took hierarchy for granted: during their studies abroad or in their service to foreign monarchs, elite Rhaetians encountered a world that asserted that a nobleman was better than a commoner. Yet in his native commune, no matter how much respect he might gain, a patrician was nominally equal to his poorest neighbor citizen. Even more galling to an aristocratic mentality, election to offices remained in the hands of the communes. Men who were knights and commanders in foreign regiments had to return home and beg or bribe their communes for offices suitable to their new dignity. Under the circumstances, it is not surprising that members of the elite increasingly turned towards the values of their aristocratic peers abroad.

---

[31] Salis-Marschlins, *Denkwürdigkeiten*, 4. Salis-Marschlins does not mention the role that bribes may have played in convincing the Schierser of his father's "upright demeanor."

Although some patricians sought wider horizons in Freestate's political institutions, the opposition between populism and oligarchy in the Freestate did not simply parallel the tension between communes and central government. Some communes, such as the Upper Engadine or the Val Lumnezia, were firmly controlled by one or two families, and were thus bastions of elite power. The central assemblies, in contrast, included delegates from communes where less influential families held sway, and could therefore be hostile to over-mighty magnates. The Planta and Salis sometimes avoided dealing with the *Bundestag*, where a majority of delegates from middling families opposed their control. Any power possessed by the "common man," meanwhile, was usually exercised directly through the communes, which often meant wresting control from a locally dominant family. The more powerful clans thus worked on a larger scale, and tried to promote their interests out of the peasants' view as much as possible.

Ironically, the elite's growing sense of superiority only inflamed the populism latent in communal political culture. When their leaders began speaking and acting like lords, Rhaetian commoners were quick to take offense. The more tightly a few families controlled the machinery of politics, the less legitimate such control seemed to the commons. Yet the elite was rarely driven from office, but actually consolidated its hold on public leadership as the century progressed. Rhaetian leaders became caught in a vicious circle of delegitimation, in which the elite's fading legitimacy made politics more venal, and the traffic in offices ever more commercial. Not virtue but hard cash became the criterion for gaining office – and cash could easily be gained through corrupt exercise of an office, especially in the Valtellina, or through pensions and bribes from a foreign power. Communal voters might not respect the leading families, but they remained willing to sell them communal and federal positions. Political corruption, in turn, only reinforced the commoners' suspicions that their leaders were unworthy of legitimate authority. The relationship between power and authority became unstable in the Freestate during the late sixteenth century, eventually giving rise to wild factionalism and popular tumults after 1600.

CONSTRAINTS ON THE NEW ELITE

The constellation of power and political discipline found in the Freestate differed sharply from that in the rest of Europe.[32] Since all but the wealthiest *Bündner* remained anchored in the life of their communes, communal discontent about the *grosse Hansen* often overlapped with factional conflicts among the leading clans. Opportunistic patricians exploited the unrest of the common man to unseat their opponents in the central government, using patronage and local leadership networks to trigger disorder. The victims used similar methods to revenge

[32] Cf. the typology of resistance proposed in Blickle, "Auf dem Weg zu einem Modell," 298–308.

themselves. Meanwhile, popular discontent rarely had a clear target. There was no distant state, as in France, trying to collect taxes and impose social discipline, nor were there "foreign" bureaucrats to hate, as there were in many of the Habsburg domains. The Freestate's nascent aristocrats were personally known to most peasants, familiar from local assemblies and daily transactions, so that disgust with oligarchic corruption was tempered by personal contact. In fact, the crowds who gathered during the great tumults expected local leaders to step forward to guide the course of events.[33] Rhaetian commoners' goals were rarely revolutionary, aiming at a transformation of the social order, but were rather reformist, hoping for a well-ordered polity in which natural leaders faithfully executed the will of the communes. Unlike peasant rebels elsewhere, the participants in Rhaetian uprisings viewed themselves neither as defenders of traditional peasant privileges against their lords, nor as the revolutionary vanguard of a new "godly law."[34] Instead, they saw themselves as their state's legitimate rulers, gathered in assembly to discipline their errant leaders. This context provides the background for understanding the constraints on elite power in the Freestate.

The contradiction between the genuine power exercised by the Rhaetian elite most of the time and the populist expectations held by the rest of the population ultimately made the Freestate ungovernable. Practice and theory drifted further and further apart after the mid-sixteenth century. Two particular aspects of this disjunction contributed to the crisis that erupted in the early seventeenth century. On the one hand, the pervasiveness of communalist ideas ensured that the increasing power of a limited group within Rhaetian society would be perceived as illegitimate. Practices congenial to oligarchic control – small and secret councils, cooptation to positions of authority, decision-making monopolized by a few powerful families – conflicted at every turn with the communal emphasis on inclusive assemblies that reached decisions by majority vote. As a result, the elite's exercise of power became a source of irritation to everyone from peasant small-holders to local leaders whose ambitions were blocked by the leading families. On the other hand, no sixteenth-century Rhaetian produced a political theory based on communal values, which might have guided the Freestate towards a new, coherent political identity. Not until the 1610s did an open debate about the foundations of authority develop, by which time foreign intervention and confessional conflict made a peaceful transformation of the political system nearly impossible. Rather than providing a clear alternative to oligarchy, communal influence remained confined to reform efforts or outbursts of popular discontent. Lacking a clear model

---

[33] Not only in Switzerland did peasants turn to local magnates to support their revolts. In France, nobles from the lowest to highest ranks often played an active role in peasant unrest. See Bercé, *History of Peasant Revolts*, e.g. 329.

[34] The line between peasant resistance and peasant rebellion is very fine. Most peasant resistance in the Holy Roman Empire, whatever its form, claimed legitimacy on the basis of inherited political and social structures. Blickle, "Auf dem Weg zu einem Modell," 303.

Elite power and popular constraint

of how popular power ought to be put into effect, the gathered citizens repeatedly turned to the very elite they distrusted in order to reform the Freestate. Not surprisingly, the changes instituted after populist outbreaks such as those in 1573 and 1607 were short lived and ineffective. The communes' power remained essentially negative: they could discipline their leaders, but they did not yet know how to rule.

Paradoxically, institutional change in the Freestate during the same period put ever more emphasis on collective rule, even as a few magnates attempted to subvert the new practices in order to consolidate their personal power. Whereas political decision-making in other European republics was moving to small councils and other privileged bodies, in Rhaetia the exercise of authority by large public assemblies continued unabated.[35] More matters went out for communal ratification under the referendum system as the sixteenth century progressed, a development that continued into the seventeenth and eighteenth centuries. Public assemblies of the entire citizenship never disappeared in Graubünden as they did in most German and Swiss cities.[36] Rhaetian political rhetoric finally reflected this trend near the end of the sixteenth century, by putting ever more emphasis on the communes' final authority in all matters. Meanwhile, a growing chorus of complaint found in elite sources indicated that the magnates, too, felt constrained by the common man's political role in Graubünden.

Members of the elite often felt threatened by the political influence of the peasants. Some of them disparaged commoners' ability to understand and judge difficult public questions, while others wrote worried, even fearful statements about the excessive freedom the common man enjoyed within the Freestate. Whereas the first response represents a European commonplace with roots going back to the Classical period, the second more accurately reflects conditions in Graubünden.[37] In both cases, however, the tone of these comments is revealing: whether disparaging the common man's ability or expressing frustration about his actual role in public affairs, elite *Bündner* always spoke of a real problem, rather than of an undesirable possibility. Popular unrest was a very real threat that could never be ignored in political calculations. Describing a brief tumult which took place in 1571, Tobias Egli expressed the common horror the Rhaetian establishment felt about popular actions:

They deposed the Amman of Davos from his seat, and condemned him to prison . . . Some men threw themselves at the feet of the peasants, and begged in the name of God and justice, that [the peasants] not do anything worse to them because of unspoken accusations and

---

[35] On European republics in general during this period, see Durand, *Républiques.*
[36] Even the Swiss rural cantons that maintained their public assemblies – Uri, Schwyz, Unterwalden, Appenzell, and Glarus – developed permanent councils of one kind or another before the sixteenth century. Peyer, *Verfassungsgeschichte*, 50–54.
[37] On the European traditions, see GG, "Demokratie," I: 821–47; and Boas, *Vox Populi.*

145

unknown facts . . . God protect us from revolts; for it would be no wonder if the earth were to open up, so irregularly [*ungeschlennglich*] do things proceed.[38]

Action by large groups of commoners could put anyone's life in danger, no matter how powerful or wealthy he was. Many elite Rhaetians simply fled when they heard that the communes were on the march. In 1607, for example, after the *Fähnli* seized Georg Beeli and Caspar Baselga, other powerful men in the Freestate hastily departed to Swiss territory. Johann Guler traveled circuitously to Ragaz, on the Rhaetian border near Maienfeld, where he met Hercules von Salis, Luci Gugelberg, the Schauenstein brothers, Joachim von Jochberg, Andreas Ruinelli, and Mayor Tscharner of Chur. Antonio Sonwig evaded eighty troops sent to catch him in the Valtellina, and joined the others. As the chronicler Bartholomäus Anhorn puts it, "When the great lords learned about the intentions of the common man, they didn't want to wait for the peasants' violence . . . "[39]

As a consequence, men in leading positions often acted cautiously, lest the common man be stirred to act. In the wake of the unrest in 1565, Johannes Fabricius, the chief Reformed minister in Chur, reported that the communes were unhappy and that measures should be taken to prevent further unrest:

the communes are not willing that matters should no longer be brought before them. Some time ago, after an Imperial representative rode around to the communes on his own authority, a statute was made, that no one should ride around the communes without permission [*eygens gwalts*]. Now the French clients . . . have brought matters so far, that an entire League was denied an audience and the right to be heard, which has made the Chadè more determined, and the common man less tractable.[40]

Foreign representatives made similar observations about how dangerous leadership in the Freestate might be. In 1564, for example, the Milanese ambassador Adrian Verbeque offered the Freestate an annual public pension of 6000 scudi in exchange for a new treaty of friendship and assistance. However, the ambassador wrote his superiors in Madrid that this sum did not include additional pensions to "principal men," which "must be arranged separately, without knowledge of the people."[41] Verbeque's superior, Sancho de Londoño, explained this need for secrecy: "The pensioners are greatly afraid that the communes will know that they are pensioners."[42] As had been shown in 1565, even the suspicion of receiving foreign bribes could put prominent men in danger of their lives. After all, one of the Spanish ambassador's tactics for raising discontent with the new French alliance had been to circulate a list of French pensioners and the amounts each of them received.[43]

A similar view appears in the memoirs of Fortunat von Juvalta. A survivor of the

---

[38] BK III: 236, (no. 237).   [39] Anhorn, *Püntner Aufruhr*, 68–69.
[40] BK II: 684–85 (no. 764).   [41] Cited in Blumenthal, *Die Drei Bünde*, 243.
[42] Haas, "Sancho de Londoño," 267.   [43] F. Jecklin, *Der Engadiner Aufruhr*, 33.

turbulent decades after 1600, Juvalta both feared and distrusted popular action. His description of the events preceding the Great Reform of 1603 reveals his conviction that the common man was incapable of sensible decisions. Juvalta opposed the plan to move the election of federal officers entirely to the communes:

One should by no means attempt this, because the common sort, who looked only to their private interests, could not be expected to show any concern for the republic or any moderation. Thus bribery and manipulation would not be abolished, but rather increased without measure; at the same time, no means for combating them would be left. As long as only single individuals violated the Reform ordinance, they could be punished by censors and judges; but if entire communes violated the law, which was sure to happen in the very first election, they would remain unpunished and the entire reform would be destroyed in no time.[44]

Juvalta expressed his fear of democracy even more bluntly a few pages further on, when he described the fate of leaders in a popular state:

For such is the character of the common type: he approves and confirms public affairs with his vote, and ascribes everything successful to himself, while blaming everything that goes badly on those who guide him; and, without being aware of it, he always treats those better favored by nature or fortune as hostile and suspicious, and seeks to topple and oppress them at the appropriate moment with malicious glee.[45]

He ended on a pessimistic note: "In tumults the worst always obtain the honors" – an statement based not on abstract conviction, but on his interpretation of the events of 1607.[46]

The common thread behind such sentiments was the fact that the Rhaetian people, once moved, were quite capable of punishing their errant leaders. Collective action by the inhabitants of the communes – whether in the form of impromptu crowds or more organized assemblies – regularly slipped out of the usual leadership's control. Increasingly institutionalized mechanisms of military assembly and popular tribunal shaped the relationship between power and authority in the Freestate between 1540 and 1620.

Fähnlilupf *and* Strafgericht, *1540–1620*

Over the course of the sixteenth century, collective action against unfaithful leaders in Rhaetia began to follow a distinctive sequence, which eventually became routine. Historians have gathered these outbursts under the name *Strafgericht* – literally, "penal court" – since they resulted in courts, made up of judges from every commune, that tried and punished those accused of acting against the Freestate. In fact, popular movements in the Freestate were characterized by several distinct stages, of which the formal court was only the last. In general, the process began

---

[44] Juvalta, *Denkwürdigkeiten*, 13.   [45] *Ibid.*, 21.   [46] *Ibid.*, 35.

when a number of districts raised their military banners and gathered in some central spot such as Chur or Thusis: this first stage was known in Rhaetian German dialect as a *Fähnlilupf* (literally, a "banner-raising").[47] The gathered militia usually encouraged more communes to join them, and if they were successful, a sort of chain reaction would bring nearly all of the communes to the assembly.[48] The second stage involved public assemblies of the citizen-soldiers, who often drafted a bill of articles intended to cleanse the Freestate of corruption and treachery. Finally, the third stage consisted in the appointment of a court, the actual *Strafgericht*, consisting of jurors from each commune and a larger number of "overseers" (*Gäumer*), who allegedly ensured honesty and incorruptibility. These courts, which often included hundreds of jurors and overseers, indicted, tried, and condemned anyone they felt had acted against the fatherland's interests. Although charges might be brought on the basis of formal statutes, many of the crimes prosecuted were purely political in character, such as supporting a foreign alliance against the communes' wishes, or speaking out against abuses by the court itself. Such popular tribunals often continued their activities for months, until they were satisfied that justice had been done (or as their opponents maintained, until they had levied enough fines to pay their bills at the local taverns). One might define the aftermath of the whole procedure as a fourth stage: once the military companies had gone home and the court had disbanded, the *Bundestag* often appointed a follow-up court to revise or nullify excesses on the part of the popular tribunal.

What distinguished the Rhaetian *Strafgericht* from other kinds of popular political action in Europe was its institutional character.[49] In the late sixteenth and early seventeenth centuries, *Strafgerichte* became an integral if unwelcome part of the political process in the Freestate. Early ones took place in 1450, 1517, and 1529, although the details are foggy. The *Strafgerichte* of 1542 and 1550 are only slightly better documented, and do not seem to have been particularly similar to one another. A clear pattern emerged only after midcentury. The tumults of 1565 and 1572 discussed in chapter 4 may have served as models for later outbreaks. By the early seventeenth century, despite opposition from the Rhaetian elite and from the central organs of the Freestate, the *Strafgericht* had become an important part of politics in Rhaetia. The first two decades of the century witnessed a proliferation of this form of political conflict. *Strafgerichte* took place in 1603 and 1607, followed by a string of some five tribunals and counter-tribunals between 1616 and

---

[47] The word was used primarily in Graubünden. SI III: cols. 1354–56. The term parallels the Latin *signa movere*.

[48] Systematic analysis in Valèr, *Bestrafung*, 130–36.

[49] Rural revolts and resistance have been the subject of a vast amount of research in the past two decades. An overview for Germany is given in Bierbrauer, "Bäuerliche Revolten." For France, see Bercé, *History of Peasant Revolts*. For early modern Europe, see Bercé, *Revolt and Revolution in early modern Europe*, tr. Joseph Bergin (Manchester: Manchester University Press, 1986), and two books by Schulze: *Bäuerlicher Widerstand*, and *Aufstände, Revolte, Prozesse*.

1620. Even after the Thirty Years' War, large popular assemblies following the same pattern took place at decisive moments in Rhaetian history, such as 1684 and 1794.[50]

The *Strafgericht* usually began when popular unhappiness reached such a peak that a few communes decided to raise their banners. The exact course of this first stage is difficult to analyze because it took place at a local level, largely without written records. Much of what we do know comes from accusations and recriminations after the fact. During this early phase, factions among the leading families could play a decisive role by triggering the outbreak in a commune where one family dominated. In 1542, for example, the Stampa family was instrumental in raising the Val Bregaglia, from where unrest spread to the entire Engadine. The *Bundestag* was able to forestall a general assembly of the military companies only by quickly setting up a penal court of its own to investigate foreign pensions.[51] Although Bartholome Stampa stirred up the communes against his rivals, the French partisans, commoners in the Bregaglia had reasons of their own to limit French influence in the Freestate. Their livelihoods depended on access to Milanese markets, which might be cut off if the Freestate appeared to be favoring France. Meanwhile, the Protestant ministers' opposition to all foreign alliances spread unhappiness to other communes as well, so that Stampa's complaints resulted in a "wild storm" of outrage.[52]

Whatever the exact causes of a *Fähnlilupf*, an assembly of the *Fähnli* always had a galvanizing effect on other communes. Separate and inchoate phenomena – factional friction, foreign pressure, and popular unhappiness – merged together once the companies were assembled, producing an institutionalized collective expression of political will. The first detailed information about how the *Fähnli* were summoned and how the impulse spread to raise the banners comes from 1565.[53] Several important conclusions can be drawn from the events between December 1564 and April 1565. First, *Fähnlilüpfe* were not simply spontaneous outbreaks at the local level; instead, widespread discontent about national policies provided the necessary precondition before any commune raised its standard. Second, the most active communes (and the magnates behind them) did everything possible to attract other communes to their cause, sending letters and messengers all over the Freestate. The participants clearly saw their actions taking place on a national, rather than merely on a local scale. Finally, not all districts sent their *Fähnli* to such assemblies willingly; some had to be coerced or did so because they feared being left out of important decisions. Once a sufficient number of communes had decided to act, however, the rest would join in. The unrest of 1565 ended

---

50 Valèr, *Bestrafung*, chapters 9 and 10.
51 Blumenthal, *Die Drei Bünde*, 139–42; Valèr, *Bestrafung*, 151–55. A contemporary description from a Protestant viewpoint, BK I: 42–45 (no. 33).
52 Blumenthal, *Die Drei Bünde*, 139. Swiss Reformed ministers had opposed military alliances since Ulrich Zwingli's day in Zurich.

without a general assembly of all *Fähnli* in the Freestate because not enough communes chose to join the movement.

In 1572, in contrast, *Fähnli* from every district streamed together in Chur, setting a pattern that was followed in 1573, 1607, and repeatedly between 1617 and 1620. As during earlier tumults, the assembly of *Fähnli* in 1572 was preceded by several months of growing popular outrage directed at leading men in the Freestate. The competition between Salis and Planta, Reformed suspicion of Catholic motives, and popular resentment against Johann von Planta's accumulation of power combined to trigger a general uprising. Five *Fähnli* appeared in Chur on March 16, 1572, and by March 23, twenty-two of them were present.[54] While Chur's Protestant ministers were instrumental in raising the hue and cry against Planta, Planta's mortal enemy Dietegen von Salis also played a major role in 1572; it was he who led the *Fähnli* of Castels down to Chur at the beginning of the tumult, setting in motion the process of assembly.[55] Although Planta's disregard for communal power provided the trigger for unrest in 1572, it is easy to see how other sources of discontent helped provoke the assembly. Protestants saw a confessional threat in Planta's bull, as well as a threat to their property; patriots saw their leaders selling out to foreign potentates rather than properly discharging their offices; common men saw corrupt magnates manipulating the political system to cheat the communes out of their income; and followers of the Salis family saw an opportunity to humble their enemies, the Planta. The pattern established in 1572, when a few activist communes set off a gathering of all the communes in Chur, also characterized most subsequent *Strafgerichte*.

Once the companies were assembled, communal ideology and practice played a central legitimating and organizing role in the second phase of most *Strafgerichte*. Most important was the idea that since the Freestate was a voluntary creation of the communes, the communes – embodied as a collectivity of arms-bearing men – retained the power to control it directly. Viewed in this light, the normal political institutions of the Freestate, such as *Bundestag* and *Beitag*, represented no more than temporary delegations of authority.[56] The formalization of the referendum system during this period, in which matters were explicitly referred to the communes for decision by a majority vote, only reinforced the communes' conviction of their own ultimate authority. Commoners consequently felt entitled to speak out whenever their agents failed to act properly, or if they felt that a matter was simply too important to handle through delegated power. Thus, while

[53] On the events of 1565, see F. Jecklin, *Der Engadiner Aufruhr*.
[54] BK III: 307 (no. 282), III: 318 (no. 287). The *Fähnli* of the Val Bregaglia had tried to come to Chur in early February, but was unable to cross the Septimer Pass because of the heavy snow. BK III: 291 (no. 274).
[55] Valèr, *Johann von Planta*, 76. See also 62.
[56] The nature and limits on the delegation of authority became an important issue in Protestant resistance theory of the period. See Skinner, *Foundations*, II: 333–38.

the communes normally exercised their oversight by sending delegates to central assemblies, they also might appear in their entirety, or in the form of a broad selection of their politically active members – namely the militarily competent adult males.[57] Once assembled, the military companies felt entitled to deliberate about every kind of public business, "in the name of and in place of the common Three Leagues according to ancient custom," as a pamphlet put it in 1618.[58]

Even when the companies assembled for other reasons, they still felt authorized to take over the Freestate's policy and business once all were present. The assembly that met at Chiavenna in January, 1585, began when the *Bundestag* ordered each League to prepare 2000 men to send to the Valtellina to suppress a feared invasion. The communes rushed to comply, though no fighting ever took place.[59] Once assembled, however, the troops proposed a set of anti-oligarchic reform articles, the Articles of Chiavenna (*Clevner Artikel*), which were subsequently ratified in modified form by the communes.[60] Although they have been neglected by historians, Rhaetian commoners repeatedly turned to these articles for precedent; they were also important for their vigorous restatement of the principle of confessional coexistence during a period of increasing tension between Protestants and Catholics.[61] Most important in the current context, however, was the way that they were proposed and ratified, which demonstrates both the authority of collective assemblies and the limits on their effectiveness.

The circumstances surrounding the actual drafting of the Chiavenna Articles are obscure. The captains appointed by the *Bundestag* ordered the troops to go home as soon as the military threat dwindled, but the *Fähnli* refused, marching instead into the Valtellina in March and establishing a commission there to investigate misfeasance by the *Bündner* office-holders.[62] Meanwhile, they also sent a set of articles to the *Bundestag* for approval. Most likely, men influential with the assembled troops used the occasion to circulate some kind of draft document that was publicly sanctioned by the soldiers after the immediate threat of a Milanese invasion had faded. The normal authorities had evidently lost control over the *Fähnli* by this point. Notably, later texts refer explicitly to "the articles established by the *Fähnli* in Chiavenna"; while this does not provide evidence about the exact procedure that resulted in the draft articles, the fact that this phrase was used soon after 1585 suggests that it contains a kernel of fact.

---

57 The communes' fighting forces were probably organized by the *Knabenschaften* or *compagnias dils mats*, the young men's associations found in most villages, which were closely tied to local power structures. Padrutt, *Staat und Krieg*, 249. Caduff, *Knabenschaften Graubündens*, 3, 21f.
58 *Grunndtlicher Bericht über den Zuostand gemeiner dreyer Pünten in Rætien*, A iiiᵛ.
59 Valèr, *Bestrafung*, 163–70; Padrutt, *Staat und Krieg*, 250–53; Pieth, *Bündnergeschichte*, 174–77; Moor, *Geschichte von Currätien*, 194–96.
60 Published in JM II: 527–31, and 540–41.
61 JVF, 116–17: article 1 established the liberty of both religions and decreed peaceful relations between Catholics and Protestants, both in the Freestate and in the subject territories.
62 Padrutt, *Staat und Krieg*, 250–52.

The earliest version of the Articles to survive is entitled "Articles, which are to be presented before the *Fähnli* at their camp and at home by the delegates of the common Three Leagues."[63] Both the title and their presence in Chur's council records indicate that the measures were submitted for approval to the communes at home, who soon ratified them. The Fähnli did not assert unlimited authority over public affairs in 1585, therefore, but only the right to make proposals.[64] A second, substantially modified copy of the articles comes from the records of the Shoemaker's Guild in Chur. In them, several provisions that were intended to rein in the oligarchs had already been weakened.[65] Article 3 of the first version sought to limit corruption in the exercise of justice in the Valtellina by forbidding any officer there from exceeding or disobeying the local statutes. The second version of article 3 seemed similar, but contained an Orwellian twist. It stated that "No officer in the Valtellina shall proceed further than the statutes provide, except in case of important reasons."[66] Similarly, article 15 of the original version provided that once the right to fill an office had been assigned to a particular district, the district should proceed to elect the officer by a majority show of hands, without bribes or gifts. The revised version dropped the stipulations about the method and propriety of election, and merely noted that "the council and commune" of the district should fill the office.[67] Over the next two years, further modifications softened the articles' restrictions on the magnates. Although no one ever challenged the authority of the *Fähnli* in 1585, therefore, their actions did not unilaterally bring about a reform of political life. Still, the principle that the assembled military companies had the authority to act directly on behalf of the communes survived to resurface after 1600.

The available evidence about meetings of the *Fähnli* suggests that each commune's company stayed together and voted as a bloc.[68] Nevertheless, most *Fähnlilüpfe* displayed some characteristics that suggest a second, more abstract way in which communal values influenced the proceedings during popular tumults: large assemblies of men might view themselves as embodying the Three Leagues in a single, national commune. This conception, closely tied to a growing national consciousness among the Freestate's inhabitants, was expressed clearly only after 1618, but scattered evidence about such views also survives from earlier tumults.[69] Of course, even if the men assembled during a *Fähnlilupf* imagined that their assembly was simply an extension of regular communal deliberation to national affairs, the truth was different. The very size of the assembled crowd resulted in a

---

[63] JM II: 527–30, col. A.
[64] Initial approval on April 5, 1585: STAG AB IV 1/6, p. 263.
[65] The modified articles are in JM II: 527–31, col. B.
[66] JM II: 527, col. B.
[67] JM II: 530.
[68] The most detailed descriptions in Anhorn, *Püntner Aufruhr*, describing a number of assemblies.
[69] Schreiber, *Entwicklung der Volksrechte*, 45–48. See also Valèr, *Bestrafung*, chapter 6, esp. 130–40.

different process and different results than at local assemblies of individual communes. In addition, whereas communal assemblies were part of existing structures of authority, *Fähnlilüpfe* represented challenges to the way authority was being exercised – challenges in the name of a related but different model of legitimacy.

The first good example of such a broad understanding of a *Fähnlilupf* comes from the Engadine in 1565. The 1200 to 2000 men gathered in Zuoz may have been no more than the military companies of distinct communes, but the language they employed reveals surprising feelings about popular sovereignty. Responding to a Swiss request that they go home, they maintained that:

[The French alliance] did not occur in an orderly fashion with the majority of votes from the communes and from the common man of the Three Leagues; the communes and every honorable confederate (except those distracted by their own interests) took it badly, that the communes' and the common man's freedom [*Fryheit*] should be oppressed and forced in such an important matter by such insolence, force, corruption and money . . . [70]

The letter continued by laying great emphasis on the political role of the common man:

[Our action takes place] no less because the common man in our neighboring communes complained, that the common man was not able to stand forth because of maneuvering, hindrance and threats from such pensioners, and was not able to say his opinion and speak, and was dishonored, and therefore justly turned to us to come to his aid. And we made a friendly appeal to these hinderers, that they should cease these actions and allow the vote of every honorable man to be counted, and that they should not disdain him; but we were unsuccessful. Thereupon we did not want to abandon the common man, but rather wanted to help maintain his privileges against the power of certain [individuals]. And when every person is able to speak his opinion, then the majority ought to be valid.[71]

Here, the populist notion that each commune's decision had to reflect open debate and free voting was paramount; more surprisingly, the letter also argued that one commune could intervene to protect the privileges of the common man elsewhere. Solidarity between the common men in different communes was not meant to abolish the boundaries between communes, yet these passages do suggest that larger assemblies might see themselves as representing the common man in general.

The Swiss delegation reporting back to the Confederacy on the situation in the Engadine wrote that "they are also all of the opinion that the common man in general, the least one as much as the mightiest, ought to be counted, along with

---

[70] F. Jecklin, *Der Engadiner Aufruhr*, 79. I have translated *fryheit* as "freedom" here, rather than as "privilege," although a more traditional usage of the word to mean "privilege" appears later in the letter.

[71] *Ibid.*, 79.

various other articles."[72] Naturally, such rhetoric might be no more than a tactic in a political struggle between elite factions beholden to foreign powers. To intrepret it, one must therefore distinguish who was making populist statements for what reason. The leaders of the Engadine uprising in 1565 – the authors of these texts – may have used populist language cynically to strengthen their position against the pro-French faction led by the Salis. Yet this does not mean that the men assembled in Zuoz under their banners were insincere in their support for the principles these statements contained. A powerful pensioner of the Spanish crown might call for an end to all alliances as a tactic to block the French alliance, whereas a common peasant who bought his grain and sold his cheese in Como might see neutrality not only as the safest way to secure his livelihood, but also as a legitimate decision reflecting popular will. That political rhetoric of this kind meant different things to different people does not imply that some people were wrong about what it meant, others correct. Especially in Rhaetia, where common men could visibly influence the course of events (even if their influence was subject to manipulation by others), the idea of popular power became more and more effective in stimulating political action.

When a large number of angry commoners assembled, events often took on a momentum of their own. While the actual assemblies are poorly documented, certain patterns emerge from the available evidence. First, such assemblies did not shy away from violence, either against the magnates by whom they felt betrayed, or against communes that took a minority position. In 1572, an armed mob sent by a *Strafgericht* seized Johann von Planta in Laax and carried him back to Chur and his death, and in 1607 an armed troop of Engadiners seized George Beeli and Caspar Baselga, laid them in chains, and saw to their eventual execution. In April, 1607, Maienfeld's *Fähnli* felt so threatened because of its minority opinions that its troops would not attend an assembly without their weapons.[73] Not much later, the *Strafgericht* in Chur sent several hundred troops to Davos to force the commune to submit; an open battle was only narrowly averted.[74]

Second, the assembled troops operated according to a very public and coercive form of majoritarianism: any important decision was reached by assembling the *Fähnli* and holding a public vote (by communes, not by heads).[75] Minority views could endanger individuals in their communes, or communes who disagreed with the rest of the assembly. Personal presence and forceful argument carried more weight under such conditions than did formal procedures, although the *Fähnli* probably drew upon their experience at communal assemblies to organize such meetings. Third, despite the general hostility towards the "big shots" displayed during *Fähnlilüpfe*, not every magnate was in danger. Even during the most tumultuous days, some members of elite families continued to lead their *Fähnli* and

---

[72] *Ibid.*, 82 (undated report from Swiss delegates). [73] Anhorn, *Püntner Aufruhr*, 20–21.
[74] *Ibid.*, 139–44. [75] See esp. *ibid.*, 20–23.

represent their communes.[76] Despite his bitter comments about the common man, for example, Fortunat von Juvalta stayed with his Engadiners throughout the tumult of 1607. After all, the communes' purpose was never revolutionary: they sought not to eliminate their leaders, but to discipline them to serving the "common good." The appearance of legality remained important, even during the embittered conflicts of 1617–19, and the *Fähnli* sought to reinforce such an appearance by recruiting educated men from the elite families as judges and scribes. The ongoing factional infighting among the magnates, moreover, meant that some families might ally themselves with a *Fähnlilupf* at any given moment.

Finally, it is remarkable that single individuals never rose to prominence, even temporarily, as leaders or spokesmen for the *Fähnli*. Uncertainty and tumultuous disorder might seem the perfect occasion for charismatic leaders to emerge, but visible leadership during a *Fähnlilupf* remained relentlessly collective. While this might be partly because magnates preferred to wield their influence behind the scenes, it also demonstrates the impact of communalism on the thinking of *Fähnlilupf* participants. A movement legitimated by communal values and directed against those who had overstepped the limits of communally granted offices provided an inauspicious environment for charismatic individualism. The greatest hostility was directed precisely at the "overmighty," thus discouraging any tendency towards the establishment of popular dictators. Neither in mythology nor in actual struggles did Rhaetian political culture allow for individual heroism or for demagogic leadership.

Popular demands for reform

When they assembled, the *Fähnli* often drafted a bill of articles intended to correct abuses in the Freestate. Such articles are a crucial source for understanding the political culture of the Freestate, since they were proposed and debated before a large number of common men. Rather than detail the specific circumstances around each surviving bill of articles, the following section will present an overview of the contents of these *Artikel-briefe* in the context of other reform efforts during the same period.[77]

---

76 The list of judges appointed by the *Fähnli* in mid-April, 1607, is instructive. Many of the judges came from families rarely heard of, but others were appointed from the major lineages: the Stampa, Travers, Tscharner, à Porta, and Salis served next to families otherwise obscure. *Ibid.*, 31–32.

77 The following sets of articles are included in this survey, which includes both articles established by the *Fähnli*, and other reform articles. Because some articles contained several provisions, the number of articles is not identical to the number of specific points discussed below. First Ilanzer Articles of April 4, 1524 (JVF, 78–83); *Bundesbrief* of September 23, 1524 (JVF, 83–89); Second Ilanzer Articles of June 25, 1526 (JVF, 89–93); articles of the *Strafgericht* of February 20, 1542 (JM II: no. 219); articles of complaint made to Swiss delegates at Davos, March 4, 1550 (EA IV.I.e: 235f); Engadine Articles of December 29, 1564 (JM II: no. 345); Engadine Articles of January 22 and

No single coherent position characterized the scores of articles written at ten assemblies of the *Fähnli* spread across sixty years, nor were the proposals made by the *Fähnli* always systematically different from reform proposals proposed by other sources. Every *Fähnlilupf* was the result of specific circumstances, and was led by specific men who often had ties to certain factions. Each set of articles had a specific context, which must be considered if the articles are not to be misunderstood. But taking a broad view does reveal certain trends about the political development of the Freestate. For example, although opinions varied about which locus of corruption most urgently needed correction, the perception was constant that corrupt magistrates threatened the Freestate. Views about how institutions ought be changed to restore right order changed a great deal, but without challenging the unwavering conviction that punishment of miscreants, combined with administrative changes, would provide the ultimate answer. Looking at these proposals synoptically over several decades provides a unique insight into the developing ideologies of common as well as elite *Bündner*.

The articles written after 1540 make it immediately apparent that the issues of the early sixteenth century no longer attracted the common man's political attention. Matters that dominated earlier documents – the relationship between secular authority and the church for the First Ilanz Articles, the maintenance of political order and public peace for the *Bundesbrief*, and the economic and social foundations of lordship for the Second Ilanz Articles – disappeared by the midsixteenth century. Religion, peace and lordship were still subjects of contention, of course, but the *Fähnli* did not address them directly. Only two religious issues drew attention from the *Fähnli* after 1540: that the two established confessions in Rhaetia should be free and should coexist in peace, and that clerics should not involve themselves in politics.[78] Nor did the *Fähnli* meddle with the fundamental organization codified in the *Bundesbrief* of 1524. Many efforts were made to modify the details of the Freestate's governance, but not by amending the *Bundesbrief* itself.[79] Even the frustrated *Fähnli* in 1618, who passed an article stating that

---

January 23, 1565 (JM II: no. 347); articles of the *Strafgericht* in Chur, May 8, 1572 (JM II: no. 411); articles of the *Strafgericht* in Thusis, May 26, 1573 (JM II: 422); reform proposal of 1584 (STAG A II 1/2452); Chiavenna Articles of February, 1585 (JM II: no. 498), with modifications of June 26, 1586 (JM II: no. 507); reform proposal of May 29, 1600 (STAC CB III Z 54, 1600, also at STAG B 1538/7, fol. 70–77); Great Reform of January 31, 1603 (JVF, 119–29); articles of the *Strafgericht* at Chur, April 10, 1607 (Anhorn, *Pündner Aufruhr*, 32–36); articles of the *Strafgericht* at Chur, July 4, 1607 (Anhorn, *Pündner Aufruhr*, 133–36); reform proposals of July 13, 1609 (STAG AB IV 5/2, pp. 17–29); articles of the assembly of the Chadè in Chur, June 14, 1617 (STAG A II LA I, 1617, June 14); articles of the *Strafgericht* at Thusis, August 3, 1618 (STAG A II LA I, 1618, August 3); articles of the *Strafgericht* at Thusis, November 12, 1618 (JVF, 129–32); articles of the assembly at Chur, June 11, 1619 (JVF, 132–34); and finally the articles of the assembly at Zizers, October 14, 1619 (JVF, 134–36).

78 The first in 1585, 1618, and 1619; the second in 1607, 1617, and 1619.
79 This even though the *Bundesbrief* specifically provided for future modifications.

"our estate should be improved," nevertheless proceeded on the basis of the *Bundesbrief*.[80] Instead, *Fähnlilüpfe* after 1550 concentrated on the problems that emerged as a *result* of the Freestate's establishment. Relations with foreign powers and the communes' control over central assemblies were the most frequent topics. Articles aimed at preventing corruption in domestic affairs were also common. Many other articles concerned the subject territories: here, the appointment and control of officers, the prevention of fiscal corruption, and enforcing the Freestate's essentially exploitative relationship with its subjects gave rise to the largest number of provisions. A few articles from each *Fähnlilupf* regulated the establishment and competence of popular tribunals, the *Strafgerichte per se*. Finally, confirmations of earlier statutes and administrative regulations typically appeared among these articles.

As the tumults from 1542 to 1565 made abundantly clear, foreign alliances frequently caused open discontent in the Freestate. The articles passed by *Fähnli* also reflect this fact: between 1565 and 1620, no fewer than 36 individual articles out of some 120 total focused on this particular problem. Reform efforts written by the *Bundestag* or by appointed commissions, in contrast, put much less stress on foreign alliances, producing only a dozen articles specifically addressing the issue; the Great Reform of 1603 did not address foreign alliances at all. The thirty-six articles proposed by the *Fähnli* fell into three groups. The most radical demanded the abrogation of all foreign alliances, sought to deny all foreign powers the privilege of sending troops across the Rhaetian passes, and called for the expulsion of all foreign ambassadors. Ironically, such articles were often promoted by the Spanish faction, which preferred no alliances to an alliance with France. A second, more moderate position proposed limiting foreign alliances to those already made with Austria and France, allowing troops to pass only with express permission from the communes, and permitting ambassadors only at the *Bundestag*, and only for a short period of time. All such articles assumed that foreign entanglements should be avoided, or at least carefully controlled. The issue of ambassadors also carried anti-oligarchic overtones, since the magnate families were the primary beneficiaries of foreign ambassadors' bribes. Neither the questions nor the possible answers to diplomatic problems changed significantly between 1565 and 1620; indeed, debate over just these matters had been going on since the late fourteenth century and would last, with interruptions, until the French Revolution. A third type of article regarding foreign alliances took a somewhat different tack. Rather than addressing the substance of alliances, these articles attempted to regulate the process by which they were reached. The most important target was foreign pensions. One assembly after another demanded that pensioners of foreign princes should not hold office in the Freestate, that communes which accepted bribes should be punished, and that

[80] STAG A II LA 1, 1618, August 3.

all foreign pensions should be distributed equally among the communes. These articles took aim at internal corruption, rather than at foreign alliances themselves.[81]

Prohibitions of pensions were directed not only at individuals, but also at communes. The radical articles of March 1565 demanded that "in each and every commune, every male person [should] swear an oath to God and the Holy Trinity, that he will henceforth accept no money, pension or gift from any foreign prince or lord, on the penalty of honor and goods."[82] The articles of 1617 also took direct aim at corrupt communes:

Sixth, the communes and districts that negotiated and that also accepted bribes and gifts on account of the Venetian alliance or the Spanish capitulation, should be punished by the established tribunal; and if they accepted promises of future [bribes or gifts], they should no longer be authorized nor entitled to participate in any more voting [*Mehren*], but should rather be excluded with their vote from the League's majorities, as well as being punished without mercy as oathbreakers . . . [83]

Confronted not only with corrupt individuals, but also with entire communes whose votes had been bought, some Rhaetian *Fähnlilüpfe* in the early seventeenth century tried to preserve the integrity of their political system by reaffirming their prohibition of foreign influence from bottom to top.

More often, though, the *Fähnli* approached this problem by treating foreign bribes as a public resource that ought to be distributed equally. In April 1607, for example, the *Fähnli* declared:

Fourth, pensions and gifts of honors to individual persons, which come from foreign princes and lords, should by all means be abolished in our land of the III Leagues, no matter the estate [of the recipients], on the penalty of death, corporal punishment, fine or loss of honor, [and] they are to be prosecuted without exception; but instead all pensions which have hitherto been given to individuals should belong to our lands in common along with the annual subsidy [*Jargelt*].[84]

Such measures had been proposed as early as 1542.[85] Not only would such a rule prevent foreign princes from bribing influential individuals, but it also fit communal ideals about the distribution of public goods. Since access to mercenaries and the privilege to cross the Rhaetian passes were public resources of the Freestate, whose members were the communes, the profits from such resources ought to go directly to those communes. Public distribution of foreign pensions thus sought to preserve the benefits of foreign alliances while minimizing the divisive consequences that accompanied their creation. That such proposals would have institutionalized the influence of donors was a small price to pay for ending the

---

[81] See Valèr, *Bestrafung*, 50–52. The Swiss Confederacy passed a similar statute in 1503. HSG I: 349.
[82] JM II: 353.
[83] STAG A II LA 1, 1617, June 14.
[84] Anhorn, *Püntner Aufruhr*, 35.   [85] Articles of 1542, article 3.

violent struggles between communes and factions who accepted large bribes from competing princes.

Fähnli articles regarding domestic affairs in the Freestate differed from those about foreign policy in that they addressed procedural matters rather than establishing policy. In part this followed from the structure of decision-making in the Freestate. Since the confederation as a whole had few domestic functions, and exercised very little authority over internal affairs of the communes, there was little here for the *Fähnli* to reform. Most important to the communes was protecting the flow of information between the *Bundestag* and themselves, while other articles sought to prevent corruption in the election and actions of communal delegates. Two other categories of articles relating to domestic affairs became common after about 1600: affirmations of the Freestate's older constitutional documents, such as the *Bundesbrief*, and detailed instructions for the tribunals being established to punish the guilty.[86]

Ensuring that delegates to the *Bundestag* approved only decisions acceptable to their communes, and ensuring that the communes were accurately informed about what took place at the *Bundestag* were two issues of great concern to the communes throughout the sixteenth century. Their concern often manifested itself in *Fähnli* articles regulating the responsibilities of delegates at the *Bundestag*. Two parallel provisions were common. First, each delegate should carry written instructions, validated with his commune's seal, specifying exactly what the delegate might approve or reject, and what he had to refer back home; and second, on his return from the *Bundestag*, each delegate should bring a written and sealed recess (*Abschied*) clearly describing all decisions that had been reached. Such demands appeared in the *Fähnli* articles of 1565 and in the articles of most of the *Fähnlilüpfe* after 1600. Reforms proposed by the *Fähnli* differed from reform measures proposed from other quarters in their emphasis on securing the channels of communication between *Bundestag* and communes. The direct correlation between assemblies of the *Fähnli* and the appearance of these specific demands shows that broader political participation was one of the communes' goals. Article 14 of March 23, 1565, laid out the entire program:

Now since the delegates often step beyond their communes' instructions, through which the communes are misled and [their authority] is not brought to bear: it might be good if every delegate were to receive his commune's instructions in writing with a seal, and that the councilors of the Chadè should afterwards bring sealed letters, that [the delegate] had carried out his commands faithfully and had not stepped beyond them. Also, whatever was discussed, that he should dutifully bring a written and sealed report back to his commune.[87]

---

[86] The numbers of individual provisions on these issues were as follows: control of delegates, sixteen; corruption, six; management of *Strafgerichte*, sixteen; and reaffirmation of older statutes, twenty-two.

[87] JM II: 352.

The communes' concern with the flow of information between commune and central assembly reflected their fear that authority was moving to the Freestate's central institutions, where wealth and corruption could more easily influence the outcome. In addition, it shows how little most Rhaetians trusted human nature. Whether a few magnates or all the assembled peasants controlled any given commune, they viewed the personal weakness of their agents as a threat to their polity. The *Fähnli* sought not institutional change, therefore, but rather the enforcement of individual accountability within the political process. If his leaders were honest, the Rhaetian common man believed, God would reward the Freestate with good fortune.

A distinctive feature that appeared in bills of articles after 1600 was the explicit reconfirmation of older constitutional documents, usually starting with the *Bundesbrief* of 1524. Such reavowals set forth the *Fähnli*'s understanding of the Freestate, in order to legitimate actions taken in defense of that understanding. The *Bundesbrief* was mentioned in nine of the ten separate bills of *Fähnli* articles between 1600 and 1620; only the assembly of August 3, 1618 did not devote an article specifically to it, although the *Fähnli* did order punishment for anyone who had "acted against our free estate, gotten involved with princes, acted against the *Bundesbrief*, or gravely misbehaved in some other way."[88] The *Fähnli* also reaffirmed other documents: the Ilanz Articles, the *Kesselbrief* of 1570 and the Great Reform of 1603 each appeared in three articles, while the *Pensionenbrief* of 1500 and the Chiavenna Articles each appeared once. Two revealing articles from 1617 and 1619 provided that the current set of articles should be read to the communes every year in the same fashion as statutes and the *Bundesbrief*: the assembled *Fähnli* apparently saw their own creations as parallel to the Freestate's founding documents.[89]

Yet drawing attention to the *Bundesbrief* as the source and symbol of the Freestate's integrity had important conceptual repercussions. The *Bundesbrief* was explicitly the product of the communes' will. Putting it at the heart of efforts to reform the Freestate, therefore, emphasized both the communes' authority and freedom, as well as the collective nature of authority in the state they had created. Evoking the *Bundesbrief* thus implied seemingly contradictory messages: it encompassed both the autonomy and authority of the individual communes, and the unity of the established Freestate. The assembled *Fähnli* represented a practical expression of the same duality. They gathered under the military banners of the individual districts and voted by commune, yet so many men gathered in one place to deliberate the future of their state formed a *de facto* national assembly, a single commune embracing the entire Freestate. It would therefore be mistaken to interpret the *Fähnlilüpfe* of the early seventeenth century simply as evidence of

---

[88] STAG A II LA 1, 1618, August 3, article 5.
[89] Article 14 of June 14, 1617, and article 6 of October 14, 1619.

fragmentation at the center of the Freestate. They could bring orderly politics to a halt, of course, but the repeated assemblies of fighting men between 1607 and 1620 also encouraged a sense of shared identity that was expressed as loyalty to the *Bundesbrief*. Long after the elite factions had descended into fanatical hatred for one another in 1619, the *Fähnli* attempted to preserve the communes' union by means of articles which both reasserted the historical foundations of the Freestate and addressed sources of corruption and conflict.[90]

The largest and most important remaining category of provisions passed by assemblies of the *Fähnli* concerned the administration of the Freestate's subjects in the Valtellina. Like reform programs from other quarters, these articles focused primarily on corruption; unlike others, however, they often went into detail about the election of officers and about administrative practice. With few exceptions, these articles sought to ensure that the profits from lordship flowed to the communes rather than to individuals, and that the allocation of profits among communes was equal or at least proportional. Lofty statements about the need to rule justly were mostly left in preambles and other documents, without having any practical consequences. Whereas corruption in the Freestate itself was seen as a threat to the communes' authority and autonomy, corruption in the Valtellina represented a threat to their income.

Taken as a whole, the articles proposed by *Fähnli* reveal certain deep-seated aspects of political culture in the Freestate. Most important is their generally reformist rather than revolutionary tenor. Born in most cases of widespread frustration directed at a narrow clique of families, the articles treated corruption, rather than institutional weakness or social injustice, as the greatest threat to the Freestate. After the great changes of the early Reformation, no popular movement sought to change the basic legal or social organization of Rhaetian society. Instead, the communes insisted on their own ultimate authority, and passed measure after measure intended to ensure that officers of the Freestate did not behave like lords possessing authority of their own. The communes' single most common demand was that delegates to the *Bundestag* act simply as messengers, carrying written instructions from their communes and returning with written reports on common deliberations. By themselves, such provisions might seem to be evidence of a corrosive particularism intended to preserve the complete autonomy of the communes. But the second most common kind of article belies this impression: after 1600, the communes went out of their way to reaffirm their commitment to the *Bundesbrief* and the common identity it stood for. Communes in this period often wrangled about whether a collective decision had been reached properly, but only rarely did they openly reject the authority of the Freestate to reach decisions at all. Even when the tensions arising from confessional division and factional strife reached a high point before 1620, the *Fähnli* in particular kept insisting that the

---

[90] Cf. the patriotic language found in Zizers Articles of 1619. JVF 134–36.

Three Leagues needed to hold together. Faced with domestic tumult and foreign pressure, the *Fähnli* spoke out for the unity and common authority of their alliance.

Along with passing articles intended to reform their polity, the gathered *Fähnli* of the Freestate also established penal courts, the *Strafgerichte* that lent their name to outbreaks of unrest in the Freestate. The organizational roots of the courts are found primarily in traditional German and military law, although mediated through the communal experience of the men in the *Fähnli*. In the very earliest examples, the practices of military justice predominated, as far as we can tell, whereas the courts established during the early and mid-sixteenth century mirrored the regular criminal procedure of the communes. A synthesis of these two trends took place in the tumults after 1565, when penal courts were established directly by the military companies. *Strafgerichte* differed from normal courts in their large size – often with fifty or more jurors – and by the presence of overseers (*Gäumer*) appointed by the companies. At the end of the sixteenth century, several efforts were undertaken to create regular panels of censors appointed by the communes, who would punish political offenses against the Freestate and, it was hoped, prevent unrest from breaking out in the form of *Fähnlilupfe*. Such panels, had they been implemented, would have detached popular justice from the military companies' control once again. The events of the early seventeenth century, however, showed that censorial justice was not effective, so that the companies continued to establish penal courts throughout the seventeenth century.

As was the case for tumultuous popular assemblies, large-scale political trials had a long history in the Freestate. The earliest recorded case of such a penal court took place in 1450, after the count of Werdenberg-Sargans tried to force the commune of Schams to accept lordly control. The evidence about this event, almost all of which comes from folktales and patriotic myths, indicates the central role that the military companies played in League justice early on. The story tells that George of Rhäzüns, a noble member of the Gray League, swore to help the count of Sargans by allowing soldiers to pass unhindered through his lordship on the way to Schams. Despite a surprise night march, however, the lords' troops were defeated by the companies of the Gray League and their allies from the Chadè, who then seized George and sentenced him to death for his participation in the "Black League" of the lords against the communes. Only the actions of his loyal servant, who plied the assembled *Fähnli* with food and drink while praising his lord's generosity, saved George, who was pardoned by the companies on condition that he reswear his fealty to the Gray League.[91]

What actually occurred in 1450 is less important than what this story – already

---

[91] The story appears in this form in sixteenth- and seventeenth-century sources: Sprecher, *Geschichte*, I: 18, and Campell, *Zwei Bücher*, II: 119. The most detailed modern description in Planta, *Geschichte von Graubünden*, 123–27. Interpreted in light of military justice in Valèr, *Bestrafung*, 141–43.

current in the sixteenth century – reveals about how Rhaetians thought unfaithful leaders ought to be punished. The lord of Rhäzüns was one of the three lords (*Hauptherren*) who had sworn membership in the Gray League; consequently, George's crime was violating his oath to the League. His trial took place not before the regular appeals court of the League (which was already well established by 1450), nor before the criminal court of a single commune. Rather, he was tried by the military companies collectively. The troops not only represented the communes as injured parties, but also acted as judges on the basis of the League they had sworn together.[92]

Subsequent *Strafgerichte* also combined military with civil procedure. A public prosecutor appointed by each commune or League (the *Kläger*), would call upon anyone who knew of persons deserving punishment to step forward and accuse them, and then called on those accused to defend themselves before a special assembly. Such inquisitorial procedures did not take place in Rhaetian communal justice, and probably derived from military trials. The assembled *Fähnli* represented the injured party, just as the assembled troops did in contemporary Swiss military justice.[93] Even after the *Fähnli* departed, the overseers (*Gäumer*) reproduced their role. Such overseers not only guarded the court from outside meddling, they also validated its verdicts. Their presence also created enormous pressure for guilty verdicts against the hated "corrupters of the fatherland."

The first concrete evidence about a court established directly by the *Fähnli* comes from 1550, although the outlines of the affair are unclear.[94] When the renewal of the French alliance triggered unrest, several communes in the Ten Jurisdictions reached for their weapons and seized two leading politicians, Valentin Gregori of Maienfeld and Johann Guler, *Landamman* of Davos.[95] The two *Fähnli* that started the affair, Castels and Klosters, raised about 300 men. Swiss mediators who reached Davos about two weeks later were told that each commune in the Ten Jurisdictions had delegated thirty armed men "only for the protection of the court, so that everyone might be treated justly."[96] The Swiss requested that the prisoners be freed, or that they at least be allowed to present evidence in their defense, but the communes refused. Instead, the rebellious assembly established a special court, "but skipped over honorable and skilled persons, who had previously presided over courts and the administration of justice."[97] This court then proceeded with both civil and criminal trials against some twenty defendants, especially Gregori and *Landamman* Guler, who were condemned to exclusion from office for seven years. When the verdicts were presented to the communes for approval, five voted to

---

[92] Valèr, *Bestrafung*, 142.
[93] *Ibid.*, 120–30.
[94] The main sources are EA IV.1.e: 230–31, and 234–41.
[95] Blumenthal, *Die Drei Bünde*, 177–87; Gillardon, *Geschichte des Zehngerichtenbundes*, 102–04.
[96] EA IV.1.e: 235.   [97] EA IV.1.e: 236.

accept milder charges, two insisted on the original indictment that called for corporal punishment, while Davos wanted to submit the question to a public assembly of the commune. After some argument, the majority opinion prevailed. After the sentences had been handed down, the Swiss again requested mercy for the defendants, but were rebuffed "in view of the [present] unrest and because of the communes"; a later request for modification of the sentences was denied "because the unrest was still heated."[98] Several features typical of later *Strafgerichte* appeared in 1550: creation of the court by large numbers of men from the communes, seizure and trials of leading figures who barely escaped with their lives, and attention to judicial procedure despite an atmosphere that made a fair trial nearly impossible.

The courts established during the larger and more violent tumults of 1565 and 1572 showed the same characteristics. The court of 1565 in the Engadine convened after over a thousand men had gathered in Zuoz; the court of 1572 followed the appearance of over twenty *Fähnli* in Chur. Confirming the tendencies visible in 1550, the court of 1572 was very large and was "protected" by an even larger number of overseers appointed by the communes. Reports differ on the court's exact size: the number of jurors reported varies between 30 and 100, the number of overseers between 210 and 600.[99] Two reasons explain why these courts tended to be large. On the one hand, since they were courts of the Three Leagues, all members of the Leagues sought to be represented. Particularly if the matter was grave, every commune wanted an agent there to ensure that its voice was heard, and to ensure that the commune got its share of the fines. On the other hand, such courts were large because the *Fähnli* saw this as a way of minimizing corruption. Fear of magnate influence could be assuaged by placing a large number of "common men" on the jury, men who had not accepted foreign pensions and who were not, it was hoped, beholden to the magnate families.[100] Leaving large numbers of overseers also ensured that the court would continue to respect the wishes of the *Fähnli*. Who appointed these overseers is harder to determine: most likely, they answered to local leaders while remaining within the constraints set by majority opinion within each commune.[101]

Historians of the Freestate have often dismissed these popular courts as outbursts of blind passion on the part of ignorant mobs, or as one more weapon in factional disputes among the Freestate's political elite. The first view, which draws upon abundant remarks by contemporary observers among the Rhaetian elite and from neighboring countries, fails to explain the course of events during

---

[98] EA IV.I.e: 239.
[99] Valèr, *Planta*, 78.
[100] See BK III: 322 (no. 289), BK III: 319 (no. 287).
[101] Padrutt's suggestion that the associations of unmarried men, the *Cumpagnias dils mats* or *Knabenschaften*, played a decisive role seems plausible. *Staat und Krieg*, 99, 249, and Caduff, *Knabenschaften*, 112, 191.

Strafgerichte, and represents a conservative attempt to portray popular action as unreasoned and elemental.[102] Aroused passions – among the magnates as well as among the "common man" – certainly influenced the course of *Strafgerichte*, but did not determine their structure or outcome. The second analysis of Rhaetian *Strafgerichte* is more useful, and contains more than a grain of truth. In the older historiography, the factions appear to be primarily confessional in character, whereas newer work emphasizes foreign influence within an oligarchic context.[103] Factional conflict certainly played an important role in the creation and course of all of these tumults: dissatisfaction with the French alliance was the trigger in 1550 and 1565, and opposition between the Salis and Planta figured prominently in 1572, as did Protestant fears of papal intervention. But an interpretation that reduces these phenomena to power struggles without considering their ideological dimension is also inadequate. Too much evidence suggests that these uprisings were informed by political values founded on communalism and popular participation. Like peasant revolts all over Europe during the early modern period, Rhaetian *Fähnlilüpfe* were deeply legitimist in their outlook; the legitimacy they were defending, however, was populist and communalist.

In fact, the Rhaetian *Fähnlilupf* and *Strafgericht* must be viewed as creative responses to threats to public order as they were perceived by a broad spectrum of Rhaetian citizens. The observable tendency toward consistent organization and practice that appeared between 1550 and 1620 testifies to the institutionalization of the entire phenomenon within the Freestate's political system. In one form or another, *Fähnlilüpfe* and popular courts occurred every ten to fifteen years for some seventy years – often enough for them to remain vivid in everyone's memory, and often enough for them to develop a tradition of their own. Despite the varying factional and confessional constellations surrounding their creation, and despite the vast differences in how effectively they resulted in "justice," *Fähnlilüpfe* and *Strafgerichte* were familiar and recognizable events by the turn of the seventeenth century. While they drew on elements which also appeared in the spectrum of popular discontent in the rest of Switzerland and across southern Germany, the particular combination of features found in Graubünden is distinctive.

By around 1600, then, two contradictory trends troubled the public life of the Rhaetian Freestate. On the one hand, some families had separated themselves from the general population through their wealth, prestige, and control over public offices. Although internally divided and not formally defined as a social estate, the upper echelons of this elite exercised tremendous influence over political affairs. On

---

[102] Such a view of peasant rebellion has been applied by conservative historians since Ranke. Cf. Schulze, "Europäische und deutsche Bauernrevolten," 11f.
[103] Blumenthal still follows the confessional model; representatives of a factional view include Padrutt, Grimm, and Färber.

the other hand, political culture in the Freestate increasingly stressed the exclusive legitimacy of collective political action. When Rhaetians spoke of their lords, they meant the assembled communes, not the emperor, the bishop of Chur, or the ambitious magnates among them. The legitimacy of collective action also justified *Fähnlilüpfe* and *Strafgerichte* – patterns of behavior that were unique to the Freestate, and that posed a major obstacle to the expansion of oligarchic rule.[104] *Fähnlilüpfe* reasserted the ultimate authority of the communes against every effort the new elite made to control them. Because the assembled communes acted on the conviction that they were participating in legitimate governance, they frequently escaped the control of the magnates who normally dominated the Freestate socially and politically.

The distinction between "elite" and "communes" is, like most analytic categories, somewhat artificial. That the political communes had become key power centers for the entire Freestate is indisputable, but that did not mean that they were all fully communal in their organization. In some communes, the elite families consolidated their hold during the sixteenth century. During a *Strafgericht*, the *Fähnli* from such a commune might support the interests of its dominant families, rather than of a larger segment of the population. Even where no single family predominated, we do not really know how the men who made up a *Fähnli* were chosen, and there is little reason to assume that they represented the entire population in an unbiased way. The individual communes were each power systems of their own, and thus prone to inequality, manipulation, and the exercise of personal power. Nevertheless, the tension between oligarchic and communal authority was a real one, as the tumults of the late sixteenth century demonstrate. Once a *Fähnlilupf* had taken place, no magnate could be certain that his commune would continue to support his faction's interests: the whole often behaved according to different rules than did the individual parts. The relative freedom of the *Fähnli* from factional control was increased by the deep divisions within the magnate class. The power and deference that magnates usually enjoyed tended to cancel themselves out in factional tension, leaving the *Fähnli* more room to heed the interests of the larger population.

A state and society in which *de facto* social dominance by one group was confronted with such ideological and institutional challenges was vulnerable to instability, as the history of the Rhaetian Freestate in the early seventeenth century amply demonstrates. Both of the trends described above increased in strength, despite the incommensurate views about society and polity they relied upon. Political realities also had ideological repercussions. Members of the most powerful families increasingly turned to hierarchical social philosophies from the surrounding world – to feudalism, to neo-Stoicism, or to loyalty to foreign rulers.

---

[104] The closest parallels are the *Mazzen*, similar collective outbursts which took place in the Valais, which was the other rural communal confederacy associated with the Swiss Confederation.

Meanwhile, more radical thinkers began celebrating popular sovereignty, encouraging the "common man" to take further control over his state. Before examining such shifts in ideas, though, we must turn to the Freestate's political fortunes after 1585.

6

Reform, communal action and crisis,
ca. 1580–1639

You'll say that the cause of such inconstancy is the form of our republic, which is made up
of democracy and oligarchy mixed together.

Johannes Fabricius, 1558[1]

Born during the brief era around 1500 when the Swiss were more than mere pawns
on the European stage, the Rhaetian Freestate flourished during the sixteenth
century, while France, Germany, and Austria were all distracted by fragmentation
and religious discord. By the end of the century, however, the international climate
in Europe had changed. France, no longer torn by civil war, renewed its struggle
with the Habsburg empire in Spain and in Austria, which was itself overcoming
internal weaknesses. After the Peace of Augsburg of 1555, moreover, tension
between Catholics and Protestants in Germany rose, exacerbated by Calvinism's
growing potency. As confessional camps consolidated, the lines of conflict between
them became clearer and more likely to align with great-power struggles over
territory and trade. The polarized European world of 1600 presented new dangers
to a small and strategically located state like the Rhaetian Freestate. Growing social
and ideological tension within the Freestate became inextricably linked with larger
battles between Habsburg and Valois, and between Catholic and Protestant all over
Europe, nearly destroying the Freestate in the process.

The Freestate's own political history after 1550 proceeded within the frameworks built up over the previous century or so: the institutional framework outlined
in 1525 and 1526, and the conceptual framework of values found in Rhaetian
political rhetoric. Power in the Freestate took a distinctive form because of
the institutions – social, economic and political – that articulated it; similarly, the
character of legitimacy in the Freestate cannot be understood without reference to
the structure of values shared by most of its inhabitants. Yet these structures were
themselves the result of how power had been distributed earlier, and how earlier
Rhaetians had conceptualized their political situation. The ongoing reciprocal
relationship between structures and the forces that animate them appears
constantly in Rhaetian politics of this period. Thus, the outcome of the struggles

---

[1] BK II: 75, (no. 82).

168

Reform, communal action and crisis

over power and authority in the late sixteenth-century Freestate depended directly on earlier conditions, including lords extinct or weakened to the point of impotence, and well-developed communal structures and values unscarred by defeat in 1525.[2] The patterns that developed from this constellation of circumstances outlined the possibilities for subsequent generations of Rhaetians, until the larger tides of European conflict swept away most of the Freestate's autonomy after 1620.

Internal political developments in Graubünden from 1580 to 1620 fall into four phases. During the first, from 1585 to 1607, it appeared that the Freestate's inhabitants might succeed in balancing popular and elite power within the republic's institutions. The *Fähnlilüpfe* of 1573 and 1585 had revealed a broad desire for reforms intended to limit the elite families and to cement the communes' control over their shared Leagues. Reform efforts continued until 1603, when the communes ratified the Great Reform, establishing a new framework for Rhaetian government at home and over the subject territories. During the same years, the Freestate reaffirmed its diplomatic ties with the Swiss. Although efforts to make Rhaetia a full member of the Swiss Confederacy failed, the Freestate nevertheless gained important support from its closer relations with the Protestant cantons. But the changing international situation, and particularly the cutting of the "Spanish Road" from Genoa through the Savoy to the Netherlands in 1601, resulted in greatly increased pressure from the outside on the Freestate's internal institutions – pressure they were ill equipped to manage.

The second phase began after a violent *Fähnlilupf* and *Strafgericht* in 1607 brought about an abrupt change in the Freestate's political life. Revealing both a frightening vulnerability to foreign manipulation and a deep gulf between Rhaetian leaders and their communes, the struggles of 1607 initiated a decade of cautious maneuvering during which the reform movement faded while factional and confessional tension increased. All Europe walked carefully during the decade after 1608, fearing and anticipating the war that finally began in 1618. Within the Freestate, a final effort in 1612 and 1613 to reestablish concord and to punish corruption proved fruitless, even as foreign manipulation became more and more blatant among the Rhaetian elite. The fronts were already drawn for the third phase, the violent domestic struggles that tore the Freestate between 1616 and 1622.

In 1616 as in earlier tumults, foreign alliances provided the trigger for a period of unrest. This time, however, the mechanisms that had previously limited disruption failed, because of heightened hostility within the Freestate, and because of vastly increased pressure from abroad. Particularly after 1618, the crucial importance of the Valtellina passes meant that both Habsburg and Bourbon focused great

---

[2] These preconditions represent a mirror-image to those proposed by Thomas Brady for Southern Germany, in his study *Turning Swiss*. Whereas the German cities had to survive in an environment of resurgent princes and defeated peasants, the Rhaetian elite had to cope with the marginalized lords and increasingly confident peasant communes.

attention on the course of events in Chur, while closer neighbors such as Venice did their best to bend the Freestate to their interests. Partly in response to such pressures, and partly owing to increased confessional tension, *Fähnlilupf* followed *Fähnlilupf* at an increasing tempo during these years. Religious and political polarization combined with personal animosity among the Freestate's magnates to lower the threshold of violence, while factional leaders urged on by foreign ambassadors became more and more willing to risk stirring up the communes in order to destroy their rivals. The result of this escalating cycle of *Fähnlilupf*, partisan court, and counter-*Fähnlilupf* was not a cleansed Freestate, however, but rather one riven by deeper and deeper divisions.

Such a pattern could not continue forever. The breaking point was reached not in the Freestate itself, but in the Valtellina. Religious tension had been growing for years there, as the mostly Catholic population resisted proselytization by the Protestant majority in Graubünden. A *Strafgericht* in 1618 increased tensions by kidnapping and murdering a popular priest, and by proscribing the leaders of the leading Catholic families in the subject territories. With support and encouragement from Spanish Milan, which saw a golden opportunity to gain control over the Rhaetian passes, the Valtellina rose against its lords on July 19, 1620. Several hundred Protestants were killed, and Milanese troops immediately occupied the valley. Since Habsburg control over the Valtellina represented a direct threat not only to Venice, but also to France's interests, the Milanese invasion immediately drew the Freestate into a maelstrom of diplomatic activity; not surprisingly, none of the major players paid any heed to the Rhaetians' own ideas about the proper resolution of either international or domestic political issues.

The Valtellina massacre and the Freestate's subsequent efforts to regain control there brought on the fourth, final phase of Rhaetian politics until 1639. The Milanese, Austrian, French, and Swiss armies that marched through the Freestate during this period overshadowed existing domestic animosities, although rivalries among the leading families remained at a fever pitch. Between 1620 and 1639, the Freestate lost its sovereignty to become a pawn in the larger conflict spreading across Europe. The Rhaetian passes remained at the crossroads of both the Habsburg and French diplomatic alliances, and neither party could allow the other free use of such an important strategic resource.[3] Only after the Thirty Years' War had entered the long stalemate that began in the mid-1630s could Rhaetians even think of acting independently, and even then, their options consisted only in finding the best possible deal among the opposing parties. The delicate diplomatic maneuvering required to save the Freestate and restore its control over the Valtellina was conducted by a few leading magnates, so that when the Freestate reemerged after 1639, the social and political balance of power was different than before the war. In a sense, this last phase no longer belongs to the developments

---

[3] Parker, *Army of Flanders*, 73–77.

discussed up to this point, since entirely different forces exercised an overwhelming influence not only on the ebb and flow of political struggle, but on the social foundations of the Freestate's communal republicanism. Nevertheless, this period represents both an important epilogue to earlier developments, and also reveals the tenacity of communal institutions even in the darkest moments of the European war.

THE REFORM MOVEMENT, 1585–1603

The tumults of 1573 and 1585 had already revealed the depth of popular resentment against the magnate families. After the troops had dispersed in 1585, the *Bundestag* therefore undertook to reform the Freestate enough to prevent such uprisings in the future, although without undermining the elite's control over the political process. On the one hand, old prohibitions against bribery during elections and against the purchase of offices were reiterated. In addition, the *Bundesbrief* was renewed and circulated to the communes, emphasizing the Three Leagues' unity.[4] On the other hand, the communally oriented parts of the Chiavenna Articles, particularly the provision that officers in the Valtellina should be elected directly in the communes, were weakened or abrogated. The *Bundestag* also invoked the *Drei-Sigler-Brief* of 1574, which prohibited communes from raising their banners, and which denied anyone the right to travel from commune to commune without the *Bundestag*'s permission.[5] The men who controlled affairs after 1585 hoped to preserve good government by limiting both overt corruption and direct communal participation in national decisions. For a time, this attempt at reform from above appeared to be succeeding.

The diplomatic scene after 1585 was active but not threatening. The Three Leagues sought closer ties with the Swiss, even petitioning unsuccessfully for direct membership in the Confederacy in 1587.[6] The Catholic cantons blocked the project out of fear of the Freestate's Protestant majority, and even Swiss Protestants feared entanglement because of the Ten Jurisdictions' nominal subjugation to Austria. Nevertheless, when Bern asked for support against Savoy in 1589, the Freestate authorized a force of 1800 troops to provide aid.[7] In the late 1580s, both Venice and Milan sought to establish a permanent alliance with the Freestate, although without success.[8] Instead, the Freestate preserved its ties to the crown of France, particularly after Henry III and Henry of Navarre joined forces against the Catholic League. Protestant Swiss and *Bündner* troops campaigned actively in

---

[4] STAG AB IV 1/7, pp. 353, 397; Ardüser, *Rätische Chronik*, 105.
[5] STAG AB IV 1/7, pp. 263, 322, 353.
[6] JM I: 245 (nos. 1059, 1061); see also EA V.1: 4–6 (nos. 3, 4).
[7] JM I: 247 (no. 1074), for six *Fähnli* of 300 men each; Ardüser, *Rätische Chronik*, 109–10 speaks of nine *Fähnli*.
[8] M. Bundi, *Frühe Beziehungen*, 224–38; JM I: 246–50 (nos. 1067, 1069, 1071, 1083, 1088–90).

France until Henry IV finally assumed the throne.[9] Relations with Austria, which had been strained owing to feuds between the Lower Engadine and the neighboring Tyrolean villages, improved after long negotiations produced a treaty in 1592 that regulated most of the local issues involved.[10]

Another flurry of diplomatic activity – more threatening this time – occurred after the French finally succeeded in 1601 in cutting off the "Spanish Road" that connected Spain and the southern Habsburg territories with the war zone in the Netherlands. With their route through Savoy and Burgundy cut off by the Treaty of Lyon, and with the reluctance of the Swiss to allow substantial troop movements through the Swiss Confederacy, Spain was now reduced to a single land route connecting its Italian and Low Country territories: from Milan through the Engadine or through the Valtellina to Tyrol, and then north of Switzerland to the Rhine.[11] Within a year of the Treaty of Lyon, the Freestate had signed a series of new defensive alliances, suggesting that the *Bündner* may have been aware of their new importance as a target of Spanish diplomatic pressure.[12] Such pressure was not long in coming, and reached a first peak in 1603, when the Spanish governor of Milan began to build a fortress on the very boundaries of the Valtellina.

Meanwhile, certain constitutional issues continued to divide the Three Leagues internally. In 1591, a dispute broke out between the Chadè and the other two Leagues about where they ought to hold their meetings. Although the *Bundestag* itself rotated among the three Leagues, the *Beitag* met almost exclusively in Chur, capital of the Chadè. The Chadè's seal alone could validate a *Beitag*'s decisions, and only the Chadè's scribe recorded its deliberations. Since three annual meetings of the *Beitag* had become customary, the Gray League suggested that these rotate like the *Bundestag*, or even better, that one of them be replaced by an annual Bundestag to be held in Ilanz in the Gray League.[13] After the Chadè refused even to consider such a proposal, claiming that "the majority of the two Leagues by their votes could not take away [the Chadè's] privileges [*fryheiten*] by force without law,"[14] the Gray League and the Ten Jurisdictions went ahead and convened a *Bundestag* in Ilanz. This assembly put the Freestate's officers in the Valtellina in a quandary: the Chadè threatened to order them away from the meeting in Ilanz, whereas the other two leagues maintained "that in all fairness the subjects had a greater obligation to obey two leagues than one."[15] Similar constitutional wrangling continued throughout the 1590s, as Rhaetian leaders attempted to balance the theoretical equality among

[9] Ardüser, *Rätische Chronik*, 100ff; Sprecher, "Beitrag zur Charakteristik," 1–15.
[10] Juvalta, *Denkwürdigkeiten*, 3–6; JM I: 250 (no. 1091).
[11] On the importance of the Spanish Road and its interruption in 1601, Parker, *Army of Flanders*, 59–74. Bolzern, *Spanien, Mailand und die katholische Eidgenossenschaft*, argues that troop movements through Switzerland were never a realistic possibility, although such movements were at all times the primary goal of the Spanish ambassadors.
[12] On the Venetian treaty, Bundi, *Frühe Beziehungen*.
[13] JM II: 555–58 (no. 219).
[14] JM II: 555.   [15] JM II: 556.

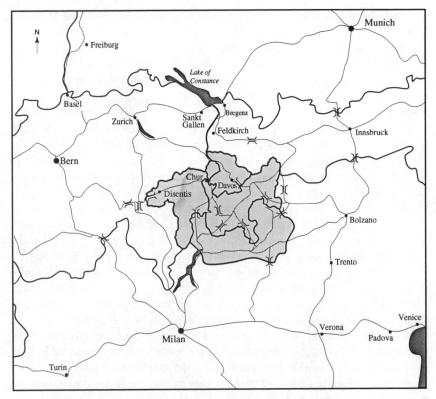

Illustration 8   The Freestate in international context.

the Three Leagues with the practical realities of governing. In the end, the Freestate's organization remained unchanged: each commune and each League was too possessive of its traditions and liberties to allow constitutional reform to proceed.

At the end of the century, the chronicler Hans Ardüser claimed optimistically that:

Because the year 1599 was the last which ended the century, it ended gently and marvelously by God's grace, and many pleasant and merry things were left at the end, so that almighty God's goodness to us poor sinners can be marveled at.[16]

But trouble lay on the horizon. Local dissatisfaction with the republic's government was growing in the villages, exacerbated by increasing foreign pressure as political tension grew in Italy and Germany. During the relatively peaceful 1590s, more and

---

[16] Ardüser, *Rätische Chronik*, 146.

more power fell to a relatively small group of men, led by Johann Guler of Davos, Johann von Planta of Rhäzüns, Johann Baptista von Tscharner of Chur, and Hercules von Salis of Grüsch. These men monopolized foreign affairs and manipulated the Freestate's government to build their personal fortunes. The endless maneuvering between them and their followers, as well as their tightening grip over the distribution of public office, provoked considerable unhappiness. As Fortunat Juvalta recalled in his memoirs, "the voices [calling for reform] became very numerous, and seemed to threaten some kind of popular action . . ."[17] Among the loudest were the Protestant clergy, who used their sermons to urge the communes to act against corruption.[18]

In an effort to forestall unrest, the *Bundestag* appointed a reform commission early in 1600, consisting of six men from each League.[19] The commissioners produced a bill of articles that addressed both the selection of officers in the Valtellina and the election of delegates within individual communes. They ordained administrative and judicial changes to improve the administration of justice in the Valtellina and to safeguard the communes' income from their Italian subjects. These articles also proposed an appeals panel to prosecute violations of the new order: the panel would consist of two judges from each League, appointed for life, who would add a third judge from each League whenever anyone complained that the new statutes had been violated. Such a standing appeals panel would have considerably strengthened the Freestate, which still lacked any central judicial machinery. In addition, the appointment of judges for life, and their broad powers to punish offenses "in whatever League or whatever commune they might occur" would have meant a significant shift in power away from the communes and towards the *Bundestag* and central authorities.[20] Yet it was not this threat to communal autonomy, nor any of the specific provisions contained in this reform proposal that blocked its adoption, but rather the stipulation that the reform should not go into effect for three years. The rumor soon spread that the delay had been arranged by some of the most powerful men in the Freestate – including Johann von Planta and Johann Guler – who did not want to lose the considerable sums they had spent to purchase high offices in the Valtellina for the upcoming years. Such blatant manipulation encouraged opponents of the reform to attack its authors, and the communes subsequently rejected the entire package.[21] As the Synodal protocol noted sadly later in 1601, "Note: Work on a reform failed this year, because the Bundestag, our leaders, and especially our magnates did not want to accept it."[22]

[17] Juvalta, *Denkwürdigkeiten*, 8.
[18] STAG B 721 (Protocol of the Rhaetian Synod), p. 157 (probably June, 1600).
[19] STAG AB IV 1/8, pp. 6, 43. Juvalta, *Denkwürdigkeiten*, 8, speaks of twelve in all.
[20] Text of the articles at STAC CB III, 254 (May 29, 1600).
[21] See Juvalta, *Denkwürdigkeiten*, 9; and Sprecher, *Rhetishe Cronica*, 250.
[22] STAG B 721, p. 162.

This failure did not put an end to the reform movement. The very next year, the Reformed ministers proposed a new series of measures, which were rejected out of hand in the Catholic part of the Freestate because of their origin.[23] The open corruption surrounding the renewal of the French alliance in 1602 raised tempers even further, increasing popular discontent already high because of two economically difficult years.[24] For many of the people, the French alliance promised instant wealth and lower taxes, if only the magnates did not swallow all the profits. As Ardüser put it:

Whereas other lands must pay fees, taxes, tribute, contributions, and tolls to princes and to lords, the Three Leagues by grace of God have the privilege [*fryheitt*] that princes and lords pay them honoraria and contributions, so that large sums of money came into the Freestate this year.[25]

Some two thousand citizens gathered in Chur at the French ambassador's request to encourage the *Bundestag* to ratify the alliance. The general excitement caused by the renewal nearly triggered a *Fähnlilupf* according to Ardüser – it was prevented only because "our masters [*Herren*] opposed it so strongly."[26]

In 1603, the desire for reform became strong enough to overcome all opposition. Led by Hartmann von Hartmannis, who had risen to knighthood and distinction in French service despite his relatively modest origins, a large number of communal representatives assembled in Chur.[27] The Protestant clergy also played a role in encouraging reform: in the Engadine, they called a special assembly, held in Zuoz in December, 1602, to consider the need for change.[28] Encouraged by Hartmannis and the clerics, a delegation of reformers traveled around the communes:

They described the rotten state of the republic, the revolting corruption, the shameless sale and dishonor of justice, the disgrace and shame that burdened the republic in the eyes of foreign nations, the current threatening dangers, and the consequent necessity for reform. They also described in detail the method they thought appropriate to achieve reform. Each individual district should choose twenty-five patriotic men, who should meet in Chur on a predetermined date, where one would explain to them everything that seemed necessary to heal the sickness found in common affairs, so that they might decide according to their collective understanding based on the majority of votes.[29]

The assembly met on January 2, 1603, convened not by the *Bundestag* but directly by the communes. About 650 representatives attended; of these, two from each district were appointed to a commission to develop a reform plan.

---

[23] STAG B 721, p. 161; Juvalta, *Denkwürdigkeiten*, 9–10.
[24] See e.g. Ardüser, *Rätische Chronik*, 171, 174–75.
[25] Ardüser, *Rätische Chronik*, 180.
[26] *Ibid.*, 181.
[27] On Hartmannis, HBLS, 4: 80.
[28] JM I: 256 (no. 1143).
[29] Juvalta, *Denkwürdigkeiten*, 10. Valèr, *Bestrafung*, asserts that districts, not communes, sent delegates, which is confirmed in STAG AB IV 1/8, p. 168.

Hartmannis and his allies came prepared with specific proposals. The commission started out by publicly reading older measures directed against corruption, such as the *Kesselbrief*, the *Drei-Sigler-Brief*, and the draft reform of 1600. Within four days, however, it began drafting articles, based on the reformers' ideas but going considerably beyond them, and within two weeks the document was complete. The communes ratified the Great Reform within a month of the first meeting, on January 31.[30] In early February, the *Bundestag* wrote Zurich that "the communes allowed [the reformers] to proceed as they had requested, and a Reform was written and adopted, and the same has already been ratified by the communes."[31] But the assembly in 1603 did not end at this point: despite admonitions from the Swiss, who rushed to quell what they saw as a dangerous disturbance, the assembly also appointed a *Strafgericht* to punish those who had "acted against our common fatherland."[32] After a few exemplary prosecutions, the court simply fined every person who had served in a Valtellina office since 1585. This action satisfied the widespread belief that all officers had diverted public revenues for their private gain, while avoiding the lengthy and inflammatory process of trying the officers one by one.[33]

In his memoirs, Fortunat Juvalta claimed that the rapid adoption of the Reform reflected widespread resentment against "those who by means of corrupt practices laid nearly exclusive claim to the offices over the subjects."[34] Indeed, reforms in the administration of the Valtellina made up the largest part of the Reform. The exact method by which officers should be elected, for example, sparked a major debate during January, 1603. Hartmannis's initial proposal sought to improve the selection process without moving it from the *Bundestag*, but the assembly of 1603, distrustful of central institutions, produced a more radical, communally oriented solution. A fixed schedule was established for distributing offices among the communes, in proportion to their size and influence. When a commune's turn came, it publicly elected four candidates, and then decided among them by lot. Officers' behavior during their terms was also put under scrutiny. A lengthy debate took place about how to choose the new auditors who would oversee the officers' financial affairs. Some thought they should be chosen from among citizens of the Three Leagues, but others argued that this would only multiply the opportunities for corruption; instead, auditors should be chosen from the subject population, which had an interest in limiting the officers' depredations. The opponents of this latter, more

---

[30] The document in JVF, 119–29. Events described in the protocol of the Three Leagues, STAG AB IV 1/8, pp. 161–84.

[31] STAG AB IV 5/2, pp. 3–4.

[32] STAG AB IV 1/8, pp. 179–81. After a first vote had found only twenty-nine communes in favor of establishing a court, the assembly agreed to allow delegates to consult with their communes. After this concession, the vote was thirty-nine in favor of holding the court. On the make up of the court (eleven judges and eleven overseers from each League), STAG D II a3c, February 3, 1603.

[33] Juvalta, *Denkwürdigkeiten*, 14–15.

[34] *Ibid.*, 11.

rigorous plan succeeded in blocking it by arguing that subjects should not be in a position to judge their masters. As a result, the new auditors were treated like any other kind of officer, being appointed by the communes in rotation.[35] Each officer's successor was also ordered to review all accounts; should any irregularities be proven, the new officer would personally receive a share of any fines levied against his predecessor.

Like the aborted reform proposal of 1600, the Reform of 1603 provided a special mechanism for enforcement. This time, the proposed court of "censors" echoed communal concerns closely: unlike the lifetime terms and the centrally organized process proposed in 1600, the new court was to be based firmly in the districts. Every district was to elect four censors. If "any commune, officer, or other individual person" informed one of them that the Reform had been violated, the censor should call upon the councils of the neighboring communes, who would create a special court to investigate.[36] One judge from each district was to be chosen by lot to serve on this court, which could levy capital punishments or fines as it deemed appropriate. The court's jurisdiction was specifically limited to violations of the Reform and of the *Drei-Sigler-Brief*, however, and all fines went to the treasury of the Three Leagues.[37] The censors were elected for six-year terms, and could not be reelected. Finally, the censors were ordered to assemble regularly "every six years to deliberate whether anyone had acted against this Reform and articles, or not, so that he who had violated them might be punished."[38] The authors clearly believed that active enforcement of the articles was necessary: the articles allowed any person to make accusations, and authorized the censors to proceed on their own even if no accusation had been made. They also gave the communes a major voice, since the communal councils had to authorize the creation of the special tribunals. At the same time, the inclusion of the *Drei-Sigler-Brief* (which forbade raising communal banners or inciting the communes to direct action), under the special courts' jurisdiction indicates that the reformers also feared uncontrolled communal unrest.

The purpose of the Reform was therefore twofold: to limit the corruption that might provoke direct communal action, but also to punish such action if it took place anyway. These purposes reflect that fact that the Reform of 1603 was drafted by leading statesmen who saw the dangers that public corruption and elite factionalism represented for the Freestate, but that it was influenced and forced through by commoners. The system before 1603 angered the voting population, which had to confront magnates who often "stole" communal offices from lesser

---

[35] *Ibid.*, 11–12.
[36] JVF, 126–27.
[37] *Ibid.*, 127. Violations within the communes were to be tried according to equity ("der billigkeit nach"), whereas officers' delicts were subject to the common law ("nach gstalt der sachen und erkhandnuss dess Rechtens").
[38] *Ibid.*

families through corrupt practices at the *Bundestag*. During the negotiations in January 1603, Hartmannis and the reformist magnates gave way to those who saw communal control as the key issue, rather than corruption *per se*. This may have been because the assembly was large enough – at over six hundred – to give members of middling families an unusually large role.

The events of 1603 also reveal a growing separation between the elite and the rest of the population. Hartmannis himself opposed many of the final measures, and was said to have died of disappointment shortly after the Reform was ratified. Juvalta reports that Hartmannis opposed direct election of officers because:

one could not expect any care for the republic or moderation from the common mob, who looked only to their private advantage. Bribery and corruption would not be abolished in this way, but would increase without measure, because no means would remain to limit them. As long as private individuals violated the reform ordinances, judges and censors could punish them; but if entire communes misbehaved, which would surely happen in the very first election, they would not be punished, and the entire Reform would soon be made fruitless.[39]

Juvalta suspected a dark conspiracy between the magnates who opposed any reform and the people "who looked only to their private advantage." After 1603, even the most civic-minded members of the Rhaetian political elite became doubtful about the logic of communal government, turning instead toward some version of patrician republicanism.[40] Other magnates turned to the resurgent aristocratic ideals that were spreading through the courts of Europe at this time.

The tumult over the Reform of 1603 had scarcely subsided when the Freestate was torn by a new conflict, this time over whether it should establish a formal alliance with Venice. After 1589, the Venetian Republic began adopting an active foreign policy towards Graubünden, whose territory formed the only non-Habsburg land connection between Venice and the rest of Europe. Not only Spanish Milan, but also Venice sought to secure its influence in Graubünden: as tension between Venice and the papacy reached a peak early in the seventeenth century, the Venetian *signoria* saw the need to keep open the roads to the rich military recruiting grounds in southern Germany. Within Graubünden, a separate pro-Venetian faction began to form as the result of lavish spending by the Venetian ambassadors; its leaders were Johannes von Salis-Samedan and his distant cousin, Hercules von Salis-Grüsch. Several early attempts at an alliance had failed because the communes feared military entanglements, but by 1603 the prospects had improved considerably.[41]

---

[39] Juvalta, *Denkwürdigkeiten*, 13.
[40] Juvalta and many of his fellows thus subscribed to the moderate historical view analyzed below in chapter 7. This position bore a strong resemblance to the republicanism of Renaissance Florence, which insisted that the individual virtue of the selected few would best promote the common good. See Pocock, *Machiavellian Moment*, esp. on Guicciardini, 219–71.
[41] On relations before 1603, M. Bundi, *Frühe Beziehungen*, esp. 224–56. See also Bouwsma, *Venice*, esp. chapter 5.

Nevertheless, several major obstacles still stood in the way. Naturally, Spanish Milan and Austria both opposed such an alliance. The Spanish governors of Milan had attempted for decades to secure the Valtellina corridor by means of a treaty with the Freestate, but had been consistently blocked by partisans of France. When the Spanish need for access through the passes increased after 1601, the Freestate bolstered its position within the French system of diplomacy by renewing the French alliance in 1602, and by forming new military alliances with the Valais in 1600 and with Bern in 1601. When the Milanese governors saw that the pro-French bloc was about to expand to include Venice – a loose but consistent ally of France – they decided to take a more aggressive tack.[42]

Two avenues stood open to the Spanish: they could threaten the Freestate's sovereignty over the Valtellina, which had once been Milanese territory, or they could apply economic pressure on the Freestate by blocking access to Milanese cattle and grain markets. Closing the borders to Milan also ruined transit trade across the Rhaetian passes, which depended on German and Italian trade goods. Either tactic opened opportunities for the Spanish faction among the Freestate's elite, who could manipulate the popular fears evoked by Milanese military actions or by a trade embargo to embarrass the dominant French faction.

Despite such threats, however, the Freestate signed a ten-year alliance with Venice in 1603. Hercules von Salis-Grüsch and Johann Guler from Davos worked out the details in advance, and mobilized strong support in the Ten Jurisdictions (which were less vulnerable to Milanese economic pressure than the other two Leagues). Early in 1603, Venice sent a new special ambassador, Giovanni Battista Padavino, who scattered pensions and gifts in every direction. Not only did sixteen men from the inner circle of the Rhaetian elite receive large pensions, but another 317 communal leaders received gifts, and each League received a public pension of 1,200 ducats for distribution to the communes.[43] Although the Spanish governor in Milan, the Count of Fuentes, tried to persuade the communes not to ratify the treaty, he lacked the resources to oppose Padavino.[44]

Milan's reaction to the treaty was swift and threatening. Not only did Fuentes impose a trade embargo, he also ordered the construction of a fortress right on the Valtellina's southwestern border. Opponents of the Venetian treaty within Graubünden stirred up a storm of recriminations, while hotter heads among the treaty's supporters called for a military campaign against the new fort. The *Bündner* also appealed to the Swiss for help; the latter counseled patience, and sent a delegation to Milan to discuss matters. Fuentes now turned to the carrot instead of the stick, and offered to sign a treaty with the Freestate himself – one which

---

[42] Bolzern, *Spanien*, esp. 249–50, 256ff. In 1592, the governor of Milan had offered to defend the Freestate even against Austria in exchange for access to the passes. JM I: 250 (no. 1090).
[43] M. Bundi, *Frühe Beziehungen*, 245–46, footnote 69.
[44] *Ibid.*, 246–56.

would have undermined the advantages enjoyed not only by Venice, but also by France. Some communes, terrified at the military threat to the Valtellina and suffering from the Milanese trade embargo, seemed inclined to accede, while others were violently opposed. Leaders of all the factions within the Freestate did everything in their power to sway communal opinion, while the clergy preached the dangers of Catholic attack or Protestant conspiracy to their excited parishioners. The *Bundestag* attempted to keep control over affairs by appointing a secret council, a measure which only increased public distrust when it was learned that the council was established at the French ambassador's request.

The Fähnlilupf *and* Strafgericht *of 1607*

In the end, the Milanese treaty was rejected, and relations with Milan became increasingly tense.[45] The general Italian war that threatened to break out in 1606, after Venice was put under papal interdict, brought matters in the Freestate to a head as well. Early in 1607, Venice called upon its Rhaetian ally to allow the passage of several thousand mercenary troops from southern Germany. The Spanish party in the Freestate set out to block this request by any means possible. They spread the rumor that the mercenaries had been promised immunity for any atrocities they might commit against the civilian population in the Freestate, and that the *Bundestag* had sold a pathway "seven arm spans wide" from the northern to the southern border. The chronicler Bartholomäus Anhorn reports that "when the common man learned that such a large number of troops would pass through the land, he was extremely upset, fearing the great damage they would do to houses and to fields; for there were many peasants [*Landleuth*] who had never wanted to enter into such an alliance with the Venetians . . . "[46] The communes immediately above Chur – heavily dependent on the pass trade to Milan – threatened to rebel if the Freestate did not close its passes to all foreign powers.

The *Beitag* responded with a call for peace and quiet, arguing that the Venetian alliance provided for the safe transit of troops according to whatever method the Freestate demanded. Far from satisfying the communal delegates, this answer instead provoked them to raise their *Fähnli*. For the first time, the Spanish party successfully triggered a tumult that spread across the entire Freestate, although events slipped catastrophically out of their hands almost as soon as the *Fähnli* assembled in March, 1607. On March 5, the first troops arrived in Chur from Churwalden, and within three weeks, all twenty-six districts were represented. Control of events moved from the *Bundestag* to a series of angry assemblies outside the walls of Chur. While the Spanish faction led by Georg von Beeli did everything it could to encourage action against the Venetian pensioners, the driving force behind events was the assembled crowd's conviction that the Freestate's

---

[45] Anhorn, *Püntner Aufruhr*, 6–7.   [46] *Ibid.*, 7.

leaders had sold themselves to foreign powers and therefore needed to be punished.[47]

Contemporary observers were unanimous about the deep hostility the *Fähnli* showed toward the magnate families and the existing government. A Bernese delegation observed in March that "the command over these Fähnli is entirely in the hands of the common man, and all noteworthy, respectable, rich, wise persons of authority have been removed from their honors and offices, and have also been shut out of all councils and decisions . . . "[48] Another Swiss observer – this one Catholic – noted in July that "the government [*Obrigkeit*] counts for nothing against the common man, and the wise people there who have a respectable amount of experience are mostly so hated by the common man that their advice is rejected . . . "[49] Anhorn also described how "the common man's feelings had become bitter about the big lords [*großen Herren*], who were thought to have despised and sold out the common Leagues."[50] Meanwhile, numerous leading figures in the Freestate demonstrated their own assessment of the situation by fleeing the country before they could be captured and tried. The assembly's early pro–Habsburg tilt eventually provoked a reaction in the opposite direction; by early summer, the pro–Venetian communes were back on top of affairs, and proceeded to execute the other party's leaders, Beeli and Caspar Baselga. Throughout the uprising, however, the troops on both sides hated the old leadership indiscriminately. Penalties imposed on one set of magnates during the first phase were by no means revoked during the second phase, and Johannes Guler remained under a death sentence should he be captured even after the pro–Venetian communes had taken control.[51]

The *Fähnli* also claimed complete freedom to act in the name of the Freestate. One of their most important acts in Chur was to repeal the *Drei-Sigler-Brief* of 1574 – the statute that prohibited the raising of communal banners. In May, the *Strafgericht* wrote to Bern that the statute was no longer in effect, since "we are concerned that if we were denied the power to assemble, our destruction would lie before our doors."[52] Therefore, the document had not only been repealed, "but chopped into pieces and trodden under their feet."[53] Viewing themselves as saviors of the corrupted Leagues, the assembled troops naturally rejected anything that denied them the right to act, or which blocked the flow of information back to the communes.

---

[47] Personal animosity played a role as well. A personal enemy of Beeli's led the commune of Ramosch to Chur. Juvalta, *Denkwürdigkeiten*, 16, 37.
[48] STAB A V 494, p. 39.
[49] LAI Hofregistratur, Akten, Reihe C, Fasz. 168, July 15, 1607.
[50] Anhorn, *Püntner Aufruhr*, 67.
[51] *Ibid.*, 163.
[52] STAB A V 494, p. 183–88.
[53] Ardüser, *Rätische Chronik*, 226–27.

Events in 1607 seemed so threatening to the Swiss that they considered sending a military force to restore order. In June, the Swiss Diet imposed an embargo on the Freestate, and in July, it discussed the exact composition of the force to be used. Religious tension between Protestants and Catholics in Switzerland brought the project to a halt, however, as did the final departure of the *Fähnli* from Chur on July 21.[54] The court established by the *Fähnli* continued its actions well into winter, although its location and its personnel changed several times. In the end, it sat in Ilanz and consisted of forty-eight judges; even in this last phase only six judges carried the names of leading families (and these may have been from minor branches).[55] By early December, the court had tried three identifiable groups, according to an Austrian agent: twenty-one men from the French and Venetian party were sentenced to fines totaling nearly 12,000 crowns, another twenty-one from the Milanese party paid over 30,000 crowns, while twelve *Neutrali* had to render a total of 1745 crowns.[56]

The alliance struggles and the *Fähnlilupf* of 1607 represented a decisive turning point. In the first place, the struggles that year intensified the hostility between the elite factions, each of which had tried to focus communal anger against its rivals. Leaders of both parties had suffered heavily, and many others had fled ignominiously, leaving all factions hungry for revenge. Moreover, the events of 1607 showed that elite conflicts and communal resentment had become inseparably intertwined, even as distrust between magnates and the rest of the population grew. No longer satisfied to watch their betters rule while they merely collected a share of the profits, the "common men" in Rhaetia – that is, the politically active members of the communes – had asserted their ultimate power over the Freestate's decision-making process. Militiamen and local leaders expressed their views on matters of international politics and constitutional policy, and their voices proved more important, for a while, than any others. Finally, the events of 1607 reminded the magnate families of the overwhelming power of direct communal action. Their fear of the communes only accelerated their turn toward more congenial ideologies such as aristocratic republicanism or noble hierarchy. Even those magnates who remained devoted to the Freestate and its institutions, such as Johann Guler of Davos, sought constitutional reforms to limit popular power. At the same time, the possibility of renewed direct action from the communes put a premium on communicating to the broader population. After 1607 the Protestant clergy moved

[54] EA v.1: 826, 830, 833; Anhorn, *Püntner Aufruhr*, 159–60. Anhorn also suggests that the Swiss commanders were not sure of their own troops, fearing that "der gemeine Mann unter ihnen (der der Püntnerischen Sachen unerfahren war) den Püntnerischen Bauren recht gab, das sie also wider ihre Oberkeit wüteten, als die das Vaterland verrahten haben solten . . . "
[55] Anhorn, *Püntner Aufruhr*, gives a complete list, 164–65.
[56] The figures from a report by Andreas Ruinelli, December 1, 1607: LAI, Hofregistratur, Akten, Reihe C, Fasc. 168. Ruinelli uses an illegible abbreviation for his monetary denominations, but comparison with Anhorn, *Püntner Aufruhr*, Chapter 13 demonstrates that he was speaking of Chur crowns (28 schillings of account, or about one and one half florins.)

to the forefront of events because of their ability to preach politics to their parishioners. Likewise, political pamphlets and songs took on a new importance after 1607, and production increased steadily to reach a peak during the years 1618–22. Rhaetia had become a state in which propaganda could be an important tool.

THE LULL FROM 1607 TO 1616

After the cataclysmic events of 1607, a cautious calm returned to the Freestate's political life for a decade. None of the problems confronting the communes and their government had really been solved, however: France, Spain, and Venice still strove to establish some control over the Freestate's strategic passes, and all of them sought out leading men in the Freestate to help them. The brothers Rudolf and Pompeius von Planta established themselves as leaders of the revived Spanish party (although Rudolf did not convert to Catholicism until 1623).[57] Hercules and Johann Baptista von Salis led the Venetian party, which worked closely with the Reformed clergy. Diplomatic relations took an ominous turn after the assassination of Henry IV of France brought about a shift in international alliances: for a few years after 1610, France and Spain sought compromise rather than confrontation, disrupting the established factional balance in the Freestate. The resulting atmosphere fostered uncertainty among the magnates, who played foreign ambassadors for the largest possible advantage, and who competed bitterly for influence over communes and local leaders.[58]

Pressure redoubled in 1613, when Venice sought to renew the ten-year alliance it had made in 1603. Both Zurich and Bern urged renewal, but the communes had learned their lesson in 1607: despite Padavino's new and generous bribes, the treaty lapsed because of communal refusal to ratify any extension. Not only did the combined Spanish–French faction oppose it, so did many moderate Protestants who preferred to strengthen the Freestate's ties with Switzerland. Only the more radical Protestants favored renewal, seeking to oppose Catholicism and "Hispanism" at any cost. The younger generation of ministers who favored a more confessionally motivated political line did not yet control the Reformed Synod and the Reformed communes, however, and their efforts to support Venice were fruitless until the Spanish party overreached itself in 1616.

During the same years, several local conflicts broke out between Catholics and Protestants within the Freestate itself. The *Bundestag* intervened in Bergün in 1601, for example, supporting the Protestants in their efforts to suppress the Catholic

---

57 Pompeius became Catholic much earlier, probably before 1605. Planta, *Chronik*, 194–95.
58 The fluidity of partisan politics appears in the fact that Rudolf von Planta received Venetian pensions and command of a Venetian regiment in 1603, worked with the French ambassador in 1612 and 1613 to block renewal of the Venetian alliance, and became leader of the Spanish party after 1616. Planta, *Chronik*, 189–91.

minority. The Protestants in Bergün had requested a preacher in the 1570s despite the bishop's objections, and had shared the village church since 1577, indicating that a shift towards Protestantism had been under way for some time.[59] The compromise reached in 1601 provided that the village church "should be cleaned of all papist superstition and ceremonies . . . and be reformed according to Evangelical teachings," though Catholics were to be tolerated.[60] In 1615 and 1616, Protestants and Catholics in the Vier Dörfer around Chur began rioting over religious disputes; the *Bundestag* intervened by setting up a court headed by the mayor of Chur, which gave the Protestants most of what they had asked for.[61] Although assemblies of the communes continued to call for "the freedom of both religions," more people in the Freestate were willing to put confessional issues at the forefront in these years, and more Catholics felt threatened by the Protestant majority at the *Bundestag*.[62]

Religious tension within the Freestate was dangerous enough, but the situation in the Valtellina was worse. The population there had remained steadfastly Catholic despite a string of measures intended to ease the spread of Protestantism. The Freestate permitted Italian Protestant refugees to settle in the Valtellina, excluded itinerant Catholic preachers and missionaries, prohibited the reading or posting of papal bulls, and seized church property to support Reformed ministers. Protestant clerics argued consistently that, as lord over the Valtellina, the Three Leagues had the obligation to control their subjects' religious lives.[63] When small Protestant congregations did appear, the Freestate's officers insisted that the local Catholics support them and yield them church buildings for their worship. Among the subjects, the "freedom of both religions" was invoked to protect and favor the Protestants against the Catholic majority.

That such a policy was bound to cause resentment among the subjects did not bother devout Protestants, of course, but religious turmoil in the Valtellina represented a real danger for the Freestate's rule there. The region was part not of the see of Chur, but of the Italian see of Como, now under Spanish influence. The bishops of Como and the archbishops of Milan were more than willing to work with their Spanish rulers to promote the Valtellina's return to Catholic (and Spanish) rule, thus saving it from the "heretics." Given that the Spanish had good military and diplomatic reasons for reasserting control over the Valtellina as well, religious trouble might easily provide them with an excuse to intervene. In 1607, the

---

[59] See JM II: 438 (no. 426), and BK III: xvi–xvii.
[60] STAG, Gemeindearchive, GA Bergün, July 5, 1601.
[61] STAG AB IV 5/12, pp. 373–412.
[62] In 1605, for example, a priest in Disentis published a pamphlet describing Carlo Borromeo's 1585 visit in glowing terms; the pamphlet was introduced by a letter from the Abbot and from the Mistral of the commune as well. Sacco, "Viaggio del B. Carlo Borromeo."
[63] Campell, "De Officio Magistratus," Evangelische Rhätische Synode, Ms. B3, pp. 27–35. Copy with identical pagination in STAG B 721.

Spanish governor Fuentes had urged immediate invasion to his Austrian colleagues in Innsbruck, and several plans for conquest were worked out during the early seventeenth century.[64]

The precarious diplomatic and religious situation in Rhaetia after 1607 moved some *Bündner* to pursue a final round of reform efforts. Late in 1608, there was an attempt to implement the special court called for in the Reform of 1603. For five years, not a word had been heard about the four censors in every district, but now that six years had passed and the unrest of 1607 had died down, moderate leaders sought to put the Reform's enforcement mechanism into effect. In a letter to the communes, the *Beitag* asked whether the censors ought to gather, and whether the Reform ought to be modified in any way.[65] The *Beitag* was careful to avoid any large assemblies, however: should the communes desire any modifications in the Reform, each district should send only one representative to Chur to deliberate. A general interest in avoiding disorder also shaped the responses to the *Beitag*'s request, as did a profound desire to keep constitutional reform separate from the growing confessional tension within the Freestate. The smiths' and shoemakers' guilds in (Protestant) Chur, for example, voted that some changes should be made, but warned that "this should take place without help or interference from the clergy, and the clergy should be warned to stay in their pulpits and not to interfere in worldly affairs to the extent which has, unfortunately, taken place in the past."[66] Many other districts simply ignored the request that censors be appointed.

A few delegates gathered in Chur in 1609 to revise the Freestate's "praiseworthy constitutions and statutes" with four problems in mind: a single person's malice could perturb the common estate, foreigners perceived the Rhaetians "as people who had no government or public order, and who had lost their old honor and good name,"[67] the Freestate's official assemblies were disobeyed by individuals and communes, and the subjects complained about arbitrary rule and the failure to punish many severe offenses. Meanwhile, many of the communes that refused to send delegates to these deliberations did so "because they thought that it was being undertaken solely for the purpose of returning the choice of officers over the subjects to the old abusive wastrels and persons . . . "[68] In fact, the changes found in the forty-one articles proposed in July 1609 had more to do with restraining communal action in the Freestate than with changing affairs in the Valtellina. Once again, raising communal banners was prohibited, and no one was allowed to appeal to the communes without the *Beitag*'s permission.[69] The method for electing

---

[64] Cf. LAI Hofregistratur, Akten, Reihe C, Fasz. 168, September 11, 1607. See also Wendland, "Republik und 'Untertanenlände'."

[65] On the following, see esp. Valèr, *Bestrafung*, 86–101.

[66] Cited in Valèr, *Bestrafung*, 87.

[67] *Ibid.*, 88.

[68] *Ibid.*

[69] STAG AB IV 5/2, pp. 17–29. Articles 1 and 2 effectively reinstated the *Drei-Sigler-Brief*.

officers for the Valtellina described in the Reform of 1603 was confirmed, but the Presidents were given the authority to reject "unsuitable" candidates.

The communes never ratified these proposals, meaning that the Reform of 1603 remained unmodified (though also unenforced). Moreover, the assembled censors never tried anyone for crimes against the Reform. Similar attempts to modify the Reform took place in 1612 and 1613, when several communes requested a gathering of censors. Once again, a group met to deliberate about changes to the Reform, this time in Davos, and once again, they produced a document whose main purpose was to prevent direct action by the communes. Not surprisingly, the proposals of 1613 had as little effect as those made in 1609.[70] Measures limiting communal authority and the communes' right to hear petitioners were unpopular among the common people, as the destruction of the *Drei-Sigler-Brief* in 1607 proved: seeing themselves as the legitimate rulers of the Freestate, the communes refused to be excluded from its business. Resistance to the changes in 1612 and 1613 was probably bolstered by magnate opposition to tighter control over their behavior in the Valtellina. Office-holding was too important a source of magnate income and prestige for major changes to go unchallenged. Unfortunately, no evidence survives about who actually took part in the assemblies of 1609 and 1613. The documents mention participation by clerics (presumably Reformed) in both cases, but without further identification, while the lay participants are entirely unknown. In any case, no changes that offended both popular convictions about the power of the "common man" and the elite's concrete interests had any change of passage by this time.

The distrust between communes and their leaders, and the hostility between magnates from different factions thus prevented any substantial changes in the Freestate's organization during the years after 1607. After 1613, foreign pressure increased once again, exacerbating internal dissension to the point that the Freestate's government nearly ceased to function. After the communes had roundly refused to renew the Venetian alliance in 1613, Venice sought other means to keep its vital lifeline to Germany open. Despite repeated prohibitions from the *Bundestag*, Venice began recruiting Rhaetian officers and soldiers to serve against Austria. In 1614, thirty-five officers and over 600 men marched off towards Venice, and in 1616, 400 men from the Ten Jurisdictions alone enlisted, despite threats of punishment from the *Bundestag*. The atmosphere that prevailed can be seen in a comment made by the departing troops: "those are Spanish prohibitions, which we don't need to obey."[71] When Venice sent its experienced ambassador Padavino in 1616 to ask again for an alliance, the French and Spanish factions responded with an alliance proposal from Milan. Neither Padavino nor his opponents, Alfonso Casati from Milan and Stephan Gueffier from France, had any success, despite

[70] Valèr, *Bestrafung*, 93–99; cf. STAG B 1178, STAG AB IV 6/19, p. 273ff.
[71] Moor, *Geschichte von Currätien*, II: 332.

great efforts by their partisans within the Freestate. Instead, the communes offended all the foreign powers by rejecting the relatively advantageous treaty proposed by Casati, while physically ejecting Padavino from the Freestate's territory.

CRISIS AND INVASION, 1616–22

The impending storm broke out late in 1616.[72] For the next four years, *Fähnlilupf* followed *Fähnlilupf* as one party after another called upon sympathetic communes to "save the fatherland and punish the guilty." Moved not only by their sense of authority, but also by their concerns about the economic implications and military consequences of one policy or another, the communes responded each time: in Chur in 1616 and 1617, in Thusis in 1618, in Chur again in 1619, then in Zizers and Davos in 1620. Until the very end, the notice that a *Fähnlilupf* was taking place resulted in participation by most of the communes, whether by a full company of troops or by a delegation sent by the council and *Amman*.[73] But even though the communes assembled in the name of the common good to prevent some perceived danger, the tribunals they established inevitably became weapons in the partisan struggle between two increasingly polarized parties. If we compare the bills of articles prepared by the *Fähnli* themselves with the subsequent actions of the *Strafgerichte* that the *Fähnli* established, it appears that the former concentrated on holding the Freestate together and reforming its political life, whereas the latter undertook vendettas directed primarily against particular magnates and communes. Indeed, the tendency of *Strafgerichte* to become partisan weapons justified further *Fähnlilüpfe*, which hoped to restore balance. Unfortunately, the agents to whom the *Fähnli* turned for leadership were moved by other concerns, and thus betrayed the task which was entrusted to them.

To presume that two identifiable camps dominated the struggles in the Freestate between 1616 and 1620, and to assert that the communes cared primarily about preserving the entire Freestate rather than promoting one faction or the other, would represent a tremendous simplification of the complex events during those years. The struggles, which took the form of tumultuous assemblies, kangaroo courts, and ultimately outright murder, did not simply concern the policies that the Freestate ought to follow, nor were they only the result of intensifying clan rivalries, although both of these certainly contributed to the process. Just as important was the question of how a communal state ought to make and stick to its decisions. To what extent was a minority bound by a majority decision? Could a

---

[72] Readers interested in a detailed political narrative should begin by consulting the contemporary historians, especially Anhorn and Sprecher. Recent secondary works include A. Pfister, *Jörg Jenatsch*, and "Il temps dellas partidas."

[73] The question of participation discussed in Valèr, *Bestrafung*, 7–11, 132.

commune change its mind, or was it bound by its oaths and promises? If a decision had been reached by corrupt means, or if a commune had been lied to, could citizens assemble anew to reconsider? Who represented the Freestate to foreign powers: the three Presidents, the *Bundestag*, the leading men who negotiated pensions and alliances, or the communes as a whole? Because the Freestate still lacked a coherent vision of its own identity and of the sources of authority within it, questions of economic or political advantage became entangled with fundamental questions of legitimacy and authority.

The result of such entanglement was that political disagreement disrupted the Freestate's ability to function at all. The very foundations of its existence were in question, which provoked two kinds of responses. First, various Rhaetians, from peasants to magnates, acted directly upon their own convictions of political order, whether by raising their communal banner, or by turning to foreign princes for support and legitimation. These actions offer clues about different conceptions of the Freestate as well as about the perceived interests of the various parties. The second response involved efforts to provide the Freestate with a coherent theory. While most of these were formulated by educated men from the magnate families or from the clergy, they nevertheless exhibited a spectrum of possible solutions to the Freestate's predicament, and will be analyzed in chapter 7 below.

Rather than describe every twist in the labyrinthine political situation between 1616 and 1622, I will focus on three key events that most deeply affected the course of politics and of political thinking during these years. The first was the *Fähnlilupf* and *Strafgericht* at Thusis in 1618, which produced some of the most radical political rhetoric of the entire period. The events and language at Thusis represented a communal and populist solution to the problem of Rhaetian nationhood, as Reformed ministers led a movement to expand the power of the Freestate's Protestant majority in the name of "democracy." The second event was the Valtellina rebellion of 1620, which effectively recast the diplomatic problems the Freestate faced. All parties within the Freestate hoped to regain the subject territories, although they continued to disagree about which foreign power was the most reliable friend. Only the common people seemed less enthusiastic: far fewer joined the military campaign to recover the lost territories in the summer of 1620 than had taken part in various *Fähnlilüpfe* during the previous years.[74] Although military actions in the wake of the rebellion brought both the Freestate and the entire Swiss Confederation to the brink of civil war, the loss of the Valtellina eventually created some pressure for cooperation among factional leaders. The third paradigmatic event took place in 1622, when the communes of the Prättigau rose up against the occupying Austrian garrison. While this rebellion drew upon religious conviction for its emotional force, it also illustrated the communes' desire

---

[74] The Swiss complained about the small number of Rhaetian volunteers in the summer of 1620. Moor, *Geschichte von Currätien*, II: 514.

to put their autonomy before all other considerations. By 1622, conflicts with foreign powers had become so threatening to the Freestate that hostility between commoners and magnates faded as the communes turned to their elite for leadership – foreshadowing the state of affairs in Rhaetia for the remainder of the *ancien régime*.

The Thusis Strafgericht *of 1618*

The *Fähnli* assembled in Thusis in July, 1618, primarily at the behest of the Freestate's Reformed clergy who feared the Spanish party's ascendancy after the Chur *Strafgericht* of 1616. Radical pastors had taken control of the Reformed Synod in April, and had stirred unrest by their sermons and by a letter they circulated among the communes. The actual outbreak of the *Fähnlilupf* in the Lower Engadine was inspired by three of the most extreme pastors, Anton Vulpius, Blasius Alexander, and Bonaventura Toutsch. Not only were the Engadiners committed Protestants, but many of them hated Rudolf von Planta, head of the Spanish faction in the Freestate. Planta had been appointed high judge in Lower Engadine by the Austrian government (which still exercised capital jurisdiction there), and had ordered the execution of a number of men for banditry. The resulting vendetta against Planta by the bandits' relatives was reinforced by communal resistance to Planta's efforts to establish a strong personal position in the village of Zernez. Personal hatred, communal resistance to an aggrandizing magnate, and interfactional competition all contributed to the outbreak in 1618.

The original tumult in the Engadine spread quickly. Spurred on by the ministers and by the leaders of the Venetian faction, the Engadiners assembled in Zuoz, sent bands of armed men to seize leading defenders of Catholicism in the Valtellina, and soon after crossed the mountains to Chur. Finding the city's gates locked against them – Chur's trade interests made it a reputed "Spanish nest" – they moved up to the more hospitable village of Thusis, where they drafted a bill of articles intended to "save the Fatherland."[75] During the previous months, the Venetian ambassador had succeeded in getting his partisans elected to communal leadership: even the primarily Catholic Gray League elected first Julius Maissen and after him Sigismund Derungs – both friends of Venice from outside the usual leading families – as presidents of the League.[76] As a result, when the Engadiners called for a general assembly, almost all of the Freestate's communes responded, full-force in many cases, but with a few men bearing the communal banner from communes where the Venetian faction was in the minority.

By early August, some 2000 men lay encamped around Thusis. In the first flush

---

[75] Moor, *Geschichte von Currätien*, II: 353–60; Planta, *Geschichte von Graubünden*, 246–47; Pfister, *Jenatsch*, 59–69.
[76] A. Pfister, *Jenatsch*, 61–62, 69–70.

of excitement, they prepared a bill of articles whose blunt language reveals their view of the situation. Many of the Freestate's problems were solved with a few words:

4. All corrupters should be removed, and the passes should be carefully guarded, but not to the damage of unsuspicious persons.
5. Concerning what we ought to punish, the majority decided to punish those who acted against our free estate [*freyen standt*], got involved with princes, acted against the Bundesbrief, or otherwise misbehaved seriously.

. . .

8. Our estate ought to be improved.[77]

The assembled troops also elected a court of sixty-six jurors supervised by nine clerics to begin punishing the "guilty." Adding clerics to a *Strafgericht* was a novelty that gave it, for the first time, a markedly confessional tone. All nine who took part were not only Protestants, but members of the activist party within the Synod. They dominated the court's proceedings for the next half year. From August until January, 1619, the *Strafgericht* proceeded against enemies of the Venetian faction and against leaders of the Catholic resistance in the Valtellina, executing the few it could capture, exiling and condemning many others, including the Planta brothers Rudolf and Pompeius.

If the *Strafgericht* at Thusis had been merely another of the partisan outbreaks that tore the Freestate apart during these years, it would not deserve special attention. But the ministers appointed as overseers of the court sought to justify their actions with a blizzard of propaganda aimed at establishing the legitimacy of the tribunal they supervised. After all, the communes and Leagues already had courts: the regular courts based on communal sovereignty, and the special court described in the Great Reform of 1603, which was specifically empowered to punish treason against the Freestate. Moreover, capital jurisdiction in Rudolf von Planta's home commune belonged not to the Freestate but to Austria. How then could the Three Leagues sentence Planta to death and to confiscation of his goods? The young ministers in Thusis responded to this challenge with an entirely novel description of the Freestate's purpose and essence, one which put the privilege of self-government above all other goods, and one which proudly and self-consciously described the Freestate as a democracy. The substance of these claims will be discussed at length below, but it is important to remember their context in the *Strafgericht* at Thusis. The ministers articulated ideas that had roots in the communal experience of most Rhaetians, and that had been followed in practice by *Fähnlilüpfe* since the mid-sixteenth century, but they were the first to express such ideas clearly. They did so because of the Freestate's desperate and dangerous position, and because of the dire threat they perceived from Catholic Spain and

---

[77] STAG A II Landesakten, 1, August 3, 1618 (perhaps a copy).

Milan – a threat which loomed ever larger during the early years of the Thirty Years' War. They also chose to call the Freestate democratic because they knew that Protestants made up a majority there, so that "democracy" legitimated Protestant control.[78] The force of circumstances demanded a rethinking of Rhaetian politics in 1618, whatever the results of that rethinking might be.

Not until March 1619 did the Spanish party manage to recover enough to trigger another *Fähnlilupf* that put an end to the court in Thusis.[79] As usual, a generous distribution of bribes – this time from the Milanese ambassador – made this possible. In addition, an ongoing power struggle in the Lower Engadine, whose details are murky but whose intensity was undeniable, upset every effort to maintain some semblance of civic peace in the Freestate. After a tense period when both "Spanish" and "Venetian" communes assembled their troops around Chur, the pro-Spanish forces gained the upper hand. Nevertheless, the assembled *Fähnli* still insisted on reswearing the *Bundesbrief*, on declaring the "freedom of the two confessions," and on the release of all prisoners held by either side.[80] The *Strafgericht* that followed, however, was no more balanced than that in Thusis. As a result the cycle of *Fähnlilupf* and counter-*Fähnlilupf* continued at an increasing pace until the summer of 1620: conditions in the Freestate at this point were close to a civil war, when the rebellion in the Valtellina and direct invasion by Austria broke the rhythm.

The Valtellina rebellion of 1620

Affairs in Rhaetia went from bad to worse during 1620. The deep divisions that separated communes and leaders were heightened by factional tension and the glowing desire that each party had for revenge. Several factional leaders were actively cooperating with foreign powers by 1620, determined to regain their prominence in the Freestate even if it was done at the head of foreign troops. No help could be expected from either France or Venice, whose ambassadors had been publicly humiliated and forcibly expelled by the communes, while the Swiss themselves were so divided by religion that they could do little to help the "wild Bündner." By the summer of 1620, the subject territories were seething with plans for an uprising.

The actual rebellion in the Valtellina only broke out in July, 1620, but signs of imminent rebellion had been spreading throughout the subject territories for several years. Enraged by the execution of the priest Nicolai Rusca at Thusis in 1618, and actively encouraged by Milanese agents, leading local families began

---

[78] This specific argument had been made since 1577. Campell, "De officio magistratus," in STAG B 721, pp. 27–28.
[79] The most detailed description of the events of 1619–20 in Moor, *Geschichte von Currätien*, II: 392–538, upon which the following paragraphs rely. See also Anhorn, *Graw-Pünter-Krieg*, 36–48.
[80] Moor, *Geschichte von Currätien*, II: 401.

planning an uprising to displace the Rhaetian magistrates and the hated Protestant congregations. An attempt to introduce Protestant worship in the village of Boalzo in 1619 led to a riot during which a Reformed minister was killed.[81] Investigations by the Rhaetian officials in nearby Teglio and Tirano uncovered evidence that several important clans were encouraging unrest in the hope of expelling the *Bündner*; the vague threats of punishment coming from Chur and Davos, however, only added an incentive to proceed with revolt, especially since the investigations focused only on wealthy and well-connected families who might pay large fines (or bribe the judges with property or cash).[82] Meanwhile, the renewal of a prohibition against preaching monks had increased popular resentment throughout the valley. Despite evidence of disaffection, and despite warnings from abroad that Milan was actively encouraging a rebellion, the *Beitag* bickered about how to respond. Plans in the Valtellina thus moved forward, and a general uprising was set for July, 1620, in cooperation with the banished leaders of the Spanish faction in the Freestate itself.[83]

The rebellion began with a massacre of the Protestants in the central town of Tirano. Despite all the signs of coming trouble, the Protestants and the Rhaetian officers who supported them were unprepared, and most of the congregation was killed in the first wave of rioting. The movement spread quickly up and down the valley, though it did not at first penetrate the separate counties of Bormio and Chiavenna. Panic-stricken letters from the Rhaetian officers reported the events to Chur, but the rapid arrival of Spanish troops prevented the Freestate from taking any measures to regain control in the valley. Not until Zurich and Bern sent an expeditionary force did a serious, if unsuccessful, attempt to reconquer the Valtellina take place.[84]

By the late summer of 1620, open warfare spread across the Freestate as well. Not only had the subject territories driven out the *Bündner* and welcomed Milanese garrisons, but the exiled leaders of the Spanish faction in the Gray League undertook an invasion of the Freestate itself in order to reestablish themselves. Paid by the Spanish and supported by the Catholic Swiss, a force led by Antonio Molina and Johann Anton Gioieri marched into the Val Mesocco even before the Valtellina massacre, but was forced back by local militias. When the rebellion broke out, the predominantly Catholic Gray League assembled its troops, but refused to send them south to campaign against the Catholic subjects. Instead, a large force camped

---

[81] *Ibid.*, 418–19.

[82] Moor stresses the uneven nature of the investigations, *ibid.*, 419.

[83] The original date planned seems to have been the 26th (old style), but changes elsewhere advanced the outbreak of the revolt by a week. Moor, *Geschichte von Currätien*, II: 437.

[84] The correspondence of this period transcribed in Anhorn, *Graw-Pünter-Krieg*, 60–107, esp. 62–63. Some forces from the Freestate conducted a brief campaign in the valley for about a week after the massacre, but were driven back by the steadily growing Spanish forces, and by their own disorganization. Moor, *Geschichte von Currätien*, II: 464–94.

at Ilanz, leading the Chadè to fear that an attack on the other Leagues was intended.[85] In September this fear increased when Uri and Schwyz sent 1500 troops to support the Gray League against the Venetian party in Rhaetia and its allies from Zurich and Bern. Not just Rhaetia, but all Switzerland seemed on the edge of civil war.

Like the *Strafgericht* at Thusis, the rebellion in the Valtellina also unleashed a flood of propaganda, this time all over Europe. Protestant literature described the massacre of the local Reformed population in the Valtellina as one more example of Catholic cruelty and rebellion, while Catholic authors praised the just action that Catholics there had taken against the unbearable tyranny of their Protestant Rhaetian masters. Within Rhaetia, the rebellion raised the question where the Freestate's political authority came from. Was the Freestate's power over the Valtellina a matter of feudal law or divine mission? How could a republic which had rebelled against its own lords now condemn the Valtellinans for doing the same? Defending the Freestate's authority required both defining it clearly, and illustrating how the undeniable abuses that had taken place in the subject territories were different from the tyranny suffered by the Rhaetians in the days of their emancipation. The revolt in 1620 also exerted a deeply polarizing effect on politics in the Freestate, because it made religious difference a pressing political issue. An overtly Catholic rebellion could only bring religion to the forefront of rhetorical debate: Protestant Rhaetians did not resist the temptation to describe the rebellion as an atrocity, whereas Catholic *Bündner* faced a troubling decision between religious solidarity and political and economic interest.

In fact, the *Bündner* no longer had any control over the Valtellina's fate, or even over their own. For the next two decades, the entire region became a battleground in the larger struggle for power and hegemony between France and Spain. Initially, France managed to secure Spanish agreement to return the Valtellina to the Freestate (the Treaty of Madrid, April 1621), but while negotiations dragged on, the Venetian party in the Freestate tried to reconquer the recalcitrant subjects by force.[86] The expedition, headed by Jörg Jenatsch, ended in disaster, and triggered an Austrian invasion of the Freestate itself in the winter of 1621–22. Austrian forces took direct control over the Lower Engadine and the Prättigau, and established a protectorate over the Chadè and the Gray League. Based on their long-standing if little-respected lordship over the conquered territories, Austria began a campaign of rigorous recatholicization that included disarming the communes, sending in Capuchin missionaries and requiring attendance at Catholic services. Abandoned by the other communes, the Prättigau submitted to hostile occupation, as Spanish officers and Austrian troops moved freely through the rest of the Freestate. The (Second) Milan articles of January 1622 decreed the

---

[85] A. Pfister, *Jörg Jenatsch*, 98; Moor, *Geschichte von Currätien*, II: 467–69.
[86] Brown, "The Valtelline," 53–54.

permanent separation of the Valtellina, and established Austrian garrisons in Chur and Maienfeld.[87]

The Prättigau rebellion of 1622

In the spring of 1622, however, the Prättigau rebelled briefly against its new Austrian lords, sparking a movement that temporarily freed the Freestate of foreign troops. By planning in secret and arming themselves with iron-tipped staves, the Prättigauer succeeded in surprising the small Austrian garrisons, who were killed or expelled from the communes in a matter of days. The angry peasants descended into the Rhine valley, where they defeated their surprised enemies in a series of skirmishes, and even forced the Austrian general Baldiron into a humiliating retreat into the Valtellina.[88] The Austrians returned within a few months, to be sure, but Protestants nevertheless made the most of this victory against the Emperor's seemingly invincible forces. A burst of pamphlets and songs celebrated the "hardy Prättigauer" who had with God's help cleansed their homeland, armed with nothing more than courage and wooden staves. By this time, however, the tone of the texts had changed. A strong confessional tone remained, to be sure, which would characterize Rhaetian polemics and politics up to the present. But the difficult problems of lordship and communal authority faded into the background. For the first time in over a century, the Rhaetians faced a situation that corresponded to their own myths: tyrannical feudal lords had attempted to subdue them by force, but the brave communes had joined together to drive out the tyrants. Confronted with genuine rule by a foreign power, the local struggles between magnates and resentful communes lost their relevance. The rhetoric of communal autonomy once again included the leading families who soon took charge of the Prättigau rebellion, along with the brave peasants themselves, thus creating the ground for the united but more oligarchic Freestate which reappeared later.[89]

RHAETIA DURING THE THIRTY YEARS' WAR, 1621–39

After the Prättigau rebellion had been suppressed, a series of further catastrophes engulfed the Freestate. Austria invaded the Lower Engadine and the Prättigau in the fall of 1622, burning most of the villages there in the process. Militarily defeated, the *Bundestag* had no choice but to accept the Peace of Lindau (September 30, 1622), which severed these regions and the Valtellina from the

---

[87] The Milan articles provided the basis for the Treaty of Lindau in 1622, as well. See Moor, *Geschichte von Currätien*, II: 666–791 for this period, with the details of the treaties at II: 667 and II: 787–91.

[88] Gillardon, *Geschichte des Zehngerichtenbundes*, 157–69.

[89] Several of these texts are discussed below, chapter 7.

remainder of the Freestate, and which made the Chadè and Gray League Austrian protectorates. The treaty foreshadowed the imperial Edict of Restitution of 1629 by returning all property taken from the Catholic church since 1526, and it provided that the Capuchins would be allowed to proselytize throughout the Freestate. Famine and plague followed the invasion of 1622–23, disrupting the patterns of village life established during the previous century. Most Reformed ministers and numerous Protestant magnates fled to Zurich, from where they conducted a vigorous but ineffective propaganda campaign against the Austrians.[90]

From 1623 until 1636, the outer political life of the Freestate was entirely determined by the foreign policies of France and Spain.[91] When these protagonists of the Thirty Years' War were openly hostile to each other, the Freestate gained direct assistance from France, as in 1624 and in 1631. When Richelieu and his advisors sought to mute their confrontation with the Habsburgs, in contrast, Rhaetia tended to slip back under Austrian occupation. The effect on Rhaetia was a long see-saw battle in which French and Austrian armies occasionally exchanged position without giving the Freestate's own government the slightest chance to regain any real autonomy. The Rhaetian magnates, meanwhile, focused on one political goal whatever the price: the recovery of the Valtellina, their most important source of income and prestige. Both sides in the greater European struggle tried to entice the magnates with scraps of control over the Valtellina: even in 1621, Governor Feria in Milan had offered to "return" the Valtellina as long as the Freestate guaranteed complete local autonomy, free transit for Spanish troops, and the exclusive practice of the Catholic religion.[92] But all such offers, whether Spanish or French, gave the magnates too little to satisfy their pride, and would have, if accepted, raised the risk of renewed unrest by the communes, which now tended to take a more rigidly confessional stance than did their magnate leaders.

The close control that the Habsburg forces established over the Freestate and the Valtellina in 1623, however, represented an immediate and dangerous threat to French diplomatic plans for the region. Unable to take direct action because of the continuing civil war with the Huguenots, France joined Savoy and Venice in 1623 to demand the return of the Valtellina to the *Bündner*; as a temporary solution to forestall open conflict between France and Spain, the valley was garrisoned by papal troops. By 1624, however, Richelieu had taken charge of French policy, and troops were dispatched to Graubünden to put the passes back in French hands. Without significant resistance, a French–*Bündner* army led by the Marquis de Coeuvres took the Valtellina back temporarily. Despite fair words to the contrary, however, France had no more intention of allowing the *Bündner* a free hand than did

---

[90] A general overview of the period, Pieth, *Bündnergeschichte*, 209–27.
[91] The following paragraphs rely also on the succinct summary, which includes the various treaties of the 1620s, in Brown, "The Valtelline," 53–62.
[92] *Ibid.*, 53.

the Spanish, as shown by the Treaty of Monzoño of 1626, which reduced the Freestate's sovereignty over the valley to purely formal terms. In the event, domestic troubles forced France to withdraw in 1627, when the Valtellina fell back into Spanish hands.[93]

All these military actions resulted in catastrophic domestic consequences for Graubünden. The winter of 1622–23 was particularly harsh, and was accompanied not only by famine but also by plague, which recurred again from 1629–31.[94] The population dropped sharply during the 1620s, while foreign presence hindered most *Bündner* from the war profiteering practiced so successfully by the Swiss during the Thirty Years' War. The turmoil of these years also shifted the balance of power within the communes and the Freestate. Two main effects seem to have dominated. In the first place, famine, epidemics, and occupation by foreign powers strengthened the position of the magnate families against the rest of the communes. Not only were the leading statesmen the only ones in a position to negotiate with the foreign commanders, but for the first time in decades, common and elite interests appeared to be in agreement. Survival and the maintenance of autonomy were the key problems that the communes faced, not the balance of power within them. Consequently, commoners seem to have been more likely to form a common front with their local magnates, even at the expense of acknowledging the latters' dominance over the political process. The "common man's" response to the series of disasters overwhelming the Freestate after 1620 seems to have been apathy, or perhaps a turn to local concerns. Relatively few men volunteered for the forces that tried to regain the Valtellina in 1620 and 1621, for example.[95] When local affairs were affected, however, as in the Prättigau, collective action remained potent and effective, though under the leadership of the magnates. The internecine struggles that had divided the Freestate since the 1570s receded in the face of overwhelming threats from the outside. Domestic conflict did not cease, of course, since different factions among the elite favored different tactics towards the great powers; but on the whole, the communes in this period did not seek to maintain an independent voice, as they had during the previous decades.

The second effect on domestic affairs in the Freestate was the rise of a kind of warlordism: a few factional leaders united nearly total power in their hands. In a period when every politician was also a general, such men as Rudolf von Salis, Rudolf von Planta and the former Reformed minister Jörg Jenatsch became the effective rulers over the Freestate. Jenatsch in particular built up a near-dictatorial

---

[93] See Moor, *Geschichte von Currätien*, II: 838–49, who lays particular emphasis on the Bundestag's outrage at the provisions of the Monzoño treaty, (as reported by Fortunat Juvalta); and Brown, "The Valtelline," 58–60.

[94] On the domestic consequences (from a robustly Protestant viewpoint), Pieth, *Bündnergeschichte*, 211–12, 216. Brown, "The Valtelline," 60, cites Venetian estimates that a fourth of the population died in 1631 alone.

[95] Moor, *Geschichte von Currätien*, II: 514.

position from 1636 until his assassination in 1639.[96] The Freestate's final foreign policy shift during this period, moving back into the Austrian orbit in 1636 in exchange for the return of the Valtellina to Rhaetian control, was the result of an aristocratic conspiracy without any communal participation. Unlike their fathers and grandfathers, the new *Grosse Hansen* of the 1630s did not need to fear popular resistance to their plans. War and its attendant miseries had weakened many of the foundations for communal participation in politics, wiping out in a few years what had taken nearly a century to build up. At the same time, a sharply reduced population decreased the economic and social strain that had contributed to popular restlessness earlier in the seventeenth century.

Although Graubünden itself was not invaded again after 1631, the military struggle among the great powers over the Valtellina continued. The high point came in 1635 and 1636, after Richelieu sent Henri de Rohan to take command of a mixed French and *Bündner* army that hoped to regain control of the strategic valley.[97] Rohan's extraordinary military successes were not matched by any French willingness to cede real control over the Valtellina to the Freestate, however; Richelieu had other plans, and Rohan was instructed to leave French garrisons in all key locations. Nor were the French willing at this point to allow the reinstatement of Protestant worship among the Catholic subjects of the Freestate, or allow the Freestate to exercise full jurisdiction in the subject territories.[98] Under the leadership of Jörg Jenatsch – by now no longer a Protestant minister, but rather a seasoned military commander and a recent convert to Catholicism – the leading magnates in Graubünden secretly negotiated a new settlement with the Austrian regent in Innsbruck and the Spanish governor in Milan. In return for accepting the exclusion of Protestants from the Valtellina and allowing the passage of Habsburg troops, the Rhaetian Freestate regained full control over its former subjects. The treaty was drafted and signed by a secret society of leading *Bündner* magnates, known as the *Kettenbund*, without any consultation with the communes.[99] When the time came to oust the French, who had garrisons within the Freestate as well as in the Valtellina, the communes unhesitatingly followed their magnates, allowing a successful change in diplomatic loyalties, and the end of French influence in the Freestate.

After this putsch, Jenatsch began to rule the Freestate by fiat, in collusion with

---

[96] A. Pfister, *Jörg Jenatsch* is the most recent biography.

[97] On this part of Rohan's career, see Johannes Bühring, *Venedig, Gustav Adolf, und Rohan*, Hallesche Abhandlungen zur Neueren Geschichte, vol. xx (Halle, 1885); and Hansmartin Schmid, *Das Bild Herzog Heinrich Rohans in der bündnerischen und französischen Geschichtsschreibung* (Chur: Bischofsberger, 1966).

[98] Moor, *Geschichte von Currätien*, ii: 908–14; Mohr participates fully in the apologetics that have surrounded Rohan and the *Bündner* change in diplomatic direction ever since the seventeenth century.

[99] On the so-called *Kettenbund* of 1636, see Pieth, *Bündnergeschichte*, 222–27; and Moor, *Geschichte von Currätien*, ii: 919–22.

the magnates who by now cared less about confessional principles than about regaining their lands and offices in the rich southern valleys. The *Bundestag* and presidents continued their functions, but entirely under Jenatsch's influence.[100] While Protestants in the Freestate rapidly came to distrust Jenatsch, it was once again the magnates that sealed his doom. When it became apparent that he was attempting to cement his control through building up his personal holdings and wealth, another conspiracy succeeded in having him murdered in 1639.[101] Now firmly in the Austrian diplomatic camp, Graubünden received control of the Valtellina in 1639, ensuring that the profits of government would once again flow into magnate coffers. While communal institutions did not fade away after this point, the communes no longer showed their earlier willingness to rise up in *Fähnlilüpfe* to defend their place in the Freestate's power structure. Instead, magnate factionalism became the dominant political paradigm for the remainder of the *ancien régime*, coexisting comfortably with the ongoing rhetoric of liberty and communal authority that had consolidated before the Thirty Years' War began. It is to that rhetorical tradition that we now turn.

---

[100] Pieth, *Bündnergeschichte*, 225–28.
[101] For the latest thought on who the secret conspirators may have been (since Jenatsch did not lack for enemies), see Mathieu, "33 Jahre."

7

Political language and political cosmology
during the crisis years

The turbulent course of events in Rhaetia during the first part of the seventeenth century has long attracted historians' attention. Rich in dramatic events – violent confrontations, battles, factional and diplomatic maneuvering – and dominated by powerful personalities such as Jörg Jenatsch and Pompeius Planta, the *Bündner Wirren* always presented a tempting subject for historical studies. For a brief time, the situation in this marginal Alpine republic attracted the concern of diplomats and generals all over Europe, as Venice, France, and Spain fought over the strategic passes of the central Alps, and as Catholic and Calvinist Europe struggled over the future of the mountain communes and their subjects in the Valtellina.

Yet the chronic instability and conflict in early seventeenth-century *Bünden* was also a political and social predicament confronting all of the Freestate's inhabitants. Foreign pressure and growing confessional hostility exacerbated the contradictions inherent in Rhaetians' views of social and political order in such a way as to call into question the foundations, and even the existence, of the Rhaetian state. How did they respond? When their political institutions broke down, and when previously tractable problems led to violence that threatened the whole structure of the Leagues, Rhaetian leaders and writers, along with peasants and townspeople, moved to restore what they saw as the correct order of affairs. Some responses took the form of actions, as described in earlier chapters: not only the reform movement after 1585, but the series of *Fähnlilüpfe* after 1617 and the revolt of the Prättigau in 1622 each represented an effort by a large number of *Bündner*, from simple farmers to wealthy patricians, to assert control over their fates in the name of their understanding of the Freestate.

Another way to respond, a verbal and ideological one, will be the subject of this chapter: during this period, an unprecedented number of propaganda pamphlets, political songs, and historical reports about the Freestate appeared. Ranging from vituperative attacks on the Freestate to impassioned defenses of its organization and institutions, these texts provide a vivid source for analyzing how different parties within and outside the Freestate interpreted its identity. These documents were all intended to persuade, not to chronicle what happened. Written mostly by educated men, they illustrate how authors whose practical experience was with the communal values and institutions of the Freestate drew upon classical, feudal, and humanist political ideas to articulate their situation. While Swiss and Rhaetian writers made few contributions to political theory during this period – for that, we must wait for Rousseau – they were caught up in the same problems and debates, trained in universities using the same texts, participants in the same European struggles as their better-known contemporaries from Bodin to Grotius. Analyzing their contributions, therefore, serves a double purpose: it provides an insight into the values and the political culture of the Freestate, but it also allows us to see how they intrepreted ideas from the broader European traditions of political thought.

The flood of persuasive literature produced during the *Bündner Wirren* took many forms, including satirical and hortatory songs, poems, prose political pamphlets, chronicles, and formal histories. Some were printed and distributed (often in several editions), others remained in manuscript but circulated widely, some consisted of official documents within various governments, and a few remained known only to their authors.[1] The predominant languages were German and Italian, but pamphlets concerning the Freestate's affairs appeared in Latin, French, Dutch, and even English.[2] Most were written by inhabitants of the Freestate, but commentators from abroad also reported on Rhaetian events. Most texts were anonymous, though scholars through the years have identified some authors; even if the individual author is unknown, we can make surmises about his position in Rhaetian society from the document itself. The following analysis will rest primarily on a selection of pamphlets and songs written between 1600 and 1640. Over one hundred short works (excluding religious tracts, reports of miracles, and the like) by Rhaetians or about Rhaetia appeared between 1523 and 1640, most of them between 1617 and 1623. Of these, some thirty surviving texts (not counting multiple editions and translations) directly addressed political affairs in the Freestate; these, together with songs and political tracts that circulated in manuscript form, provide the core of the analysis below.

Beyond sorting Rhaetian political literature by its external characteristics, we can also categorize it on the basis of its content. In many cases, we can associate a text with a given party during the early seventeenth-century struggles in Rhaetia. The prose political pamphlets are easiest to identify in this way, since the authors often explicitly attacked the opposing party while promoting their own faction's goals. A preponderance of the texts was clearly anti-Spanish, a smaller group virulently anti-French. Pro-Catholic and pro-Reformed pamphlets appeared as well,

---

[1] This chapter rests on an analysis of some 120 texts, of which 99 were published. They are listed by *title* in the bibliography, and will be cited by title below. Among them are 76 pamphlets, 24 political songs, and 14 manuscript tracts.

[2] Between 1523 and 1640, 68 per cent of political texts published in or about Graubünden were in German, 12 per cent in French, 8 per cent in Italian. Notably absent are texts in Romantsch. In addition, a large number of Italian pamphlets reporting diplomatic events exist which are not part of this analysis.

although surprisingly many pamphlets either avoided confessional issues or argued for "the freedom of both religions." After the Freestate's internal conflicts had burst into open violence in 1620, new publications concentrated on reporting and commenting about major upheavals such as the Valtellina massacre and the Prättigau rebellion, both of which attracted interest all across Europe.

My central question will be the general standpoint each author adopted about the existence and character of the Freestate. Seen very broadly, four major positions emerged: a conservative and legalistic tendency that defended the Freestate's existence in terms of feudal privileges and laws; a moderate patriotic position that emphasized the historical myths of the Freestate, appealing to the "courageous ancestors" who by their blood and sweat freed the Rhaetians from bad lords; and finally two different radical views that questioned the very basis of the Freestate. The two radical positions reached opposite conclusions about Rhaetian affairs. The first, the radical-populist, went beyond the rejection of "bad lords" found in the moderate patriotic pamphlets; instead, these pamphlets equated all lords with tyrants and all subjects with slaves. The violently anti-aristocratic tone here contrasted with relatively positive statements about the "common man" in Rhaetia. Although none of the radical-populist texts presented an abstract theory of popular government, a few pamphlets mentioned rule by the common man and even "democracy" as distinctive virtues that characterized the Freestate. Almost all were Protestant in their confessional tone, ranging from moderate assertions of "religious freedom" to hysterical anti-papalism. The second radical standpoint, the radical-critical, denied the autonomy of the Freestate, and portrayed its freedom as no more than peasant usurpation. Often associated with a strongly Catholic viewpoint, these pamphlets and songs countenanced the continued existence of the Leagues only within a framework of subjection to princes outside and patricians inside. The most unrestrained of these pamphlets used such immoderate language that they reveal a certain "aristocratic rage" against the social order of the Freestate. All the radical pamphlets, whether positive or negative, echoed the sense of crisis and incoherence that plagued the Freestate in the early seventeenth century.

Of course, any typology of political arguments carries the risk of artificially separating what belongs together and joining what could be separated. This is particularly true of Rhaetian political rhetoric during the early seventeenth century. Rhaetian authors of that period wrote as we might expect in a crisis during which not only the distribution of power, but also the basic principles of their political order were at stake: a few argued for simple if extreme standpoints, but the majority grasped eagerly, even desperately, at ideas from widely varying sources to help explain and solve their current dilemmas. Their goal was not theoretical purity, whether political or religious, but immediate solutions to a growing sense of disorder and irresolvable conflict. The problem addressed by these authors was not the general character of the political good, but what specific measures should be taken to realize that good under the present circumstances. These measures, being practical, necessarily depended on the prevailing practice of politics in the Freestate; each author's understanding of practice, therefore, influenced the way he connected his vision of the Freestate with the specific actions he proposed. The question "What sort of entity should the Freestate be?" was not identical to the question "What values should be promoted by the political life?" although the two were obviously related.

Consequently, the four main approaches – conservative-legal, historical-patriotic, radical-populist, and radical-critical – consisted of clusters of frequently associated ideas, rather than clearly delineated groups of texts. Many texts mixed legalistic *loci communes* and historical commonplaces indiscriminately with novel trains of thought. While it is true that certain correspondences did appear between confessional orientation, partisan position, and foreign alignment, the turbulent course of events ensured that complex and often incoherent constellations of discourse were common. Nor can we find a single spectrum of opinions, ranging from some hypothetical right to left. The ease with which seemly incompatible positions mingled is itself evidence of the deep-seatedness of the crisis in Rhaetian society and politics, showing that the very terms of the debate were often unclear or incommensurate. Although the following meander through the fields of Rhaetian political rhetoric is guided by a movement from conservative through moderate to radical, the reader should remember that arguments which I have separated were sometimes printed side by side on the same page. Still, each rhetorical paradigm drew upon the political practice and institutional structure that had evolved over the previous century. Particularly for the radical-populist texts, which departed widely from contemporary European political theory, it is important to see how the political reality of the Freestate made certain ideas thinkable and believable, ideas which would have been viewed as subversive or utopian in most European political contexts of the time.

European ideas provided the raw material, so to speak, for much Rhaetian rhetoric. Pamphlets and songs were not themselves theoretical, but their authors were most often men familiar with the political theories of their time. This becomes particularly evident in the histories and memoirs composed by such men as Fortunat von Juvalta and Fortunat Sprecher von Bernegg. The first was influenced by neo-Stoic ideas (also evident in his Latin poetry) while the latter avows his debt to classical methods of historiography.[3] Even the village minister Bartholomäus Anhorn, less educated than other chroniclers, naively laid out his duty to be historically accurate in his chronicles, citing "the pagan historian Sallustius" and Cicero along with Phillipe de Commynes, Pietro Bembo, and Sleidan as his models for writing "*nudam historiam.*"[4] But even when terms central to contemporary

---

[3] Juvalta, *Denkwürdigkeiten*. A selection of Juvalta's poems published as *Raeti Commentarii*. Sprecher also cites a list of humanist historians as his sources and inspirations: Sprecher, *Rhetia*, 4–6.
[4] Anhorn, *Püntner Aufruhr*, iii–vii.

theoretical debates turned up in Rhaetian texts – terms such as "absolute power", "democracy", or "sovereignty" – they functioned in a different context, and thus carried a meaning different from their broader European usage. Rhaetian authors were not passive transmitters of ideas; rather, they reinterpreted what they had learned in light of the daily practice of communal and League politics with which they were familiar. Only when understood in this way can a modern reader make sense of the extraordinary manifesto that the *Strafgericht* of Thusis issued in 1618: "The form of our government is democratic, and the power to elect and depose all magistrates . . . lies with our common man."[5] This single sentence linked the Aristotelian category of democracy with the late medieval idea of the "common man" through an assertion of popular sovereignty that transcended the latter doctrine's high medieval roots.[6]

The seeds of the troubles after 1617 were fundamentally no different from those during the previous century: the conflicts of interest caused by foreign intervention, and the implicit contradiction between communalist ideology and leadership by a self-conscious elite. But the larger context was different in 1618, partly because of greater stakes in the competition between Venice, Spain, and France over the Freestate's passes, partly because of the growing social separation between patrician and peasant within the Freestate, partly because both religious confessions felt more threatened than they had been previously. The polemicists of the *Bündner Wirren* reached back to familiar conceptual models in an effort to overcome these obstacles, stretching to fit a republic of semi-sovereign communes into established political world-views. Whether the Freestate's radical populists could have elaborated their principles into a coherent ideology strong enough to quell the conflict tearing apart the Freestate cannot be known: when foreign intervention moved from bribes and threats to invasions, the terms of the debate changed decisively. New formulations stopped appearing after the terrible years in the early 1620s, leaving claims about popular power incomplete and discredited. By the end of the troubles in 1639, the distribution of power in Rhaetian society had shifted in favor of the magnates, with the result that communal values and populist rhetoric became confined to a narrow range of situations. The tenacity of populist rhetoric in the face of this situation suggests that it was indeed deeply rooted in the practice of the communes, but circumstances hindered its further development until the mid-eighteenth century. For a few years around 1620, though, traditionalist, absolutist, and democratic ideas about political order all competed in the words and actions of the Rhaetian people.

---

[5] *Grawpündtnerische Handlung*, fol. A ii^v: "Die Form unsers Regiments ist Democratisch: unnd stehet die erwellung unnd entsetzung der Oberkeiten . . . bey unserem gemeinem man . . . " (All citations from the 52-page edition of 1618.)

[6] The best analysis of the political theories of the Swiss confederacy in the sixteenth century is Reibstein, *Respublica Helvetiorum*.

CONSERVATIVE RHETORIC ABOUT THE FREESTATE

Among the flood of pamphlets and similar texts written about the Freestate in the early seventeenth century, a few took a conservative and legalistic position. Their essential claim was that the communes and Leagues existed, or should exist, entirely within a traditional, fundamentally feudal structure of authority. The valleys and towns of the Freestate, according to this view, were fiefs of various lords, and were endowed with specific privileges by those lords; that these privileges sometimes included complete self-government, or that some lordships had been purchased by the people who inhabited them, did not affect the origins of legitimate authority. Such conservative rhetoric about the Freestate did not question the existence of the Three Leagues and their common institutions: after all, these had been in existence for well over a century, had been recognized by emperor and other princes in treaties and agreements, and were documented by letters of infeudation and privileges.

What distinguished the conservative position, rather, was first an emphasis on the purely legal dimension of the Freestate's status, and second an anti-political tone which discouraged direct action in defense of the Freestate. The emphasis on freedom common to all Rhaetian political discourse appeared in the conservative pamphlets primarily in the sense of inherited privilege and public order. Above all, the conservative position was a defensive one: it argued that every man should obey his established authority, while attempting to demonstrate that the communes and Leagues constituted such an authority because of legitimate concessions from their lords. We can find passages reflecting the conservative position both before and after the crisis of 1618–20, but the effect is quite different depending on the context. Before the Freestate's survival came into question because of civil war and foreign invasions, the conservative position reflected the *de facto* legal situation in the Leagues. Most communes still valued the specific privileges they had negotiated with their lords, although the favorable situation after 1524 had led many communes to usurp considerable additional authority. Even after a century of effective autonomy, concrete disputes often returned to the charters and judgments of the late Middle Ages. Given the local balance of power, it was typically the lords who appealed to older documents to preserve their remaining rights, while communes often sought new agreements.[7] After 1622, however, as a result of the shifting balance of power, it was the communes, not the lords, who saw in the old letters a bulwark for their position; consequently, several narrowly legal defenses of communal rights were published during this period.

A manuscript tract from 1607 clearly outlined the conservative position on the Freestate's identity. Entitled "Reasons why the general penal courts [*Strafgerichte*]

---

[7] As late as 1615, the communes in the lordship of Rhäzüns negotiated new, highly favorable agreements with the house of Austria. LAI Ferdinandea, Fasz. 206, Rubrik 193 (September 22, 1622).

in the Leagues are intolerable to all men who love peace and honor," the phrasing in its early sections suggests a pro-Austrian author from either Switzerland or the Freestate.[8] The author first established the purpose of the Swiss and Rhaetian confederacies: God had established them for the sake of freedom and peace. Their alliances clearly established what each League should hold in common and what should be held separately, and also specified the exact obligations each party had to its allies and to its lords.[9] Most importantly, because the Confederates knew that fairness and justice pleased God, whereas injustice incited him to wrath, the Swiss and Rhaetian alliances protected the rights of every "prince, lord, and city."[10] However, in recent years "a certain pride and insolence has grown in the Leagues among the common man, through abuse of the privileges he had attained," so that everyone fomented rebellion against those who had served in the government or who were wealthy.[11] The author continued by portraying the *Bundesbrief* of 1524 and other constitutional documents as efforts to prevent unrest and to ensure that every confederate would be judged by his legitimate authority.[12] Narrating the events leading up to the *Fähnlilupf* of 1607, the author presented the entire affair as an "outcry and raging of the common man,"[13] before whom no honorable gentleman was safe.

A second section of the tract analyzed the causes of the uproar. "Those in the eight communes [in the Prättigau]," the author maintained, "are born to rebellion, and inclined by nature to innovations."[14] The best way to counter such tendencies was to follow the *Bundesbrief*, and to recognize that the Prättigauer were natural subjects of the house of Austria: "as long as the other two Leagues do not permit and require them to carry out their obligations to their lord, no blessing from God, no peace and quiet can be hoped for in these lands."[15] The text breaks off shortly after this point, but the import is clear. On the one hand, the freedom of the Three Leagues was a divine gift for the sake of peace and order; the author was clearly not advocating the abolition of the Leagues altogether. On the other hand, the existence of the Leagues must not interfere with each lord's legitimate rights and authority over his subjects. Thus, holders of this conservative position saw no conflict between the freedom of the Three Leagues and the judicial and administrative

---

8 "Ursachen warumben die Algemaine Strafgerichten in Pündten allen Ehr- und rhue liebenden unträgenlich seyendt . . . 1607."
9 "Ursachen warumben," fol. 1.
10 *Ibid.*, fol: 2.
11 *Ibid.*, fol. 2: "Doch ist nit ohn dz seid etlich jaren hero in den Pündten bey dem gemainen Mann, durch mißbrauch der erlangten freihaitten etwas hoch: und ubermuth zuegenomben, also das ein jeder sich understanden umb ein Jetwederen abdanckh muetwilliger wiß nach aufrueren trachten, deme so Im Regiment sich brauchen laßen, oder sonst von Gott mit Reichthumb begabet..."
12 *Ibid.*, fol. 3.
13 *Ibid.*, fol. 5.
14 *Ibid.*, fol. 7: "dz die in der 8. gerichten merenthails zue aufrueren erboren, und von Natur zu ernewerungen geneigt."
15 *Ibid.*, fol. 9.

power of individual lords. The proper balance between the two had to be sought through the correct interpretation of the various legal documents that defined the relationship between communes and lords.

Although the author did not discuss the internal organization of the communes, he explicitly attacked the common man, who had misinterpreted his God-given privileges and become proud and insolent. Holders of the conservative position did not understand political authority as something that could be negotiated between lord and subject, or as something which ought to be adjusted to reflect changing circumstances. Certainly the common man had no business attempting to change or reform the terms of his subjection. In a sense, this text denied the value of politics (in the modern sense) altogether.[16] God ordained lords and subjects; he erected kingdoms and confederations and, by his grace, specified the relationships between them. When subjects tampered with his arrangements, divine displeasure resulted in rebellion and disorder, as demonstrated by the events in 1607. For conservative authors, the troublesome question of how authority flowed between communal assembly, local magistrates, and lords simply did not exist: since the lord was the source of communal privileges, obedience to him was the first priority. Well-documented and customary privileges merely outlined the shape of this obedience, although they, too, were divinely sanctioned. Politics, according to this view, simply involved the correct identification of the ordained channels of authority; once these were reestablished, order and peace would result.

This conservative document's practical conclusion, therefore, was that the relationship between communes and lords was an ongoing one defined by formal documents and legally binding custom. While acknowledging the freedom of the Swiss and Rhaetian Confederacies, the author made no mention of the reasons for their autonomy, nor that they had fought several wars to maintain it. Conservative authors skimmed over the historical context to alight on the natural relationship they still perceived between lord and subject. In this particular document, conservative claims served to defend noble prerogatives from communal usurpation.

Communes could also take this conservative view. In 1622, the commune of Mesocco was involved with a dispute with its former lords, the Trivulzio, who used the Milanese invasion as an excuse to reassert their claims to lordship over the valley. The Mesoccans responded with a pamphlet that accepted the legal frame-work of feudal authority, but argued that the actual documents demonstrated that they had purchased their autonomy from the Trivulzio in 1549.[17] The first

---

[16] I follow Moses Finley here in defining politics as self-conscious reflection and action by a relatively large number of persons about the proper ordering and conduct of public business. *Politics in the Ancient World*, esp. 50–57.

[17] "Factum tale in risolutione." The editor's dating of the manuscript to the late sixteenth century is unlikely. Not only is there a German published text with an identical title from 1623, but the Italian text makes reference to the "pace perpetua l'anno passato in Milano et il presente in Lindau,"

paragraph described the lordship that the house of Sax had possessed over the valley for many centuries, having the authority to judge the civil and criminal cases between men in the valley. After a dispute about the sale of the valley to the Trivulzio, Giovanni Giacomo Trivulzio had brought the valley into alliance with the Gray League, "without any reservation of the Holy Roman Empire nor of any other matter," and since that time the lord and the valley had been full members of the Gray League.[18] The author continued by narrating the many lawsuits which had taken place between the valley and its lords, culminating in the final purchase of the Trivulzios' rights in 1549, as ordered by a neutral court of the Three Leagues. However, disputes about the final resolution resulted in still more suits; the last adjudication in 1580 imposed perpetual silence, and explicitly affirmed "the Valley of Mesocco had never been subjected to the Holy Roman Empire."[19]

Nevertheless, the latest Trivulzio heir was now (in 1622) claiming the valley as an imperial fief. The author protested that this claim was nonsense: all the documents and history showed that not the emperor, but rather the Gray League was "the master and supreme prince" over the valley.[20] The magistrates in Mesocco obviously feared that their status was vulnerable, now that Austria had effectively taken control over the Three Leagues, and were afraid that an imperial court might reinstate the Trivulzio. This pamphlet, phrased in careful legal language, represented an effort to block such a move within the framework of feudal law: the authors presented the matter as one of tracing who was the legitimate lord over the valley, rather than attempting to marginalize or eliminate lordship altogether. Here, as in the 1607 tract, no mention appears of any tyranny that drove the inhabitants to seek their freedom. During the dangerous times of the 1620s, ambitious claims about the just liberation of the Leagues were not likely to get far; instead, conservative rhetoric that did not challenge the legal order of the Empire seemed a safer tactic.

Similar legalistic arguments appeared in pamphlets defending the autonomy of the Prättigau after the rebellion in 1622. Here, the situation was more complex than in the Mesocco. The position of the duke of Tyrol as lord over eight of the Ten Jurisdictions had long been recognized, although with few practical implications. Working together with the historian and statesman Johann Guler, Bartholomäus Anhorn wrote two pamphlets in 1622 defending the League of the Ten

---

referring to the Milanese articles of February 6, 1621 (or perhaps the second set, of January 15, 1622), and the treaty of Lindau, September 30, 1622.

[18] *Ibid.*, 153: "senza niuna riserua del Sacro Romano Impero [sic], ne d'altra cosa, come constà per la Confederatione chiamata la Carta de Cinq. Sigilli . . . ," (punctuation modernized).
[19] *Ibid.*, 154. That such a claim was historically nonsensical did not disturb the author of the pamphlet.
[20] *Ibid.*, 155: "oue non obliga li detti Popoli ad hauer licenza dal Imperatore, ma si bene dalla Legha Grisa come Mastrato et Prenicipe supremo di tutto quello che si ritrouava nel distretto, et dominio della detta Legha . . . "

Jurisdictions, and justifying its rebellion "allowed by nature and all laws."[21] Anhorn made broad claims for the ancient freedom of the Rhaetians, regained by throwing off the yoke of tyrannical lords, and he maintained that calling the Prättigauer "subjects" (*Untertanen*) was no different from enslaving them. The general thrust of his pamphlet was that the Rhaetians were an inherently free people who were only exercising their natural rights in rising up against the Austrian occupation – hardly a conservative position.

Yet the pamphlet also relied heavily on the region's history of feudal lordship to bolster its case, and included an appendix with the texts of thirty-nine charters, which made up nearly half its total length. The letter of 1289 by which the counts of Werdenberg and Vaz gave a group of Walser families the valley of Davos in fief (*Lehenbrieff der Landtschafft Davoß*), was of central importance.[22] It is tempting to point out a seeming contradiction here. If the Rhaetian people had always been free, as historians since Ulrich Campell had argued, then grants of privileges from foreign lords proved little – at most, that earlier lords had recognized the freedom of the Rhaetians. If, in contrast, the status of the people in the communes of the Prättigau in fact depended on grants of privileges, then the principle of subjection to lords' authority was indisputable, and the justice of using force to resist Austria's presence became questionable. Anhorn and Guler clearly subscribed to the first position, but could not neglect the second argument during the critical situation of 1622. They used arguments based on feudal law and custom only where they were strongest, whereas the remaining text of the pamphlet shows that their overall understanding of the true nature of the Leagues and the Freestate was quite different. For a seventeenth-century thinker, the two viewpoints may have operated at different levels. In a society founded on the principle that legal status varied from individual to individual, custom and law pertained to the exact status of specific persons; the "liberty of the Freestate," in contrast, remained an abstract and global concept which defined the relationship between different collectivities.[23] Most of Europe saw no conflict between collective freedom and individual subjection in this period, after all. In the specific context of the Freestate, Anhorn followed Campell by interpreting the ties between communes and their lords in a narrowly contractual sense: the free peasants of Davos had entered into a contract with the counts of Werdenberg, according to the stipulations recorded in the charter of infeudation. Should the lord's successors violate that contract, becoming

---

[21] Citation from the subtitle. The texts are: *Kurtze Wahrhaffte Relation, Was massen in Verwichnen Monat Aprilis*, reprinted identically as *Graubüntische Handlung: das ist, Kurtze und Warhaffte Relation, was massen*. An expanded edition was published later in 1622, entitled *Pündtnerischer Handlungen Widerholte unnd vermehrte Deduction*. My citations are taken from the 1877 edition of the latter, whose editor incorrectly attributes the text to Guler alone. (The correct identity of the author was established by Gustav Scherer.)

[22] *Pündtnerische Handlungen*, 89–91.

[23] Cf. Bierbrauer, *Freiheit und Gemeinde*, esp. 204ff.

bad lords, the peasants were entitled to resist "by nature and according to every law."

Especially in Switzerland, where feudal and non-feudal practices and ideas about ruling were inextricably mixed, Anhorn's position was understandable. Moreover, we must remember that his text had rhetorical goals: Anhorn hoped to elicit sympathy and aid, whereas an accurate description of either theory or practice in the Freestate was of secondary interest. Still, his use of legal arguments based on feudally granted privileges, together with the clearer rhetoric of the 1607 tract and the Mesocco pamphlet of 1622, help outline the conservative view of what kind of entity the Freestate was. According to this position – the most common one found in the fifteenth and even sixteenth centuries – the Freestate was an autonomous construct within the existing framework of law and custom, and thus represented neither a threat to good hierarchical order nor an incitement to peasant rebellion. Lords, too, were bound by law: Rhaetian authors who took the conservative position often stressed this point to protect what they had gained by grant and by good custom. But as European rulers began to reconceive the character and origins of their authority, such a conservative position became increasingly ineffective. It is revealing that when Anhorn's legal arguments failed him, he began contrasting "free confederates with power over themselves" with the "slaves and subjects" of a "monarchy long-sought" by Spain, or even with the "*absolutum dominium* and unlimited power" now sought by the Archduke Leopold.[24] Novel threats needed to be confronted with different rhetoric. Thus, as the Freestate developed beyond its fifteenth-century roots, new models of its nature flourished as well. While the conservative position reemerged in moments of stress, most Rhaetian political rhetoric in the early seventeenth century moved towards quite different viewpoints.

MODERATE HISTORICAL-PATRIOTIC TEXTS ABOUT THE FREESTATE

Many political texts written about the Rhaetian Freestate in the late sixteenth and early seventeenth centuries proceeded from a position I have labelled historical-patriotic. The historical dimension of this political cosmology lay in the passionate conviction that the Rhaetian people's freedom was a heritage from the dawn of recorded time, and that their entire history revolved around the problems of preserving that freedom from one threat after another. Drawing upon the humanist historiography of Aegidius Tschudi and Ulrich Campell, this view extended the Rhaetian past far beyond the surviving documents of the feudal age, to the eponymous hero Rhetus the Tuscan. The patriotic dimension of historical-patriotic literature reflects a growing national consciousness in the Freestate after

---

[24] *Kurtze Warhaffte Relation, Was massen*, B i^v: "freyen ihren selbst mechtigen Pundtsleuten . . . ," versus "Sclaven und underthanen . . . " On the Spanish monarchy, *ibid.*, B ii^r. The line about *absolutum dominium* appears in *Pündtnerischer Handlungen*, 21.

1550. Signaled by expressions of loyalty to "the Fatherland" (*Vaterland* became a common term during this period), a commitment to the Freestate's distinct political identity pervaded not only pamphlets and songs, but also the learned histories written in this period. Campell's *Historia Raetica* remained the seminal work in this respect, although it circulated only in manuscript form until the nineteenth century; Guler's *Raetia* of 1616 and the early parts of Sprecher's *Historia Raetiae* follow Campell closely on the early history of Graubünden. As in Switzerland, Rhaetian patriotism in the early seventeenth century focused closely on a history of late medieval emancipation, which was depicted as a return to autochthonous freedom. The current political order was portrayed as the fruit of recent ancestors' labor, won through their sweat and blood. It was this connection which gave historical-patriotic texts their internal cohesion and compelling emotional power.

All over Europe during the late sixteenth century, thinkers were turning to historical models to explain or challenge the political arrangements they saw around them. Whether in France, where François Hotman's *Franco-Gallia* attempted to reverse the hierarchy of king and people, or in the Netherlands, where the ancient liberties of the Batavians helped legitimize resistance against Phillip II, or in England, where Sir Edward Coke was soon to elaborate the principles of the "Ancient Constitution," historical thinking played a remarkably prominent role during this period.[25] J. G. A. Pocock's classic analysis of the situation in England illustrates how changing interpretations of England's past and its relation to the present formed a conceptual background before which many of the polemics of the English Revolution were staged. Pocock's work is especially important because of the close connection it uncovers between the experience of practicing common lawyers and the political cosmologies which they developed. English political rhetoric was different from that in France partly because of the daily practice and limited education of many English lawyers and political thinkers. A similar point can be made in Graubünden, especially with regard to the historical-patriotic thinkers: they grew up in a political environment which deeply affected the way they interpreted classical political ideas and current developments.

Ulrich Campell composed his *Historia Raetica* between 1570 and his death around 1584.[26] He was encouraged to do so by his fellow Reformed minister Josias Simmler in Zurich, who was himself writing a comprehensive history of the Swiss Confederation. When Campell got to the sixteenth century in his monumental text, he began using contemporary documents and eyewitness accounts to provide a colorful and variegated narrative; the earlier parts of his history, however,

---

[25] The first chapter of Pocock's *Ancient Constitution* provides an excellent introduction. For Hotman, see Donald Kelley, *François Hotman: A Revolutionary's Ordeal* (Princeton: Princeton University Press, 1973). On the Batavians, see the entertaining chapter by Simon Schama in his *The Embarrassment of Riches* (New York: Knopf, 1987), 51–125.

[26] On Campell, Wartmann, "Einleitung"; and Fontana, *Rechtshistorische Begriffsanalyse*, esp. 97–125.

represented a reinterpretation of evidence already gathered and published by Aegidius Tschudi and Johannes Stumpf.[27] Nevertheless, Campell was no blind imitator. From the beginning, he wrote with a different attitude to Rome and the Empire than his German-Swiss colleagues, even describing his native Romantsch language as the result of polluting Latin with German influences.[28] His chronicle tied the history of the region into a single narrative of subjection and liberty.

Campell's most original contribution lay in his interpretation of Rhaetian history after the fall of Rome, which he presented as a tale of Rhaetia falling into servitude and working its way back out. By means of suggestive chapter headings, he first guided the reader from "Rhaetia subjected to servitude" through "Rhaetia enslaved" to "Silent Rhaetia, obscure and ignoble."[29] A ray of hope appeared in his Chapter 23, describing the events of the mid-thirteenth century. There he described "Rhaetia, subjected until now, begins to hope for liberty," followed by "Rhaetia hopes greatly for liberty during these days" and "Rhaetia near to recovering her liberty," reaching his climax with the heading which stood proudly above his chapters 40 through 87, "The Rhaetians are free." Clearly, Rhaetian thinkers like Campell were by no means immune to the wave of historical explanation of national origins sweeping Europe at this time. Moreover, as in other nations, the author's sense of history closely reflected his ideas about his present situation. Writing in a communal republic, Campell could tell a different kind of story than historians of the European monarchies did. His version of Rhaetian liberation became canonical for the historical-patriotic rhetoric written during succeeding generations.

The patriotic views of moderate authors shared the conviction found in conservative texts, that the structure of communes and Leagues had been ordained by God. Where the two views differed was on whether the freedom embodied in the Leagues was prior to the communes' relationship with their lords, or proceeded from that relationship as the conservatives believed. In 1615, the historian Fortunat Sprecher composed and published a song, "Ein schön neu Lied zu Ehren der drei Bünde," which concisely portrayed the ancient origins of the Rhaetian people's freedom. The first stanza made Sprecher's position quite clear:

> I am the old Rhetus, I come from Tuscany.
> To preserve my freedom, and to escape the bonds of servitude,
> I gave up my fatherland, and many possessions and lands,
> Together with many a brave fighter, I brought myself to safety.[30]

---

[27] Wartmann, "Einleitung," xxvii–xxx, and footnote 71, p. lxiv–lxvii.

[28] *Ibid.*, xxxiii; Campell, *Historia*, I: 16.

[29] My analysis here based on Fontana, *Begriffsanalyse*, 103–04. Wartmann, "Einleitung," xxxvii, and the associated footnote 72, p. lxvii, implies that the headings are Campell's own.

[30] Sprecher, "Ein schön neu Lied zu Ehren der drei Bünde," 5: "Rhetus bin ich der alte / komm aus Toscanerland, Die Freyheit zu behalten / u[nd] zmeiden Dienstes bandt / Hab sVaterland aufgeben / darzû groß hab und Guot / Mit manchem khünen Degen / mich gsetzt in sicher Huot."

The subsequent stanzas fleshed out the story: long before Christ, Rhetus and his people were attacked by the Gauls and overwhelmed. Rather than accept the yoke of such a crude tribe, the Tuscans retreated to the "ringwalls" in the high mountains so as to preserve their "free estate."[31] In his prose chronicle of Rhaetian history, Sprecher took the same view, even rendering Horace's praise of the ancient Rhaetians as follows:

> For the Rhaetian in every age
> His precious freedom was of great concern,
> So that he disregarded the fear of death,
> As long as he died a free man.[32]

Like his model Aeneas (and Brutus and all the other Trojan and republican founders so popular in late medieval and humanist historiography), the character Rhetus embodied the idea that the Rhaetians had always been free people, and that their collective freedom was more valuable to them than even their homeland.[33] Sprecher reinforced this notion in the stanzas which followed, repeating the myth that the Rhaetians had later fought the advancing Romans with such courage that they became allies, rather than subjects to Augustus and his heirs.[34] Sprecher's song simply denied that Rome had ever ruled Graubünden, whereas his more detailed prose works argued that the decay of Roman power freed the Rhaetians from Rome.[35]

Sprecher's song also illustrated the dilemma of a Protestant humanist, who both feared and admired the Roman tradition. Loathing the power of contemporary Counter-Reformation Rome, Sprecher insisted that Rome's ancient rise to world dominion had been a direct threat to the Rhaetians' freedom: "[Rome's power] did not want to tolerate us / our freedom galled them / they wanted to bring everything / into their power by force."[36] His conception of national history required him to argue that the "alpine Rhaetians at the sources of the Rhine and the Inn were not all forced under the yoke,"[37] yet the further course of his work adopted the borders and institutions established under Roman rule. The myth of Rhetus clashed with the

---

31 *Ibid.*, 5–6.
32 Sprecher, *Rhetische Cronica*, 17: "Dem Rhetier ist zu aller Zeit / Anglegen gweßt die schön Freyheit / Daß er den Todt nit sihet an / Nun daß er sterb ein freyer Mann."
33 On ancient origin myths in Switzerland, in contrast with princely territories, Marchal, *Frommen Schweden*, 95–96.
34 Sprecher, "Schön neu Lied," 6 (Stanza 14).
35 Sprecher, *Rhetische Cronica*, 8–9. His *Historia von denen Unruhen und Kriegen* (1701 ed.), 8, argues "dann weil kein Hauptmann oder Befehlshaber mehr vorhanden war / ist wol zu erachten / das selbiges als seiner pflicht ledig und loß / den dienst und fleiß welchen es zu vor dem Römischen Fürsten geleistet, zu seinem eignen nutz und frommen werde angewendet haben . . . "
36 Sprecher, "Schön neu Lied," 6: "Da thete sich erhaben [sic] / der Römer Herrschaft groß / Wolt uns das nicht vertragen / die Freyheit sy verdroß / Sy woltend alles bringen / mit Macht in ihren Gewalt . . . "
37 Sprecher, *Rhetische Cronica*, 19. See also his *Geschichte*, I: 12–14.

record of the historical Rhetia Prima under Roman dominion, yet Sprecher drew upon both depending on the circumstances. Sprecher the historian tacitly accepted the truth of Roman rule in his works intended for educated readers, but he glossed it over in a song written for popular dissemination. Meanwhile, Sprecher the humanist continued to write in Latin using Roman authors as his sources. Only an extensive study of Sprecher could determine how the different dimensions of his historical understanding were woven together, but looking at the purpose and character of each text he wrote illuminates why each perspective predominated where it did.

Only late in the tale as told by Sprecher and his fellow moderates did any lords appear over the Rhaetian people:

> Soon some lords appeared, who wanted to be too mighty /
> by increasing their own power, and bearing down on our freedom.
> But their violence and tyranny could not endure in the long run /
> To defend against this / a free alliance was made
> By the people of the Gray League / for which they are famous.
> This greatly harmed all the lords / but nothing could help them.[38]

However little this chronology had to do with the real course of events, it served to reinforce Sprecher's key claim: dominion over the Rhaetians was a late and temporary phenomenon. Having already dismissed the possibility that Rome had conquered the region, he also rejected the authority of medieval lords because they transgressed beyond the authority lent to them, becoming tyrants. As Sprecher's contemporary Adam Saluz put it in his *Rhetus* of 1621:

O God, how marvelously my old free government
Escaped from the hands of the Tyrants.
They were the source of great mischief
And many strong castles and fortresses were seen on the mountains and in the valleys.
Most of these were built by the hand of foreign nobles,
Whom I [Rhetus] allowed to nest in the land in good faith.
Building themselves a home was not the end of it;
They stretched things beyond the breaking point, and turned to tyranny.[39]

When the people organized themselves into Leagues to resist, according to Sprecher, the Pope and Emperor had first threatened, then attacked, but to no avail.

---

[38] Sprecher, "Schön neu Lied," 7: " . . . Bald fand man etlich Herren so woltend seyn zu groß / Ihr eignen Gwalt vermehren, der Freyheit gen ein Stoß. In d'Länge nicht mocht währen / Ihr Gwalt und Tyranney / Derselben sich zerweeren / verbunden sich ganz frey / Ds [sic] Volk im grauen Pundte / den Ruhm man ihnen giebt / Diß dHeerschaft hoch verwundte / half sy doch alles nicht."

[39] Saluz, "Rhetus," 8: "O Gott wie wunderbarlich / Mein alt frey Regiment / Kam wider seer gefahrlich / Vß der Tyrannen hend: Von Inen war entsprossen / Vil Mutwils vberall / Manch veste Burg und Schlosse / Sach man in Berg vnd Thaal. Die mertheils sind erbauwen / Durch frömbdes Adels Handt / Die ich vß gut verthrauwen / Ließ nisten in daß Landt: Ein Wonung zu bereyten / Da blieb es nicht darbey / Sy vberspanten dseyten / Griffen zur tyranney."

The three Leagues not only survived, but also joined with the Swiss Confederacy "to bravely expel the power of mighty princes." As everyone could see, the Rhaetians preserved their freedom through this second period of tyranny, as well.[40] Sprecher could thus sweep to the conclusion of his song, urging his fellow confederates to abjure the honors and riches offered by foreign princes, lest God take away their fine freedom.

Sprecher's song represented a particularly lucid rendering of Rhaetian history from a moderate, historical-patriotic standpoint. Aside from the central emphasis on the antiquity of the region's freedom, this view also emphasized how important the active defense of that freedom had always been. Owing to its short-ness, however, the song only touched on several important questions, including God's role in the unfolding of Rhaetian destiny, and the internal organization of the society that was endowed with such enviable freedom. In fact, these lacunae were not uncommon for the historical-patriotic position. Like most Europeans of their era, *Bündner* believed their republic to be ordained by God, but the moderates' understanding of their own history emphasized the labors of their ancestors, who – with God's help, to be sure – had bravely defended the Fatherland's freedom against threats of foreign domination. The moderates also shared the assumption of their age that human society was divided into unequal estates, and that political rule belonged to the better sorts, in republics just as much as in aristocracies and monarchies. Given this assumption, it was the liberty of the Freestate rather than its constitution that was distinctive and important. Thus neither sacred history nor constitutional doctrine appeared prominently in historical-patriotic rhetoric, whose goal was to spur loyal service to the existing order in the Freestate, not to encourage religious transformation or political change.

Some authors did address the questions of divine providence, particularly in longer works. Saluz's *Rhetus*, for example, described how God used "marvelous means" to rescue the Freestate from lords' violence. In answer to Rhetus's hot tears and prayers, "He [God] was no longer willing to observe such great tyranny, He struck down that violence, loosed me, and set me free."[41] Saluz was quick to deny that the liberation of the Rhaetians had anything to do with rebellion, however, since Rhetus "was never known to call anyone lord, but dear God himself."[42] God's favor appeared clearly in battles where the *Bündner* defeated their enemies, demonstrating that "God fortified my [Rhetus's] government and estate, which I passed

---

[40] Sprecher, "Schön neu Lied," 7 (stanza 20).
[41] Saluz, "Rhetus," 8: "Der mocht nit lenger schauwen / Solch große tyranney / Den gwalt thet er zerhauwen / Vnd macht mich loß und frey."
[42] *Ibid.*: "Man sprach: Ich wölt mich schwingen / Vngehorsam vß dem gwalt / Da ich doch aller dingen / Zuvor in keiner gstalt: Kein Herren wußt zu nennen / Als nur den lieben Gott / Den ich noch heut erkennen / Der halff mir Vß dem spott."

on to you in the best condition."[43] Conrad Buol's 1617 song, "Ein schön Danklied um die Freyheit," used similar language. Buol was a Protestant minister from the radical faction that oversaw the *Strafgericht* of Thusis in 1618, which helps explain his attention to God's role in defending the Freestate. The song's first line asserted "We are free confederates and Swiss through God's power." Buol went on to describe how God had led the people to reject Austrian aggression in 1499.[44] After a long description of the Swabian War, Buol concluded with a prayer:

> For this victory and benefit
> Let our Lord be praised,
> He alone protected us,
> So that we were not scorned:
> He preserved our League,
> And maintained our free estate.
> He increased the honor of our pious ancestors
> Through our own hands.[45]

Typically for political rhetoric from the Freestate, Buol emphasized the human dimension of God's providence, insisting that God's action through *"our own hands"* had resulted in the rescue of freedom and increased honor for the brave ancestors. Whereas conservative rhetoric discouraged popular political action because it usurped the business of lords, moderate rhetoric took a stance more consistent with the Freestate's political culture by emphasizing the role of human action within the framework of divine providence.

Rarely did authors attempt to establish a detailed narrative about divine intervention in the Freestate's political affairs; instead, God appeared either as a well-inclined lord who inspired and supported human action, or else as an angry father who punished the Freestate for its people's moral failings. Even clerical authors tended to separate repentance and conversion from practical political action. A manuscript tract by the Reformed minister Daniel Anhorn written in 1621 illustrates this point exceptionally clearly.[46] After establishing that God was the true lord of the world, and that his providence would ultimately determine the outcome of the Rhaetian struggle to regain the Valtellina, the younger Anhorn proceeded to outline the specific reasons for God's present wrath. In doing so, he clearly separated them into "spiritual, inner reasons" and "political reasons." The former included God's testing of the faithful, and His disgust at the lukewarm faith shown

---

[43] *Ibid.*, 9: "Mitt hin thet Gott bevesten / Mein Regiment vnd Standt / Wie ichs beim allerbesten / Euch geben in die handt . . . "
[44] Buol, "Ein Schön Danklied," 1: "Frey Pundtsleut vnd Eydgnossen / Sind wir durch Gottes Kraft / Drey Pündt kün vnverdrossen / Gelobt sey dEidtgnoschafft."
[45] *Ibid.*, 5: "Vmb disen sig und güte / Sey hochglobt vnser Gott / Er allein hat vns bhütet / Das wir nit wurdend zspott:/ Den Pundt hat er erhalten / Vfrecht den freyen stand / Das lob der frommen alten / Gmehret durch vnser hand."
[46] Anhorn, "Vertraulicher Discurs," unpaginated ms. in VAD 219.

by some Protestants in the Freestate; the latter revolved around corruption in government, both in the Valtellina and at home in the Freestate.[47] Anhorn's proposals to correct the current sad state of affairs were similarly divided: on the one hand, he counseled appeals to the king of France, who could help in negotiating with the Spanish; on the other hand, he reminded his beloved "Grisonen" that they should trust only in God, rather than in their own powers and abilities.[48] He even commented, "Since God too is a God of means, for our sake, you lords the Grisons will have to take such external means into your hands."[49] Without denying for a moment that God's will legitimated and determined their political fate, Rhaetian authors nevertheless clearly separated political action from religious transformation. Just as the Leagues themselves were the result of human will, though sanctioned by oaths witnessed by God, so the defense of those Leagues was clearly seen as a matter for human, not divine action. Provided that human action was in keeping with Christian morality and God's desire for peace and order in the world, the Rhaetians could expect God to sanction their defense of freedom. As a proverb still seen painted on houses in Graubünden today has it, "*Igl um propona, il Dieu dispona*": man proposes, but God disposes.

Historical-patriotic texts remained vague about what form of government the Freestate should have, and avoided linking national autonomy to a certain internal organization. Some possibilities were excluded, however. Given the region's traditional identity as part of the Empire, no basis for an independent Rhaetian monarchy existed: *Bündner* monarchists were necessarily imperialists, and did not write tracts in the historical-patriotic mode. Any argument for an autonomous Rhaetian principality was similarly restricted by the historical rights of the see of Chur: only the bishop could make a traditionally founded claim to be prince in Rhaetia. Given the events of the sixteenth century, including the Reformation and the emancipation of the communes from the bishop's control, such a view of the Freestate found no adherents among the moderates. Under these circumstances, it is not surprising that nearly all political rhetoric in the Freestate was republican; what is important, however, is that this republicanism could be passive, as in the historical-patriotic view, or active as among the populist radicals.

The political content of historical-patriotic texts focused primarily on relations between the Freestate and the rest of the world. Depending as they did on a historical justification of the Freestate's autonomy, these texts confronted several specific problems of political order in fairly consistent ways. The first problem had to do with why the Rhaetians had rejected their lords in the fifteenth century. Unlike the radical populists, the moderates did not wish to reject the principle of

---

[47] The "Geistliche und innerliche" causes are found on fols. 11ʳ to 28ʳ, the "Politische ursachen" from fols. 28ᵛ to 49ᵛ.

[48] The former advice, e.g. *ibid.*, fols. 51ʳ, 56ʳ; the latter from fols. 72ʳ to 78ᵛ.

[49] *Ibid.*, fol. 79ʳ: "Politischer Rath: Wyl nun aber auch Gott ain gott der mittlen ist, umb unßert willen, so wërdend dan ir Herren Grisonen, sölche ußerliche mittel auch müßen zuhanden nemmen."

nobility altogether, since it was part and parcel of the social ideology of estates that they shared with most sixteenth-century Europeans. They therefore defined the situation facing their medieval forebears as one in which lords had transgressed the limits of their legitimate power, and thus become tyrants. Indeed, the term "tyranny" played an essential role in both moderate and populist rhetoric, representing the opposite of liberty.[50] *Bündner* wrote of tyranny not just in songs and pamphlets, but in all sorts of other texts as well: histories and chronicles, letters, diplomatic correspondence, and even lawsuits. But whereas radicals considered any kind of lordship within the Freestate tantamount to tyranny, the moderates defined only abusive lordship in this way.

A Latin pamphlet of 1622 went into the matter in some detail. Entitled *Solida ac necessaria confutatio argumentorum* [51] the pamphlet was written to refute the claims made in a widely-distributed Italian text from the Valtellina that had justified the Valtellina massacre as legitimate resistance to Rhaetian tyranny.[52] The author of the Latin refutation, intent on defending the Freestate against such accusations, expressed his shock that the Italian subjects had not only rebelled against their legitimate lords and fathers, but were now attempting to excuse or even glorify their action.[53] He then proceeded to outline the specific claims that the Valtellinans had made. The second one had to do with tyranny: "they say: the lordship of the Rhaetians over the men of the Valtellina had been a tyrannical yoke, which they had shaken off by divine and human law."[54] The rest of the pamphlet attempted to refute this allegation, which allows us to deduce the Rhaetian author's conception of tyranny in the first place.

The author started by claiming that, if Rhaetian administration were tyrannical, it would have to be so either in religious or political affairs. Turning first to religion, he averred that, even though the majority in the Freestate was Protestant, "nevertheless they always left the profession and practice of the Roman Catholic religion free, having conceded the full means for all the things which pertain to the intact exercise of that religion."[55] The pamphlet used a revealing argument to reject the subjects' complaints that their churches and cemeteries had been profaned, and that they had been forced to build churches for the Protestants:

---

[50] This was true not only in Graubünden. See the extended discussion in Kelley, *Beginning of Ideology*, 276–87, on late sixteenth-century France.

[51] Haller's *Bibliothek der Schweizer-Geschichte*, V: 888, attributes the pamphlet to Fortunat Sprecher.

[52] *Solida ac necessaria confutatio* is a response to a lost Italian pamphlet that was also translated into German as *Ursachen unnd Motiven / was die Veltliner Bewegt / sich der Tyranney der Grisoner . . .*, along with several other translations. An English edition appeared in 1650, *The cruell subtilty of Ambtioin* [sic].

[53] *Solida ac necessaria confutatio*, A ii^r.

[54] *Ibid.*, 2: "Dicunt: Raetorum in Vallistellinae homines dominium fuisse jugum tyrannicum: quod ipsi jure divino, & humano excusserint."

[55] *Ibid.*, 3: "Semper tamen illis mansit libera Religionis Catholicae Romanae professio et usus, concessa omnium, quae ad integram illius Religionis administrationem pertinent plena facultate."

are not even the Evangelicals citizens and members of the community? And ought not our subjects patiently endure this law, which the free communes imposed on themselves as well? If these are tyrannies, then the Kings of France are tyrants, and the Emperors, and many princes and magistrates in Germany, who have given the same privilege [i.e. to practice either Catholic or Reformed religion] to their subjects.[56]

Because the law established the freedom of both religions, and ordained that communes provide the means for the exercise of both, the Freestate's policy could not be called tyranny. This passage rested on the assumption that tyranny was the opposite of law; if an established law was applied equally to all, then no tyranny was present. The emphasis on citizenship was also important: it was as citizens and members of their communes that the Valtellina Protestants were entitled to certain benefits, including burial in the public cemetery and a space for their worship. That the author called the Valtellinans citizens in one breath and subjects (*subditi*) in the next shows that he did not consider the two categories mutually exclusive – unlike the radical populist rhetoric to be considered below. Above all, the pamphlet tried to defuse the issue of religious oppression, which provided fertile ground all over Europe for theories of resistance to authority: each abuse that the Valtellina manifesto characterized as religious oppression was, according to this rejoinder, nothing more than the legal exercise of secular authority, unrelated to any plan to favor Protestants over Catholics. With the exception of the radical-critical texts, almost all of the Freestate's political rhetoric took such a *politique* position about the separation of religion from politics.

Turning to the question of political tyranny, the pamphlet provided a list of behaviors that defined a tyrant, but that the Rhaetians had never displayed:

Their [the subjects'] privileges, immunities, laws, and oaths have always remained firm, established, and protected; no fortresses were built up in the manner of tyrants; no unaccustomed taxes were imposed; the buildings were not plundered; honest women were not violated; and the innocent were not killed. May such crimes be far, far, from our people![57]

The author was surprisingly willing to admit that some abuses in the exercise of justice had taken place on account of greed; he denied, however, that these were sufficient to justify rebellion.[58] Obviously, a Rhaetian writer with an eye on his own history could not simply reject resistance against tyranny out of hand, for such a position would affect the Freestate just as much as subjects in the Valtellina.

---

[56] *Ibid.*, 4–5: "An non Evangelici & ipsi sunt Cives, & Communitatum membra? An non subditi patienter hanc legem ferre debent, quam liberae Communitates sibi etiam impositam voluerunt? Si haec tyrannia sunt; Tyranni Galliarum Reges, tyranni Imperatores, tyranni multi Principes, & Magistratus in Germania, qui eandem libertatem subditis suis concesserunt."

[57] *Ibid.*, 7–8: "Privilegia, immunitates, leges, jura ipsorum semper firma, facta, tecta manserunt: Arces nullae extructae more tyrannorum: vectigalia nulla insolita imposita: non direptae aedes: non violatae honestae foeminae: non trucidati innocentes. Absit, absit A populis nostris tanta immanitas."

[58] *Ibid.*, 8.

Instead, the author sought to define the political abuses in the Valtellina as corruption, which was reprehensible but not tyrannical. His criteria for recognizing tyranny can be derived from the list of tyrannical behaviors which the author provided: along with destroying the legal system, a tyrant oppressed his victims by building fortresses, by imposing new taxes, by destroying homes, and by violating women.

Not surprisingly, these were the very characteristics which contemporary Rhaetian writers highlighted in their texts describing the Freestate's own rebellion in the fifteenth century. The construction of castles was a favorite theme, especially in songs,[59] while the immensely popular song "Pündtnerisch Hanengeschrey" of 1621 dwelt at length on the crimes of the tyrants:

> They robbed without measure or end,
> and dishonored plenty of virgins,
> Sent many people to prison,
> Brought many people into fear and poverty,
> Even threw some people to their deaths,
> Spilling innocent blood.[60]

Having such a clear model of tyranny allowed the author of the Latin pamphlet of 1622 to draw a clear distinction between genuine oppression and the mere abuses suffered by the population of the Valtellina. At same time, however, the Rhaetian definition of tyranny from the historical-patriotic viewpoint did set distinct limits on what any government in the Freestate could do. In effect, autocratic government of any kind, whether feudal or absolutist, was excluded. In this sense, the historical-patriotic school was passively rather than actively republican in tone.

Another problem which affected the scope of political discussion in historical-patriotic texts had to do with the relative novelty of the Rhaetian Leagues themselves. However antique Rhaetian freedom might have been, the Leagues themselves were much newer. Historians could not appeal to an "ancient constitution" of the Freestate: the constitution of the Three Leagues as a whole was precisely dateable to 1524, with forerunners no earlier than the mid-fifteenth century. Moderates might depict the Leagues as defenders of an older freedom, populists might celebrate them as the founders of contemporary freedom, but both standpoints recognized them as historically specific associations for the purpose of political action. The particularism natural to federal politics also made it difficult to appeal to the ancient institutions of the few communes – such as Chur – about which any statements at all could be made before the high Middle Ages, since such a tactic would have evoked either indifference or hostility from the inhabitants of all

---

[59] E.g. in Saluz's "Rhetus," 8; and in "Das bündnerische Hahnengeschrei (1621)," 9.

[60] "Das bündnerische Hahnengeschrei," 9: "Die hand geraubt ohn maaß und ziel / Jungfrauwen auch geschent gar viel / Viel Leut in Gfengnuß g'stossen / Viel Leut gebracht in angst und noth / Viel Leut gestürzt gar in den Todt / Vnschuldig Blut vergossen."

the other communes. Each commune had its own proud legends of liberation: the Walser communes had their thirteenth-century colonizers' privileges, other communes had long histories of negotiation and conflict with their ecclesiastical or secular lords, while some, like "the free men of Laax" had eccentric backgrounds that faded into the past without clear origins. It was the Leagues that overcame this confusion by creating a single framework for Rhaetian liberty. The political predicament in the Freestate differed in this respect from the European monarchies, where some constitutionalists sought to describe an age of popular liberty that preceded the establishment of the monarchy. Rhaetian history, in contrast, obligated the historical-patriotic school to argue for modern federalism, not because the Leagues were old, but because they provided the Freestate with its very existence. We saw above how the historical-patriotic interpretation of tyranny excluded certain political possibilities without actively specifying an ideal form; in a similar fashion, the recent origin of the Leagues and their central place in the Freestate's identity blocked the historical-patriotic school from searching the older past for the perfect system of government. All that authors like Sprecher and Saluz asked of the ancient past was Rhaetian liberty itself.

Yet Rhaetia's "ancient liberty" contributed important elements to the coherence of the moderates' political cosmology. In the first place, it allowed them to refute the charge that the Freestate was founded on rebellion against its rightful lords.[61] It also legitimated the Leagues themselves as defenders of custom and right, yet did not threaten the status quo in either the Valtellina, where the Rhaetians ruled by right of lordship, or in neighboring territories. Rhaetia's autochthonous liberty guaranteed it a peaceful place in the European framework of feudal monarchies, equivalent to an allod. The historical model proposed in these texts derived all the Three Leagues' legitimate institutions from the alliances that joined them. By stressing the importance of (divinely aided) human action in the preservation of ancient liberty, the relatively recent origins of the Freestate's practical organization could be integrated into a larger historical view. Meanwhile, the voluntarism and particularism embodied by the Leagues provided an infertile ground for specu-lation about the best possible social and political order. In this way the moderates could portray the Freestate as one peaceful estate in a Christian world where the political hierarchy of monarchies and the social hierarchy of estates could continue undisturbed.

This impression is reinforced by disparaging references to the common mob that adorn some historical-patriotic texts. It was one thing to be anti-aristocratic and republican, it was quite another to believe that the common man had a place in political life. A manuscript report from 1607, for example, explained how the people reacted to accusations of corruption: "When the common man heard this, he was enraged and armed himself with the communal banners, and out of pure

---

[61] Marchal, "Antwort der Bauern," documents the importance that the Swiss put upon this point.

simplemindedness he allowed himself to be misled and convinced that the big shots were traitors who had sold out the fatherland . . . "[62] Adam Saluz's long poem of 1618, "Prosopopeia Raetica," concentrated on the corruption of the Freestate's leaders; the author ascribes a purely reactive and negative role to the common people, whose involvement in politics was merely further evidence for the failure of the ruling group. Not only were disorder and hostility on the increase among the magnates, but the common man was following the bad example of his betters:

> And then the common man, too,
> Wants to get a feather from the goose.
> He doesn't realize that, for a mere morsel,
> he's pawning himself and his wife and children.[63]

In the following lines, Saluz warned the elite about the dangers of becoming the servants of foreign potentates by accepting their bribes and blandishments:

> Oh think, how just a few years ago,
> You saw an example of the common mob's ignorance,
> Their fierce and merciless raging,
> Which cannot be stilled without shedding blood,
> Without respect for anyone's person,
> And not sparing favor or service.
> You should consider this carefully,
> And not prepare yourself this kind of bath,
> Don't give the common man an excuse,
> For such wild behavior.[64]

Saluz here threatened the elite with the specter of popular political action, which the events of 1607 had shown to be unpredictable and violent. If leaders were virtuous, however, the common man would "praise, honor, and obey" them.[65] For Saluz as for most of the moderates, popular engagement in affairs of state was above all simply evidence that the magistrates had failed.

The key to the moderates' understanding of domestic politics must be sought in their concept of unity. Unlike feudal reactionaries or absolutist monarchists, who

---

[62] STAG B 694, p. 174 (in a copy from after 1666): "Do der gmein man daß hört, ward es erzürnd rüsscht uff mit den fendlinen, und uß luter einfaltigkeit ließ er sich verfüeren, und überreden, die große hanßen weren verräther, hetten daß vatterland verkauft..."

[63] Saluz, "Prosopopeia Raetica," 51: "So will daby der gmeine Mann, ein fåderen von der ganß auch han / Denckt nit / daß er vmb ein Morëndt / Sich selbs / sein Wyb und Kind verpfëndt;"

[64] *Ibid.*, 53: "Ach dënkt doch wie vor wenig Jar / Ihr ein Exempel gsähen hand / Deß gmeinen Pöffels Vnuerstand / Ihr grimmig vnbarmhertzig wüten / Daß ohn Blut sich nicht laßt begüten / Ohn alles ansähen der persohnen / Thut weder gunst noch anhang schonen / Daß sollen Ihr doch wol bedänken / Kein solliches Bad üch überhäncken / Dem gmeinen Mann nicht Vrsach geben / Zue einem sollchen wilden lëben."

[65] *Ibid.*

proposed a categorical distinction between those who ruled and those who were ruled, Rhaetian and Swiss moderates idealized the state of unity in which such distinctions were irrelevant. This did not mean, in their view, that the people took active part in politics, but rather that magistrates and people enjoyed a complete harmony embodied in the acts and decisions of the magistrates. This paradigm of correct political order, similar to the medieval concept of popular sovereignty and to the political philosophy of Johannes Althusius, challenged neither the hierarchy of social estates nor the relationship between the Rhaetian communes and their various lords. Nevertheless, it can only be called moderate in a Swiss context, since it rejected the *a priori* superiority of a hereditary noble class. By doing so, it transformed the meaning of "estate" even while preserving the concept's importance.

This transformation, too, can be illustrated in detail from Saluz's "Prosopopeia Raetica." One of the poem's central arguments was that the Freestate's current travails had resulted because "no one wants to remain in his estate."[66] This accusation was directed not at the peasants who participated in *Fähnlilüpfe* and popular tribunals, but rather at the patricians and oligarchs who hung themselves on foreign princes. Saluz drives the point home a few lines further on by playing on the multiple meanings of the German phrase *gemeiner Stand*: he notes that "Because you [*Bündner*] have a common (e)state, You also have honor or shame in common."[67] The phrase has at least three meanings here: a shared political organization or state (as in the terms *Reichsstand* or *Eidgenössischer Stand*) embodied in the Three Leagues; a shared social estate in the formal sense, because neither clerics nor nobles formed an estate within the Freestate; and the "common" social status of commoners. In Saluz's description of the idyllic past:

> Our pious fathers enjoyed all this /
> in peace, and preserved it /
> After they endured a great deal /
> before winning their freedom /
> And they let themselves be satisfied /
> With whatever God the lord sent them /
>
> Good and rural, without pride and splendor /
> They honored the work of their hands /
> They considered leisure shameful /
> Nor were there any excesses in the land.[68]

---

[66] *Ibid.*, 50: "Wie Ihr das heutiges tags thund tryben / Keiner in seinem standt will bleiben."

[67] *Ibid.*, 57: "Weil Ihr doch habt ein gemeinen stand / Hand Ihr auch gemein ehr oder schand."

[68] *Ibid.*, 49–50: "Daß haben üwere fromme Alten / Im friden bsässen und erhalten / Nachdem sy hatend vil erlitten / Ehe sy die freyheit hand bestritten / Und ließent sich an dem begnüegen / Wie's Gott der Herr ihn thet zufüegen / Guot landtlich / ohne stoltz und pracht / Ihrer Handarbeit namens acht / Müssigang hieltend sy für ein schand / Kein überfluss sach man im Land."

His ideal was a society with only one estate, namely those who worked; he compared it favorably to the present, when the *Junkerschafft* was large, and everyone wanted to join the nobility and get rich.[69]

At one level, Saluz's model completely inverted the traditional doctrine of the three estates, which insisted on the exclusive privilege of the second estate to rule, in favor of a doctrine of social unity. Saluz seemed to argue that peace resulted when society consisted of a single estate, at least in Rhaetia. At the same time, however, he continued to rely on the principle of social estates and social hierarchy: disorder in the Freestate resulted from the Rhaetian elite's attempt to escape its estate by attaching itself to foreign nobility. The descendants of Rhaetian peasants, Saluz seemed to be saying, should not try to act like noblemen. Yet his comments about the "base mob" demonstrate that Saluz was not arguing for democratic sovereignty. What he was saying, instead, was that everyone should do the work God had given him, whether it was to rule or to farm. In contrast to the medieval view that those who fought were therefore entitled to rule and to judge, Saluz implied that ruling, too, was a profession – one which went to men qualified for it, to be sure, but not one which set them qualitatively apart from the rest of the Rhaetian people. Such a view was consistent with the opinion, strong in Rhaetian political culture, that magistrates were officers whose authority was not based on their persons, but on the will of the commune. If this was the case, separation between ruler and ruled was evidence of corruption, whereas political unity also gave proof of a sound social order.[70]

RADICAL–POPULIST RHETORIC ABOUT THE FREESTATE

While the ideas brought together in the historical-patriotic understanding of the Freestate's history and identity formed a stable nexus which could be used to explain the past and provide counsel for the future, they also contained enough contradictions and gaps to stimulate further thinking. Like any ideology, the historical-patriotic paradigm neither perfectly described the Freestate's political practice nor completely answered every question that could be directed at it. As the tumults of the early seventeenth century eroded the practical consensus that had enabled the Freestate to function in the European political world, and as Rhaetians found themselves confronted with the problem of explaining the conflicts and violence after 1617, some thinkers began moving beyond the moderate historical-patriotic framework. New and creative political ideas that radically reframed the problems of political life in the Freestate began to appear. A later section of this

---

[69] *Ibid.*, 50. Such view had Swiss antecedents in the early sixteenth century, especially in the play *Das Spiel von den Alten und Jungen Eidgenossen*, ed. Friederike Christ-Kutter, Altdeutsche Übungstexte, vol. XVIII (Bern, 1963).

[70] Saluz compares separation with unity explicitly in lines 379–98.

chapter will consider those writers who concluded that the Freestate's existence was in fact *not* justified; here we will look at those who, while affirming that the Freestate should be a distinct and autonomous polity, maintained that it was founded not on some ancient freedom descended from Rhetus and the Tuscans, but rather on the will of the people expressed through their universal participation in political action. Such a populist, democratic position was extremely uncommon for seventeenth-century Europe, and it is worthwhile to see how it came to be defined and promoted in the Rhaetian Freestate.[71]

Two provisos must be introduced at once. First, no clear and systematic program of popular sovereignty on the basis of universal political participation was ever penned during the Freestate's crisis years. Graubünden was not blessed with a Machiavelli or an Althusius or a Locke of its own, who could have formulated a coherent theory explaining the Freestate's institutions in light of a broader concept of popular authority. Instead, various authors argued in passing for popular sovereignty, even though the passages that implied a populist view often stood side by side with arguments founded on a historical-patriotic understanding, or sometimes even with conservative arguments about feudal privileges. The text closest to a coherent populist position, the widely circulated *Grawpündtnerische Handlungen deß M.DC.XVIII jahrs*, was primarily a piece of propaganda intended to justify the actions of the *Strafgericht* of Thusis in 1618 – not an easy task – that used several radical propositions to frame a much more conventional interpretation of the crimes and punishments adjudicated in Thusis.

A second proviso concerns the relationship between democratic ideas and democratic practice in the Freestate. While political practice in the communes and the entire Freestate represented an essential background that made democratic rhetoric understandable in the Freestate, the insistence on popular decision-making found in these texts must not be confused with a description of how the Freestate was actually ruled. Common citizens did play an unusually large role in Rhaetian politics, it is true; but as we have seen, this role was limited on the one hand by the complex remnants of feudal authority, and on the other by the rising power of an increasingly self-conscious patrician elite. It is significant and revealing

---

[71] The closest antecedents appeared in early sixteenth-century Switzerland, but faded after the Reformation. Stricker, *Selbstdarstellung*, 63–101. Overtly populist ideas did flourish during the English Revolution. Revisionist historians have emphasized how limited the Levellers' commitment to democracy was, yet the Levellers did assume a greater role for subjects and commoners than did most contemporaries. In France, Calvinist debate about church government around 1572 is also comparable, though of brief duration, as is some Leaguer rhetoric. Kingdon, "Calvinism and democracy"; Francois Crome, *Dialogue d'entre le Maheustre et le Manant*, ed. Peter M. Ascoli (Geneva: Droz, 1977). Republican rhetoric from the Netherlands was much less democratic in character. See esp. Kossman, "Popular sovereignty"; and Eco Haitsma Mulier, "The language of seventeenth-century republicanism." Martin van Gelderen's *The Political Thought of the Dutch Revolt* (Cambridge: Cambridge University Press, 1992), which appeared after this study was complete, provides valuable details about Dutch political language without changing the larger picture.

that political propaganda should use populist arguments, but the fact remains that these texts were primarily propaganda. Nor should the Rhaetian radicals' populism be interpreted as a plea for individualistic democracy in a modern mold. The commune rather than the individual was the source and legitimating principle of popular politics for the Rhaetian radicals, just as for their more conservative peers.[72] In some respects the radicals' view of freedom paralleled the Rhaetian paradigm of ownership and labor: individuals enjoyed a liberty which was defined and managed communally, just as the peasant worked his own land under the conditions set by communal control.

An examination of populist rhetoric immediately reveals its connections with the historical-patriotic consensus which preceded it. The radicals derived their political principles by expanding the questions and shifting the conclusions found in more moderate texts. Nevertheless, the radical-populist texts reached different conclusions using different arguments, thus revealing distinctive conceptions about the fundamental character of political life in the Freestate and in general. By replacing a historical argument with one based on the abstract desirability of freedom, and by closely associating the Freestate's liberty with the specific form of government practiced there, the radicals reached a uniquely Rhaetian synthesis of ideas which differed not only from contemporary European political theories, but also from the historical-patriotic rhetoric which predominated in Switzerland at the time. Moreover, the close association between political freedom and spiritual freedom proposed in the radical texts represented a rejection of both conservative tradition and orthodox Protestant political theory. Despite its origins as propaganda and its relatively brief appearance in the late 1610s and early 1620s, radical Rhaetian populism represented a genuine alternative to other political ideas current at the time, an alternative whose roots are found in the confluence of the European political tradition with the social life and political practice of the mountain communes.

The authorship of radical rhetoric is one of its striking features: almost all of the texts which adopted the position were composed by Reformed ministers, mostly from the faction which took over the Rhaetian Synod during 1618. While this fact might tempt us to resurrect theories that claimed some direct or indirect connection between Calvinism and democracy, the evidence from the Freestate does not support such a conclusion. Instead, a steady development took place starting in the mid-sixteenth century, during which the Freestate's Reformed clergy moved from a traditional Reformed position of obedience to established magistrates, within certain limits, to a reconception of their office and their position as citizens within their communes. The appearance of radical political rhetoric in

---

[72] This distinction is central to Benjamin Barber's analysis of Rhaetian politics in *The Death of Communal Liberty*. For a historical analysis which carefully delineates the meaning of *Freiheit* in Swiss rural regions, see Bierbrauer's *Freiheit und Gemeinde*.

the Freestate coincides with the moment when some of the ministers – the authors of the texts in question – decided that their office required them to act as citizens who were specially qualified to advise the highest magistrate, namely the people as a whole.[73]

The pamphlet published by the ministers at Thusis, *Grawpündtnerische Handlungen deß M.DC.XVIII jahrs*, was the first and most coherent exposition of the radical populist position in Graubünden. Written to explain and defend the actions of the *Strafgericht*, it was widely distributed in the Freestate and outside, provoking several responses. More evidence than usual survives about how and when it was composed, although the details remain obscure. Several seventeenth-century sources attributed the pamphlet to Johann à Porta, head of the panel of ministers at the *Strafgericht*, and to Johann Peter Guler, son of the politician and historian Johann Guler of Davos.[74] While an attribution by the enemies of the *Strafgericht* cannot be certain, it seems reasonable that à Porta may have at least supervised the writing and publication of the pamphlet, even if he was not the sole author. This pamphlet gained European importance in part through its wide dissemination: along with four German editions, there were two printings of an Italian version, two separate translations into French, a Dutch and an English translation, and perhaps a Latin version published in Prague, all before 1620.

The political theory implicit in radical-populist texts from Rhaetia displayed four distinct but interrelated features: it claimed that freedom was an abstract good desired by all and granted by God to the Rhaetians; it contained clear assertions of popular sovereignty, together with a defense of the common man's capacity to make political decisions; it explicitly associated spiritual with political liberty, while simultaneously denying that confessional motives had any place in the political process; and it exhibited a strong sense of national identity as a republic, coupled with the expectation that monarchs and princes were naturally hostile to "free estates." Populist rhetoric reached several of these stands by transforming the views found in conservative and moderate ideas. Thus, although freedom was a central concern for all Rhaetian political thought, the radicals detached it from the historical background – feudal in the conservative case, ancient and Tuscan in the moderate case – that was used to interpret it according to other views. Moderate rhetoric, along with the actual records of the Freestate's government, routinely acknowledged the supreme authority of the councils and communes, but only the radicals followed through to speak of a democratic polity in which the good counsel of the people was contrasted with the corruption of the men actually leading the Freestate. Similarly, the idea that both religions were free in the

---

[73] Head, "Rhaetian ministers."

[74] HBLS 5: 469 incorrectly lists *Heinrich* à Porta as one of the overseers at Thusis. Sprecher and other authorities, however, speak of Johann à Porta of Davos. Sprecher, *Geschichte*, I: 76. See also "Kurtz Beschribene Pündtnerische Handlungen" (unpaginated), 4th paragraph, 11th paragraph, which names both authors.

Freestate was not new, but the focus on the close association between spiritual and political freedom was. And finally, patriotism was equally a distinguishing feature of the historical-patriotic view, but the radicals laid greater emphasis on the importance of republican consciousness and on the inevitable hostility which aristocrats would harbor against a genuine republic. Thus, despite important continuities, every central issue addressed by radical rhetoric received a different solution from that proposed by moderates or conservatives during the great political and religious debate of the *Bündner Wirren.*

The pamphlet *Grawpündtnerische Handlungen* opens with an uncompromising statement about the importance of freedom:

Among all of the temporal blessings and gifts, which God is accustomed to bestow on the human race, spiritual and worldly liberty of conscience and of self-government is by no means the least, because one can preserve one's soul, honor, body and goods through its legitimate use, and enjoy these things without vexatious compulsion and pressure. Therefore it has always and everywhere been desired and sought after by everyone as a precious valuable treasure.[75]

This statement by itself goes far beyond anything found in conservative Rhaetian rhetoric, since freedom is presented as an abstract good coming directly from God. The slow transformation of the ideal of liberty which had taken place during the sixteenth century reached its endpoint here: no longer tied to the idea of privileges which had been granted by some human agent, "freedom" in this passage was prior not only to the lords who had ruled Rhaetia during the Middle Ages, but also to human historical experience altogether. Instead of resulting from history, freedom had become its goal.

The radicals' abstract definition of freedom did not mean that they placed it entirely outside the actual history of their people, however. In the second paragraph of *Grawpündtnerische Handlungen*, à Porta and Guler went on to situate freedom in the past, the present and the future of the Freestate. They started with the past:

we the inhabitants of old Upper Rhaetia, known today as the Three Gray Leagues, gained both freedoms, maintained and preserved them in long and honorable succession, and also fully enjoyed their pleasant usefulness, through the blessing of God and the power of his might, which appears in the upright courage of our pious ancestors . . .[76]

---

[75] *Grawpündtnerische Handlungen*, A ii^r: "Under allen zeitlichen gnaden unnd gaben / die der liebe Gott dem menschlichen geschlecht zuo verleihen pfleget: ist geistliche und weltliche freyheit des gewüssens unnd selbster regierung mit nichte die geringste: weilen man durch sölcher rechtmessigem gebruch seel / ehr / leyb und guot erhalten kann / und ohne verdrießlichen zwang und trang der selbigen geniessen. Dennenhar sie als ein kostlich kleinot je und allwegen von menniglichem innigklich ist erwünscht und begert worden."

[76] *Ibid.*: "Dieweil dann wir die eynwoner alten hoher Rhetien / diser zeit die drey Grawe Pündt genant / durch den sägen Gottes und die krafft seiner stercke / so sich in der redlichen dapfferkeit unserer frommen Altforderen erscheint / dise beyderley freyheit erlanget / durch lange succession loblich besessen / und erhalten / auch ihrer lieblichen nutzbarkeit wol genossen . . . "

The text went on to maintain that the presidents, councils and communes ought to value and love their liberty today, so that it might be passed on to subsequent generations in the future. Like the moderates, the radicals recognized that freedom was something which had been gained in the past, but their emphasis was different: not ancient history, but God's blessing demonstrated by the liberation of one's ancestors formed the core of Rhaetian political identity. The radical position did not deny the reality and importance of past experience – neither rationalism nor apocalypticism played a role in this or in most radical texts[77] – but it avoided the assertion that the Freestate's modern liberty derived from the ancient freedom possessed by Rhetus and the Tuscans.

An especially clear illustration of how radical-populist thought differed from the historical-patriotic tradition was the song "Das bündnerische Hahnengeschrei," printed and translated repeatedly during the seventeenth century. The song's subtitle indicated that it did start from a historical viewpoint: not only did it speak of "upper Rhaetia," referring to the Roman provincial boundaries, but it also urged the Rhaetian confederates to return to their ancient manliness and courage. Nevertheless, the story of the Rhaetian past found in this song differed significantly from the work of Campell and Sprecher. The first two stanzas placed the Freestate's liberty in historical context:

> About the good liberty of the Grisons,
> And about the courage of your ancient heroes,
> I wish to sing to you Leagues.
> These were gained through blood,
> And ever preserved through blood,
> Through manliness, spears and blades.
>
> Your ancestors, mark well my confederates,
> Were not free as you are,
> But were all servants.
> Look how the cliffs in the mountains and the valleys
> Are all occupied with castles:
> Tyrants inhabited them.[78]

Significantly enough, the author addressed his song to his *Grisonen*, not to the *Rhetier*: for him, the core of Rhaetian historical identity reached back only to the fifteenth century AD, rather than to the sixth century BC.[79] Although the song went

---

[77] The distinction explained in Pocock, *Ancient Constitution*, 125–27, 235–41.

[78] "Das bündnerische Hahnengeschrei," 9: "Von der Grisonen Freyheit gut / Von euwer alten Helden muth / Wil ich euch Pündten singen. Durch Blut hand sie erworben die / Durch Bluot erhalten je und je / Durch Manheit / Spiess unnd Klingen. Die Alten / merckt ihr Pündtner mein / Sind nicht wie jhr gefreyet gseyn / Sie waren Knecht allsammen. Schauw wie die Felsen / Berg vnd Thal / Mit Schlösser sind besetzet all / Darin hand g'wont Tyrannen."

[79] Some radical texts did appeal to the "pious old Rhaetians," e.g. "Kurtzer Bericht, Wie und welcher gestalt," esp. fol. 11. But the references to a Tuscan origin of freedom were confined to mere

on to describe the liberation of the Freestate from its tyrannical lords in a way consistent with the historical-patriotic paradigm, these opening lines gave it a quite different thrust. Whereas Campell described how liberation during the late Middle Ages returned the Rhaetian people to their ancient liberty, "Das bündnerische Hahnengeschrei" presented the story of a people establishing its liberty in the first place. Accordingly, the Freestate's modern autonomy rested not on the fact that the Rhaetians had previously been free, but on the fact that their tyrannical lords had been driven out. Historical-patriotic rhetoric narrated the defense of liberty against bad lords, but this song celebrated the wresting of liberty from lords who could not be other than tyrannical. Even though the events upon which each story was founded were essentially the same, the conclusions implicit in them varied considerably: an essentially conservative story about preserving one's ancient condition was confronted with a activist story about liberation from tyranny.

Consequently, radical rhetoric rarely touched on the virtues of Rhetus and his fellows. Authors like à Porta and Guler accepted the historical sequence outlined by historical-patriotic chronologies, but they believed the most important moments had taken place when their recent ancestors had earned their freedom with God's help. They were willing enough to call themselves the inhabitants of Rhaetia (noting that it was now known as the Three Leagues), and were proud of the long history of freedom they could claim. This pride, however, rested not on an ancient founder's virtue that was to be emulated by his descendants, but rather in the "pleasant usefulness" of a good which God had granted the Freestate. Their emphasis was not on a freedom which the Rhaetians must preserve because they had inherited it, but on a freedom they must preserve because freedom itself was a great benefit from God.

History thus moved out of the central role it played in historical-patriotic rhetoric, although it still retained its importance for demonstrating that the Freestate's status had resulted from the substitution of freedom for tyranny. Implicit in this transformation of history's importance was a shift in the attitude toward societies in time.[80] For the radicals, the Freestate's contemporary autonomy and freedom were essentially self-justifying because they were direct benefits granted by God. The past was important only in that it showed God's hand at work supporting the process by which the Rhaetian people had become free. While no Rhaetian populist ever advanced a purely rational explanation of political freedom, the populist position took a decisive step away from the view that the right order of current affairs should be sought primarily in the distant past.

phrases, compared to extensive historical arguments from the fifteenth and sixteenth centuries. Swiss antecedents for this view e.g. in Bullinger's "Lucretia," 61, which described how the Romans had "seized their liberty with force."

[80] This issue central to Pocock's more recent work, esp. *The Machiavellian Moment* and "Time, institutions and action: an essay on traditions and their understanding," in *Politics, Language and Time*.

If freedom was a divine gift, but some people lacked it because they were subject to lords, then it necessarily followed that dominion by others was the opposite of a gift from God – either a punishment or a Satanic stratagem.[81] The way the radicals changed their definition of liberty, from a historical possession to an abstract good, thus led directly to their virulently anti-aristocratic stand. Implicit in their rhetoric was the notion that lordship was identical with tyranny, and subjection to a lord therefore identical with slavery. While *Grawpündtnerische Handlungen* did not follow this train of thought to its rhetorical conclusion, the songs written around 1620 did. For example, "Das bündnerische Hahnengeschrei" asserted that "Your ancestors, my Bündner, were not free as you are, they were all servants [*Knecht*]."[82] The point was made even more strongly in "Lobspruch der dapferen und mannhafften Prätigäuweren" (1622) written to celebrate the Prättigau rebellion. After describing the peace and quiet long enjoyed by the Three Leagues as "a free people, who lived since old times in unity, without the burden of princes,"[83] the song described how after the Austrian invasion in 1621 "the yoke of slavery"[84] was imposed, and how the Capuchin monks were brought in who "tyrannized after their custom, and molested free conscience, forcing [the Prättigauer] not only into servitude of the body, but also forcing pious souls to fall and collapse into eternal sorrow . . . "[85] In contrast to moderate rhetoric that claimed that the legitimate rights of the Austrians over the Prättigau had always been respected, this song equated actual Austrian lordship with tyranny.

Some of the strongest expressions of the radical view appeared, ironically, in Bartholomäus Anhorn's pamphlet *Kurtze Warhaffte Relation, Was massen*, already discussed above for its use of conservative and moderate ideas. Intent on exploiting every possible argument, Anhorn adopted the radical notion that subjection was identical to slavery even while he insisted that the Ten Jurisdictions' freedom was not "*de facto*, negotiated in a willful and self-aggrandizing way against oath and duty . . . "[86] Anhorn mentioned the various occasions when the Habsburgs had confirmed the privileges of the Ten Jurisdictions, down to and including the *Erbeinung*, the hereditary treaty which had regulated relations between Freestate and Austria since the Reformation. "It is therefore clear to see," he maintained,

---

[81] The Satanic interpretation e.g. in *Ursachen und Motive / Warumb die Gemeine drey Bünde*, A ii[r].

[82] "Das bündnerische Hahnengeschrei," 9.

[83] "Lobspruch," 114. On the authorship of this song, see Zinsli, *Politische Lieder*, 30f.

[84] "Lobspruch," 116: "der Sclaven Joch . . . " References to slavery are absent from older Rhaetian political documents.

[85] *Ibid.*: "D'Caputzyner bald kommen sind / Z'breden, abzführen wyb und Kind / Nach Ihrem sit tirranisiert / Die freye gwüßne molestiert / Zwingen nit nur in Dienstbarkeit / Den Leib, sonder in ewigs leidt / Z'stürtzen, z'verfellen fromme Seelen . . . "

[86] *Kurtze Warhaffte Relation, Was massen*, 9: "Und soll niemands hie meinen / als wann diß alles *de facto* mutwilliger und eygenthätlicher weiß / wider Eyd und Pflicht biß dato were von dem X. Grichten Pundt verhandlet worden . . . " (because it had all been confirmed by the House of Austria up to the present).

"that the Imperial Majesty negotiated and compacted with the Ten Jurisdictions not as *slaves* and subjects, which is how one wants to treat them now, but as free confederates with power over themselves."[87] Anhorn used the same dualism throughout the pamphlet: free men were those who had power over themselves, while those who did not were subjects (*Untertanen*) and slaves. Even while he was arguing that the Freestate's privileges ought to be respected because they had been properly granted by previous lords, Anhorn also drew upon a world-view that implicitly denied that lords had any right to exercise dominion in the first place. The double vision implicit in the pamphlet's subtitle, which referred to the "Defense of body and soul as allowed by Nature and by all laws" was carried out in Anhorn's text as well. The Ten Jurisdictions' liberty was guaranteed not only by the old law which looked to charters and confirmations, but by the law of nature which determined that subjection was no more than slavery, and that dominion was therefore tyranny.[88]

Yet calling all dominion by all lords illegitimate raised the question of how a people ought to arrange its political affairs. Both Classical and medieval political theory and Rhaetian political practice suggested some kind of popular sovereignty as the answer. Not only had Aristotle and other Classical philosophers discussed democracy as one form of rule which needed to be considered seriously; medieval rhetoric, too, had often used the aphorism "*Salus populi suprema lex*," and anti-papal and anti-imperial theorists such as Marsiglio of Padua had derived political models in which political power derived from popular consent, even if it was exercised by those best suited to rule on account of their piety, education, or wealth. More recently, the history of the Swiss Confederation and of the Freestate provided concrete models of common men joining into self-willed political associations for the purpose of maintaining peace and establishing order. Majoritarian decision-making was a fundamental component in the organization of Rhaetian communes, further reinforcing the idea that the common man had an active role to play in politics. Given all these precedents, it was not surprising that Rhaetian publicists developed an argument for popular sovereignty in the Freestate. The argument remained latent in moderate rhetoric, however, which separated the establishment of freedom (by ancient historical precedent) from its current exercise (by a federation of communes). Only in the radical rhetoric of the *Bündner Wirren* was the connection made between Rhaetian freedom and republican government, and only there do we find the claim that the Freestate was a democracy.

Once again, it was *Grawpündtnerische Handlungen deß M.DC.XVIII jahrs* which laid out the claim most clearly:

---

[87] *Ibid.*, 10: " . . . so ist handgreifflich / das ja ir Key: May: mit dem Zehen Grichten Pund / nicht als mit *Sclaven* und underthanen / darfür sie jetzunder wollen gehalten werden / sonderen mit freyen ihren selbst mechtigen Pundtsleuten abgehandlet und geschlossen haben."

[88] Notably missing is an appeal to God's law, such as that found during the German Peasants' War.

The form of our government is democratic: and the election and deposition of the magistrates, all kinds of officers, judges and commanders, both in our free and ruling lands and in those which are subject to us, belongs to our common man; he has the power, according to his majorities, to create statutes and to abolish them, to establish alliances with foreign princes and estates, to dispose questions of war and peace, and to deliberate about all other matters pertaining to the high and lesser magistrates.[89]

This was an extraordinary set of claims to make in the early seventeenth century, since the authors systematically attributed all of the characteristics of sovereignty, legislative as well as judicial, to the common man in the Rhaetian communes. The paragraphs that followed reinforced the forthright view expressed in these lines. À Porta and Guler first described how certain "particular persons" had recently drawn all authority and power to themselves by means of their great wealth and power.[90] Because of such abuses, "discerning persons, and even the common man" had attempted to bring about "reformation and improvement according to appropriate methods," which had been blocked by the corruptors' partisans and by the general mistrust in which the common man held his leaders.[91]

Another attempt at reform, appealing to the communes to appoint a reform commission, had also been in vain, the pamphlet continued,

and thus the common population [*Landvolck*] lost all hope of achieving any good results through a small number of persons deputized for this purpose, and plainly saw that one could overcome the tyrants in no other way than with a larger number of the people: not in regard to violent resistance, but only in regard of gaining the majority and hindering all kinds of corruptions and wrongful inducements.[92]

---

[89] *Grawpündtnerische Handlungen*, A ii^v: "Die form unsers Regiments ist Democratisch: unnd stehet die erwellung unnd entsetzung der Oberkeiten / allerley Amptleüten / Richtern und Befelchshabern / so wol in unsern befreyten unnd herrschenden Landen / als auch uber die / so uns underthenig sind / bey unserem gemeinen man: welcher macht hat / dem mehren nach / Landtsatzungen zu machen / und wider abzuthun / Pündtnussen mit frömbden Fürsten und Stenden aufzurichten / uber Krieg und Frid zu disponieren / und alle andere der hohen und minder Oberkeit gebürende sachen zuverhandlen." The English edition, B ii^{r-v}, reads as follows: "The forme of our Common-wealth is *Popular*, and the choosing and displacing of the supreme Magistrate, Officers, Iudges, and Commissioners in our free Countries and of our Subiects, standeth meerely in the power of our *People*, who have absolute authority by pluralitie of voices, to establish and abrogate Lawes, Leagues, and Affiances with Princes and forraine States, to make Warre or Peace, and to order and gouerne all other businesses belonging to the higher and lower Magistrate."

[90] *Grawpündtnerische Handlungen*, A ii^v.

[91] *Ibid.*, A iii^r: "Welche klägliche sachen / wiewol sie ein zeit lang mit etwas näbel verdeckt waren: so haben doch verstendige leut / ja auch der gemeine man / ihre *effect* und würckungen so sehr gespürt / daß mancher frommer Landtman sölches beweinet / und mit Reformation unnd verbesserung in gebürender procedur ihme gern begegnet were: es hat aber wegen ihres mechtigen anhangs / und deß gemeinen mans gegen menniglichem mißthrawens nichts fruchtbarlichs verrichtet mögen werden." The radicals' ambivalence concerning the common man is discussed below.

[92] *Ibid.*, A iiii^r: " . . . dardurch dem gemeinen Landvolck alle hoffnung entfallen / einiches guotes zuo erhalten / durch ein kleine anzal der hierzuo deputierten personen / und augenschinlich gesehen / daß man die tyrannen in kein andern weg / als durch ein grössere anzal deß volcks uberwinden könne

The rule of the corrupt and tyrannical few could only be hindered by a politically active majority, according to the radical understanding of politics. The failure of previous reform efforts demonstrated the futility of delegating power to any limited group, since such groups were all too easily corrupted themselves. The pamphlet used this interpretation to justify the communes that had raised their banners and assembled at Thusis for the purpose of punishing the leaders who had been "tyrannizing" them – specifically the brothers Rudolf and Pompeius Planta. Like his uncle Dr. Johann Planta, Rudolf was accused of attempting to make himself "a general and universal lord over the land" by means of the many tyrannical actions that the pamphlet alleged against him.[93] Unlike historical-patriotic texts which focused their attention on *external* threats to Rhaetian freedom, and which described the "tyrants" of the fifteenth century as "foreign lords," radical texts accused the Freestate's own leading figures of tyrannical behavior aimed at excluding the common man from politics.

The authors of *Grawpündtnerische Handlungen* did express a few reservations about the common man's abilities to rule well. The passage mentioned above, in which "discerning persons" were clearly distinguished from the common man in general, was not the only one of its kind. The authors also worried that the common man in the communes was too easily manipulated, and they bemoaned the fact that the miscreants had "moved the common man first to one, then to the other opinion, or just deceitfully claimed to have done so without the common man's even knowing it."[94] Picking up on a theme also found in moderate rhetoric, they worried that the Planta brothers and their party were giving the people just cause to distrust their own magistrates, thus disrupting the desirable unity of the Freestate.

Despite these comments, however, the pamphlet maintained a remarkably positive attitude towards the common man as political actor. Whereas the vast majority of contemporary literature about the "people" disparaged their wisdom and steadfastness, the authors used the final section of their pamphlet to argue exactly the opposite:

If our population were as irresponsible as these slanderers claim, then we (like our accusers, the instigators of all irresponsibility) would have accepted and rejected all sorts of alliances every year. For it is surely not to their credit, that the honorable upright alliances were not abrogated; rather, it is to the credit of the honest population's faith and constancy, and to the credit of some honest leaders and councillors. And if we have failed to fulfill some of the obligations in our alliances, the blame belongs to no one except these faithless natives of our country, who allowed themselves to be obliged by money like day-laborers, and who misled

---

/ nit von wegen gewalthätigen widerstands / sonder allein von wegen der ubermehrung der stimmen / und der hinderhaltung allerley *corruptionen* und falschen *persuasionen.*"
[93] *Ibid.*, D iii[r]: " . . . sich zuo einem Generalen / und algemeinen Landtherren machen . . . "
[94] *Ibid.*, A iii[r]: " . . . unnd den gemeinen man jetz zuo einer / dann zuo der andern meinung oder [sic] vermögen / oder doch söliches ime unwüssend / hinderlistig vom jme fürgegeben."

the common man (who is the highest magistrate here) with invented stories and falsely portrayed dangers.[95]

Clearly illustrated here was the radical populists' conviction that, rather than being fickle and inconstant as the entire European tradition would have it, the people were essentially faithful and competent in political affairs. Earlier Rhaetian authors from Joann Travers to Ulrich Campell had warned about the fury of the people, but this passage stood tradition on its head: not the people, but the treacherous few who were seeking to take over the state were the fickle, the faithless, and the dishonorable. The people might be intimidated, confused, or misled, but they would make good choices given the opportunity. This passage, together with the forthright assertions of popular sovereignty found elsewhere in the text, made it an unambivalent manifesto for democratic values. By shifting the focus of freedom from historical privilege to universal good, by coupling freedom with republican government, and by defending the political competence of the common people, the authors of *Grawpündtnerische Handlungen* moved decisively away from both conservative and historical-patriotic understandings of the Freestate's nature and destiny.

A further distinctive feature of radical rhetoric appeared in the close connection it posited between spiritual and secular freedom, between freedom of conscience and freedom of self-government. Both concepts, which were mentioned at the opening of *Grawpündtnerische Handlungen* and in other texts adopting the radical position, could be read several ways. They could refer to the coexistence of the Catholic and Rhaetian Reformed churches in the Freestate, they could be used in a confessional sense to assert the Valtellinans' obligation to contribute to the support of Protestant worship, and more abstractly, they could illuminate the radicals' views about the proper relation between spiritual and secular affairs. The last issue had been the subject of tremendous debate all over Europe during the late sixteenth century. Not only can we find out which European ideas had the greatest impact on the Rhaetian ministers' thinking by reading their texts, but we can also see how their experience as citizens of a peasant republic affected their interpretation of the ideas they read.

Before 1600, relatively few authors attempted to establish an explicit parallel

---

[95] *Grawpündtnerische Handlungen*, F iii[r]: "Wann unser Landvolck so leichtfertig were / wie dise Lestermeüler von uns ausgeben: so hetten wir mit ihnen / als den anstiffteren aller leichtfertigkeit / järlichen allerley Pündtnussen angenommen und wider aufgesagt. Dann es warlich nicht an ihnen erwunden / daß die aufrechten redlichen Pündtnussen nicht sind aufgesagt worden: sondern ist gestanden an der threüw und standhafftigkeit deß redlichen Landvolcks / und etlichen der selbigen redlichen Vorstenderen unnd Rähten. So wir aber etwas an Pundsgenößischen pflichten ermanglen lassen: ist die schuld niemanden / als disen unsern threuwlosen Landkinderen zuozuomessen / die sich von andern zuo sölchem mit gelt als die taglöner dingen lassen / und denn [sic] den gemeinen man / so bey uns die höchste Oberkeit ist / mit erdichtem fürgeben / und felschlich fürgemaleten gefahren / vom rechten weg abwendig gemacht haben."

[96] BK II: 531–32 (no. 634).

between the liberty of the Freestate and the freedom of its churches. One of the earliest examples dated to 1564, when Johannes Fabricius wrote Heinrich Bullinger expressing his concerns about the upcoming renewal of the French alliance: "The Rhaetians," he claimed, "cannot enter any alliance which is dangerous to the liberty of their country or the church."[96] Fabricius, himself Reformed minister in Chur, was reluctant to have the Freestate supporting the bitter enemies of his faith, as his further comments revealed. The kernel of the radicals' later conviction that the secular liberty of the Freestate correlated with the religious liberty of its churches already appeared in Fabricius' words, but without being developed. Fabricius's *libertas ecclesiae* still pertained to the church, rather than to the Rhaetian people, whereas the texts from the seventeenth century clearly described both religious and political freedom as God's gifts to the Rhaetians. Moreover, in 1564 the liberty of the church was not yet defined as "the liberty of the two churches," a change which gained its legal and rhetorical foundation only with the Chiavenna Articles of 1585.[97] Fabricius's radical successors, although they too were Protestant ministers, interpreted "freedom of soul and body" to allow equal political status for Catholic and Protestant communes within Graubünden.

It is striking how hard the radicals strained to deny that their actions after 1617 were confessionally motivated. Responding to the justified accusation that the *Strafgericht* at Thusis displayed a strong anti-Catholic bias, à Porta and Guler replied:

They say that they are being persecuted by a particular faction. It is the faction which desires to preserve, protect and defend God's honor and word, and its upright honorable servants of *both religions*. It is the faction which desires to maintain our Fatherland's freedom according to the old statutes and decrees.[98]

A few lines later they again denied being confessionally motivated, saying "Why are we of both religions in our Fatherland so well united? Why do men from both religions sit on this court, and punish equally the miscreant clergy and laymen of both religions?"[99] No matter how dubious these claims were in truth, the idea that Rhaetia's freedom transcended the division between Catholic and Protestant predominated in the radical rhetoric of the *Bündner Wirren*.[100] The overtly Protestant pamphlet *Ursachen und Motiven* of 1620 explicitly combined religious freedom with popular sovereignty when it described how the Reformed synod,

---

[97] Campell still denied this point in 1577. For him, the toleration of Catholicism within the Freestate depended primarily on the desire for peace. "De officio," STAG B721, 29.

[98] *Grawpündtnerische Handlungen*, F iᵛ (emphasis mine): "Sie sagen / es sey ein sonderbare *Faction* / die sie verfolge. Es ist die *Faction*, die Gottes ehr und wort / unnd dessen auffrichteig / redliche diener beyder Religionen begert zuo furderen / zuo erhalten / zuo schutzen und zuo schirmen. Es ist die *Faction*, die da begert vatterländische Freyheit / laut der alten Statuten und Satzungen zu mantenieren."

[99] *Ibid.*, F iiʳ.

[100] Some further examples in "Lobspruch," 121, lines 313–18.

disturbed about the state of affairs in the Freestate, had appealed that "everyone should publicly propose whatever he believed might be useful, and especially that the common man *of both confessions*, who is the sovereign, should be informed about the state of affairs in best form, and shown the origins of all the evils . . . "[101] For a Protestant text to admit that Catholics shared equally in dominion over their state was unprecedented in European literature of the early seventeenth century.

Acknowledging that citizens from both religions were politically competent meant that religious criteria could not intrude into secular affairs. If they did, the secular unity that was universally accepted as essential for the Freestate's survival would be broken: only by rigorously separating the secular from the religious could both freedoms be maintained. Thus, the elevation of "spiritual and worldly freedom of conscience and of self-government" as the highest good resulted in a firm theoretical distinction between religion and politics, and in an active rejection of the confessionalism which characterized most of Europe at the time. At the same time, however, it freed the ministers, who were citizens too, to take an active part in political life. Because populism established government as a universal problem that required the attention of all citizens, it transcended the traditional view of social estates dedicated exclusively to praying, ruling, and working.

Yet spiritual and secular freedom could carry another, confessionally loaded sense as well. When Protestants in the Freestate spoke of freedom of religion, their target was often the subject population in the Valtellina. By insisting on "freedom" for the few adherents of the Reformed church there – which meant having the Valtellina communes build or hand over churches and pay for ministers – Rhaetian Protestants were following a pattern common all over Europe: "religious liberty" meant freedom for the ruler's own religion. A tract by Ulrich Campell in 1577 even argued that democracy in the Freestate justified forced conversion in the Valtellina. Campell wanted to answer the following question: how could the subjects be coerced towards Protestantism when both religions – the Catholic and the Reformed – were explicitly permitted within the Freestate itself? His line of argument was straightforward. Assuming that magistrates had a general obligation to oversee their subjects' religion, he made the following claim:

Now in Rhaetia (where a democratic magistrate flourishes, that is, the part of the population with the larger number of votes is recognized as the supreme magistrate, and commands,) the people in the communes which embraced the Evangelical faith and profess it greatly exceed the various Papists in the Rhaetian Leagues, not only in votes, but in number of men . . . [102]

---

[101] *Ursachen und Motiven / Warumb die Gemeine drey Bünde* . . . , B i^r, (emphasis mine).

[102] Campell, "De officio," STAG B721, 27–28: "Iam cum in Rhetia (ubi Democraticus viget Magistratus, i.e. potior suffragiis populorum pars pro supremo Magistratu agnoscitur atque imperat) populi Communitates qui Evangelicam fidem amplexi, eam confitentur, diversam Papistarum in foederata Rhetia partem, non suffragiorum modo, sed et virorum numero longe superent . . . "

His conclusion followed naturally, that the Rhaetian magistrate – that is, the people – could and should force their subjects to be instructed in Protestantism.

A half-century later, the pamphlet discussed above, *Solida ac necessaria confutatio*, illustrated that some Protestants' view of "freedom of religion" among the subjects had not changed much: because the Freestate had established a statute guaranteeing the free exercise of either confession, the subjects should patiently endure the burdens this statute put on them – even though the sovereign communes themselves usually banned the practice of the minority religion within their own borders.[103] As the seventeenth century progressed, moreover, the more tolerant popular attitude that the *Fähnli* had expressed in 1585 faded, to be replaced by an enduring confessional distrust that has characterized Graubünden in more recent times.

The radical populist authors shared the strong sense of national identity found among the moderates, but they connected it more closely to a republican form of government. Here again, *Grawpündtnerische Handlungen deß M.DC.XVIII jahrs* framed the issue most clearly: in the initial, theoretical part of the pamphlet, the authors' train of thought flowed directly from the Freestate's freedom and its current endangerment to their statement that the form of government was democratic.[104] Both moderates and populists took it for granted that the Freestate did, in fact, form a single coherent polity. This assumption presented no theoretical difficulty for the moderates, who looked back to the Tuscan origins and Roman organization of *Rhetia prima*: since the region owed its freedom to a single founder and its boundaries to its history as a single Roman province, unity was its natural political condition. Most of the radicals implicitly relied on this argument as well when they spoke of the *Rhetierland*, but the secondary role that history played in their political cosmology limited the effectiveness of appeals to ancient unity.

Consequently the radicals also emphasized the leagues and the *Bundesbrief* as sources of common identity for the Freestate. The Bündner formed a single *Volk* in the seventeenth century because their ancestors had fought side by side, spilling their blood and their "sour sweat," and because they had sealed their cooperation through the very oaths and alliances which contemporary *Bündner* also swore to and lived under. This viewpoint had several advantages: besides providing a conceptual foundation for the Freestate's unity, it also established a logical connection between liberty and the Freestate's present institutional structure. Fittingly enough, the first publication of the *Bundesbrief* took place under the aegis of the radicals in 1619. Besides the *Bundesbrief* (using the text of 1544 but claiming it had been established in 1471), the pamphlet contained both Ilanz Articles, the *Pensionenbrief* of 1500, the *Kesselbrief*, and the Reformation of 1603, as well as

---

[103] *Solida ac necessaria confutatio* . . . , 3–5.   [104] *Grawpündtnerische Handlungen*, A ii^{r–v}.

the recently passed Zizers Articles of 1619. The collection was prefaced by a short poem markedly populist in tone:

> Where human customs are wickedness,
> And all good order is avoided;
> Where the strongest is master,
> And the rich man deceitfully oppresses the poor man,
> And where no one fulfills his obligations to the rest,
> That government will soon be obliterated.[105]

Evidently the editors of the collection believed that the greatest threat to their political survival came not from the unruly common man, but rather from the powerful and the wealthy.

Radical-populist authors filled their works with patriotic language. Their texts abounded with appeals to "honor and freedom of the Fatherland" and the "boundaries of duty to the Fatherland,"[106] to "good men and patriots,"[107] and "beloved Fatherland."[108] A song from 1622 pleaded that everyone should come and help who was "firmly patriotic [*gut vatterländisch*] and no longer [pro]-Spanish, [pro]-Austrian or the like."[109] This emphasis combined with the assertion of popular sovereignty in passages that emphasized that the common man who ruled the Freestate was at the same time the peasant in his commune. In "Lobspruch der tapferen Prättigauer," for example, the song explained how "such great deeds were accomplished by unarmed peasants [who became] good soldiers, which their dear posterity will find amazing," and how the peasants lost not a single man in the battle at Fläsch.[110] The song also included a passage reminiscent of Adam Saluz's social criticism, charging that the Spanish partisans had hoped to become lords or gain great honor through their betrayal of the Freestate.[111] "Das bündnerische Hahnengeschei" typified the tyranny of the lords in a conflict between a *Herr* and a *Pauer* in Guardaval.[112] Throughout the corpus of radical-populist rhetoric, the failings of the powerful families and "big shots" (*Grosse Hansen*) were compared unfavorably to the good will of the general population.

The anti-aristocratic bias of populist thought also resulted in a certain sense of solidarity with other republican states. This was most obvious with regard to the Swiss Confederacy, which Rhaetians viewed as a polity parallel to their own.

---

[105] *Landtsatzungen Gemeiner dreyer Pündten*, title page: "Wo freffen sindt der menlichen sitten, Und guote ordnung bleibt vermitten: Wo je der sterckste meister ist: Der Reich den Armen truckt mit list: Wo keine dem andren leist sein pflicht: Das Regiment bald zgrund wird gricht."

[106] *Grundtlicher Bericht über den Zustand gemeiner dreyer Pündte*, B ii^r, C i^r.

[107] "Lobspruch," 118.

[108] *Grawpündtnerische Handlungen*, F ii^r.

[109] "Lobspruch," 121.

[110] *Ibid.*, 118–19, lines 121–24, 175.

[111] *Ibid.*, 115, lines 53–60.

[112] "Das bündnerische Hahnengeschrei," 9.

Indeed, the Republic of the Three Leagues was closely allied with many of the cantons, and delegates from the Freestate regularly attended the Confederate Diet.[113] On the cultural level, many elements of Swiss national mythology appeared in Graubünden: plays celebrated Wilhelm Tell,[114] appeals for unity referred to Brother Claus von der Flüe, while Rhaetian youths were educated in Zurich and Basel. Although the relationship was not without tensions, as revealed in 1607, the Rhaetians correctly saw the Swiss as the political entity most like them on the European stage.

The radicals also believed that monarchs and princes were naturally hostile to republics. The pro-Venetian faction in the Freestate was particularly fond of making this point. In 1603, for example they argued that:

The governments of Venice and the Three Leagues had the same form, since they were two free estates [*Ständ*], and therefore they ought to be able to reach an agreement more easily. The king of Spain was a great monarch. Now all monarchs were hostile to free estates, and therefore used all sorts of means to bring these under the yoke, so that they might tyrannize them as was their desire . . . [115]

The Venetian party had close connections with the radical wing among the Reformed ministers, who also assumed that no foreign prince could mean well by the Freestate. In 1620, the Freestate even exiled the French ambassador because of his intrigues; in a published letter written to the King, they informed him that although they intended to maintain their ancient alliance with him, "We have never gained any other fruit from ambassadors and their secretaries than sedition, civil wars, and ultimately the ruin of our country."[116] The ministers' fears echoed Swiss sentiments familiar since Zwingli's time a century before, that foreign princes would use their wealth and power to corrupt the leadership of communal republics.[117]

The ideas found in radical-populist rhetoric in the Rhaetian Freestate thus expressed a closely linked and relatively coherent set of ideas about the nature of human freedom, the Freestate's place in history, its appropriate form of government, and its relations with other powers. Most of the texts conveying this viewpoint appeared over a very short time. The first printed text to set out populist views unambiguously was *Grawpündtnerische Handlungen* in 1618, which remained the strongest statement of this view. A burst of songs and pamphlets published in 1620, 1621, and 1622 completes the roster of radical texts in this era, except for one Swiss song printed in 1631. Radical-populist rhetoric flourished during the deep crisis affecting the Freestate for five years after 1617, rather than before or

---

113 Oechsli, "Benennung," 170–72.
114 Flugi, "Abriss der ladinischen Literatur," 12.
115 Anhorn, *Graw-Pünter-Krieg*, 7.
116 *Copie d'vne Lettre Escripte av Roy de Franc*, A iii[r].
117 Close Swiss antecedents discussed in Bernhard Stettler, "Einleitung," *75–*90.

after.[118] Yet while radical views expressed in public rhetoric appeared like a quick-blossoming flower after 1618, the fundamental views and assumptions that characterized these texts had a history both before and after the crux of the *Bündner Wirren.* Just as historical-patriotic paradigms were disseminated through learned chronicles and published histories, and just as conservative views continued in legal correspondence with Austria and with regard to the Valtellina, so also radical views had their echoes in other texts such as reform articles, and to a lesser extent in the preambles to communal statute books. Each of the visions of the Rhaetian state analyzed in this chapter had its practical and institutional correlates.

RADICAL–CRITICAL RHETORIC ABOUT THE FREESTATE, AND ARISTOCRATIC RAGE

At the height of the disorders from 1618 to 1620, a few authors produced texts attacking the Reformed minsters and the Venetian party, who had the upper hand at that time. Consisting of several poems and one prose pamphlet, this material concentrated on violent and colorful personal attacks on the authors' enemies. Since they were written as libels rather than as substantive arguments, we can hardly claim that they conveyed any coherent political theory, yet they did display a strong aversion to popular participation in the affairs of state on the part of "coarse beasts and worthless ragpickers."[119] Several of them also analyzed the causes of the Freestate's current disorder, suggesting that the proper magistrates had been usurped by the Protestant ministers who were sources of "rebellion, envy and hatred."[120] In effect, though, these radical-critical texts questioned whether the Freestate had any right to exist at all. If the Rhaetians were as anarchic and dishonorable as the authors suggested, then the words of an Austrian chronicler of the invasion of 1621 only made sense: "and may Almighty God grant that such a peace is made, in which one does not allow these coarse, bestial people so much freedom, so that at least later events will not be even worse than their beginnings."[121] The violent criticism in the radical-critical texts left no room for the autonomous self-governing Freestate envisioned by moderates and populists alike.

The radical-critical texts were almost all explicitly Catholic in their orientation,

---

[118] All printed polemics from this era of Rhaetian history show the same temporal distribution. Of the 104 pamphlets counted here, 76 (73 per cent) were published between 1618 and 1622. In Germany, 40 per cent of an important collection of seventeenth-century pamphlets was published in the same years. Parker, *Thirty Years' War*, 110–11.

[119] "Kurtz Beschribene Pündtnerische Handlungen deß 1618.19 und 20. Jahrs," paragraph 12. Haller's *Bibliothek* attributed the text directly to Pompeius Planta, an attribution which Phillip Zinsli also found plausible. Zinsli, *Politische Gedichte*, 71.

[120] "Pasquille vom Thusner Strafgericht: Aliud I," 38–39.

[121] *Kurtzer Bericht, und Warhaffte Erzehlung, welcher gestalt*, A iiᵛ.

just as the majority of the radical populist ones were written by Protestants.[122] But again, in parallel with populist propaganda, explicitly confessional attacks were avoided in favor of a critique of the Reformed clergy's behavior in secular affairs. Neither party's political rhetoric was altogether free of statements touching on theological and ecclesiological problems, of course, but in no case was religious doctrine the central concern. The distinction may seem subtle – after all, calling a group of clerics "servants of the devil" was certainly a confessional sort of thing to do – yet the clerics were attacked for their injustice, tyranny, or personal failings, not for teaching heresy *per se*. While there is no doubt that confessional hostility was on the rise in the Freestate after 1600, and that more people were willing to act out of primarily confessional motives, the texts addressing *political* problems rarely availed themselves of overtly religious arguments until after the Valtellina massacre.

These texts also remind us of another important dimension to political strife in the Freestate, a dimension suppressed in the measured language used by the moderates or the proud pronouncements of the populists. Coarse, vituperative, and aggressive as they were, radical-critical polemics exposed a profoundly emotional dimension to the *Bündner Wirren*: the radical ministers, the partisan oligarchs, and even the moderates did not simply disagree, they also hated one another passionately, on the basis of conviction or for the infliction of past wrongs. The *Strafgerichte* and tumults after 1617 were also expressions of revenge, deep-seated hostility, and fanatical contention, and the primary actors were moved as much by personal and emotional forces as by their ideas about political order and propriety. After all, Jörg Jenatsch personally led the band that assassinated Pompeius Planta in 1621, breaking his head open with an axe; when Jenatsch was murdered in turn eighteen years later, the rumor spread immediately that Planta's relatives were behind his death, and that they had used the very same axe which Jenatsch had employed so bloodily.[123]

The high point of the personal attacks came in Pompeius Planta's pamphlet, "Kurtz Beschribene Pündtnerische Handlungen deß 1618.19 und 20. Jahrs." Planta employed the most aggressive language possible – though not without certain flashes of humor – to defame and disgrace his opponents. The inhabitants of the Lower Engadine had been "rogues, thieves and murderers" for at least a hundred years, nor were the other *Fähnli* which assembled at Thusis and Zizers any better, so that "if God wanted to punish a land, he would appoint no other people than these." The leader of the men from the Val Müstair was a "bewhored man,

---

122 Only one radical-critical text, "Pasquille vom Thusner Strafgericht: Aliud II," 39–41, claims to have been written by a Protestant, even though it contains a strong attack on clerical interference in secular affairs
123 On the assassination of Planta, see *Blutige Sanfftmuet* . . . The scholarly debate about Jenatsch's murder is summarized by Mathieu, "33 Jahre," 502–06. On the story of the same axe, see A. Pfister, *Jörg Jenatsch*, 409.

who was always comfortable with rebellions, Caspar Carl by name." While plundering the region around Chur, young Johann Peter Guler stole a store of nuts which he sold to his own troops, after which he was known as the "nut-commander." Once assembled in Zizers, the Fähnli appointed "a judge who was always drunk, crazy, and not fit to be a sowherd." One secular leader after another was called a traitor to the land, a murderer, a thief.[124]

Planta reserved his real vitriol, however, for the Reformed ministers, especially the ones who had served at Thusis. Johann à Porta was the son of a black magician who had been killed by lightning, while he himself had been "wrought in hell." Blasius Alexander was "a public thief, incestuous, a perverter of children, and a traitor to his country."[125] Jörg Jenatsch was described in more detail:

The fifth was Georgie Jenatsch, a godless lad well suited criminally – when he lived on welfare in Zurich [as a student], he had more whores than schoolbooks, and he can outfox practiced deceivers when it comes to lying and treachery.[126]

When the ministers preached the word to their troops, the latter "became so zealous, that as soon as the sermon was over, they had to capture, torture, steal, or do even worse things." According to Planta, the ministers in Thusis "led such a life, that if someone were resurrected from Sodom and saw how they behaved, he would have been amazed that God did not rain down sulphur and pitch."[127]

As the pamphlet rants on in this vein, spilling out one dishonorable accusation after another (in an age excruciatingly sensitive to honor), the reader is led to wonder about the author's extraordinary rage.[128] Moderate and radical texts, too, spoke of treachery, they too used strong language to castigate what they portrayed as violence and injustice, but never did they resort to calling their opponents whore-mongers or perverters of children.[129] The language in Planta's pamphlet was so intemperate that a deeper reason than mere political advantage may have lain at the heart of it. The most probable roots, aside from the personal character of the author, must be sought in the profound hostility he displayed towards his own people. As a self-conscious aristocrat with both historical and theoretical grounds for seeing himself and his peers as the natural leaders of the Freestate, Planta was confronted with a political system that had steadily eroded the legitimacy of his leadership, and repeatedly persecuted his immediate family in the name of popular government.

---

[124] "Kurtz Beschribene Pündtnerische Handlungen," paragraphs 13, 18, 16, 27 and 30, respectively.
[125] *Ibid.*, paragraphs 19 and 20.
[126] *Ibid.*, paragraph 20: "der fünfft war Jöry jenatsch, stund dißen Gottloßen Bursch freffenlich wol an, da er zu Zürich im muß haffen saß, hatte er mehr huren alß Schulbucher, mit liegen und betriegen kan er wolgeubte Bößwicht uberlistigen."
[127] *Ibid.*, paragraphs 21 and 25 respectively.
[128] Contemporaries recognized the shocking nature of Planta's allegations : his murderers justified their act by the calumnies he had introduced against them. Zinsli, *Politische Gedichte*, 71.
[129] Such extreme attacks did appear during the French religious wars after 1572. Cf. Kelley, *Beginning of ideology*, 287.

When, after 1618, the state seemed to be in the hands of the very people whom he felt entitled to command, and leadership had fallen to a group of ministers from client families, Planta's steadfast political opposition was compounded with an emotionally violent reaction. His just claim to influence was being ignored in favor of those with the least possible claim to it. When the ministers and populists at Thusis drove the Planta faction out of the Freestate, and then disseminated a pamphlet asserting that Rhaetia had a democratic government, Planta and a few of his peers turned their backs on a system in which they had hitherto participated, setting out instead on a course of personal aggrandizement in the name of patrician authority and established order.

A earlier poem published in 1618 helps locate this shift. The "Kurtz Beschribene Pündtnerische Handlungen" of 1620, described above, reached very bleak conclusions about the people of Graubünden:

I shall not describe the rest of their unjust un-Christian acts, which are fresh in our memory, because I fear that foreign princes would be greatly displeased by them, and would think that we Bündner were no longer men, but devils. Someone might wonder, what devil had given these people occasion to exercise such tyranny? He should know that since ancient times, everyone always called us Bündner faithless *Churwahlen*, and we still keep that title, and want to keep it in the future . . . [130]

The earlier poem, "Beschreibung eines wunderlichen Gesichts," although it too included vituperative attacks on the author's lay and clerical opponents, did not yet reach radically negative conclusions about the Freestate as a whole. Instead it confined devilishness to the Reformed ministers and their supporters in the Venetian party. In the course of the poem, which took the form of a dream reported by the author, a troop of devils comes to praise the works of the ministers, remarking "We devils ourselves don't know whether we or they are worse."[131] The devils report each minister's crimes and failings, though in vaguer terms and without the sexual misdeeds which appeared in the later prose text; they also identify the lay leaders of the Venetian party (including Hartmann von Planta, cousin to Pompeius). The devils end their appearance by saying that they too must be on guard, lest the ministers and Venetians destroy their kingdom, too.[132]

The poem's author – who described himself in the title as a "distinguished confederate" – ended his work with a warning to all *Bündner* to beware the disorders that occurred when ministers sat on courts and rendered verdicts. We could hardly call the author's view of the Freestate optimistic, since he portrayed it overrun by devilish clerics who propagated injustice, yet he still wrote his song as a warning and plaint,

---

[130] "Kurtz Beschribene Pündtnerische Handlungen," paragraphs 36–37. The term *Churwahlen* was the German term for Romantsch-speakers.
[131] "Beschreibung eines Gesichts," 34.
[132] *Ibid.*, 36.

> To bemoan the pain in my heart /
> And the afflicted state of our common estate /
> Our beloved Fatherland.[133]

The prose pamphlet of two years later, in contrast, may have started on a patriotic note, claiming to be written by "an honorable Confederate and lover of the Fatherland," but soon the mounting violence of its language dispelled any positive impression about the Freestate's current population or institutions. Rhaetia could be the author's fatherland only in the most general sense, not including its current institutions or leaders. The concluding remarks cited above moved beyond pessimism to self-hate, beyond disappointment to rage. Of course, the authors of radical-critical texts such as the two in question would never have favored a populist, or even a historical-patriotic view of the Freestate. But the challenge to their place in the Freestate that appeared in the radical-populist texts pushed these writers from aristocratic conservatism to a radical denial of the very possibility of virtue within the Freestate.

One more poem from the radical-critical position illustrates how central the authors' social anxiety was in shaping their views. Titled only "Postscripta," the anonymous manuscript began with a general attack on the ministers, but then specified the danger they represented:

> If they should have their will /
> The country would soon be subject to them;
> If we don't pick these ticks off soon [?]
> Our old freedom will be gone and lost.
> So Rhaetia, open your eyes /
> Don't let the ministers steal your authority.[134]

The poem left no doubt at all: the ministers were at the root of the Freestate's unrest, because they refused "to learn to stay in their estate, and to leave worldly affairs to those God has ordained to rule them."[135] The "estate" of the ministers had more than one implication, since it could refer either to the clerical estate in the old model of three estates, or to the low social estate from which the ministers originated. In either case, the author assumed the conservative view that a man's estate was his destiny, and should determine his actions. Unlike the radical-populists, who also wanted church and state kept separate, but who argued

---

133 *Ibid.*, 28: "Zubeklagen mein Hertzen leidt / Vnd den gemeinen betreübten Standt / Vnßers geliebten Vatterlandt."

134 "Pasquille vom Thusner Strafgericht: Postscripta," 37–38, lines 18–23: "Solt es nach Ihrem Willen gahn / wer daß Landt baldt ir Vnderthan; lißt man nit zeitlich Ihnen d'zächen ab / alde Freyheit / du bist schabab. Drumb Rhaetia / thue auf deine Augen / Laß dich von Predicanten deins gwalts nit brauben: . . . " The third line is obscure: Zinsli suggests *Zecken* for *zächen*, but other readings are imaginable.

135 *Ibid.*, lines 27–30: "daß sy beim standt, lernendt verbleiben vnnd zuehandt, weltliche sachen die lohn füehren / die Gott hatt g'ordnet zue regieren."

that a minister could also be a citizen, this poem preserved ruling for those born to rule – a position which excluded not only the ministers, but also the common man.

In the end, as we have seen, the conservative magnates turned to foreign powers to reestablish their authority. Rudolf Planta invaded the Freestate together with Austrian troops after his brother had been murdered by the Venetian faction in 1621. Nor did the radical critique of the Freestate implied in these texts ever become rhetorically effective. On the one hand, their language was too personal and too vehement in its hostility. On the other hand, the changing terms of political debate after 1621 narrowed the rhetorical field to historical-patriotic and conservative views which were easier to defend before a European audience. Neither the radical-populist position nor the radical-reactionary views of the authors examined above had a place under the vastly different circumstances of foreign invasion and European war. The radical-critical texts are nevertheless interesting, particularly for their reemphasis of the personal and emotional dimension of Rhaetian politics in the early seventeenth century. In addition, they remind us of the tenacious strength of hierarchical and aristocratic assumptions. The Rhaetian magnates rarely reflected about their claims to legitimate leadership, and few may have noticed the growing strength of openly aristocratic viewpoints among the elite. But when their *de facto* control over the Freestate's supposedly communal institutions was challenged, they reacted energetically and often violently.

During and after the Thirty Years' War, political rhetoric in the Freestate stabilized around the moderate historical position, which allowed the magnate class room to exercise power without directly challenging the authority of the communes. The communes reacted by turning to a particularist conservatism which blocked almost all institutional innovations for the next hundred and fifty years. We may speculate that only the outbreak of a European war saved the magnate position in 1620: wartime conditions favored consolidation over innovation, while the elite was bolstered by contact with its ideological allies from the rest of the continent. Communalist populism, which sprouted only under the unusual conditions found in the Freestate during the early seventeenth century, began to wither, unable to unfold against old and new ideas about hierarchy and dominion. When the idea of popular government reappeared in Europe a century later, it took the form of natural law and individual rights, profoundly different from the corporate autonomy and historically legitimated freedom found in the Freestate of the Three Leagues.

Democracy in early modern Graubünden

This study set out to investigate the political debate that took place in the Rhaetian Freestate in the early seventeenth century, and to determine the foundations and contours of the system that was at stake. During the political crisis of 1607–20, a few Rhaetian authors found it plausible and expedient to call their form of government "democratic," and to ascribe all political authority to "the common man" in the Freestate of the Three Leagues. My argument has been that the unusual social order, institutional organization, and political practice that Rhaetian citizens experienced in their communes provided a substrate for such statements, a political culture that included widely accepted assumptions and beliefs about the Freestate's past and about the nature of legitimate authority within it. When foreign pressure and social tension both increased after 1600, such unreflected ideas became the common ground from which most contemporary polemicists argued, even if they occasionally borrowed vocabulary and concepts from other sources.

I also maintain that while the origins of Rhaetian political culture must be sought in the social practice of local communities, its subsequent elaboration depended on the political and institutional development of the Freestate as a whole. The rural commune, with its specific combination of autonomous family labor and collective economic and social discipline, effectively incubated certain ideas about the sources of legitimate authority, and about specific methods for reaching decisions and distributing common resources and burdens. When the weakness of local lords provided communal inhabitants with the opportunity to emancipate themselves, they formed leagues that drew upon principles familiar from village life. The political sphere created by such leagues soon gave birth to federally organized institutions and usages that, while no longer directly based on communal life, still reflected communal ideas about authority and legitimacy. Finally, after social developments in Rhaetia led to a growing disjunction between ideas about power and its actual exercise, various writers set forth theories about political order, seeking to justify their own actions and to save the Freestate from imminent collapse. Some Rhaetian writers drew upon humanist historical views, Aristotelian principles, or widely shared views about feudal authority to describe a state that never fitted into any of those categories, but a few attempted a novel synthesis that went beyond existing models to describe the Freestate in terms of political liberty and popular rule.

Conclusion

The Freestate of the Three Leagues was not the only communally organized republic in Europe during this period, of course: not only the Swiss Confederation and its individual cantons, but also the German and Italian city-states and the Dutch Republic drew upon communal values to justify their autonomy. Urban and even rural communities within princely states continued to rely on similar principles as well, following the medieval practice of subordinating horizontal organization to vertical hierarchy and thus preserving substantial self-government in an increasingly aristocratic world.[1] Yet the extent to which communalism became the sole legitimating principle in Rhaetia was unique among territorially extensive states during the early seventeenth century. The aristocratic views that formed a reactionary fringe in the political language of Graubünden would have been unexceptionable almost anywhere else, whereas the views that made up the moderate-historical mainstream might have seemed dangerously republican in many European kingdoms. Only the Freestate's first long century of independence, during which a state founded on communal principles nourished both institutions and concepts, can explain this reversal of European norms. Moreover, the texts that illustrate *Bündner* political language were not speculative treatises or utopian fantasies, but rather represented deadly serious moves in the game of communal and international politics that took place from 1600 to 1620. For this reason we can assume that authors deployed arguments that they hoped would convince and move their audience: the various explanations of the Freestate's existence that are found, in different texts or even within single ones, thus reveal the range of arguments that might be both cognitively and emotionally compelling to the politically active population of the Freestate.

The late sixteenth and early seventeenth centuries were a period of intense ferment in European political theory, and it is interesting to consider how the Rhaetian experience relates to contemporary changes in the definition of politics and the state. Both Jean Bodin's theory of legislative sovereignty and Johannes Althusius's theory of corporate politics expressed ideas that resonate with certain events or statements found in Graubünden during the same period. The Rhaetian state also matured just before absolutism and natural law became the key competing visions of authority that would define political theory for the next two centuries. The voluntarism behind the Rhaetian communal ideal rested on medieval ideas about consent, but it went beyond medieval values to foreshadow the social contract invented by Hobbes and Locke. The political debates we have seen in Rhaetia coincided with changes taking place all over Europe, so that it seems reasonable to ask what connections there might have been.

Definitions are important, here: for example, a modern criterion for "democracy" tends to be universal participation, whereas for Aristotle, "democracy" was

---

[1] See esp. Mack Walker's portrayal of German towns in the seventeenth and eighteenth centuries, *German Home Towns*, 11–144.

essentially rule by the many citizens who were free but poor, rather than by the few rich or by one individual.[2] Similarly, the concept of sovereignty was in flux during the early modern period, shifting from a judicial to an explicitly political context.[3] In addition to the formal characteristics of democracy, modern viewpoints also emphasize the importance of practice in evaluating forms of government, just as Aristotle did: "whenever the free are not numerous, but rule over a majority who are not free, we still cannot say that it is a democracy . . . "[4] Sovereignty likewise depends not only on a political entity's formal relationship with others, but on whether it can make decisions that are in fact not subject to appeal to a higher authority. On both these counts, the Rhaetian Freestate possessed a marginal status that reflected not only its own historical roots in medieval forms of governance, but also the changing meaning of these categories at the time.[5]

In formal terms, it was plausible to describe the Freestate as a democracy, as European authors including Bodin did: "the Grisons . . . which are of others the most popular, and most popularly governed of any Commonweale that is."[6] Rhaetia was obviously no monarchy itself, nor did its nominal inclusion in the Holy Roman Empire make it part of a larger monarchy. The emperor neither exercised nor claimed final authority in the Freestate after 1499; even when Austrian troops invaded the Lower Engadine and the Prättigau in 1620, they did so in the name of Habsburg feudal claims, not as imperial agents. Nor was the Freestate an aristocracy: with minor exceptions, no privileged group possessed an *a priori* claim to political authority. Instead, the Freestate's political institutions were systematically organized to put decisions before assemblies of common citizens. The formal *Bündner Referendum* for important issues and the widespread use of majority voting illustrate the spread of democratic forms during the sixteenth and early seventeenth centuries. Needless to say, popular decision making in Graubünden did not take place in a social vacuum; social power and even violence were regularly applied to affect the outcome of nominally democratic decisions. Formally, however, there can be little doubt that the Freestate's constitution (written and unwritten) was significantly democratic in character by the early seventeenth century.[7]

---

[2] Aristotle, *Politics*, 4.4.   [3] Quaritsch, *Souveränität*.

[4] Aristotle, *Politics*, 4.4.

[5] The following comments follow the traditional categories monarchy – aristocracy – democracy. Although they by no means form the only scale on which one can place political entities, this spectrum seems appropriate if "democracy" is in question.

[6] *Six Books of a Commonweale* (original 1606, facsimile Cambridge: Harvard University Press, 1962), 247.

[7] Nor was citizenship or the ability to be elected so restricted in the communes that Aristotle's comment cited above would apply: free men were in fact numerous, whereas the unfree within the Freestate were limited in numbers. Note, however, that women, who were free in most legal senses, were still disenfranchised. From a feminist viewpoint, the Freestate was far from democracy. Their exclusion from politics because of gender was only reinforced by the communal emphasis on bearing arms.

Conclusion

At the level of practice, the situation could become complicated, as we have seen. A relatively limited group of wealthy families did in fact take the lion's share of offices and monopolized routine decision-making in the Freestate. Nevertheless, the regular popular assemblies that seized authority from the magistrates and the *Grosse Hansen* in order to exercise it in the name of the common man put severe limits on oligarchic power. Rhaetian magnates were too dependent on communal support to be able to rule the Freestate by themselves. Many German territories were struck by occasional peasant revolts, as were most of the Swiss cantons from time to time, but nowhere else did mass assemblies of citizens regularly take the government out of the elite's hands. The Rhaetian *Fähnlilupf* and *Strafgericht* were not in fact revolts: their purpose was not to reject unjust authority from above, but to reaffirm the principle that authority came from below. For all the oligarchic tendencies that can be observed there, the Freestate was not an oligarchic state. In theory and to a substantial extent in practice, ultimate authority in Graubünden lay with the "many."

At the same time, we must recognize the differences between Rhaetian and later European forms of democratic thought. Recently, Peter Blickle has proposed some relatively direct connections between regions where communalism was widespread and those in which "assemblies of estates became representative institutions in the modern sense."[8] If he is right, communal democracy of the kind found in Graubünden was an important condition for the appearance of truly representative government on the Continent – or more pessimistically, the suppression of communalism in Germany after 1525 explains the absence of genuine republicanism there. Yet Blickle's optimistic view underrates the fundamental difference that remained between the ideas of citizenship and authority in the Rhaetian Freestate and those found in the later liberal tradition. The legitimating principle for *Bündner* populism rested on the widespread medieval value of "the common good" – the *Gemeinnutz* that permeates documents from this period.[9] As we have seen, Rhaetian political myths left little room for either the exemplary individual virtue celebrated by civic humanists or for the pre-political "natural" liberty proposed by Enlightenment theories of natural law.[10] Instead, both liberty and obligation were constituted by the individual's oath to his commune, in the act of will that defined the relationship between individual and community. Individuals who found themselves at odds with their commune could dissent in the name of justice – a

---

[8] Blickle, "Kommunalismus, Parlamentarismus, Republikanismus," 540.

[9] The "common good" discussed in Rublack, "Political and social norms." Winfried Schulze has recently discussed a rare sixteenth-century text that took the opposite position: "Von Gemeinnutz zum Eigennutz."

[10] Civic virtue led to modern concepts of representation in a way that communal virtue never did. In this sense I agree with J. G. A. Pocock that the civic humanist tradition took the central role in the evolution of European and American republican thought, although the "common good" remained a shared value for forms of liberalism ranging from Guiccardini to Mill.

transcendent value guaranteed by God – but not in the name of liberty, since the latter gained its substance for the individual precisely through his participation in the commune. More often, individuals and communes alike appealed to their *Freiheiten* – their privileges in the late medieval sense. In contrast, *Freiheit* – liberty as an abstract good – became a characteristic of entire communities. The Freestate was democratic, to be sure, but it was "the common man in his commune," rather than individual common men who ruled it.

As to sovereignty, the Freestate's situation was more ambiguous, sufficiently so to reveal the uncertain meaning of the concept when applied to sixteenth-century polities. The same authors who spoke of the communes or the common man as the highest power in the Freestate did not hesitate to acknowledge Habsburg dominion over eight of the Ten Jurisdictions. The same Rhaetians who insisted on their God-given freedom seemed eager to treat the population of the Valtellina as subjects owing obedience to their lords, even when Rhaetian dominion was acknowledged to be brutal and corrupt. It is a commonplace to point out that nowhere in the Holy Roman Empire was sovereignty the simple undivided prerogative of kings that Bodin and his followers idealized. But Rhaetia illustrates with special clarity that sovereignty was not simply fractured among many different holders, but rather that multiple and incommensurate models of dominion and authority continued to coexist. The bitterness of social and political conflict in Graubünden derived in part from a new elite's attempt to discredit the very foundations of public authority that had been established during the sixteenth century. The common citizens, meanwhile, conceived of a highest secular authority that was voluntary in character and communal in location, and consequently resisted the reimposition of a model of authority that was based on royal concession or personal status. Yet few Rhaetians were ready to discard the traditional claims of lordly authority outright. Long after the two systems appeared to be visibly clashing, at least to a modern observer, Rhaetian thinkers maintained that there was no contradiction between them, or at least that their claims could be separated and harmonized.

One way to see how the Rhaetian political experience cut across the epochal European transition "from divine cosmos to the sovereign state" is to look at the place that an originary contract played in its ideological life.[11] An imagined social and political contract, as is well known, played a decisive role in the rise of natural law and liberal theories of the state in the work of authors from Hobbes and Locke to Rousseau.[12] The Rhaetian Freestate, too, was founded on an explicit political

[11] The quoted expression is the title of Stephen L. Collins's recent book, *From Divine Cosmos to Sovereign State: An Intellectual History of Consciousness and the Idea of Order in Renaissance England* (Oxford: Oxford University Press, 1989).

[12] The term "natural law" is quite ambiguous; I use it here as explained by Norberto Bobbio, *Thomas Hobbes and the Natural Law Tradition*, tr. Daniela Gobetti (Chicago: University of Chicago Press, 1993), esp. 1–25.

contract whose definitive version appeared in the *Bundesbrief* of 1524. Rhaetia, it might seem, was a political entity whose existence rested solely on the free will of its contracting members, and thus demonstrated the historical plausibility of a contractual social and political theory.[13] By the early seventeenth century, the Rhaetian conviction that their confederation rested on their autochthonous or God-given right to ally for the purpose of establishing peace and prosperity brought them surprisingly close to the theories of the great seventeenth-century English thinkers. Yet in many respects, Rhaetian political ideas remained deeply attached to medieval social ideology as well. Even radical authors who defended Rhaetian liberty also thought that every man should remain in his estate, and that social order depended on a clear subordination of the individual to his community. Nor were they willing to give up the principle that lordship was the natural order of the political universe, even if lordship in their corner of Europe was exercised collectively rather than individually.

Even more revealing is the fundamental pessimism of Rhaetian constitutional documents. Modern democracy is an essentially optimistic creed that assumes that individuals can create and sustain a state that will promote the welfare of all by respecting the rights of every single individual. Government, for the modern world, is not a consequence of human sinfulness and the need to keep corrupted human nature in check, but rather an expression of the human potential to promote the good on a scale larger than the individual. Rhaetian constitutional documents did not share this optimism. The First Ilanz Articles opened with a lament about the inevitability of human corruption:

Now since the fall of the first man, down through the length of years and changes, has in these times made sinfulness creep before reason, and because it is therefore necessary, for the teaching and permanent knowledge of those who will come after us, to commit those things to the evidence of written truth which are intended to live eternally and indestructibly, we therefore declare . . . [14]

The *Bundesbrief*, too, opened with brief comment about how "human nature changes from time to time," with the clear implication that such changes were rarely for the better.[15] A century later, this attitude had changed little: the first published version of the Rhaetian constitutional documents opened with a poem stressing the

---

[13] That the original contracts in Hobbes and Locke were imaginary and heuristic does not mean that a genuinely contractual polity would have been uninteresting to them.

[14] JVF, 78: "Wann von dem Fall des ersten menschen Durch lange der Jaren und verenndrung diss zittes die sinlichkeit der vernunfft hinschlicht, Unnd desshalb nott ist, zuo underrichtung unnd ewiger gedechtnusse den kunftigen die ding unnd sachen, so unnzerstörlich ewig leben söllen, der zügnusse geschrifftlicher warheit zu bevelchen; Bekennend wir..." The passage is difficult to translate. Comparison with the Second Ilanz Articles suggest that *sinlichkeit* should be translated "sinfulness," as a variant of *Sündlichkeit*. The "*welich*" that the editor inserts in the passage (or that was crossed out in the manuscript), serves no purpose.

[15] JVF, 83: "Dwill sich aber das mentschlich wässen, von zytt zuo zytt verendren thuot . . . "

251

destructive consequences of human greed, which therefore needed to be kept in check by political institutions.[16]

It is not surprising that frightened village preachers and angry magnates in the remote villages of Graubünden did not take the conceptual steps that were only beginning to emerge among intellectuals at Oxford and Louvain and Herborn at the turn of the seventeenth century. Rhaetian politics and Rhaetian ideology are not interesting for their breakthroughs, but rather for the way they straddled the medieval and the modern political worlds, often uncomfortably or awkwardly. Still, despite its unusual characteristics, the Freestate was caught up in the general political development of all of Europe. But because the Freestate was so different, studying developments there provides a novel perspective on processes elsewhere, in the universities, in the council chambers, and in the streets and fields. While they started from similar preconditions, and expressed themselves in the same vocabularies as other Europeans, early modern *Bündner* lived in a polity far different from their neighbors, a fact which can be seen in the novel ways they understood their own history and traditions. Social practice, power, and language changed together as communalism superseded feudal dominion in the Rhaetian Alps.

In the end, the Freestate was neither stable nor strong enough to survive the early seventeenth century unscathed. While the rhetoric of commune and republic remained, the distribution of power after the end of the Thirty Years' War again favored the new elite – now overtly aristocratic in its bearing – over the radical claims inspired by the communes' frustration around 1618. Graubünden's political language became a fossil, as it were, revealing the turbulent dynamics of communal power in a society where such turbulence no longer threatened the control exercised by a small group of magnates. The political immobility that spread throughout the Empire after 1648 did not stop at Rhaetia's borders. Separated from Switzerland by its pro-Austrian policies, the Republic of the Three Leagues after 1648 remained a state without a coherent theory, even though it contained a people not subjected to any lords. Only the epochal changes at the end of the *ancien régime* stimulated a new burst of political debate about the Freestate's foundations, just in time for the next great European crisis that ultimately brought the Freestate into the Swiss Confederation in 1803.

---

[16] *Landtsatzungen gemeiner dreyer Pündten*, (Zurich: Joh. Rud. Wolffen, 1619), title page.

Bibliography

ARCHIVAL AND MANUSCRIPT MATERIALS

Staatsarchiv Graubünden, Chur (STAG)
A I   Urkunden
A II/1-2 and Akten   Landesakten, Abschiede and Ausschreiben
A II/4   Ausgabebüchlein
ASp. III/6   Hochgerichte, Gerichte und Nachbarschaften
ASp.III/8i   Reproductions, Sammlung A. Pfister
AB IV/1   Bundestags- oder Landesprotokolle
AB IV/3   Protokolle des Oberen Bundes
AB IV/5   Amtliche Schreiben, Ausschreiben, Strafgerichtsprotokolle
AB IV/6   Dokumentensammlung Mohr, Kopialbücher
AB IV/7b   Archivbücher Sammlung Janett
AB IV 8   Archivbücher des Veltlins
B   Handschriften aus Privatbesitz
D II   Dauerdepositum Archiv Salis-Planta, Samedan
Z   Familienarchiv Planta
Regesten der Gemeindearchive
Gemeindearchiv Davos (GA Davos)
B50–51: Rats- und Landsgemeinde Protokoll, 1578–1617
Archiv der Evangelisch-Rhätische Synode Graubündens
B3: Synodal-Protokoll, 1572–1608
B4: Acta Synodi 1608–41 (copy)
Staatsarchiv Bern (STAB)
Unnütze Papiere, vol. 45, nos. 213–26
Pündten-Bücher: A V 492/B–496/F
Stadtarchiv Chur (STAC)
C II Z 54, "Zizerserband"
C III Z 45 "Schmiedezunft," vols. 1–2, 18
Ratsakten, 1500–1649
Ratsprotokolle
Landesregierungsarchiv Innsbruck (LAI)
Ältere Grenzakten
Lauf. Fasz. 81, 84, 87
Ferdinandea, Fasz. 206, Rubrik 193

Bibliography

Oberösterreichische Hofregistratur
  Protokollen und Repertorien (1572, 1573, 1607)
  Hofregistratur, Akten, Reihe C, Fasz. III/1–3, (nos. 71–73)
  Hofregistratur, Kriegssachen, Sonderreihe "Unruhen in Graubünden"
Kantonsbibliothek St. Gallen, Vadianische Handschriftensammlung (VAD)
  Mss. 219–25: Bartholomäus Anhorn, "Graw-Pündter Krieg"
  Mss. 230, 233–35, 239

PAMPHLETS AND TRACTS

Note: items printed in Phillip Zinsli, "Politische Gedichte aus der Zeit der Bündner Wirren 1603–1639. Texte," JHAGG, 40 (1911): 107–239, and 41 (1911): 23–120, are listed by their *number* in that collection. Page references to these materials follow the internal pagination of the two parts. The following additional abbreviations are used to indicate the location of copies:
  Freytag: Gustav Freytag Sammlung (microfiche)
  LB: Schweizerische Landesbibliothek, Bern
  KGr: Kantonsbibliothek Graubünden, Chur
  StUB: Stadt- und Universitätsbibliothek, Bern
N.p. signifies that the publisher is not identified.

Abriss einer wunderseltzamer / mehr dann Sathanischen Spinnstuben. N.p., 1620. One-page print. A copy is bound in VAD 233.

Actes et Procedures des Grisons de l'Année 1618. Par lesquels sont clairement et veritablement racontés, les justes et urgentes raisons; de l'Assemblée du Commun peuple, avec la réele procedure, de la Justice Criminelle de Thusis. La Haye: Arnoult Meuris, 1619. Freytag 4832. Copy at KGr Be 94.

"Allgemeine Beschreibung / Deß erbärmlichen Zustands / in welchem sich anjetzo die drey Ligen der Grawbündter befinden." Appendix to *Uberkomnuss und Capitulation Endtzwischen Der Kön May. zu Hispanien und den Herren der 2. Pündten / deß Grawen- und Gotteshaus Bund / und der Herrschafft Meyenfeldt . . . Anno 1622 den 15. Jenner / zu Meyland auffgericht und beschlossen*, pp. 27–34. N.p, 1622. Copy at StUB H.XXII.30 (9).

"An den Autoren des Kelchkriegs." 1621. Zinsli, no. 22.

Anonymous. Letter addressed to Holy Roman Emperor, *ca.* 1550–54. STAG AI/3b, no. 134.

Artickel so die zwen Pündt, Desgleichen Burgermayster, Radt, von Gemayn der Stat Chur (Two similar editions. The text is that of the First Ilanz Articles.) Zwickau: n.p., 1523. Copy at KGr Be 225.

Außführliche / Umbstendliche und warhaffte Beschreibung des graußamen und unmenschlichen Veltliner Mords 1620. (Handwritten note found in the copy bound into VAD 220: "Pro Bartholomeo Anhorn 1620," in the author's hand.) N.p. (probably Zurich), n.d.(1620?).

"Bericht über die Ereignisse im Veltlin nach dem bewaffneten Eingreifen der Franzosen gegen die päpstlichen Truppen." Anonymous ms., 1623. STAG BI540/24.

"Beschreibung eines Gesichts." Zinsli, no. 9a. (See "Kurze und Warhaffte Beschreibung," below.)

Blutige Sanfftmuet Der Caluinischen Predicanten. Warhaffte Relation auß einer Glaubwürdigen Person Sendschreiben / so den 6. Martij diß 1621. datirt. Was massen der Edel und Gestreng

Bibliography

Herr Pompeius à Planta von dreyen Predicanten und andern Caluinischen Mördersbrüdern in Engadein in seinem Schloß unfürsehens uberfallen / unchristlicher weiß zu Todt geschlagen / und jämmerlich zerflaischt worden. N.p., 1621. Freytag 5139.

"Der Bündner Spiegel." Attributed to Bartholomäus Anhorn, 1621. Zinsli, no. 36.

"Der Bündnerische Fagaus (1629)." Printed in Fortunat Sprecher, *Geschichte*, I: 236ff. (An incomplete version in Zinsli, no. 29.)

Capitolatione e Conventione tra Sua Maestà, li Signori delle due Leghe Grisa, e Cadè, et Signoria de Mayenfeld, et quelli della Valtellina, et Contado di Bormio. Milan: n.p., 1622. Copy at KGr LB O Gr (Mandate).

Capitulationi e Conventioni Fatte con I Signori Grisoni L'Anno MDCIIII. (Milan?): n.p., 1604. Copy at KGr BE 225.3.

Ilg chiet d'ils Grischuns. N.p., 1665. (Translates three German songs, including "Pündtnerisch Hanengeschrey.")

Colloquium oder Gespräch Eines Schweitzerischen Kühmelckers / Holendischen Käßkramers / unnd Venedischen Seiffensieders / auch etlicher anderer incidenter zu kommenden Personen vom jetzigem der Christenheit Zustandt / darinn etliche gefährliche und schädliche Rathschläg an Tag gegeben werden / zu dieser Ziet sehr nothwendig zu wissen / damit ein jeder frommer uffrichtiger Christ wissen könne / wem er mit gutem gewissen vertrawen dörffe. N.p., 1620. Copy at StUB XXII.29 (14).

Copie d'une lettre escrite au Roy de France et de Navarre, par les trois Ligues des Grisons. La Haye: Hillebrant Jacobssz, 1620. Copies at KGr LS C. B225, 10; BE 225, 9. (A translation of the same text was published in Dutch by the same publisher at the same time.)

The cruell subtilty of Ambtioin [sic], *discovered in a discourse concerning the King of Spaines Surprizing The Valteline. Written in Italian by the Author of the Historie of the Counsell of Trent. Translated by the Renowned Sir Thomas Roe.* London: William Lee, 1650. (Translation of "Ursachen unnd Motiven / was die Veltliner Bewegt," or of its Italian version.)

Decret public, faict en l'Assemblée générale des Grisons a Coire, le 14. Iour de Septembre 1620, stile Antien. La Haye: Hillebrant Jacobssz, 1620. Copies at KGr B2108, 6; BE 225,11.

Discours sur l'affaires de la Valteline, et des Grisons dedié au roy d'Espagne. Paris: 1625. Copy at StUB H.XXII.54 (4).

Discours sur l'estat lamentable auquel sont reduites les trois ligues des Grizons. N.p., 1622. Copy at StUB H.XXII.54 (3).

Discours sur l'estat présent des affairs des Grisons, ou sont representées au vray les justes causes pour lesquelles les peuples dudit pais se sont assemblez: avec les procedures tenües par la justice Extraordinaire, establie à Tousane en la haute Ligue Grise, contre quelques vns de leurs Compatriots, conuaincus de perfidie & de trahison . . . Traduit d'Alleman en François, par S.W. N.p., 1618. Copy at LB A 13357.1. (Translation of *Grawpündtnerische Handlungen deß M.DC.XVIII jahrs.*)

Discours veritable sur l'estat des Trois Ligues Comunes des Grisons: Comprenant ce, que s'est passé en ces pays depuis le massacre et meurtres commis en la Valteline. N.p., 1621. Copies at KGr LS Sp., StUB H.XXI.4.IV (2). (Translation of *Grunndtlicher Bericht uber den Zustand.*)

"Factum Tale in risolutione della Valle Misolcina al Sig.r Conte Triuultio." Ed. A. M. Zendralli. *Quaderni Grigionitaliani*, 22, 2 (1953), pp. 153–55. (Probably a translation of

Bibliography

Factum tale, oder Wolbefügte gründ, welche ein Ersame Gemeind des gantzen Mesaxer Thales im Ob. Grawen Pundt zu beschirmung ihrer Vaterländisch Freyheit wider die ansprachen des Herren Grafen Theodori Trivultzen zu Meyland einführen. N.p., 1623. I have not located a copy of the latter pamphlet, which is cataloged but not present at KGr.)

Fatti de Grisoni nell'Anno 1618. Ove si manifestano chiaramente, & con verità le legitime, & vrgentissime cause della Congregatione del popolo commune, & delli modi legitimi, che l'honorabile giudicio censorio, congregato in Tosana nella Ligia Grisa con piena, & perfetta potestà, è stato costretto di usar contra alcuni loro infedelli Patrioti. N.p., 1618.(Two editions of this pamphlet were printed, identical except for differing decoration on the title page. It is a translation of *Grawpündtnerische Handlungen*.)

Die Geschicht und kurtz begriffene Historia des Kriegs gemeyner Aydgenossen mit sampt den dreyen Pündten, im lande das man nennt Veltlinn in Meylandt. N.p., 1531. Freytag 1652.

"Ein gesicht, so einen Pündtner in einer Nacht erschinen." Zinsli, no. 9.

"Glückwünschung Herrn Blasii Alexandri (1622)." Zinsli, no. 40.

Graubüntische Handlung: Das ist: Kurtze Wahrhaffte Relation, Was massen in Verwichnen Monat Aprilis, den Einwohnern des Zehen Gerichten Pundts in alter hohen Rahetia, durch des Hochloblichen hauses Oesterreich nachgesetzte Oberste und Befelchshaber, die in der Natur und allen Rechten erlaubte Defensions Leibs und der Seelen abgetrungen worden. N.p., 1622. (Identical to *Kurtze Wahrhaffte Relation, Was massen*, attributed to Johannes Guler but probably written by Bartholomäus Anhorn.) Copy at KGr C. B2108, 9, Sp.

Grawpündtnerische Handlungen deß M.DC.XVIII jahrs, Darinnen klärlich unnd wahrhafftig angezeigt werden die rechtmeßigen unnd notzwingenden ursachen der zusammen kunfft deß gemeinen Landvolcks / und ordenlichen processuren / so ein eersam Strafgericht / zuo Tusis im oberen Grawenpundt versampt / uß gegebnem volkomnem gewalt / wider etliche ire untreüwe Landkinder füren müssen. N.p., 1618. (Three separate printings of this pamphlet exist from 1618. A 52 page edition in quarto and another of 39 pages contain the identical text, while a 28 page edition is somewhat abridged. A fourth German edition appeared in 1619 under the title *Grawpündtnerische Handlungen. Das ist: Vollkommener Bericht / wie die in Grawpündten angestellte und verübte Verrähtereyen entdeckt / und die Thaten gestrafft worden.* Copies of all these at KGr. In addition, translations into Italian [two editions], French [two separate translations], Dutch, English and perhaps Latin were published.)

"Grundtliche Widerlegung Eines ehrenvirigen Pasquils unnd unmenschlichen lästerschrifft, so nüwlicher zeit unter dem titel Kelchkrieg . . . ausgegangen." By Bartholomäus Anhorn. 1621? Ms. VAD 220, unpaginated.

Grunndtlicher Bericht über den Zustand gemeiner dreyer Pünten in Raetien: Und was sich syder den im Veltlin begangen Mordthaten in bemelten dreyen Pündten weiter zugetragen. N.p., 1621. Copies at LB A 12243.5; KGr LS Sp. C. BE 3, 24.

Guthertzige Helvetische / Tellische und AntiTillische warnung. Das ist Ein Kurtze fürbildung / wie hoch nohtwendig es seye / daß ein Lobliche Eydgnoschafft / sich ihrer berümpt Altvordern / glücklichen beispil nach / in rühmlicher Einigkeit / zusamen halte / und der / von vielen Wilden Thieren umbgebne Schweitzer Stier / dieselbe als seine geschworne Feind / mit einem Zornigen anblick / und unerschrocknem gegensprung / auß seiner Weid vertreibe. N.p., 1625. Copy at StUB H.XXII.29.

256

"Der heroische Wildemann, das ist ein neuw Lied, wie die Mannhaffte Leuth in dem 10 Grichten Bundt in alter hocher Rhaetia, durch Gottes Hilff mit ihren Brüglen, die Spanische und Leopoldische uß dem Land geschlagen habent (1622)." (Several published versions.) Text in Zinsli, no. 31.

"Ein hüpsche nüw Lied zuo lob unnd ehren gesungen den Dryen Pündten / unnd dem Land Wallis / wie sy ein pundt zusammen gemachet den 3. Augusti des 1600. Jars." Zurich, 1601. Reprinted in Zinsli, no. 5.

"Kurtz beschribene Pündtnerische Handlungen, deß 1618., 19. und 20. Jahrs." (Attributed to Pompeius von Planta. Copy inserted into Anhorn, "Pündtner Krieg," by the copyist Heinrich Spätt.) VAD 235, unpaginated.

"Kurtze unnd einfalte Beschreibung deß Barbarischen unnd jämerlichen mortt unnd verfolgung der waren Christen im Veltlein, gmainer Dryen pünden underthonen landen. Welche zum teil von Ihren eignen landleüten, zu teil aber von ausßlendichen bestelten Banditen geschächen unnd verrichtet worden im Julio deß 1620 Jars." (Probably by Bartholomäus Anhorn. Ms. with corrections and changes.) VAD 220, unpaginated.

Kurtze Wahrhaffte Relation, Was massen in Verwichnen Monat Aprilis, den Einwohnern des Zehen Gerichten Pundts in alter hohen Rahetia, durch des Hochloblichen hauses Oesterreich nachgesetzte Oberste und Befelchshaber, die in der Natur und allen Rechten erlaubte Defensions Leibs und der Seelen abgetrungen worden. N.p., 1622. Freytag 5194.

Kurtzer Bericht, und Warhaffte Erzehlung, welcher gestalt die Hochfürstliche Durchl. Ertzhertzog Leopoldt, von Oesterreich, etc. Die Drey Pündten und Chur mit Kriegesmacht erobert unnd Sieghafft eingenommen den 14. Nouembris Im Jahr, 1621. Augsburg: Andreas Aperger, 1621. Freytag 5049.

"Kürtzer Bericht Wie und welcher gestalt die Spanische faction in den 3 Pundten uber handt genommen. Sonderlich von Anno 1603 biß auff 1621 Jahrs." Ms. copy by Heinrich Spätt, *ca.* 1621, VAD 233, unpaginated. (The text is the same as the pamphlet *Ursachen und Motiven, Warumb die Gemeine drey Bündt.*)

"Kurtzer einfaltiger unnd unpartheyischer Bericht, auss wass ursachen und mittel, der Landtkrieg in den drey Grawen Pündten alter freyer hoher Rhaetia, sambt der Rebellion ihm Landt Veltlin, unnd selber Mordt entstanden seye, so diss lauffende MDCXX Jahres Ihm werckh ist. Item durch waß mitel dessen Landkrieg widerumb möge gestillet unnd abgelegt werden." (Ms. fragment which breaks off, *ca.* 1620.) VAD 239, pp. 337–402.

Kurtzer grundtlicher Bericht des leidigen aufflauffs in den 3 Grawen Pünden. Durch Glückhold, Redner v. Hinderleygen beschriben. N.p., 1607.

"Kurtzer waarhafter bericht des zustandes gmeiner dreien Grauwen Pündten darin wir ietzdann sindt, mit anzeigung." (Anonymous ms., perhaps composed by Rhaetian Synod, October 1, 1607.) LAI Hofregistratur, Kriegssachen, Reihe C, Fasz. 169.

"Kurze und Warhaffte Beschreibung Eines wunderlichen Gesichts, so einem fürnemen Pundtsman zu hohen Realta, nit weit von Tusis gelegen, in einer nacht erscheinen, in welchenn deß Straffgrichts Ritterliche Thadten, so sie mit dreyen Pärsohnen Begangen, beschriben oder erzehlt worden. Allen fromen Pündtneren zu einem Guthertzigen Wahrnung an Tag geben." (Ms. copy by Heinrich Spätt of original text *ca.* 1618.) VAD 235, unpaginated. Text also in Zinsli, no. 9a.

"Kurzer Bericht, wie es den fünf Kath. Orten ergangen (1621)." Zinsli, no. 27.

"Kurzer und Warhaffter Bericht des Kelchen Kriegß, so von den Calvinischen Püntneren und Zwinglischen Züricheren unnd Berneren Im Veltlin volbracht worden." (Ms. copy of a pamphlet, made by Bartholomäus Anhorn, bound together with his ms. rebuttal.) VAD 220, unpaginated.

"Kurzer unnd Warhaffter Bericht des Kelchen Kriegß, so von den Erzketzern Calvin, Bündtner, Zwinglischen, Zürchern, und Grauern in Veltlin, von dem 15. august Anno 1620 bis dato her, vollbracht worden (1621)." Reproduced in *Illustrierter Flugblätter aus den Jahrhunderten der Reformation und der Glaubenskämpfe*, ed. Wolfgang Harms. Coburg : Die Kunstsammlungen, 1983, p. 59. Text reproduced in Zinsli, no. 23.

Landtsatzungen gemeiner dreyer Pündten in alter hoher Raetia gelegen: Zu underschidenlichen mahlen abgesetzt und dises MDCXIX jahrs / fürohin steiff und stet zuhalten angenommen und gelobet. Zurich: Joh. Rud. Wolffen, 1619. Copies at KGr Bd 11/3, 11/4; StUB H.XXII.121.

"Ein Lied von dem gehepten Bündner Krieg (1631)." Zinsli, no. 44

"Ein Lied von dem harten Streit vor Tiran (1620)." By Heinrich Rynacher. Zinsli, no. 18.

"Ein lied zu Ehren Gemeinen Löblichen dreyen Pündten in alter hoher freyer Rhetien ober Teutschlandt und zuo sonderen geflissner Dankerzeigung gegen dem Edlen / Gestrengen...H. Johann Guler von Weineck / Rittern / gewessnen Landthaubtman Veltlins und Landtamman uff Davos etc. (1615)." By Fortunat Sprecher. Zinsli, no. 2.

"Lobspruch der dapferen und mannhafften Prätigäuweren im 10. Grichten Bundt, alter hoher Rhaetier Landts, waß Gott durch ihre Brügel gegen ihren feinden den Spaniern, Italieneren, und österrychischen gewürkt hat, Inn dißen letzten betrübten Zeiten." N.p., 1622. Reprinted in Zinsli, no. 33.

"Ein lustiges Lied von dem Veltliner Land (1621)." Originally printed in *Drey Warhafftige Newe Zeytungen*. Prague: Peter Fabrici, 1621. Copy at StUB H.XXII.54.3 (2); text in Zinsli, no. 17.

"Ein neu Lied (über den begehrten Pass) (1612)." Zinsli, no. 8.

"Neue Zeitung über die Vorgänge des 1621. Jahrs (1621)." Zinsli, no. 28.

"Ein new Lied und Frolockung uber die Pündtnuss, so dises Jahr zwischen den dreyen Pündten Rhetier Landts und der statt Bern auffgerichtet worden (1602)." By Michael Stettler. Originally printed in Bern: Johannem le Preux, n.d.; text in Zinsli, no. 6.

"Ein new Lied, Gedicht vom redlichen alten Eydtgenossen der nichts anders begert, betrachtet und sucht, dan Nutz, Frommen unnd Wolfahrt des gemeinen Vaterlandts (1621)." Zinsli, no. 25.

Newe zeittung und beschreibung der zwiträchtigen kriegshandlung, so sich kürtzlich zwischen den dreyen Pündten und Aydgenossen, wider den Castellan von Müß, zugetragen und verloffen haben. N.p., 1531. Freytag 1654.

Over-Rhetische ofte Grysonsche Acten ende Proceduren des Jaers M.CD.XVIII. Vaer inne claerlichen ende waerachtichlicken verhaelt werden / de rechtveerdighe ende noodt-dwinghende oorsaken / der Verganderinghe des ghemeenen Landt-volcks / ende wetterlicke Procedure / die de eersame criminele Justitie / tot Tussis in Over-Rhetian vergadert / uyt tracht van henluyden ghegeven macht / tegens etlicke har ontrouwe Landtsaten / heeft moeten ghebruycken. s'Graven-Hage: Aert Meuris. 1619. Copy at KGr LS C. B2108, 5b. (Translation of *Grawpündtnerische Handlungen deß M.DC.XVIII jahrs.*)

Bibliography

"Pasquille vom Thusner Strafgericht, 1618." Zinsli, nos. 9a–f.

The Proceedings of the Grisons in the yeere 1618. Originally published London: n.p., 1619. Facsimile edition, Amsterdam/New York: Theatrum Orbis Terrarum/Da Capo Press, 1971. (Translation of *Grawpünterische Handlungen deß M.DC.XVIII jahrs.* Short-Title Catalogue, 12390.)

"Prosopopeia Raetica (1618)." By Adam Saluz. Zinsli, no. 10.

Pündtnerisch Hanengeschrey: Das ist ein new Lied, darin die gemeinen Pundsleut oberen Retierlands umb Rettung und erhaltung irer wolhergebrachten teuwren Freyheit willen / zur alten Mannheit und Tapfferkeit vermahnet werdend. In der Weiß / Der Marggraff schiffet uber Rheyn / etc. N.p., 1621. Copy at LB A 11166.6; text reprinted in Zinsli, no. 4.

"Der Pündtnerische Brügel Krieg, welche die dapfferen und mannhafften Prättigäuwern wider ihre Feynd zu handen genommen (1622)." Two published editions; text in Zinsli, no. 32.

Pündtnerische Handlungen Widerholte unnd vermehrte Deduction. Darinnen weitläuffig dargethan und erwiesen wird, was massen die Einwohner deß zehen Grichten Pundts in Alter Rhätia, von deß Hochlöblichen Hauses Oesterreichts nachgesetzten Obristen unnd Befelchshabern widerrechtlich überfallen: in die eusserste dienstbarkeit gewetten, grausamer weyß tyrannisiret und geplagen: unnd deßwegen ihnen die in der Natur, unnd allen Rechten erlaubte Defension Leibes und der Seelen im verwichenen Monat Aprilis abgetrungen worden. Sampt einem Warhaften Bericht, was zwüschend beyden Partheyen biß dato denckwürdiges fürgeloffen. N.p., 1622. Freytag 5181. (Revision of *Kurtze Wahrhaffte Relation, Was massen in Verwichnen Monat Aprilis.*) Reprinted 1877, ed. Conradin von Moor.

"Reimen über den zuostand des Pundtnerland und straffgericht dises jahrß 1607." Manuscript, *ca.* 1607. STAG B1538/13:384.

Relation, als sich im Jahr 1620 mit Ihr. König. Maiest. in Spanien, wie auch IFD Leopoldisch Kriegsvolk mit den Grawbündtern, Veltlinern un Engetheinern kürtzlich zugetragen hat . . . Attributed to Wilhelm Peter Zimmerman. Augsburg: David Franck, 1621. Copy at KGr LS C. B2108, 7c.

"Rheti-Berchtoldus (1602)." By Antonius à Graffenried. Originally printed in Bern: Johannem le Preux, 1602; text reprinted in Zinsli, no. 7.

"Rhetus. Ein schön new Lied und Freundtliche erinnerung des Uralten Greysen Rheti an seinen Grawe Püntner (1621)." By Adam Saluz. Originally published n.p., 1621; text reprinted in Zinsli, no. 3.

"Ein schön Dancklied umb die Freyheit Welche der Barmherzig Gott, einer werden Eydtgnoschafft und loblichen dreyen Pündten im Schwabenkrieg (dessen ein kurzer begriff hierin verfasst) sonderbar und wunderbar auß gnaden erhalten hat (1617)." By Conrad Buol. Originally printed in Bern: Abraham Weerlin, 1617; text in Zinsli, no. 1.

Sendschreiben eines getrewen Teutschen Patrioten / welches er an seiner guten Freund und Landsleut einen abgehen lassen: Aus welchem zu sehen / Wie es mit dem den 15/25 Aprill Anno 1621. in Hispanien zu Madril [sic] getroffenen Accord, betreffend die Restitution des Lands Veltlyns / der Herrschafft Worms / und etlicher orten der Graffschafft Cläven / den Grawpündtnern in Alter Hoher Raetien zugehörig / biß uff Dato den 5. Tag Septembris St. N. nach verscheinung V. gantzer Monaten / eigentlich sey beschaffen. Allen Freyen Ständen / zur Warnung und Nachrichtung / an tag gegeben. N.p., 1621. Freytag 5143.

259

Bibliography

Solida ac necessaria confutatio argumentorum quibus Sceleratissimi Parricidae Rhaetorum provinci Vallistellinae, non modo scelera sua immania palliare satagunt, sed Reges etiam & Principes, ut patrocinum sui suscipiant, permovere volunt ausu indignissimo & plane nefario. Attributed to Fortunat von Sprecher. Augustae Trebocorum: Christophori ab Heyden, 1622. Copies at KGr LS C. B2108, 9a; StUB H.XXII.30 (6).

Sommaire description de l'Estat present des Trois Ligues. N.p., 1624. (This is apparently an abbreviation of *Discours veritable sur l'estat des Trois Ligues Comunes des Grisons*, which is itself a translation of *Kurtzer Vergriff der jetzigen Pündtnerischen Zustands*.)

Summarische Relation: Von den im Namen der Hochfürstlichen Durchleucht Ertzhertzog Leopolden zu Oesterreich / durch dero Generaln / dem Hoch- und Wolgebornen Herren / Herren Alwigen Grafen zu Suls unnd Lanndtgrafen im Kleckgew / gegen den Engadeinern, Tauuasern und Brättigöwern fürgenommnen Kreiegsexpedition und in zehen Tagen erlangten volkommner Victori. Augsburg: Sara Mangin, 1622. Freytag 5195.

Summarischer Begriff. Aller Frantzösischen Verhandlungen in Pündten von Anno 1602. biß Anno 1640. Attributed to Johan Simeon von Florin. N.p, n.d. Copy at LB A 3023.4.

"Summarischer Bericht des gegenwärtigen Zustandes gemeiner drei Bünde bis den 22 Juli 1607." Anonymous manuscript, *ca.* 1607. STAG B1548/2. Another copy as "Summarischer Bericht des Zustandes gem. Drei Bünde bis zum 22. Juli 1607." STAG B694/4, pp. 172f.

"Der traurige Bündner Spiegel." Zinsli, no. 37.

Trewhertzige Ermahnung an die drey Pündt, das sie nit die Meylandische Artikel verachten / sonder mit dem König in Hispanien söllen Pündtnuß machen / unnd mitt ihme gutte Fridenspacta ingehn / unnd sich so unbesinnet von Franckreich nit zertrennen / dann es werden uns die Frantzösichen Ambassatorn nit verderben lassen sondern fordern vermög der Pündtnuß beystendig sein. N.p., 1621. One-page print. Copy at StUB H.XXII.29 (16).

Trewhertzige vermahnung an die drey löbliche Bündt gemeinen Rhetierlandts: Darinn sie zu hinlegung innwendiger Uneinigkeit / und hingegn zur wahren Einigkeit / wie in gemein zu rechtschaffner Christlicher buß und bekehrung zu Gott / vermahnet werden. By Antonio de Molina. N.p., 1608. Copy at KGr Bg 260.

Uber dise nachkommenden Schlußreden wellend wir der pfarrer zu S. Martin zu Chur . . . ainem yeden antwurt und bericht geben auß hayliger geschrifft news und alts Testaments, auff den Pundtstag der zu Ilantz angesehen ist auff Sontag nach Epiphanie, Anno 1526. N.p., 1526. Freytag 3298.

"Ursach der letzt geschechen Resolution [sic] wider die Tiranney der drey Pündten." Ms., 1620. STAG B1572.

Ursachen und Motiven, Warumb die Gemeine drey Bündt in alter hoher Rehtia oder Graupünden gelegen, etlicher frembder Fürsten und Herren Gesandten Residentz, in jhren Landen ferner nicht zugestatten, sich entschlossen. N.p., 1620. Freytag 5029. (This pamphlet exists in two German editions, and in Italian and French translations. The text is very similar to that in "Kürtzer Bericht Wie und welcher gestalt die Spanische faction in den 3 Pundten uber handt genommen.") Ms. in VAD 233.

"Ursachen unnd Motiven / was die Veltliner Bewegt / sich der Tyranney der Grisoner (so sie vermittels ihrer Vögt und Blutrichter ein zeitlang wider die Catholischen deren orten verübt) mit gewalt zuwidersetzen," in *Veltlinischer Blutrath und Straffgerichtt*, by Nicolai Elias, (pseudonym), with the false imprint Franckenburg: Gottlieb Warmund,

Bibliography

1621, pp. 32–44. Freytag 5009. (This text translated as *Cruell Subtilty of Ambitioin*, and similar to "Ursach der letzt geschechen Resolution [sic] wider die Tiranney der drey Pündten," and "Warhaffte Historische Relation / waß die Veldtlyner verursachet.")
"Ursachen warumben die Algemeine strafgericht in den Pündten. allen Ehr: und rhue liebenden unträgenlich seyendt, also dz man dieselbe nit mügen abgeschafft werden, nit müglich ist das ein frummb Erlich Mann müge bey seinen hauß und hof verbleiben, 1607." Anonymous manuscript (copy), May 19, 1607. LAI Hofregistratur, Kriegssachen, Reihe C, Fasz. 168.

Veltlinisch Blutbad, Und Außführliche umbständliche unnd warhaffte Beschreibung deß grausamen und unmenschlichen Mordts, so in dem Land Veltlyn, gemeinen dreyen Pünden gehörig, Anno 1620. den 9. Julij und folgende tag, alten Calenders...ist geübt worden. Zürich: Johann Rudolff Wolffen, 1621. Freytag 5054.

Veltlinische Tyranney, Das ist Außführliche Umbstendliche und Wahrhaffte Bescheibung Deß Grausamen und unmenschlichen Mordts so in dem Landt Veltlin gemeinen dreyen Pündten gehörig...ist geubet worden. Zürich: Johann Rudolff Wolffen, 1621. Freytag 5154. (The imprint indicates that this edition is a reprint of *Veltlinisch Blutbad*. The British museum attributes this text to Caspar Waser of Zurich.)

Veltlinischer Blutrath und Straffgericht, Das ist: Kurtzer und warhaffter Bericht, von den ursachen deß im Veltliner Thal entstandnen Kriegs, dabey etlichermassen außgeführt wird, ob: und was Spanien wegen deß Herzogthumbs Mayland darbey interessiert. Auch was es mit der fünfften Monarchia von ein gestalt / daruon so vil underschidliche Discurs dise Jahr hero spargiert worden. Item / was man sich deßwegen in Teutschland / unnd hergegen in Holland danach endung des 12 Jährige anstands / Gott der Allmächtig deren orten was widrigs verhengen solt, zubefahren . . . By Nicolai Elias (pseudonym), with false imprint Franckenburg: Gottlieb Warmund, 1621. Freytag 5119.

Vera narratione del massacro degli evangelici, fatto da' papisti i rebelli, nella maggior parte della Valtellina, nell'ann M.DC.XX addì IX. iuglio, e giorni seguenti, stilo vecchio. N.p., 1621. (Translation of *Veltlinische Tyranney*, by V. Paravicino [according to British Museum: see Freytag 5154].)

"Vertraulicher Discurs an die Herren Grisonen in alter freier hoher Rhätia, durch Lucium Brittanum redivivum." By Daniel Anhorn. Manuscript composed in 1621. VAD 219, unpaginated. Copy in VAD 233.

"Viaggio del B. Carlo Borromeo Cardinale di S. Prassede Archivesco di Milano Fatto al Monastero di Tisitis principal Communita delle Eccelse tre Leghe nell'anno 1581." By Giovanni Sacco, (i.e. Johann Sax). Originally published Milan: Gio. Iacomo Como, 1605. Reprinted in ZSKG 18 (1924): 136–65, ed. Gion Cahannes.

"Warhaffte, erschrökliche und unerhörte newe Zeitung Von der urplötzlichen Undergang deß wolbekandten Fleckens Plurs in Bergell (1618)." Originally published in Embs: Bartholome Schnell, 1618; text reprinted in Zinsli, no. 12.

Warhaffte Historische Relation und Bericht. Was sich in den gemeinen dreyen Bünden. inn altem hohen Rhetia gelegn, seythero dem vorgangenen unmenschlichen verübten Blutbad de Anno 1620. in Veltlin, biß auff gegenwärtige Zeit nämlich zu anfang diß Monats Junij, Anno 1621. begeben und zugetragen. N.p., 1621. Two similar editions at Freytag 5134, 5135.

Warhaffte Historische Relation, was die Veldtlyner verursachet habe, sich von der Graw Pündtnern umbillicher Regierung abzuwerffen, in Monat Julio und Augusto diß 1620. Jahrs.

261

Bibliography

Auß dem Italienischen getruckten Exemplar in unsere teutsche Sprach transferiert. Augsburg: Andreas Aperger, 1620. Freytag 5009.

Warhaffte Relation Dessen Was sich in Gemeinen Dreyen Pündten, in alter hoher Retia gelegen, seyd dem unmenschlichen verübten Mord im land Veltlin, biß auff gegenwertige zeit, nemlich zu anfang des Monats Junij zugetragen. N.p., 1621. Freytag, 5133. (Nearly identical to *Warhaffte Historische Relation und Bericht. Was sich in den gemeinen dreyen Bünden* . . .)

Warhaffte Verzeichnuss dess Prättigöws (map). N.p., 1622. Copy bound in VAD 234.

"Ein warhafftiges newes Lied auß dem Land Pünten und Veltlyn (1620)." Zinsli, no. 24.

PUBLISHED SOURCES

Ämtliche Sammlung der älteren Eidgenössischen Abschiede, 1245–1798. 8 sections in 22 vols. Various publishers, 1856–86.

Anonymous (attr. to Jan Aliesch). "La Cronica [ladina dal 1575 al 1588 scritta in rimas]." In *Rhätoromanische Chrestomathie,* vol. v, ed. Caspar Decurtins, pp. 299–324. Erlangen: A. Deichert and Fr. Junge, 1888–1919. Reprinted Chur: Octopus, 1982–85.

Anhorn, Bartholomäus. *Barth. Anhorn's Püntner Aufruhr im Jahre 1607.* Ed. Conradin von Moor. Chur: Verlag von C. Nigg, 1862.

   Graw-Pünter-Krieg, beschrieben von Barthol. Anhorn 1603–1629. Nach dem manuscript zum ersten Mal herausgegeben. Ed. Conradin von Moor. Chur: Verlag der Antiquariatsbuchhandlung, 1873.

   "Politisches und religiöses Testament des Chronisten Bartholomäus Anhorn." Ed. Fritz Jecklin. *Anzeiger für schweizerische Geschichte,* n.s. 25, 3, vol. 7 (1894): 89ff.

Anhorn, Bartholomäus, Jr. *Heilige Wiedergeburt der Evangelischen Kirchen / in den gmeinen dreyen Pündten / Der freyen hohen Rhaetiae: Oder Beschreibung derselbigen Reformation / und Religionsverbesserung: Sampt dero Ferner zustand / grossen Verfolgungen / wider sie angespunnen / mortdtlichen prattiquen und Gnädiger Erhaltung Gottes.* Brugg: Ranhard Amman, 1680. (Text composed by Bartholomäus Anhorn Sr., edited and published by his grandson, B. Anhorn Jr.)

Ardüser, Hans. *Hans Ardüser's Rätische Kronik, herausgegeben auf Veranstaltung der bündnerischen naturhistorischen Gesellschaft.* Ed. J. Bott. Chur: Buchdruckerei von Gebr. Casanova, 1877. Reprinted Walluf bei Wiesbaden: Sandig, 1973.

   Warhaffte und kurzbegriffene Beschreibung etlicher herrlicher und hochvernampter Personen in alt. fr. Rhätia. Lindau: Hans Ludwig Brem, 1598.

Campell, Ulrich. *Raetiae alpestris topographica descriptio.* Ed. Chr. Kind. *Quellen zur Schweizer Geschichte,* o.s. vol. vii. Basel: Felix Schneider, 1884.

   Ulrici Campelli Historica Raetica. Ed. Placidus Plattner. *Quellen zur Schweizer Geschichte,* o.s. vols. viii and ix. Basel: Felix Schneider, 1887–90. Ed. and tr. by Conradin von Moor as *Ulrich Campells zwei Bücher rätischer Geschichte.* 2 vols. Chur: Leonhard Hitz, 1849–51.

Decurtins, Caspar, ed. *Rhätoromanische Chrestomathie.* 13 vols. Erlangen: A. Deichert and Fr. Junge, 1888–1919. Reprinted Chur: Octopus, 1982–85.

Guler von Wyneck, Johannes. *Raetia; das ist, außführliche und wahrhaffte Beschreibung der dreyen loblichen Grawen Bündten etc.* Zürich, 1616.

Bibliography

"Die Erneuerung des Bundesschwurs in Graubünden: Eine Oration Johannes Gulers bei der Eidesabnahme im Jahre 1605." Ed. J. Ferdmann. *Davoser Revue*, 16, 9 (1941): 179–83.

Haffter, Ernst, ed. *Georg Jenatsch*. Vol. II: *Urkundenbuch, enthaltend Exkurse und Beilagen*. Chur: Hitz'sche Buchhandlung, 1895.

Jecklin, Constanz, ed. "Urkunden zur Staatsgechichte Graubündens." *Jahresbericht der Historisch-antiquitarische Gesellschaft Graubündens*, 20 (1890): 41–63; 21 (1891): 21–133. (Two parts separately paginated into a single sequence.)

Urkunden zur Verfassungsgeschichte Graubündens. (Als Fortsetzung von Mohr's Codex Diplomaticus). Chur: Sprecher und Plattner, 1883. Also published in *Jahresbericht der Historisch-antiquitarische Gesellschaft Graubündens*, 1883, 1885, and 1890.

Jecklin, Fritz, ed. *Materialien zur Standes- und Landesgeschichte Gem. III Bünde (Graubünden), 1464–1803*. Vol. I: *Regesten*. Vol. II: *Texte*. Basel: Basler Buch- und Antiquariatshandlung, 1907 and 1909.

"Eine neue Quelle für die Geschichte des bündnerischen Strafgerichts vom Jahre 1572." *Anzeiger für schweizerische Geschichte*, n.s. 33, 3, vol. 9 (1902): 72–84.

"Ein Pasquill gegen Landrichter Gallus v. Mont und Hauptmann Sebastian v. Castelberg vom 7. Januar 1585." *Bündner Monatsblatt* (1926): 354–60.

Jenatsch, Jörg. *Jörg Jenatsch: Briefe, 1614–39*. Ed. Alexander Pfister. Chur: Jörg-Jenatsch-Stiftung, 1983.

Juvalta, Fortunat von. *Denkwürdigkeiten des Fortunat von Juvalta, 1567–1649*. Ed. Conradin von Moor. Chur: O. Hitz, 1848.

Raeti Commentarii vitae et selecta poemata. Ed. Luzius Hold. Chur: Andreas Traugott Otto, 1823.

Lemnius, Simon. *Die Räteis von Simon Lemnius: Schweizerisch-deutscher Krieg von 1499: Epos in IX Gesängen*. Ed. and tr. Placidus Plattner. Chur: Sprecher und Plattner, 1874.

Meyer-Marthaler, Elisabeth and Franz Perret, eds. *Bündner Urkundenbuch*. 3 vols. Chur: Verlag Bischofsberger, 1955–85.

Niger, Franciscus. *Rhetia. Eine Dichtung aus dem 16. Jahrhundert von Franciscus Niger aus Bassano*. Ed. and tr. T. Schiess. Chur: Manataschal, Ebner, 1897.

Padavino, Giovanni Battista. *Del Governo e Stato dei Signori Svizzeri Relazione di Giovanni Battista Padavino, Segretario dell'eccelso Consiglio dei Dieci*. Ed. Vittorio Ceresole. Venice: Tipografia Antonelli, 1874.

"Relatione de Grisoni fatto del secretario Padavino (1603–1607)." Ed. Vittorio Ceresole. *Rätia, Mittheilungen des geschichts-forschenden Gesellschaft von Graubünden*, 2 (1865): 186–247.

Relatione del segretario Padavino, ritornato dal paese de' Signori Grisoni presentata nell'Ecc.^mo Collegio a'20 Agosto 1605. Ed. A. Giussiani. Como: Premiata Tipografia Editrice Ostinelli di Bertolini Nani e C., 1904.

Pasquali, Carlo [Charles Paschal]. *Caroli Paschali legatio Rhätica*. Paris: Peter Chevalier, 1620. Translated as *Karl Paschal, König Ludwigs des XIII Geheimer Staatsraths Geschichte seiner Gesandtschaft in Bündten*. Chur: Bernhard Otto, 1781.

Rohan, Henri duc de. *Memoires de duc de Rohan sur le guerre de la Valtelline*. 2nd series, vol. v, *Nouvelle collection des memoires pour servir à l'histoire de France*. Ed. M. Michaud. Lyon: Guyot Fréres, 1853.

Salis-Marschlins, Ulysses von. *Denkwürdigkeiten*. Ed. and tr. Conradin von Moor. Chur: Pargätzi & Felix, 1858.

Sammlung Schweizerischer Rechtsquellen. Section XV, *Rechtsquellen des Kantons Graubünden*. Series B, *Die Statuten der Gerichtsgemeinden*. Part 1, *Der Gotteshausbund*. Ed. Andreas Schorta. Aarau: Verlag Sauerländer, 1980– . Part 2, *Der Zehngerichtenbund*. Ed. Elisabeth Meyer-Marthaler. Aarau: Verlag Sauerländer, 1985– .

Schiess, Traugott, ed. *Bullingers Korrespondenz mit den Graubündnern*. Vols. XXIII–XXV, *Quellen zur Schweizer Geschichte*, o.s. Basel, 1904–06. Reprint Nieuwkoop: B. de Graaf, 1968.

Simmler, Josias. *Von den Regiment der Lobl. Eÿdgenoßschaft Zwey Bücher*. Ed. and revised Hans Jacob Leu. Zurich: David Gessner, 1722.

Sprecher von Bernegg, Florian. "Beitrag zur Characteristik bündnerischer Staatsmänner des 16.Jahrhunderts: Sechs Briefe des Ritters Florian Sprecher von Bernegg zu Davos an seine Ehegattin Dorothea, geb. Büsch." In *Archiv für die Geschichte der Republik Graubünden*, vol. I, part. 2, ed. Theodor von Moor, pp. 1–16. Chur: Leonhard Hitz, 1848.

Sprecher von Bernegg, Fortunat. *Das christliche Leben und selig Sterben des thüren Helden und thrüwen Vatters des Vatterlands, Herrn Obersten Joh. Gulers von Wyneck. . . samt der Lychpredig. . . gehalten durch Herrn Georg Salutz etc*. N.p., 1637. Reprinted 1819.

Geschichte der bündnerischen Kriegen und Unruhen. 2 vols. Ed. and tr. Conradin von Mohr [Moor]. Chur: Leonhard Hitz, 1856. (Tr. of *Historia motuum et bellorum*.)

Historia motuum et bellorum postremis hisce annis in Rhaetia excitatorum et gestorum. Coloniae Allobrogum (i. e. Geneva?): n.p., 1629

Historia von denen Unruhen und Kriegen/ so in denen hochloeblichen Rhaetischen Landen vor Jahren entstanden und durch Gottes Beystand gluecklich zu Ende gebracht worden. St. Gallen: Tobias Hochreutiner, 1701. (Tr. of *Historia motuum et bellorum*.)

Pallas Raetica, armata et togata. Basel: I. J. Genathius, 1617. Reprinted as *Rhetia, ubi eius verus situs, politia, bella, foedera, et alia memorabilia accuratissime describuntur*. Lugdunum Batavorum: Ex officina Elzeviriana, 1633.

Rhetishe Cronica, oder kurtze und wahrhaffte Beschreibung Rhetischer Kriegs- und Regiments-sachen… erstlich lat, hernach v. Authore vermehrt u. ins D. übersetzt. Chur: n.p., 1672. (Tr. of *Pallas Raetica*.)

Sprecher von Bernegg, Fortunat, and Phillip Cleverius. *Die Rätia-Karte von Fortunat Sprecher von Berneck und Phillip Cleverius aus dem Jahre 1618*. Ed. G. Grosjean. Dietikon: Bibliophile Drucke, 1976 (facsimile of 1618 edition).

Travers, Joann. "La canzun della guerra degl chastè da Müsch." In *Zwei Historischer Gedichte in ladinischer Sprache aus dem 16. und 17. Jahrhundert. Zum ersten Male herausgegeben, übersetzt und mit einem Abriß der ladinischen Literatur eingeleitet*, ed. Alfons von Flugi, pp. 42–54. Chur: Leonhard Hitz, 1865.

Tschudi, Aegidius. *Die uralt warhafftig Alpisch Rhetia / sampt dem Tract der anderen Alpgebirgen / nach Plinii / Ptolemei / Strabonis / auch anderen Welt und gschichtschribern warer anzeygung . . .* Basel: n.p., 1538.

Wagner, R. and L. R. von Salis, eds. *Rechtsquellen des Cantons Graubünden*. 4 sections in 2 vols. Special imprint from the *Zeitschrift für schweizerisches Recht*, vols. 25–28. Basel: C. Detloff's Buchhandlung, 1887.

Bibliography

Wietzel, Gioerin."Gioerin Wietzels Gedicht vom Veltlinerkriege." In *Zwei Historischer Gedichte in ladinischer Sprache aus dem 16. und 17. Jahrhundert. Zum ersten Male herausgegeben, übersetzt und mit einem Abriß der ladinischen Literatur eingeleitet*, ed. Alfons von Flugi, pp. 55–113. Chur: Leonhard Hitz, 1865.

Zinsli, Philipp. "Politische Gedichte aus der Zeit der Bündner Wirren 1603–1639. Texte." *Jahresbericht der Historisch-antiquitarische Gesellschaft Graubündens*, 40 (1911): 107–239; 41 (1911): 23–120 [also paginated separately].

SECONDARY MATERIAL

Aubin, Hermann. "Zur Entwicklung der freien Landgemeinden im Mittelalter. Fehde, Landfrieden, Schiedsgericht." In *Deutsches Bauerntum im Mittelalter*, ed. Günther Franz, pp. 191–218. Darmstadt: Wissenschaftliche Buchgesellschaft, 1976.

Bader, Karl Siegfried. *Der deutsche Südwesten in seiner territorialstaatlichen Entwicklung*. Stuttgart: K. F. Koehler Verlag, 1950.

Das Schiedsverfahren in Schwaben vom 12. bis zum ausgehenden 16. Jahrhundert. Tübingen: H. Laupp, Jr., 1929.

"Staat und Bauerntum im deutschen Mittelalter," in *Adel und Bauern im deutschen Staat des Mittelalters*, ed. Theodor Mayer, pp. 109–129. Darmstadt: Wissenschaftliche Buchgesellschaft, 1967.

Studien zur Rechtsgeschichte des mittelalterlichen Dorfes. Vol. I: *Das Mittelalterliche Dorf als Friedens- und Rechtsbereich*. Cologne and Vienna: Böhlau Verlag, 1981. Vol. II: *Dorfgenossenschaft und Dorfgemeinde*. Cologne and Graz: Heinrich Böhlaus Nachfolger, 1974.

Barber, Benjamin R. *The Death of Communal Liberty: A History of Freedom in a Swiss Mountain Canton*. Princeton: Princeton University Press, 1974.

Baron, Hans. "Calvinist republicanism and its historical roots." *Church History*, 8 (1939): 30–42.

The Crisis of the Early Italian Renaissance. 2nd edition. Princeton: Princeton University Press, 1966.

Baum, Wilhelm. *Sigmund der Münzreiche. Zur Geschichte Tirols und der habsbürgischen Länder im Spätmittelalter*. Bozen: Verlagsanstalt Athesia, 1987.

Baumgartner, Frederic J. *Radical Reactionaries: The Political Thought of the French Catholic League*. Geneva: Librarie Droz, 1975.

Bercé, Yves. *History of Peasant Revolts: The Social Origins of Rebellion in Early Modern France*. Cambridge: Polity Press, 1990.

Revolt and revolution in Early Modern Europe: An Essay on the History of Political Violence. Manchester: Manchester University Press, 1987.

Berger, Hans. "Der Churer Pfarrer Saluz (1571–1645), seine Kollegen und seine Zeit." *Jahresbericht der Historisch-antiquitarische Gesellschaft Graubündens* (1961): 1–98.

Bierbrauer, Peter. "Der Aufstieg der Gemeinde und die Entfeudalisierung der Gesellschaft im späten Mittelalter." In *Kommunalisierung und Christianisierung. Voraussetzungen und Folgen der Reformation 1400–1600*, ed. Peter Blickle and Johannes Kunisch, pp. 29–55. Berlin: Duncker & Humblot, 1989.

Bibliography

"Bäuerliche Revolten im Alten Reich: Ein Forschungsbericht." In *Aufruhr und Empörung? Studien zum bäuerlichen Widerstand im Alten Reich*, ed. Peter Blickle, pp. 1–68. Munich: Verlag C. H. Beck, 1980.

Freiheit und Gemeinde im Berner Oberland, 1300–1700. Bern: Historischer Verein des Kantons Bern, 1991.

"Das Göttliche Recht und die naturrechtliche Tradition." In *Bauern, Reich, und Reformation: FS Günther Franz*, ed. Peter Blickle, pp. 210–34. Stuttgart: Eugen Ulmer, 1982.

Bilgeri, Benedikt. *Der Bund ob dem See*. Stuttgart: Kohlhammer, 1968.

Billigmeier, Robert Henry. *A Crisis in Swiss Pluralism: The Romansh and Their Relations with the German- and Italian-Swiss in the perspective of a millennium*. The Hague, Paris, and New York: Mouton Publishers, 1979.

Bisson, T. N. "The military origins of medieval representation." *American Historical Review*, 71 (1966): 353–73.

Black, Antony. *Guilds and Civil Society in European Political Thought from the Twelfth Century to the Present*. London: Methuen, 1984.

Blickle, Peter. "Auf dem Weg zu einem Modell der bäuerlichen Rebellion–Zusammenfassung." In *Aufruhr und Empörung? Studien zum bäuerlichen Widerstand im Alten Reich*, ed. Peter Blickle, pp. 293–308. Munich: Verlag C. H. Beck, 1980.

The Communal Reformation: The Quest for Salvation in Sixteenth-century Germany. Tr. Thomas Dunlap. New Jersey: Humanities Press, 1992.

"Communal Reformation and peasant piety: the peasant Reformation and its late medieval origins." *Central European History*, 20, 3–4 (1987): 216–28.

"The criminalization of peasant resistance in the Holy Roman Empire: toward a history of the emergence of high treason in Germany." *Journal of Modern History*, 58, Supplement (1986): 588–97.

Deutsche Untertanen. Ein Widerspruch. Munich: Beck, 1981.

"Herrschaft und Landschaft im Südwesten." In *Bauernschaft und Bauernstand, 1500–1970. Büdinger Vorträge 1971–1972*, ed. Günther Franz, pp. 17–42. Limburg-Lahn: C. A. Starke Verlag, 1975.

"Der Kommunalismus als Gestaltungsprinzip zwischen Mittelalter und Moderne." In *Gesellschaft und Gesellschaften: Festschrift zum 65. Geburtstag von Professor Dr. Ulrich im Hof*, ed. Nicolai Bernard and Quirinus Reichen, pp. 95–113. Bern: Wyss, 1982.

"Kommunalismus, Parlamentarismus, Republikanismus." *Historische Zeitschrift*, 242 (1986): 529–56.

"Kommunalismus und Republikanismus in Oberdeutschland." In *Republiken und Republikanismus im Europa der Frühen Neuzeit*, ed. Helmut Koenigsberger, pp. 57–76. Munich: R. Oldenbourg, 1988.

"Die Krise des Ständestaats. Tirol als Modell zur Lösung des Konflikts von 1525." In *Die Bauernkriege und Michael Gaismair*, ed. Fridolin Dörrer, pp. 45–55. Innsbruck: Tiroler Landesarchiv, 1982.

Landschaften im Alten Reich. Die staatliche Funktion des gemeinen Mannes in Oberdeutschland. Munich: Beck, 1973.

"Rechtsautonomie durch Kirchenkritik. Die Eidgenossen wehren sich gegen Bann und Interdikt." In *Ansichten von der rechten Ordnung: Bilder über Normen und*

Bibliography

Normenverletzung in der Geschichte, ed. Benedikt Bietenhard, Peter Hug, Regula Ludi, Rolf Maurer, Brigitte Schnegg, and Albert Tanner, pp. 98–112. Bern and Stuttgart: Verlag Paul Haupt, 1991.

"Die Reformation vor dem Hintergrund von Kommunalisierung und Christianisierung. Eine Skizze." In *Kommunalisierung und Christianisierung. Voraussetzungen und Folgen der Reformation 1400–1600*, ed. Peter Blickle and Johannes Kunisch pp. 9–28. Berlin: Duncker & Humblot, 1989.

The Revolution of 1525: The German Peasants' War from a New Perspective. Tr. Thomas A. Brady Jr, and H. C. E. Midelfort. Baltimore and London: Johns Hopkins University Press, 1981.

Blickle, Peter, ed. *Aufruhr und Empörung? Studien zum bäurlichen Widerstand im Alten Reich*. Munich: C. H. Beck, 1980.

Blumenthal, Duri. *Die Drei Bünde 1535 bis 1565, unter besonderer Berücksichtigung der Bündnisverhandlungen mit Frankreich und Mailand*. Zurich: Zentralstelle der Studentenschaft, 1990.

Boas, George. *Vox Populi: Essays in the History of an Idea*. Baltimore: Johns Hopkins Press, 1969.

Bolzern, Rudolf. *Spanien, Mailand und die katholische Eidgenossenschaft: Militärische, wirtschaftliche und politische Beziehungen zur Zeit des Gesandten Alfonso Casati (1594–1621)*. Luzern and Stuttgart: Rex Verlag, 1982.

Bonjour, Edgar. "Fortunat von Juvalta." In *Die Schweiz und Europa*, vol. II. Basel and Stuttgart: Helbing und Lichtenhahn, 1961.

Bonorand, Conradin. *Die Engadiner Reformatoren Phillip Gallicius, Jachiam Tütschett Bifrun, Durich Chiampell. Voraussetzungen und Möglichkeiten ihres Wirkens aus der Perspektive der Reformation im allgemeinen*. Chur: Evangelischer Kirchenrat Graubünden, 1987.

"Stand und Probleme der Forschung über die Bündner Geschichte der frühen Neuzeit seit 1945." *Jahresberichte der Historisch-antiquarische Gesellschaft Graubündens* (1979): 85–130.

Borchardt, Frank L. *German Antiquity in Renaissance Myth*. Baltimore and London: Johns Hopkins Press, 1971.

Boringhieri, Paolo, "Geschlechter und Gesellschaft des alten Zuoz im Spiegel der Estims des 16. Jahrhunderts." *Bündner Monatsblatt*, nos. 6/7 (1983): 165–98.

"Pussaunza, richezza e poverted a Zuoz 1521–1801." *Annalas de la Società Retorumantscha*, 102 (1988): 79–201.

Bosl, Karl and Karl Möckl, eds. *Der moderne Parlamentarismus und seine Grundlagen in der ständischen Repräsentation*. Berlin, Duncker & Humblot, 1977.

Bouwsma, William J. *Venice and the Defense of Republican Liberty*. Berkeley: University of California Press, 1968.

Brady, Thomas A., Jr. "Der Gemeine Mann und seine Feinde: Betrachtungen zur oberdeutschen Geschichte im 15. und 16. Jahrhundert." In *Stände und Gesellschaft im Alten Reich*, ed. Georg Schmidt, pp. 223–30. Stuttgart: Steiner Verlag Wiesbaden, 1989.

"From the sacral community to the common man: reflections on German Reformation studies." *Central European History*, 20, 3–4 (1987): 229–45.

Bibliography

Turning Swiss: Cities and Empire, 1450–1550. Cambridge: Cambridge University Press, 1985.

Brown, Horatio F. "The Valtelline." In *The Cambridge Modern History*, vol. IV: *The Thirty Years' War*, ed. A. W. Ward, G. W. Prothero, and Stanley Leathes, pp. 35–63. Cambridge: Cambridge University Press, 1906.

Brunner, Otto. *Land and Lordship: Structures of Governance in Medieval Austria.* Tr. Howard Kaminsky and James Van Horn Melton from 4th German edition. Philadelphia: University of Pennsylvania Press, 1992.

Land und Herrschaft. Grundfragen der territorialen Verfassungsgeschichte Südostdeutschlands im Mittelalter. 3rd edition. Brünn, Munich and Vienna: Rohrer Verlag, 1943.

"Das 'ganze Haus' und die alteuropäische Ökonomik." In Otto Brunner, *Neue Wege der Verfassungs- und Sozialgeschichte*, pp.103–27. 2nd edition. Göttingen: Vandenhoeck & Ruprecht, 1968.

Brunold, Ursus and Lothar Deplazes. *Geschichte und Kultur Churrätiens. Festschrift für Pater Iso Müller OSB zu seinem 85. Geburtstag.* Disentis: Desertina, 1986.

Bücking, Jürgen, "Habsburg-Tirol und die Erhaltung des Bistums Chur im frühen 17. Jahrhundert." *Schweizerische Zeitschrift für Geschichte*, 20, 3 (1970): 303–20.

Michael Gaismair, Reformer, Sozialrebell, Revolutionär. Seine Rolle im Tiroler "Bauernkrieg" (1525/32). Stuttgart: Klett-Cotta, 1978.

Bühring, Johannes. *Venedig, Gustav Adolf und Rohan. Ein Beitrag zur allgemeinen politischen Geschichte im Zeitalter des Dreissigjährigen Krieges aus venezianischen Quellen.* Halle: Max Niemeyer, 1885.

Bundi, Gian, "Das Geständniss des Dr. Johann Planta (1572)." *Bündner Monatsblatt*, no. 3 (1920): 73–79.

"Dr. Johann v. Planta-Räzüns und sein Lehensherr. Ein Beitrag zur Geschichte des Planta Prozesses." *Bündner Monatsblatt*, no. 2 (1916): 33–48

Bundi, Martin. *Frühe Beziehungen zwischen Graubünden und Venedig.* Chur: Gasser, 1988.

Stephan Gabriel. Ein markanten bündner Prädikant in der Zeit der Gegenreformation. Ein Beitrag zur Politische- und Geistesgeschichte Graubündens im 17. Jahrhundert. Chur: Bischofsberger, 1964.

Zur Besiedlungs- und Wirtschaftsgeschichte Graubündens im Mittelalter. Chur: Calven-Verlag, 1982.

Bundi, Martin, Ursula Jecklin, and Georg Jäger. *Geschichte der Stadt Chur.* Vol. II. *Vom 14.–17. Jahrhundert.* Chur: Calven Verlag, 1986.

Caduff, Gian. *Die Knabenschaften Graubündens. Eine volkskundlich-kulturhistorische Studie.* Chur: Kommissions-Verlag F. Schuler, 1932.

Cahannes, Johannes. "Die Pilgerreise Carlo Borromeo's nach Disentis im August 1581." *Zeitschrift für schweizerische Kirchengeschichte*, 18 (1924): 136–65.

Camenisch, Emil. *Bündnerische Reformationsgeschichte.* Chur: Bischofsberger & Hotzenköcherle, 1920.

"Notizen über Ulrich Campell aus seinen letzten Lebensjahren." *Bündner Monatsblatt*, no. 3 (1920): 79–83.

Carlen, Louis. "Les communautés des pasteurs en Allemagne, Autriche et Suisse." *Recueils de la Société Jean Bodin pour l'histoire comparative des institutions*, 44 (1987): 113–26.

Bibliography

Die Landsgemeinde in der Schweiz: Schule der Demokratie. Sigmaringen: Jan Thorbeke Verlag, 1976.

Caroni, Pio. "Dorfgemeinschaften und Säumergenossenschaften in der mittelalterlichen und neuzeitlichen Schweiz." *Recueils de la Société Jean Bodin pour l'histoire comparative des institutions,* 44 (1987): 191–222.

Castelmur, Anton von. "Die Leibeigenen der III Bünden in der Herrschaft Maienfeld." *Bündner Monatsblatt,* no. 12 (1929): 377–80.

"Ein Versuch zur Einführung der ständischer Verfassung im Bistum Chur." *Zeitschrift für schweizerische Kirchengeschichte,* 18 (1924): 96–108.

Clavadetscher, Otto. "Die Bauernunruhen im Gebiet der heutigen Eidgenossenschaft. Mit einem Excurs über die Beziehungen Gaismairs zur Schweiz." In *Die Bauernkriege und Michael Gaismair. Protokoll des internationalen Symposions 15.–19. November 1976,* ed. Fridolin Dörrer, pp. 153–60. Innsbruck: Tiroler Landesarchiv, 1982.

"Die Herrschaftsbildung in Rätien." In *Die Alpen in der europäischen Geschichte des Mittelalters,* pp. 141–58. Sigmaringen: Jan Thorbecke Verlag, 1965.

"Wandlung der Rechtssprache im 13. Jh. nach bündnerische Quellen." In *Festschrift Karl Siegfried Bader.* ed. F. Elsener and W. Ruoff, pp. 85–100. Zürich, Cologne and Graz: Schulthess and Böhlau, 1965.

Clavuot, Otto. "Kurze Geschichte des Gotteshausbundes (eine zusammenfassende Übersicht)." In *Festschrift 600 Jahre Gotteshausbund,* ed. P. Jörimann, pp. 529–58. Chur: Calven Verlag, 1967.

Pövel e domini in Engiadina. Separats ord las Annalas da la Società retorumantscha, Annada 15. Disentis: Società retorumantscha, 1977.

Cole, John R. and Eric Wolf. *The Hidden Frontier: Ecology and Ethnicity in an Alpine Valley.* New York and London: Academic Press, 1975.

Dahm, Karl-Wilhelm, Werner Krawietz, and Dieter Wyduckel, eds. *Politische Theorie des Johannes Althusius. Rechtstheorie. Zeitschrift für Logik, Methodenlehre, Kybernetik und Soziologie des Rechts,* Supplement 7. Berlin: Duncker & Humblot, 1988.

Deplazes, Lothar. *Alpen, Grenzen, Pässe im Gebiet Lukmanier-Piora (13.–16. Jahrhundert). Mit Anhang: Akten und Urteile des Val Termine-Prozesses unter Gilg Tschudi als Obmann (1560) sowie eine Quellenauswahl 1435–1899.* Disentis: Staatsarchiv Graubünden and Desertina Verlag, 1986.

Dilcher, Gerhard. "Reich, Kommunen, Bünde und die Wahrung von Recht und Friede: Eine Zusammenfassung." In *Kommunale Bündnisse Oberitaliens und Oberdeutschlands im Vergleich,* ed. Helmut Maurer, pp. 231–47. Sigmaringen: Jan Thorbecke Verlag, 1987.

Dreyfuss, Heinrich. "Die Entwicklung eines politischen Gemeinsinns in der schweizerischen Eidgenossenschaft und der Politiker Ulrich Zwingli." *Zeitschrift für schweizerische Geschichte,* 6, 1 (1926): 61–127; 6, 2 (1926): 145–93.

Duby, Georges. *The Three Orders: Feudal Society Imagined.* Chicago: University of Chicago Press, 1980.

Durand, Yvés. *Les républiques au temps des monarchies.* Paris: Presses Universitaires de France, 1972.

Durnwalder, Eugen. *Kleines Repertorium der Bündner Geschichte.* Chur: F. Schuler, 1970.

Ebel, Wilhelm. *Die Willkür: Eine Studie zu den Denkformen des älteren deutschen Rechts.* Göttingen: Verlag Otto Schwarz & Co., 1953.

Bibliography

Elsener, Ferdinand. "Das Majoritätsprinzip in konfessionellen Angelegenheiten und die Religionsverträge der schweizerischen Eidgenossenschaft vom 16. bis 18. Jahrhundert." In *Zeitschrift der Savigny-Stiftung für Rechtsgeschichte*, 86 (*Kanonistische Abteilung*, vol. 55) (1969): 238–81.

"Zur Geschichte des Majoritätsprinzips (pars maior und pars sanior) insbesondere nach schweizerischen Quellen." *Zeitschrift der Savigny-Stiftung für Rechtsgeschichte*, 73 (*Kanonistische Abteilung*, vol. 42) (1956): 73–116, 560–70.

Färber, Silvio. *Der bündnerische Herrenstand im 17. Jahrhundert: Politische, soziale, und wirtschaftliche Aspekte seiner Vorherrschaft.* Zürich: Zentralstelle der Studentenschaft, 1983.

Fehr, Hans-Jürg. "Die Freiheitsbewegung im Oberengadin." *Bündner Monatsblatt*, nos. 3/4 (1974): 49–80.

Feller, Richard and Edgar Bonjour. *Geschichtsschreibung der Schweiz.* Basel and Stuttgart: Bennno Schwabe & Co. Verlag, 1962.

Fetz, J. F. *Geschichte der kirchen-politische Wirren im Freistaate der III Bünde.* Chur: by the author, 1875.

Finley, Moses I. *Democracy Ancient and Modern.* 2nd edition. London: Hogarth Press, 1985.

Politics in the Ancient World. Cambridge: Cambridge University Press, 1983.

Fontana, Giatgen-Peder. "Ländliche Gemeinde in Graubünden bis 1800." In *Die ländliche Gemeinde: Historikertagung in Bad Ragaz, 16.–18.10.1985*, ed. Alois Stadler, pp. 43–60. Bozen: Athesia, 1988.

Rechtshistorische Begriffsanalyse und das Paradigma der Freien. Ein methodischer und rechtssemantischer Begriffsbildungsversuch der mittelalterlicher Freiheit unter besonderer Bezugnahme auf die Historiographie Graubündens. Zurich: Schulthess, 1987.

Franz, Günther. *Geschichte des deutschen Bauernstandes vom frühen Mittelalter bis zum 19. Jahrhundert.* Stuttgart: Eugen Ulmer, 1970.

Ganseuer, Frank. *Der Staat des 'gemeinen Mannes'. Gattungstypologie und Programmatik des politischen Schrifttums von Reformation und Bauernkrieg.* Frankfurt am Main: Peter Lang, 1985.

Ganzoni, Rudolf Anton. *Beiträge zur Kenntnis des bündnerischen Referendums.* Zurich: Zürcher und Furrer, 1890.

Genicot, Léopold. *Rural Communities in the Medieval West.* Baltimore and London: Johns Hopkins University Press, 1990.

Geschichtliche Grundbegriffe. Historisches Lexikon zur politisch-sozialen Sprache in Deutschland. 7 vols. Eds. Otto Brunner, Werner Conze, and Reinhart Koselleck. Stuttgart: E. Klett, 1972–92.

Gierke, Otto von. *Das deutsche Genossenschaftsrecht.* Graz: Akademische Druck- und Verlagsanstalt, 1954. Selections edited and translated as *Community in Historical Perspective. A Translation of Selections from "Das deutsche Genossenschaftsrecht"*, ed. Antony Black, tr. Mary Fischer. Cambridge: Cambridge University Press, 1990.

Gillardon, Paul. "Die Bevölkerung der VIII Gerichte im Frühling 1623." *Bündner Monatsblatt*, no. 6 (1930): 161–74; no. 7 (1930): 193–218.

"Die Erwerbung der Herrschaft Maienfeld durch die III Bünde und ihre Einrichtung als Landvogtei 1504–1509." *Bündner Monatsblatt*, no. 6 (1936): 161–82.

Bibliography

Geschichte des Zehngerichtenbundes. Festschrift zur Fünfhundertfeier seiner Gründung 1436–1936. Davos: Buchdruckerei Davos, 1936.

Graus, Frantisek. "Verfassungsgeschichte des Mittelalters." *Historische Zeitschrift,* 243, 3 (1986): 529–89.

Grimm, Paul Eugen. *Die Anfänge der Bündner Aristokratie im 15. und 16. Jahrhundert.* Zurich: Juris Verlag, 1981.

Grundmann, Herbert. "Freiheit als religiöses, politisches, und persönliches Postulat im Mittelalter." *Historische Zeitschrift,* 183, 1 (1957): 23–53.

Haas, L. "Sancho de Londoño und seine Denkschrift von 1565 über die Drei Bünde." In *Festschrift Oskar Vasella zum 60. Geburtstag am 15. Mai 1964 überreicht von Schülern und Freunden,* pp. 247–71. Fribourg: Universitätsverlag, 1964.

Haffter, Ernst. *Georg Jenatsch. Ein Beitrag zur Geschichte der Bündner Wirren. Mit Urkundenbuch und Beilagen.* Davos: Richter, 1894. Second section also published separately, Chur: Hitz'sche Buchhandlung, 1895.

"Zur Charakteristik von Bartholomäus' Anhorns des Älteren Grauw Püntner Krieg und 'Ein schryben von Chur von Genatzen unruw,' (vom 14./24/ Mai 1639)." *Anzeiger für schweizerische Geschichte,* n.s. 28, 5, vol. 7 (1897): 546ff.

Haitsma Mulier, Eco. "The language of 17th-century republicanism in the United Provinces." In *The Languages of Political Theory in Early-Modern Europe,* ed. Anthony Pagden, pp. 179–95. Cambridge: Cambridge University Press, 1987.

Haller, Gottlieb Emmanuel von. *Bibliothek der Schweizer-Geschichte und aller Theile, so dahin Bezug haben.* Bern: Hallerschen Buchhandlung, 1785–88.

Hamm, Bernd. *Zwinglis Reformation der Freiheit.* Neukirchen-Vluyn: Neukirchner Verlag, 1988.

Handbuch der Schweizergeschichte. Zurich: Verlag Berichthaus, 1972–77.

Hauser, Alfred. "Zur soziologischen Struktur eidgenössischen Bauerntums im Spätmittelalter." In *Bauernschaft und Bauernstand, 1500–1970. Büdinger Vorträge 1971–1972,* ed. Günther Franz, pp. 16–64. Limburg-Lahn: C. A. Starke Verlag, 1975.

Head, Randolph. "Rhaetian ministers, from shepherds to citizens: Calvinism and democracy in the Republic of the Three Leagues, 1550–1620." In *Later Calvinism: International Perspectives,* ed. W. Fred Graham, pp. 55–69. Kirksville, Mo.: Sixteenth Century Journal Publishers, 1994.

"Social order, politics, and political language in the Rhaetian Freestate (Graubünden), 1470–1620." PhD thesis, University of Virginia, 1992. Ann Arbor: University Microfilms, 1992.

Hilfiker, Max. *Thomas Massner 1663–1712.* Chur: Buch- und Offsetdruck Casutt AG, 1978.

Historisch-Biographischer Lexicon der Schweiz. 7 vols. and supp. Ed. Heinrich Türler, Marcel Godet, Victor Attinger *et al.* Neuenburg: Administration des Historisch-biographischen Lexikons der Schweiz, 1921–34.

Hofmann, Hasso. *Repräsentation. Studien zur Wort- und Begriffsgeschichte von der Antike bis ins 19. Jahrhundert.* Berlin: Duncker & Humblot, 1974.

Hsia, R. Po-chia. *Social Discipline in the Reformation: Central Europe 1550–1750.* London: Routledge, 1989.

Hübscher, Bruno. "Das bischöfliche Archiv Chur." In *Archivalia et Historica (Festschrift*

Bibliography

Anton Lagiarder), ed. Dietrich Schwarz and Werner Schnyder, pp. 33–49. Zurich: Verlag Berichthaus, 1958.

Huter, Franz."Baüerliche Führungsschichten in Tirol im 16.–18. Jh." In *Bauernschaft und Bauernstand, 1500–1970. Büdinger Vorträge 1971–1972*, ed. Günther Franz, pp. 65–88. Limburg-Lahn: C. A. Starke Verlag, 1975.

Isler, Egon. *Der Verfall des Feudalismus im Gebiet der Ostschweiz im XIV. und XV. Jahrhundert*. Lichtensteig: Maeder, 1935.

Jecklin, Fritz. "Allerlei Bündnergeschichtliches aus dem k. k. Statthalterei Archiv zu Innsbruck." *Bündnerisches Monatsblatt*, n.s. 7, no. 11 (1902): 195–202.

Der Engadiner Aufruhr des Jahres 1565. Chur: Sprecher and Valer, 1904. Also published in *Jahresbericht der Historich-antiquarische Gesellschaft von Graubünden*, 1904.

"Einteilung der Hochgerichte und möglichst vollständiges Ortsverzeichnis der drei Bünde dieses Kantons, 1805." *Bündnerisches Monatsblatt*, n.s. 8, no. 2 (1903): 35–42.

"Jörg Blaurock vom Hause Jacob: Ein Märtyrer der Wiedertäufer." *Jahresbericht der Historisch-antiquarische Gesellschaft Graubündens*, 21 (1891): 1–20.

Jenny, Rudolf, *Staatsarchiv Graubünden*. Vol. 1: *Das Staatsarchiv Graubünden in landesgeschichtlicher Schau*. 2nd edition. Chur: Calven Verlag, 1974.

Staatsarchiv Graubünden. Gesamtarchivplan und Archivbücher-Inventare des Dreibünderarchivs, der Helvetischen und des Kantonalen Archivs. Chur: Verlag Bündner Tagblatt, 1961.

Der traditionelle Vazeroler Bund von 1471 und das Bündnis zwischen dem Grauen und dem Zehngerichtenbund vom 21. März 1471. Chur: Staatsarchiv Graubünden, 1969.

"Über die Pündten Bücher im Berner Staatsarchiv." *Jahresbericht der Historisch-antiquitarische Gesellschaft Graubündens* (1948): 123–32.

Keller, Hagen. "Mehrheitsentscheidung und Majorisierungsproblem im Verbund der Landgemeinden Chiavenna und Piuro (1151–1155)." In *Civitatum Communitas (Festschrift Heinz Stoob)*, vol. 1, ed. Helmut Jäger, pp. 2–41. Cologne and Vienna: Böhlau Verlag, 1984.

Kelley, Donald R. *The Beginning of Ideology: Consciousness and Society in the French Reformation*. Cambridge: Cambridge University Press, 1981.

Foundations of Modern Historical Scholarship: Language, Law and History in the French Renaissance. New York and London: Columbia University Press, 1970.

Kind, Christian. "Das zweite Strafgericht in Thusis, 1618." *Jahrbuch für schweizerische Geschichte*, 7 (1882): 277–326.

Kingdon, Robert M. "Calvinism and democracy: some political implications of debates on French reformed church government, 1562–1572." *American Historical Review*, 69, 2 (1964): 393–401.

Koenigsberger, Helmut G. "'Riksdag', 'Parliament' und Generalstaaten im 16. und 17. Jahrhundert." *Zeitschrift für historische Forschung*, 17, 3 (1990): 305–25.

Koenigsberger, Helmut G., ed. *Republiken und Republikanismus im Europa der Frühen Neuzeit*. Munich: R. Oldenbourg, 1988.

Konstanzer Arbeitskreis für mittelalterliche Geschichte. *Die Alpen in der europäischen Geschichte des Mittelalters: Reichenau-Vorträge 1961–1962*. Sigmaringen: Jan Thorbecke Verlag, 1965.

Bibliography

Die Anfänge der Landgemeinde und ihr Wesen, 2 vols. Sigmaringen: Jan Thorbecke Verlag, 1964 [repr. 1986].

Kopp, Max. *Die Geltung des Mehrheitprinzips in eidgenössische Angelegenheiten vom 13. Jahrhundert bis 1848 in seiner Bedeutung für die Alte Eidgenossenschaft*. Winterthur: Schellenberg, 1959.

Kossman, Ernst H. "Popular sovereignty at the beginning of the Dutch *ancien regime*." *Low Countries History Yearbook/Acta Historiae Neerlandicae*, 14 (1981): 1–28.

Liebeskind, Wolfgang A. *Das Referendum der Landschaft Wallis*. Leipzig: Theodor Weicher, 1928.

Liver, Peter. *Abhandlungen zur schweizerischen und bündnerischen Rechtsgeschichte*. Chur: Calven Verlag, 1970.

"Alpenlandschaft und politische Selbstständigkeit." *Bündner Monatsblatt*, no. 1 (1942): 1ff.

Beiträge zur rätischen Verfassungsgeschichte vom 12. bis zum 15. Jahrhundert mit besonderer Berücksichtigung des Tumleschgs und des Heinzenbergs, Chur: Bündner Monatsblatt, 1947–48.

"Geschichtliche Einleitung." In *Sammlung Schweizerischer Rechtsquellen*, Section xv, *Die Rechtsquellen des Kantons Graubünden*, Series B, *Die Statuten der Gerichtsgemeinden*. Part 1: *Der Gotteshausbund*, vol. II, *Unterengadin*, ed. Andreas Schorta, pp. 17–58. Aarau: Verlag Sauerländer, 1981.

"Die staatliche Entwicklung im alten Graubünden." *Zeitschrift für Schweizerische Geschichte*, 13, 2 (1933): 206–45.

"Die Stellung des Gotteshausbundes in der bischöflichen Feudalherrschaft und im Freistaat Gemeiner Drei Bünde." In *Festschrift 600 Jahre Gotteshausbund*, ed. P. Jörimann, pp. 129–183. Chur: Calven Verlag, 1967.

Vom Feudalismus zur Demokratie in den bündnerischen Hinterrheintälern. Chur: Sprecher, Eggerling, 1929.

Lötscher, Valentin. *Der deutschen Bauernkrieg in der Darstellung und dem Urteil der zeitgenössischer Schweizer*. Basel: Helbing und Lichtenhahn, 1943.

Lüdi, Heidi. "Praktizieren und Trölen. Wahlkorruption und Ämterkauf in den Landsgemeinde-Orten der alten Schweiz." Ms, University of Bern, 1990.

Lutz, Robert H. *Wer war der Gemeine Mann? Der dritte Stand in der Krise des Spätmittelalters*. Munich and Vienna: Oldenbourg, 1979.

Maissen, Felici. "Die ältesten Druckschriften über den Erzpriester Nicolò Rusca." *Zeitschrift für schweizerische Kirchengeschichte*, 54, 3 (1960): 211–39.

Die Drei Bünde in der zweiten Hälfte des 17. Jahrhundert in politischer, kirchengeschichtlicher, und volkskündlicher Schau. Vol I: *1647–1657*. Aarau: Sauerländer, 1966.

Major, J. Russell. *Representative Institutions in Renaissance France*. Madison: University of Wisconsin Press, 1960.

Maleczek, Werner. "Abstimmungsarten. Wie kommt man zu einem vernünftigen Wahlergebnis?" In *Wahlen und wählen im Mittelalter*, ed. Reinhard Schneider and Harald Zimmerman, pp. 79–134. Sigmaringen: Jan Thorbecke Verlag, 1990.

Marchal, Guy. "Die Antwort der Bauern: Elemente und Schichtungen des eidgenössischen Geschichtsbewußtseins am Ausgang des Mittelalters." In *Geschichtsschreibung und Geschichtsbewusstsein im Späten Mittelalter*, ed. H. Patze, pp. 757–790. Sigmaringen: Jan Thorbecke Verlag, 1987.

Bibliography

Die frommen Schweden in die Schweiz: Das «Herkommen der Schwyzer und Oberhasler» als Quelle zum schwyzerischen Selbstverständnis im 15. und 16. Jahrhundert. Basel: Helbing und Lichtenhahn, 1976. 138,

"Nouvelles approches des mythes fondateurs suisses: l'imaginaire historique des Confédérés à la fin du XVe siècle." *Itinera*, 9 (1989): 1–24.

Margadant, Silvio. *Graubünden im Spiegel der Reiseberichte und landeskundlichen Literatur des 16. bis 18. Jahrhundert.* Zürich: Juris Verlag, 1978.

Mathieu, Jon. *Bauern und Bären. Eine Geschichte des Unterengadins von 1650 bis 1800.* Chur: Octopus Verlag, 1987.

"33 Jahre nach Pfisters Jenatsch-Biographie: Neue Forschungsergebnisse und -perspektiven." In Alexander Pfister, *Jörg Jenatsch: Sein Leben und seine Zeit*, 4th edition, pp. 491–510. Chur: Terra Grischuna, 1984.

"Eine Region am Rand: Das Unterengadin 1650–1800," 2 vols. Chur: By the author, 1983.

Mathieu, Jon and Hansruedi Stauffacher. "Alpine Gemeindedemokratie oder aristokratische Herrschaft? Eine Gegenüberstellung zweier Schweizerischen Regionen im Ancien Régime." *Itinera*, 5/6 (1986): 320–60.

Maurer, Helmut, ed. *Churrätisches und St. Gallisches Mittelalter. Festschrift für Otto P. Clavadetscher zu seinem 75ten Geburtstag.* Sigmaringen: Jan Thorbecke Verlag, 1984.

Mayer, Ernst. "Zur rätischen Verfassungsgeschichte." *Zeitschrift für schweizerische Geschichte*, 8, 4 (1928): 385–504.

Mayer, Johann George. "Hinrichtung des Dr. Johann Planta, Herrn von Rhäzuns." *Anzeiger für schweizerische Geschichte*, n.s. 5 (1886–89): 195–99.

Mayer, Theodor. "Über die Freiheit der Bauern in Tirol und in der Schweizer Eidgenossenschaft." In *Deutsches Bauerntum im Mittelalter*, ed. Günther Franz, 177–90. Darmstadt: Wissenschaftliche Buchgesellschaft, 1976.

Mayhew, Alan. *Rural Settlement and Farming in Germany.* London: Batsford, 1973.

Meuli, Anton. *Die Entstehung der autonomen Gemeinden im Oberengadin.* Chur: Sprecher & Valer, 1902.

Meyer, Bruno. *Die Bildung der Eidgenossenschaft im 14. Jahrhundert. Vom Zugerbund zum Pfaffenbrief. Schweizerische Zeitschrift für Geschichte*, Supplement 15. Zurich: Leeman, 1972.

"Freiheit und Unfreiheit in der alten Eidgenossenschaft." In *Das Problem der Freiheit in der deutschen und schweizerischen Geschichte (Mainauervorträge 1953)*, ed. Theodor Mayer, pp. 123–58. Lindau and Konstanz: Jan Thorbecke Verlag, 1955.

Meyer-Marthaler, Elisabeth. *Studien über die Anfänge Gemeiner Drei Bünde.* Chur: Bischofsberger, 1973.

Michelet, Henri. *Le Valais: au temps de son extension territoriale, 1475–1569. Récit des événements et aperçu des grands problèmes valaisans de l'époque.* Saint-Maurice: Editions rhodaniques, 1982.

Midelfort, H. C. Erik. "Adeliges Landleben und die Legitimationskrise des deutschen Adels im 16. Jahrhundert." In *Stände und Gesellschaft im Alten Reich*, ed. Georg Schmidt, pp. 245–64. Stuttgart: Steiner Verlag Wiesbaden, 1989.

Mitterauer, Michael. "Grundlagen politischer Berechtigung im mittelalterlichen Ständewesen." In *Der moderne Parlamentarismus und seine Grundlagen in der ständischen*

274

Bibliography

Repräsentation, ed. Karl Bosl and Karl Möckl, pp. 11–41. Berlin: Duncker & Humblot, 1977.

Möckli, Silvano. *Die schweizerischen Landsgemeinde-Demokratien*. Bern: Verlag Paul Haupt, 1987.

Moor, Conradin von. *Geschichte von Currätien und der Republik "gemeiner drei Bünde" (Graubünden)*. 3 vols. Chur: Verlag der Antiquariats-Buchhandlung, 1871.

Müller, Iso. "Die Abtei Disentis im Kampfe gegen die Cadi zu Anfang des 17. Jahrhunderts." *Jahresbericht der Historisch-antiquitarische Gesellschaft Graubündens* (1948): 53–95.

"Die Entstehung des Grauen Bundes 1367–1424." *Zeitschrift für schweizerische Geschichte*, 21, 2 (1941): 137–99.

Geschichte der Abtei Disentis von den Anfängen bis zur Gegenwart. Zürich and Cologne: Benziger, 1971.

Näf, Werner. "Frühformen des 'modernen Staates' im Spätmittelalter." *Historische Zeitschrift*, 171, 2 (1951): 225–43.

Netting, Robert McC. *Balancing on an Alp: Ecological Change and Continuity in a Swiss Mountain Community*. Cambridge: Cambridge University Press, 1981.

Neuschel, Kristen B. *Word of Honor: Interpreting Noble Culture in Sixteenth-Century France*. Ithaca and London: Cornell University Press, 1989.

Oakley, Francis. *Omnipotence, Covenant, and Order: An Excursion in the History of Ideas from Abelard to Leibniz*. Ithaca and London: Cornell University Press, 1984.

Oechsli, Wilhelm. "Die Benennung der Alten Eidgenossenschaft und ihre Glieder." *Jahrbuch für schweizerische Geschichte*, 41 (1916): 51–230; and 42 (1917): 87–258. Excerpt published as "Die Entstehung der Namen 'Graubünden' und 'Bündner'." *Bündner Monatsblatt*, no. 8 (1916): 257–265.

Oestreich, Gerhard. *Neostoicism and the Early Modern State*. Ed. Brigitta Oestreich and Helmut Koenigsberger, tr. David McLintock. Cambridge: Cambridge University Press, 1982.

Strukturprobleme der frühen Neuzeit. Ed. Brigitta Oestreich. Berlin: Duncker & Humblot, 1980.

Oexle, Otto Gerhard. "Die funktionale Dreiteilung als Deutungsschema der sozialen Wirklichkeit in der ständischen Gesellschaft des Mittelalters," in *Ständische Gesellschaft und soziale Mobilität*, ed. Winfried Schulze, pp. 19–51. Munich: Oldenbourg, 1988.

Padrutt, Christian. *Staat und Krieg im Alten Bünden. Studien zur Beziehung zwischen Obrigkeit und Kriegertüm in den Drei Bünden vornehmlich im 15. und 16. Jahrhundert*. Zürich: Fretz und Wasmuth, 1965.

Pagden, Anthony, ed. *The Languages of Political Theory in Early-Modern Europe*. Cambridge: Cambridge University Press, 1987.

Pappa, Christian. *Zur Entstehung des schweizerischen Nationalbewußtseins in Graubünden*. Zurich: Buchdruckerei Fluntern, 1944.

Parker, Geoffrey. *The Army of Flanders and the Spanish Road 1567–1659*. Cambridge: Cambridge University Press, 1972.

Peyer, Hans-Conrad. "Die Anfänge der schweizerischen Aristokratien." In *Könige, Stadt und Kapital. Aufsätze zur Wirtschafts- und Sozialgeschichte des Mittelalters*, ed. Ludwig

Schmugge, Roger Sablonier, and Konrad Wanner, pp. 195–218. Zurich: Verlag Neue Zürcher Zeitung, 1982.

Verfassungsgeschichte der Alten Schweiz. Zurich: Schulthess Polygraphischer Verlag, 1978.

Pfister, Alexander. *Jörg Jenatsch: Sein Leben und seine Zeit.* 4th edition. Chur: Terra Grischuna Buchverlag, 1984.

"Partidas e combats ella Ligia Grischa, 1494–1794." *Annalas de la Società Retorumantscha,* 40 (1926): 71–208.

"Il temps dellas partidas ella Ligia Grischa, 1600–1639." *Annalas de la Società Retorumantscha,* 45 (1931): 165–228; 46 (1932): 1–85.

Pfister, Rudolf. *Kirchengeschichte der Schweiz.* Vol. II, *Von der Reformation bis zum Zweiten Villmerger Krieg.* Zurich: Theologischer Verlag, 1974.

Pfister, Ulrich. "Politischer Klientelismus in der frühneuzeitlichen Schweiz." *Schweizerische Zeitschrift für Geschichte,* 42, 1 (1992): 28–68.

Pieth, Friedrich. "Das altbündnerische Referendum." *Bündner Monatsblatt,* no. 5 (1958): 137–53.

Bündnergeschichte. Chur: F. Schuler, 1945.

"Das Streit zwischen dem Grauen Bund und dem Gotteshausbund um den Vorrang 1549/50." *Bündner Monatsblatt* (1951): 355–65.

Pithon, Remy. "La Suisse, théâtre de la guerre froide entre la France et l'Espagne pendant la crise de Valteline (1621–1626)" *Schweizerische Zeitschrift für Geschichte,* 13, 1 (1963): 33–53.

Planta, Peter von. *Chronik der Familie von Planta, nebst verschiedenen Mittheilungen aus der Vergangenheit Rhätiens.* Zürich: Orell Füssli, 1892.

Planta, Peter Conradin von. *Geschichte von Graubünden in ihren Hauptzügen gemeinfaßlich dargestellt.* 2nd edition. Bern: K. J. von Wyß, 1894.

Plattner, Wilhelm. *Die Entstehung des Freistaates der III Bünde und sein Verhältniss zur alten Eidgenossenschaft.* Davos: Hugo Richter, 1895.

Pocock, J. G. A. *The Ancient Constitution and the Feudal Law: A Study of English Historical Thought in the Seventeenth Century. A Reissue with a Retrospect.* 2nd edition. Cambridge: Cambridge University Press, 1987.

"The concept of a language and the *métier d'historien:* some considerations on practice." In *The Languages of Political Theory in Early Modern Europe,* ed. Anthony Pagden, pp. 19–38. Cambridge: Cambridge University Press, 1987.

The Machiavellian Moment: Florentine Political Thought and the Atlantic Republican Tradition. Princeton: Princeton University Press, 1975.

Porta, Petrus Dominicus Rosius à. *Historia Reformationis Ecclesiarum Raeticarum.* Vol. I: Chur: Societatis Typographicae, 1771. Vol. II: Chur and Lindau: Jacobi Otto Sumtibus, 1777.

Quaritsch, Helmut. *Souveränität. Entstehung und Entwicklung des Begriffs in Frankreich und Deutschland vom 13. Jahrhundert bis 1806.* Berlin: Duncker und Humblot, 1986.

Reibstein, Ernst. *Respublica Helvetiorum: Die Prinzipien der Eidgenössischen Staatslehre bei Josias Simmler.* Bern: Verlag Paul Haupt, 1949.

Rebel, Herrmann. *Peasant Classes. The Bureaucratization of Property and Family Relations under Early Habsburg Absolutism 1511–1636.* Princeton: Princeton University Press, 1983.

Bibliography

Robbi, Jules, *Ritter Johannes Guler von Wyneck*. Chur: Bischofberger & Hotzenköcherle, 1911.

Robisheaux, Thomas. *Rural Society and the Search for Order in Early Modern Germany*. Cambridge: Cambridge University Press, 1989.

Rohe, Karl. "Politische Kultur und Ihre Analyse: Probleme und Perspektiven der politischen Kulturforschung." *Historische Zeitschrift*, 250, 2 (1990): 321–46.

Rublack, Hans-Christoph. "Political and social norms in urban communities in the Holy Roman Empire." In *Religion, Politics, and Social Change: Three Studies on Early Modern Germany*, ed. Kaspar von Greyerz, pp. 24–60. London: George Allen Unwin. 1984.

Ruser, Konrad. "Die Talgemeinden des Valcamonica, des Frignano, der Leventina und des Blenio und die Entstehung der Schweizerischen Eidgenossenschaft." In *Kommunale Bündnisse Oberitaliens und Oberdeutschlands im Vergleich*, ed. Helmut Maurer, pp. 117–51. Sigmaringen: Jan Thorbecke Verlag, 1987.

Sabean, David. *Power in the Blood: Popular Culture and Village Discourse in Early Modern Germany*. Cambridge: Cambridge University Press, 1984.

Sablonier, Roger. *Adel im Wandel. Eine Untersuchung zur sozialen Situation des ostschweizerischen Adels um 1300*. Göttingen: Vandenhoeck & Ruprecht, 1979.

"Das Dorf im Übergang vom Hoch- zum Spätmittelalter. Untersuchungen zum Wandel ländlicher Gemeinschaftsformen im ostschweizerischen Raum." In *Institutionen, Kultur und Gesellschaft im Mittelalter, Festschrift Josef Fleckstein*, ed. Lutz Fenske *et al.*, pp. 727–45. Sigmaringen: Jan Thorbecke Verlag, 1984.

Salis-Soglio, Nicolaus von [Pader Benedictine Emaus]. *Die Familie von Salis. Gedenkblätter aus der Geschichte des ehemaligen Freistaates der drei Bünde in Hohenrhätien (Graubünden)*. Lindau: Johann Thomas Stettner, 1891.

Scheurer, Rémy. "Les Grisons dans les communications entre la France, Venise et l'Orient au milieu du XVIe siècle." In *Cinq Siècles de Relations Franco-Suisses: Hommage a Louis-Edouard Roulet*, pp. 37–49. Neuchâtel: Editions de la Baconnière, 1984.

Schlumbohm, Jürgen. *Freiheitsbegriff und Emanzipationsprozeß*. Göttingen: Vandenhoek & Ruprecht, 1973.

Schlumpf, Viktor. *Die Frumen Edlen Puren. Untersuchung zum Stilzusammenhang zwischen den historischen Volksliedern der Alten Eidgenossenschaft und der deutschen Heldenepik*. Zurich: Fretz und Wassmuth Verlag, 1969.

Schmid, H. "Beat à Porta, Bischof von Chur von 1565–1581." *Bündner Monatsblatt* (1952): 358–66.

Schmidt, Heinrich Richard. "Über das Verhältnis von ländlicher Gemeinde und christliche Ethik: Graubünden und die Innerschweiz." Ms, Historisches Institut, University of Bern, 1989.

Schneider, Reinhard and Harald Zimmerman, eds. *Wahlen und wählen im Mittelalter*. Sigmaringen: Jan Thorbecke, 1990.

Schnyder, Werner. *Handel und Verkehr über die Bündner Pässe im Mittelalter zwischen Deutschland, der Schweiz und Oberitalien*. 2 vols. Zürich: Schulthess Polygraphischer Verlag, 1973–75.

Schreiber, Paul. *Die Entwicklung der Volksrechte in Graubünden*. Chur: Sprecher und Eggerling, 1921–22.

Bibliography

Schulze, Winfried. *Bäuerlicher Widerstand und feudale Herrschaft in der frühen Neuzeit.* Stuttgart-Bad Cannstatt: Fromman-Holzboog, 1980.

"Europäische und deutsche Bauernrevolten der frühen Neuzeit – Probleme der vergleichenden Betrachtung." In *Europäische Bauernrevolten der frühen Neuzeit.* Frankfurt a.M.: Suhrkamp, 1982.

"Von Gemeinnutz zum Eigennutz: Über den Normenwandel in der ständischen Gesellschaft der frühen Neuzeit." *Historische Zeitschrift,* 243, 3 (1986): 591–626.

Schulze, Winfried, ed. *Aufstände, Revolten, Prozesse: Beiträge zu bäuerlichen Widerstandsbewegungen im frühneuzeitlichen Europa.* Bochum: Klett-Cotta, 1983.

Europäische Bauernrevolten der frühen Neuzeit. Frankfurt a.M.: Suhrkamp, 1982.

Schweizerisches Idiotikon. Wörterbuch der schweizerdeutschen Sprache. Ed. Friedrich Staub and Ludwig Tobler. Frauenfeld, J. Huber, 1881– .

Scott, Tom. "The common people in the German Reformation." *Historical Journal,* 34, 1 (1991): 183–92.

"The communal Reformation between town and country." Ms. of paper read at German Historical Association, Washington, DC, October 1990.

"Peasant revolts in early modern Germany." *Historical Journal,* 28, 2 (1985): 455–68.

Simonet, J. Jakob. "Die Ilanzer Disputation von 1526." *Zeitschrift für schweizerische Kirchengeschichte,* 21 (1927): 1–16, 103–24.

Skinner, Quentin. *The Foundations of Modern Political Thought.* 2 vols. Cambridge: Cambridge University Press, 1978.

Sprecher von Bernegg, Joh. Andreas. *Kulturgeschichte der Drei Bünde im 18. Jahrhundert.* 2nd revised edition, ed. Rudolf Jenny. Chur: Bischofberger, 1976.

Stadler, P. "Vom eidgenössischen Staatsbewustsein und Staatensystem um 1600." *Schweizerische Zeitschrift für Geschichte,* 8, 1 (1958): 1–20.

Steiner, Paul. *Die religiöse Freiheit und die Gründung des Schweizerischen Bundesstaates.* Bern and Stuttgart: Verlag Paul Haupt, 1976.

Stettler, Bernhard. "Tschudis Bild von der Befreiung der drei Waldstätte und dessen Platz in der schweizerischen Historiographie," in Aegidius Tschudi, *Chronicon Helveticum.* Ed. Bernhard Stettler, 3:*9–*128. *Quellen zur Schweizer Geschichte,* n.s., Series 1, vol. 7/3. Bern: Allgemeine Geschichtsforschende Gesellschaft der Schweiz, 1980.

Stolz, Otto. "Die Landstandschaft der Bauern in Tirol." *Historische Vierteljahresschrift,* 28 (1934): 699–736; 29 (1935): 109–44.

Stricker, Hans. *Die Selbstdarstellung des Schweizers im Drama des 16. Jahrhunderts.* Bern: Verlag Paul Haupt, 1961.

Truog, Jakob Rudolf. *Aus der Geschichte der evangelisch-rätischen Synode, 1537–1937. Im Auftrag des evangelischen Kirchenrates auf der Synodalfeier 1937.* Chur: Manatschal und Ebner, 1937.

Vahle, Hermann. "Calvinismus und Demokratie im Spiegel der Forschung." *Archiv für Reformationsgeschichte,* 66 (1975): 182–212.

Valèr, Michael. *Die Bestrafung von Staatsvergehen in der Republik der III Bünde. Ein Beitrag zur mittelalterlichen Rügegerichtsbarkeit und zur Geschichte der Demokratie in Graubünden.* Chur: F. Schuler Verlags-Buchhandlung, 1904

Geschichte der Zensur und der Amtsehrbeleidigung im alten Graubünden, von der Reformationszeit bis zur Gegenwart. Chur: Sprecher und Valer, 1907

Bibliography

Johann von Planta. Ein Beitrag zur politischen Geschichte Rhätiens im XVI. Jahrhundert. Zürich: F. Schulthess, 1888.

"Sechs Jahrhunderte Davoser Geschichte." In *Landbuch der Landschaft und Hochgerichts-Gemeinde Davos im Eidgenössischen Stand Graubünden,* ed. Geschichtsforschende Gesellschaft in Davos (separately paginated, 1–83). Davos: Verlagsanstalt-Buchdruckerei Davos, 1912.

Vann, James. *The Making of a State: Württemberg 1593–1793.* Ithaca and London: Cornell University Press, 1984.

Vasella, Oskar. "Bauernkrieg und Reformation in Graubünden 1525–1526." *Zeitschrift für schweizerische Geschichte,* 20, 1 (1940): 1–65.

"Der bäuerliche Wirtschaftskampf und die Reformation in Graubünden, 1526 bis etwa 1540." *Jahresbericht der Historisch-antiquitarische Gesellschaft Graubündens* (1943): 1–183.

"Bauerntum und Reformation in der Eidgenossenschaft." *Historisches Jahrbuch,* 76 (1957): 47–63.

"Die bischöfliche Herrschaft in Graubünden und die Bauernartikel von 1526." *Zeitschrift für schweizerische Geschichte,* 22, 1 (1942): 1–86.

"Der Bruch Bischof Paul Zieglers von Chur mit den Drei Bünden im Jahre 1524," *Zeitschrift für schweizerische Geschichte,* 23, 2 (1943): 271–78.

"Die Entstehung der bündnerischen Bauernartikel vom 25. Juni 1526." *Zeitschrift für schweizerische Geschichte,* 21 (1941): 58–78.

"Krise und Rettung des Bistums im 16. Jahrhundert." In *1500 Jahre Bistum Chur.* Zurich: NZN-Verlag, 1950.

" Zur Entstehungsgeschichte des 1. Ilanzer Artikelbriefes vom 4. April 1524 und des Eigenössischen Glaubenskonkordates von 1525." *Zeitschrift für schweizerische Kirchengeschichte,* 34 (1940): 182–92.

Viazzo, Pier Paolo. *Upland communities. Environment, Population and Social Structure in the Alps since the Sixteenth Century.* Cambridge: Cambridge University Press, 1989.

Wackernagel, Hans Georg. "Fehdewesen, Volksjustiz, und der staatlicher Zusammenhalt der Alten Eidgenossenschaft." *Schweizerische Zeitschrift für Geschichte,* 15 (1965): 289–313.

Walker, Mack. *German Home Towns: Community, State, and General Estate 1648–1871.* Ithaca and London: Cornell University Press, 1971.

Wartmann, Heinrich. "Einleitung." In Ulrich Campell, *Chronica Historica Raetica,* ed. Placidus Plattner, pp. v–lxviii. *Quellen zur Schweizer Geschichte,* o.s. vol. IX. Basel: Felix Schneider, 1889.

Weber, Hermann. *Avers. Aus Geschichte und Leben eines Bündner Hochtales.* Chur: Terra Grischuna, 1985.

Wendland, Andreas. "Republik und 'Untertanenlände' vor dem Veltlineraufstand (1620)." *Bündner Monatsblatt,* no. 3 (1990): 182–213.

Willi, Claudio. "Benedikt Fontana im Laufe der Zeiten." In *Festschrift 600 Jahre Gotteshausbund,* ed. P. Jörimann, pp. 351–75. Chur: Calven Verlag, 1967.

Wunder, Heide. *Die bäuerliche Gemeinde in Deutschland.* Göttingen: Vandenhoeck & Ruprecht, 1986.

Bibliography

"Peasant communities in medieval and early modern Germany," *Recueils de la Société Jean Bodin pour l'histoire comparative des institutions*, 44 (1987): 9–52.

Zinsli, Philipp. *Politische Gedichte aus der Zeit der Bündner Wirren 1603–1639*. Zurich: Buchdruckerei Gebr. Leemann & Co., 1909.

Index

agrarian conflict, 14; after 1526, 120; and the
Ilanz Articles, 69–72; within villages, 17; *see
also* peasant rebellion
agriculture, 25–27, 39–42; cheese production, 27,
83; common labor, 84; and elite families,
137–39; grazing rights, 84
Alexander, Blasius, 189, 242
alliances: authority of *Bundestag* over, 108; calls
for ending, 157; between Chadè and Ten
Jurisdictions (1450), 57, 59; between Chur and
Gray League (1440), 57; outside Graubünden,
112; exceptions to, 57; fiscal effects of, 116;
military, with Swiss, 61, 64; between
Oberhalbstein and Rheinwald, 86; among
Three Leagues before 1524, 56, 58; *see also*
foreign affairs; Leagues
Alps, effects on Graubünden, 2, 10–11, 36,
39
Althusius, Johannes, 222, 247
ambassadors: expulsion of, 239; hostility to, 157;
manipulation of communes by, 110
Anhorn, Bartholomäus, 207–09; as historian,
202
Anhorn, Daniel, 215
appeals, to communes, judicial, 106–07; *see also*
Drei-Sigler-Brief
Aristotle, 231, 247
arms-bearing: as criterion for citizenship, 75;
ideological role in *Fähnlilupf*, 150
army, Rhaetian, 64; effects on social consensus,
65; finances of, 117; role in foundation of
Freestate, 100
assemblies: before 1524, 59; business at, 107; of
censors, 186; communal, 74–78, 103;
framework for, in *Bundesbrief*, 95; need for, 95;
procedure at, 105, 109; role in political
process, 99; types of, 96; *see also Beitag*;
Bundestag
assemblies, of *Fähnli*, 149; authority of, 150, 155;
as national commune, 152; procedures at, 152;
reform programs, 155–62; violence at, 154; *see
also Strafgericht*
Ausschreiben, 105, 110

Austria, 23; invasion of Freestate (1622–23),
194–95; relations with, 116; *see also* foreign
affairs; Habsburgs
authority: in conservative rhetoric, 206;
delegation within communes, 14; in federal
organizations, 102; lack of central, in
Freestate, 90; in medieval social ideology,
20–22
Avers, 51, 92

Basel, Treaty of (1499), 62
Baselga, Caspar, execution, 154, 181
Bavier, Johann, 104
Beeli, Georg, 180; execution, 78, 154, 181
Beitag, 97–99, 185; actual practice at, 102–04;
calls for abolition of, 104, 132; compared to
Bundestag, 98; early evidence of, 64; limits on
power of, 105; matters treated at, 104–09;
oligarchy in, 104; presidents as members of,
97; *see also* assemblies; *Bundestag*
Black League (1450), 162
Blickle, Peter, 12, 15, 19, 20, 28, 75, 249
Bodin, Jean, 247
Boringhieri, Paolo, 138
Bormio, Rhaetian claims to, 62
Bregaglia, 43, 50
bribes: at *Bundestag*, 108, 111; at communal level,
115, 128; dangers of accepting, 146, 221;
distribution of, 115, 158; from foreign powers,
116, 121, 122, 157, 179; *see also* corruption
Brunner, Otto, 29–32, 75
bull, papal (1571), 129
Bundesbrief (1524), 66–68, 86; on assemblies, 95;
dispute resolution in, 68; enforcement of
obedience to, 112; majoritarian provisions, 81;
pessimism in, 251; political significance of,
68–69; publication of, 237; reconfirmation of,
43, 160, 171; relation to Leagues, 101; role in
reform programs, 160; as source of unity, 237
Bundestag, 96–98; actual practice at, 102–04;
compared to *Beitag*, 98; corruption at, 108;
delegates to, reform of, 159; enforcement of
decisions by, 112–13; limits on power of, 105;

281

Index

Index

Index

CAMBRIDGE STUDIES IN EARLY MODERN HISTORY

Early Modern Democracy in the Grisons: Social Order and Political Language in a Swiss Mountain Canton, 1470–1620
RANDOLPH C. HEAD

Titles available in paperback marked with an asterisk*

The following titles are now out of print:

French Finances, 1770–1795: From Business to Bureaucracy
J. F. BOSHER

Chronicle into History: an Essay in the Interpretation of History in Florentine Fourteenth-Century Chronicles
LOUIS GREEN

France and the Estates General of 1614
J. MICHAEL HAYDEN

Reform and Revolution in Mainz, 1743–1803
T. C. W. BLANNING

Altopascio: a Study in Tuscan Society 1587–1784
FRANK MCARDLE

Gunpowder and Galleys: Changing Technology and Mediterranean Warfare at Sea in the Sixteenth Century
JOHN FRANCIS GUILMARTIN JR.

The State, War and Peace: Spanish Political Thought in the Renaissance 1516–1559
J. A. FERNÁNDEZ-SANTAMARIA

Calvinist Preaching and Iconoclasm in the Netherlands, 1544–1569
PHYLLIS MACK CREW

The Kingdom of Valencia in the Seventeenth Century
JAMES CASEY

Filippo Strozzi and the Medici: Favor and Finance in Sixteenth-Century Florence and Rome
MELISSA MERIAM BULLARD

Rouen during the Wars of Religion
PHILIP BENEDICT

The Emperor and his Chancellor: a Study of the Imperial Chancellery under Gattinara
JOHN M. HEADLEY

The Military Organisation of a Renaissance State: Venice c. 1400–1617
M. E. MALLETT AND J. R. HALE

Neostoicism and the Early Modern State
GERHARD OESTREICH

Prussian Society and the German Order: an Aristocratic Corporation in Crisis c. 1410–1466
MICHAEL BURLEIGH

The Changing Face of Empire: Charles V, Philip II and Habsburg Authority, 1551–1559
M. J. RODRIGUEZ-SALGADO